The Orthodoxy of
Amoris Laetitia

The Orthodoxy of
Amoris Laetitia

Pedro Gabriel

RESOURCE *Publications* · Eugene, Oregon

THE ORTHODOXY OF AMORIS LAETITIA

Copyright © 2022 Pedro Gabriel. All rights reserved. Except for brief quotations in critical publications or reviews, no part of this book may be reproduced in any manner without prior written permission from the publisher. Write: Permissions, Wipf and Stock Publishers, 199 W. 8th Ave., Suite 3, Eugene, OR 97401.

Resource Publications
An Imprint of Wipf and Stock Publishers
199 W. 8th Ave., Suite 3
Eugene, OR 97401

www.wipfandstock.com

PAPERBACK ISBN: 978-1-6667-3328-0
HARDCOVER ISBN: 978-1-6667-2778-4
EBOOK ISBN: 978-1-6667-2779-1

JANUARY 31, 2022 3:01 PM

For information contact :
pedrogabrielbooks@gmail.com

Nihil Obstat
Imprimatur
Mons. António Coelho de Oliveira
Vicar General of the Diocese of Porto
December 6, 2021

Excerpts from papal and other Vatican documents. Used by permission of © Libreria Editrice Vaticana.

Excerpts from "A Conversation with Cardinal Schonborn". Used by permission of La Civilta Cattolica English Edition.

Excerpts from "Case Study in Communion." by Paul Keller. Used by permission of Paul Keller and Crux.

Excerpts from "Risposte Amichevoli." by Rocco Buttiglione. Used by permission of Rocco Buttiglione and Edizioni Ares.

Excerpts from "Pope Francis, the Family, and Divorce." by Stephen Walford. Used by permission of Stephen Walford.

Excerpts from "*Amoris Laetitia* and Canon 915," by Patrick Travers. Used by permission of Patrick Travers.

Excerpts from "Entender a Wojtyla," and "Para Comprender *Amoris Laetitia*," by Rodrigo Guerra López. Used by permission of Rodrigo Guerra López.

Excerpts from "Weakness, and Wounded and Troubled Love," by Tom Ryan. Used by permission of Tom Ryan.

I consecrate this book to Our Lady of Fatima, patroness of my home country and saint of my devotion; and also to St. Peter the apostle, the first pope and my namesake. May God, through the intercession of these saints, show me the path to truth and help me assist the church in this time of need. May I never fall into error, but rather help bring clarity where there is confusion, and unity where there is disunity. May I, useless servant, always be an instrument of his will, and never of my own.

Amen.

Contents

List of Tables and Illustrations | ix

Preface | xi

Acknowledgements | xxi

List of Abbreviations | xxiii

Introduction: A Call to *Metanoia* | xxv

Section I | Some Introductory Remarks

Chapter 1   Is *Amoris Laetitia* Magisterial? | 3

Chapter 2   The Question of Assent | 14

Section II | Clarifying *Amoris Laetitia*

Chapter 3   The "Multiple Interpretations" Objection | 31

Chapter 4   Who Is Allowed to Receive Communion? | 48

Chapter 5   External Validation | 58

Chapter 6   Misinterpretations | 68

Chapter 7   The Teaching on Mitigating Circumstances | 85

Chapter 8   The Problem of Scandal | 106

Chapter 9   The *Dubia* | 115

Section III | A Harmonious Development

Chapter 10 The Anatomy of a Development: A Proposal | 137

Chapter 11 Does *Amoris Laetitia* Contradict *Familiaris Consortio*? | 152

Chapter 12 Does *Amoris Laetitia* Contradict *Veritatis Splendor*? | 165

Chapter 13 Does *Amoris Laetitia* Contradict Any Other Authoritative Church Statement? | 180

Chapter 14 A Very Interesting Precedent | 202

Chapter 15 The Newman Trial | 211

Section IV | Some Practical Examples

Chapter 16 A Case Study | 237

Chapter 17 The Portuguese Reception | 246

Conclusion | 259

Recommended Reading | 263

Bibliography | 265

List of Tables and Illustrations

Table 1. External validation using the Buenos Aires criteria

Figure 1. Doctrinal evolution models

Figure 2. Doctrinal development with shift of emphasis

Figure 3. Hermeneutics models

Figure 4. Hermeneutics of reform for the divorced and remarried

Preface

ONE BEAUTIFUL MARCH MORNING in 2016, I woke up to find Catholic social media in an uproar. Some of my Portuguese friends, who like me were involved in apologetics, informed me of what had just happened: Pope Francis had allegedly changed perennial doctrine by allowing divorced and remarried people to receive communion, even while maintaining sexual relations.

This seemed like a blow to me, since I had spent the preceding months reassuring my friends (who feared this might happen all the way through the 2014–15 synods on the family) that Pope Francis would never do such a thing. I had invoked the principles of papal primacy and church indefectibility to dispel inordinate fears that a Vicar of Christ would ever bind his flock into error. It seemed like I had been proven wrong. The foundations of my faith were shaken: could I trust the church's teachings anymore?

I had learned a lesson during Benedict XVI's pontificate: never rely blindly on media reporting. So I did what I had learned during the previous papacy: not to be swept away by the tsunami of scandal, but to consult the primary sources instead. This strategy had never failed me before; it had saved me from many heartbreaks. So I downloaded the PDF directly from the Vatican website and read *Amoris Laetitia* for myself, from beginning to end.

By doing so, I arrived at two conclusions. First, the media was actually correct: Pope Francis had indeed opened up the possibility of communion to some divorced and remarried people who were previously banned from receiving the Eucharist. But I also learned that Pope Francis had done this with care so as not to create a magisterial conundrum. In fact, he had solved this tension with an extremely elegant solution: he had applied the sound doctrine of mitigating circumstances to the problem of the divorced and remarried.

For years, Catholics in social media and forums had encouraged people who struggled with sexual sin (eg. masturbation or pornography) to make an examination of conscience before receiving communion: "Are you in mortal sin?" Please note, they did not simply ask them "Did you sin?" but rather "Are you in *mortal* sin?" Only mortal sin precluded the sinner from the Eucharist, and not every sexual sin fitted the requirements for a mortal sin: subjective culpability had to be ascertained. Pope Francis just extended this logic one step further, to people to whom this process was barred before: the divorced and remarried. *Amoris Laetitia* was orthodox, after all!

However, when I came back to social media to present my findings to other people, they did not sigh with relief, nor did they accept my explanations. A strange phenomenon had taken hold of the Catholicosphere: it seemed like there was an epidemic of amnesia regarding some basic tenets of moral theology. Suddenly, Catholics were saying that those who had divorced and remarried and who engaged in sexual activity were in mortal sin, without any qualifier. It was *always* mortal sin, they said. When I pointed out that that was not true, they would just double down: of course it was a mortal sin! It was like the teaching of mitigating circumstances, universally accepted and previously non-polemical, had never existed.

❈❈❈

All of this did not happen in a vacuum. The massive cultural changes in the twentieth century led to an emptying of the pews and an ever decreasing influence of the Catholic Church in worldly affairs. The church tried to respond to this by convening an ecumenical council from 1962 to 1965: the Second Vatican Council. Nevertheless, even if the church implemented many liturgical and pastoral reforms in the wake of this council, it continued to wane, at least in the West (where its presence had traditionally been very strong).

One of the major sources of conflict between the Catholic Church and this modern world was matters of sexuality. In no other area was Catholic doctrine more rejected as outdated, burdensome, and irrational. Shortly after Vatican II, Pope St. Paul VI published *Humanae Vitae*, reaffirming the church's teachings on the immorality of artificial contraception. This document was almost universally rejected, including by a significant number of Catholics.

As the secular worldview began to separate procreation from sexuality more and more, it developed a sexual anthropology of its own, completely antithetical to Catholic principles. As it became more prevalent, both in society and in academia, this anthropology started to take hold of policies and political programs. Abortion began to be viewed as a human right, with the ensuing death of millions of unborn children every year. Homosexuality also gradually came to be viewed as a legitimate expression of sexuality, and homosexual relations as ontologically no different from marriage. Fornication, masturbation, pornography: all were seen as normal and ethical, and in fact necessary for a healthy development. Governments, therefore, saw it as their duty to educate children with this philosophy, regardless of their parents' opinions. Finally, divorce rates skyrocketed, since this modern sexual anthropology could not but influence the way society viewed marriage as a whole.

A clash between secularized people and orthodox Catholics was inevitable. Catholics who had remained faithful to the fullness of doctrine felt more and more alienated, as the society around them was transformed according to principles they deemed immoral. They needed to push back.

One of the ways this was achieved was through political engagement in the public arena. The pro-life movement was formed in defense of the human rights of the unborn child, and sought political allies against its ideological enemies: the liberal left-wing. One of the hotspots of this strife was the United States of America, where political polarization has increasingly grown stronger, especially in recent years.

The other way was through a renewal of the apologetics movement. The advent of the Internet allowed orthodox Catholics to bypass the classical means of communication (which mostly ignored them, or misconstrued them) and to expound their principles and ideas, directly and unfiltered, to their own readership. Again, the vitality of this new online apologetics movement was especially vigorous in the USA. American apologetics began to shape Catholic thought around the globe.

❖ ❖ ❖

Around this time, I was embarking on a deep study of the basics of my religion, inspired by Benedict XVI's intellectual prowess. Of course, it was inevitable that, during my research, I would come into contact with

American apologetics sites and forums. I devoured the threads and articles I came across. Increasingly, Catholic tenets and values started to make more sense to me. Gradually, I had a conversion of the mind and let go of every major instance of disagreement I had with the church's doctrine: I had embraced the orthodox way, including *Humanae Vitae*.

However, as indebted as I was to the American apologetics movement, I noticed that something was not quite right. It seemed like many apologists' views of the faith were profoundly influenced by American ideals that were simply not universal. This is by no means a detraction from American culture: every country and nationality would be prone to interpret the faith through the lens of its own culture. Still, I could not help but notice that there had been an infiltration in the church: not an infiltration of people, who surely are well-intentioned in their defense of the faith, but rather an infiltration of ideas and ideologies extraneous to Catholicism.

As Catholics sought political alliances against the aggressively anticlerical and anti-Catholic left-wing, many adopted the programs and agendas of their allies, even if these did not quite fit with Catholic social doctrine. No secular ideology can completely fall in line with Catholic principles, but many Catholics increasingly turned a blind eye to the problems in their own political camps. They adopted a culture war mentality: in an "us-versus-them" mindset, every single act from "us" needs to be defended against the attacks of "them," lest failing to do so results in a weakening of one's political position.

On the other hand, as Catholics became more emboldened to proclaim their polemical views more forcefully in the public square, some of them started to view the church hierarchy as weak. They blamed this weakness on a mindset and praxis which some outlets derogatively called the "Church of Nice," i.e., a saccharine "niceness" that avoided proclaiming hard, inconvenient truths. Some even associated this weakness with the reforms initiated during the Second Vatican Council. Groups of young people rediscovered pre-conciliar liturgies and thought they had been robbed of an esthetical and spiritual experience that was rightfully theirs. Antagonism towards Vatican II grew in some sectors of the church involved in this Catholic renaissance.

It was then that I saw a disconnect between the apologetics movement and the Catholic faith it pointed to. Time after time, I would read the actual church documents from primary, authoritative sources and feel like the commentaries from certified apologists and popular pundits had missed the mark. It seemed like they were trying to read church doctrine according to a preconceived image of the church that did not always correspond to reality. Sometimes they would try to ignore the discrepancies between their opinion and church teaching, choosing to focus solely on those parts of doctrine they felt were more urgent to expound to the secularized world. Other times, however, the discrepancies were just too obvious to go unnoticed.

So certain members of the apologetics movement started to include an objective extraneous to it: to find arguments to justify the cognitive dissonances their positions created. They devised theologically sophisticated arguments to square Catholicism with their political positions. They found ways to dress up some difficult teachings as negotiable, and told Catholics they could just disagree with most of Catholic social doctrine on the grounds of "prudential judgment," or treat Vatican II as if it had been merely a pastoral council, with little to no doctrinal weight. People who would decry secularized Catholics as "cafeteria Catholics" (a term Pope St. John Paul II used to describe those who pick and choose which doctrines they agree with) would then dissect authoritative episcopal or papal documents, underlining in gold what they thought should be assented to and in red what should not be assented to.

These arguments were given a veneer of authority, for they were firmly and confidently expounded by theologians, apologists, commentators, and pundits who had gained notoriety for defending orthodox principles in areas where the vast majority of society disdained Catholicism. Consumers of this type of media began to trust these popular figures more than in their bishops, whom they deemed too weak to defend doctrine decisively and unwaveringly in the midst of a hostile society. And even if this apologetics movement was heavily influenced by American ideals and circumstances, it started to shape Catholicism around the rest of the world as well, especially online apologetics from other countries.

Nowhere was this problem more concerning than on the topic of who should be admitted to communion. It was not uncommon to check the comment sections of Catholic websites and find people openly advocating for the excommunication of some politician, or even any public sinner who might be causing scandal, even if they had no authority to do so. This created the idea among many that they, the laity, had the responsibility of judging whether the Eucharist was being profaned or not, since bishops and priests would be too irresolute to enforce what they perceived to be the right Eucharistic discipline.

❖❖❖

Then came Pope Francis, elected in 2013. Mere minutes after his presentation at the balcony of St. Peter's Basilica, the well-known website *Rorate Caeli* published an article titled "The Horror." In fact, many Catholics in social media were reacting with horror, as the Holy Father had chosen a non-traditional papal name (he was the first in history to choose "Francis"). What was worse, that name was actually associated with liberal sensitivities, since St. Francis of Assisi's love for poverty and nature made him particularly attractive to left-wing advocates of social justice and ecological care. To add insult to injury, the pope eschewed the typical papal regalia during his presentation, and chose instead a more humble attire. He seemed to fit into the typical left-wing stereotype of what a pope should be.

In the following years, the situation seemed to deteriorate. The pope's strong emphasis on social justice made it unsustainable to cling to the arguments previously designed by the aforementioned apologists to align Catholicism with their own right-wing views. By this point, however, the ideas that had been absorbed by these Catholics for years did not allow them to think of Catholicism in any other way. Either Catholicism was something completely different from what they had been taught to believe before . . . or the pope was wrong.

Those suffering from an ingrained "us-versus-them" mentality felt like they had no other choice but, for the first time, to catalogue the pope himself as one of "them." The Catholic Church now needed to be defended by faithful Catholics not just from the world, but from the pope himself. This idea (which they did not create, but certainly adopted) was called "recognize and resist." In other words, they would "recognize" the pope, but "resist" his allegedly erroneous teachings.

From 2013 to 2016, the resistance to Pope Francis's teachings and reforms kept building in Catholic media. Every one of Francis's utterances was viewed with increasing suspicion. It became an undeniable truth among certain Catholics that Francis wanted to undermine sound doctrine, even if he had not explicitly taught anything heretical. On the other hand, Francis could not be accused of heterodoxy or heresy as of yet, since everything he said could be traced back to the previous two pontificates (even if those sayings had been largely ignored by the Catholic establishment before).

But all of that changed in 2016.

Preface xvii

By publishing *Amoris Laetitia* and changing the discipline regarding Eucharistic access to the divorced and remarried, Pope Francis had finally done something that no other of his immediate predecessors had done before. In fact, it seemed like he actually and blatantly contradicted St. John Paul II and Benedict XVI. The accusations that had simmered in the previous three years had finally found an outlet. *Amoris Laetitia* had become the proof of the pope's heterodoxy. From now on, *Amoris Laetitia* could be invoked as a validation of the suspicions raised against Francis since his election.

In this context, it is no wonder that my (or any other) arguments in favor of the orthodoxy of *Amoris Laetitia* were met with skepticism. However, this context also shows why I think a book defending the orthodoxy of this apostolic exhortation is urgent. For, in the meantime, the apologetics movement has started to produce arguments meant to undermine papal authority, something utterly incompatible with Catholicism's very own DNA.

❦ ❦ ❦

Structure of the book: This book is an attempt to refute the arguments posed by the adherents of the "recognize and resist" position, who have taken a critical approach towards *Amoris Laetitia* and Pope Francis. I struggled to find a charitable yet succinct term that would encompass all of the Catholics belonging to this highly heterogeneous group. The term I came to use was "papal critic." I think it is not uncharitable to use this term, since one of the keystones of their position is that it is possible for a faithful Catholic to voice legitimate criticisms of the pontiff. In any case, the term "papal critic" should not be construed as a judgment on their soul, nor as a derogatory expression, and should always be read according to the definition I just provided.

Whenever I deal with one of those critical arguments, I will provide footnotes with relevant quotes from well-known figures advocating such claims. However, these quotes are merely examples, because each of them represents a common and oft-repeated argument. I do not want to refute individual persons, but rather standard talking points that most people acquainted with this debate will be able to recognize. Not all papal critics will have used all of the arguments present in this book; but all of these arguments have been advanced at one time or another by some papal critics, and are relatively widespread across Catholic news outlets and social media.

Many of the chapters in this book originate in articles I wrote for the website *Where Peter Is* (http://wherepeteris.com), a site created by a group of Catholics troubled by the attacks against the holy father and the Catholic doctrine of papal primacy. I have decided to organize this book by dividing it into four sections:

- Introduction: An appeal to a *metanoia* of the mind. Just like Pascal's wager is not meant to be an argument in itself, but to open up minds to his apologetics, likewise this introduction is meant to emphasize that the reader has nothing to lose from taking the thesis of this book seriously. What if the pope is indeed orthodox? If there is even a sliver of a chance that this might be true, should we not take it? If there is a way to reconcile Pope Francis's teachings with sound doctrine, should this not be met with joy and expectation, instead of suspicion—especially since the pope's reliability on teachings of faith and morals should be the default position for the faithful?

- First Section: Some brief introductory remarks, where the groundwork for the actual arguments is laid.

  - Chapter 1: An assessment of *Amoris Laetitia*'s magisterial weight.

  - Chapter 2: An explanation of the narrow limits allowed for dissent from an act of authentic magisterium of the pope, contrary to common arguments by many commentators stating the opposite.

- Second Section: A search for *Amoris Laetitia*'s most likely interpretation, and of its theological foundations.

  - Chapter 3: An evaluation of the various interpretations of this document, and whether they allow us to find an interpretation more in line with Pope Francis's manifest mind and will.

  - Chapter 4: An exegesis of the apostolic exhortation's controversial eighth chapter, so as to try to interpret it on its own terms.

  - Chapter 5: A validation of the conclusions drawn from the previous chapter, by taking recourse to other papal acts besides the document itself.

- Chapter 6: A dispelling of some of the most common misinterpretations of the document.

- Chapter 7: An exposition on the Catholic teaching of mitigating circumstances, since this seems to be the central axis around which the most likely interpretation of *Amoris Laetitia* revolves, and without which the text cannot be properly understood.

- Chapter 8: A comment on the issue of scandal, since this can be used as an objection to the implementation of the apostolic exhortation.

- Chapter 9: An explanation as to why the *dubia* sent to the pope by four cardinals, far from clarifying the issue, have sadly contributed to increasing the confusion around it.

● Third Section: A demonstration of how *Amoris Laetitia* constitutes a legitimate development of doctrine.

- Chapter 10: A proposal for a model explaining the mechanics of this development, so as to better illustrate its orthodoxy to those who may have trouble envisioning how this can be possible.

- Chapter 11: A hermeneutic of continuity between *Amoris Laetitia* and *Familiaris Consortio*.

- Chapter 12: A similar attempt to explain the continuity between *Amoris Laetitia* and *Veritatis Splendor*.

- Chapter 13: A refutation of the supposed contradictions between *Amoris Laetitia* and other authoritative church documents besides the ones already mentioned.

- Chapter 14: An exposition of a curious precedent for *Amoris Laetitia*, involving the pastoral application of *Humanae Vitae* in place since the time of John Paul II.

- Chapter 15: A demonstration of the legitimacy of the doctrinal development present in *Amoris Laetitia*, according to the principles laid out by the most important theologian on the topic, Saint Cardinal Henry Newman.

● Fourth Section: An illustration of how *Amoris Laetitia* can be applied in practice.

- Chapter 16: An exposition of a hypothetical case study.

- Chapter 17: An assessment of the guidelines issued by three Portuguese dioceses, since each one of them contains details that may help illustrate different facets of the practical application of *Amoris Laetitia*.

❈ ❈ ❈

Disclosures: I am a practicing Catholic and I proclaim my fidelity to every single doctrine of the church, in every single matter, be it sexual or social. I also believe in the church's infallible doctrine on the indissolubility of marriage, and neither I, nor anyone of my proximate circle, has ever been divorced at the time of the writing of this book. I also believe that people in mortal sin should not receive the Eucharist. I have been faithful to every single teaching of Pope Benedict XVI and see my fidelity to Francis as a simple extension of what I did during the previous pontificate. I also take the authority of *every* successor of Peter seriously, both pre- and post-conciliar. I have no ideology nor political party. I am neither liberal nor conservative. I am neither traditionalist nor progressive. I am simply Catholic and try to let myself be guided by the church to wherever its teachings may take me.

Acknowledgements

I wish to thank my beautiful wife Claire Navarro Domingues for her support, for reviewing these writings, and for her input on church governance.

I thank Stephen Walford and Mike Lewis for all their support and encouragement throughout this project. I thank Mike also for inviting me to contribute to *Where Peter Is*, prompting me to write many of the chapters of this book.

I thank Stephen Little for his work in copyediting this book, and also David Wanat for his beta reading.

I would also like to thank Austen Ivereigh and the Reverend Vicar Patrick Travers for their bibliographical suggestions and help.

Finally, I send special thanks to Father Paul Keller for graciously allowing me to use his case study on chapter 16; to Filipe d'Avillez, reporter for the Portuguese Catholic radio station Rádio Renascença, for his English translation of the Lisbon guidelines; and to Prof. Rocco Buttiglione, Prof. Rodrigo Guerra López, and Father Tom Ryan for allowing me to quote their books and articles.

List of Abbreviations

Biblical Abbreviations

1 Cor—First Epistle of the Apostle St. Paul to the Corinthians

1 Tim—First Epistle of the Apostle St. Paul to Timothy

Acts—Book of the Acts of the Apostles

Exod—Book of Exodus

Gen—Book of Genesis

Isa—Book of Prophet Isaiah

John—Gospel according to St. John

Jas—Epistle of the Apostle St. James

Luke—Gospel according to St. Luke

Mark—Gospel according to St. Mark

Matt—Gospel according to St. Matthew

Ps—Book of Psalms

Rom—Epistle of the Apostle St. Paul to the Romans

(Note: All of the biblical quotes were taken from the Douay-Rheims, except in the cases where they were quoted as embedded in other documents, in which case the version of said document was followed.)

Non-biblical Abbreviations

AAS—*Acta Apostolicae Sedis*

AL—*Amoris Laetitia*

CCC—*Catechism of the Catholic Church*

CDF—Congregation for the Doctrine of the Faith

DCPF—*Doctrinal Commentary on the Concluding Formula of the Professio fidei*

DV—*Donum Veritatis*

EG—*Evangelii Gaudium*

FC—*Familiaris Consortio*

LG—*Lumen Gentium*

PCLT—Pontifical Council for Legislative Texts

SSPX—International Priestly Society of St. Pius X

VS—*Veritatis Splendor*

WPI—*Where Peter Is* website

Introduction

A Call to Metanoia

METANOIA HAS BEEN TRADITIONALLY understood (and rightfully so) in Christian theology as conversion, repentance, turning our backs on an old life of sin. But this word was engendered in ancient Greece, before Christianity even began. Etymologically and originally it meant "to change one's mind" (*meta* means "go beyond"; *noein* means "mind").[1]

Why has Christianity changed the meaning of this word? For Christians, the greatest change of mind one can experience is a conversion to a greater communion with God's will. However, just as the new definition developed a deeper, wider meaning for the word, returning to its original roots may help us rediscover this word with a new Christian perspective.

❊❊❊

As Pope Benedict XVI has remarked, there can be no *orthopraxis* (i.e., correct conduct) without orthodoxy (correct thought).[2] Of course, one may accidentally do the right thing even when one has a defective moral compass. However, in the end, our thoughts, values, prejudices, and perceptions shape and structure the way we act. If we wish to start a path of conversion, and be consistent with it, we need to reexamine the way we think.

In this sense, I would like to focus on *metanoia* as a change of mind. This is especially important for a certain sector of the church composed of people (like myself) with a certain interest in theology and church affairs, and who usually engage in apologetics online. It is my firm belief

---

1. *Catholic Dictionary*, s.v. "Metanoia."
2. Messori, *The Ratzinger Report*, 23.

that this community, just like the rest of humanity, is in deep need of *metanoia*.

Given its particular vocation, this community is prone to over-intellectualize the faith. We spend most of our time engaging in debates and polishing arguments, sometimes overestimating the effectiveness of purely intellectual preaching. Sometimes, this may result in an estrangement from the average Catholic in the pews—someone who may have a more pietist approach to the faith. It can even result in what Pope Francis calls a kind of "Neo-Gnosticism": the more a person knows about the faith, the more holy he thinks he is.[3]

So it could be argued that urging *metanoia* as a "change of mind" for this community might actually exacerbate the problem. After all, the hurdle lies precisely in an over-emphasis of the intellect. However, I disagree with this for two reasons. First of all, it will be very hard for these people to let go of their intellectualized approach to the faith—and thank God for that! That is my approach too, and I would not be truly myself if I would be forced to act my faith in a way that is foreign to my own being. The church—thankfully so—is not and never has been anti-intellectual, contrary to widespread atheist propaganda. Rather, the church nurtures and develops everything truly human in us, including our God-given minds. Catholicism needs as many intellectuals as prayer warriors or activists.

Secondly, it must be stressed that an exaggerated intellectualization actually goes against true orthodoxy. If we are focused on church teaching, we must know that church teaching itself cautions us about an exclusively intellectual approach to the faith, to the detriment of other aspects of our life that are also important. It is part of our orthodoxy that everything that is good may become an idol, if its importance is so overestimated that it is set on a pedestal above God. This includes reason. As Benedict XVI, himself a brilliant intellectual, remarks in his encyclical *Deus Caritas Est*:

> Being Christian is not the result of an ethical choice or a lofty idea, but the encounter with an event, a person, which gives life a new horizon and a decisive direction.[4]

The statement above is also doctrine. It is orthodoxy. A proper understanding of Christianity must acknowledge this. We cannot have a

---

3. Francis, *Gaudete et Exsultate*, 45.
4. Benedict XVI, *Deus Caritas Est*, 2.

reductionist view of Christianity, as if it were only a set of ideas, dogmas, and checklists. Ultimately, Christianity is a conversion permeating our whole life. But for that to happen, we need to set our mind to accommodate this fact. Hence, we need a *metanoia* of the mind.

❖ ❖ ❖

I am reminded of the ancient philosopher Xenophanes, who believed that, if horses and cattle had hands, they would sculpt gods in the likeness of horses and cattle.[5] I have seen a similar argument being touted by atheists, parodying one of our most foundational doctrines: allegedly, God did not make man in his image; rather man fashioned God in man's image.[6]

I have always thought this showed a serious misconception about the faith. I can assure the reader the God I worship is not made in my image and likeness. If he was, he would certainly do many things differently, and act more in accordance with my ideas. One of the core frustrations of the religious man (a constructive frustration, necessary for spiritual growth) is the acknowledgement of how different God is from one's desires and preconceptions.[7] Progress in the path of faith means accepting this fact with increasing docility, and conforming our wills to his.[8]

Yet, even though I see the atheists' argument as based on a misconception, I can certainly understand where they are coming from. It is true

---

5. Wikipedia, s.v. "Xenophanes."

6. An example of this reasoning can be seen in Thomson and Aukofer, "Science and Religion."

7. See Isa 55:8–9: "For my thoughts are not your thoughts: nor your ways my ways, saith the Lord. For as the heavens are exalted above the earth, so are my ways exalted above your ways, and my thoughts above your thoughts."

8. This is such a constant in Catholic asceticism and mysticism, that examples are superabundant. One such instance can be seen in John of the Cross, *Ascent of Mt. Carmel*, 3.3.4: "If he [a man] sets store by knowledge, this is simply and utterly impossible; for countless imperfections and follies insinuate themselves into such knowledge, some of which are so subtle and minute that, without the soul's realization thereof, they cling to it of their own accord. . . . You will say likewise that by so doing the soul deprives itself of many good thoughts and meditations upon God, which are of great profit to it and whereby God grants it favours. I reply that to this end purity of soul is of the greatest profit, which means that there clings to the soul no creature affection, or temporal affection, or effective advertence; which I believe cannot but cling to the soul because of the imperfection which the faculties have in their own operations." See also Thomas à Kempis, *Imitation of Christ*, book 3: "And he is truly learned, who does the will of God, and forsakes his own will."

that many religious people unwittingly give a bad example, providing evidence that man often fashions God in his own image.

To better illustrate what I am getting at, let us take one example that resonates with most papal critics: the heresy of modernism. Pope St. Pius X defined modernism as "the synthesis of all heresies."[9] I believe he is correct, but not for the reason people of a traditionalist bent usually give. Modernism is usually defined as the idea that the Catholic Church must adapt its teachings to modern society's expectations and values, no matter how antithetical they are to Catholic doctrine.[10]

In this sense, modernism is the synthesis of all heresies, but not because modernity has within it some kind of malignant potential corrupting everything it touches. Rather, modernism is the synthesis of all heresies because it is caused by the sin of pride.[11] In fact, in his seminal anti-modernist encyclical, Pius X defines the pride lying at the heart of the modernist movement as:

> That confidence in themselves [that] leads them to hold themselves up as the rule for all . . . which allows them to regard themselves as the sole possessors of knowledge . . . which rouses in them the spirit of disobedience.[12]

In sum, this pride leads us to think that when we disagree with church teaching: it is the church that is wrong, not us. This is one of the things that makes modernism so dangerous.

I think modernism is indeed the synthesis of all heresies in this regard, because this attitude underlies the core source of all heresies and evils: original sin. There is a common misconception in atheist quarters: that God wanted to keep Adam and Eve in ignorance by forbidding them to taste from the fruit of the tree of knowledge. Atheists wrongly interpret

---

9. Pius X, *Pascendi Dominici Gregis*, 39.

10. Vermeersch, "Modernism": "A remodelling, a renewal according to the ideas of the twentieth century—such is the longing that possesses the modernists. 'The avowed modernists', says M. Loisy, 'form a fairly definite group of thinking men united in the common desire to adapt Catholicism to the intellectual, moral, and social needs of today' (*Simples réflexions sur le décret 'Lamentabili' et sur l'encyclique 'Pascendi' du 8 September, 1907*, p. 13). 'Our religious attitude,' as *Il programma dei modernisti* states (p. 5, note l), 'is ruled by the single wish to be one with Christians and Catholics who live in harmony with the spirit of the age.'"

11. Pius X, *Pascendi Dominici Gregis*, 40.

12. Pius X, *Pascendi Dominici Gregis*, 40.

this as yet another anti-intellectual stance of the Bible.[13] But we know from a correct biblical exegesis that when Adam and Eve ate from the tree of knowledge, it was not because they craved knowledge, but because they wanted a life on their own terms, independent of God.[14] Satan himself illustrates this, for he tempts them: "in what day soever you shall eat thereof . . . you shall be as Gods."[15]

This attitude is perfectly countered by Jesus, the new Adam, in the garden of Gethsemani. Foretelling his own death, Jesus prays to the Father to spare him. Nevertheless, in the end, he yields by saying: "Thy will be done."[16] This cry is mirrored by the Virgin Mary's *fiat*,[17] for she is the new Eve crushing the head of the ancient serpent. As Catholic author Caryll Houselander magnificently writes, "What is conversion but the *fiat* of Our Lady echoed again and the conception of Christ in yet another heart?"[18]

It is fitting, therefore, that this should be conveyed in our most fundamental prayer, the one that God himself taught us so that we should know how to pray: "Thy will be done on earth as it is in heaven."[19]

❊ ❊ ❊

Let us return to the point where we acknowledge that the ultimate error of the modernist is the pride leading him to think that the church is wrong, rather than himself. In this sense, it may be true that many liberal Catholics are applauding Pope Francis, not because they think he is expounding correct doctrine (in fact, they tend to be unconvinced and unimpressed by doctrinal statements) but because they think he is a kind of Trojan horse that will be used to change the church into the form they

---

13. Clarence Darrow, as quoted in an eulogy by Emanuel Haldeman-Julius in 1938, would have said: "Do you, good people, believe that Adam and Eve were created in the Garden of Eden and that they were forbidden to eat from the tree of knowledge? I do. The church has always been afraid of that tree. It still is afraid of knowledge." ("Clarence Darrow Quotes.")

14. *CCC* 398, quoting St. Maximus the Confessor, defines the Fall as man wanting to be "like God," but "without God, before God, and not in accordance with God." See also Levering, *Christ and the Catholic Priesthood*, 114.

15. Gen 3:5.

16. Mark 14:36; Luke 22:42.

17. Luke 1:38.

18. Houselander, *The Reed of God*, 49.

19. Matt 6:10.

want. But should Pope Francis say something against their progressive ideals, their support wanes.[20]

Ironically, many conservative Catholics, who rail against modernists and liberals for doing this, seem to fall into the same error. Francis makes them uneasy, but they view that as Francis's fault, not as a call for their own conversion from any error they may espouse.[21] Their theological baggage makes them think they have everything figured out, so the pontiff cannot ask them to change their mind.

Those who have fallen prey to this error want to change the church, not change themselves. The only difference between them and the modernists is that the former want to change the church to what (they think) it once was, while the latter want to change the church to what (they think) it will be. While the externals are diametrically opposite, the heart remains the same in both situations. A *metanoia* is sorely needed.

❦❦❦

The apologetics community, of which I am part, recognizes the need for a *metanoia* of the mind, or otherwise its whole existence would be absurd. After all, apologetics is predicated on changing other people's minds. The problem is, we may be tempted to recognize this need in others while failing to apply it to ourselves first and foremost. We may become so dazzled with our own apologetics that we start to confuse it with actual church doctrine.

So, when a pope or ecumenical council or a bishop teaches something that contradicts an idea that some Catholics have held for years, their first reaction may be not to conform to the church, but to find ways to justify themselves so as to remain unchanged. This is particularly serious if they have for years incentivized people on how they should change their deeply held beliefs to accommodate church teaching. If we become unable to heed our own advice, Jesus's parable of the speck and the beam may then speak against us.[22]

Sometimes, this rationalization is done by taking a very clear and straightforward church document and deconstructing it into

---

20. Pepinster, "The Pope's Liberal Supporters Feel That He's Let Them down."

21. For example, some reactions from papal critics towards Pope Francis's warning against doctrinal rigidity are documented in this article from critical website *Church Militant*: Moyski, "Clergy and Laity Offer Strong Response to Pope's 'Rigid' Comments."

22. Matt 7:3–5.

meaninglessness.²³ This can be done in order to assert that the document does not say what it actually (and clearly) says.²⁴ We should be wary, especially if we disagree with the plain reading of the document in the first place, lest we introduce our own bias into the mix. Or this deconstruction can be done to try to undermine the magisterial source issuing the document, claiming that it is therefore unreliable.²⁵

Another common *modus operandi* consists in proof-texting church documents, separating them from the magisterial context conferring them authority, and selecting whatever validates one's preconceived ideas while rejecting anything which does not fit. This person holds onto a private interpretation of tradition and then insists all Catholics are bound to hold to that interpretation.²⁶ When someone acts like this, he ceases to be an apologist for the church's actual teaching. Rather, he becomes an apologist for his own opinions. If the church contradicts him, the church is the one that must yield. All these strategies serve one sole purpose: to prevent one from changing one's mind. In other words, to avoid *metanoia*.

❈ ❈ ❈

It may also happen that the individual claims to be undergoing *metanoia*, while in fact keeping himself stagnant in his *status quo*. I have come across two of such tactics.

One may say, "What do you mean I need to convert? Every day I try to convert! I go to confession and keep myself from sinning, so as to get

---

23. As an example, Chris Johnson published an article in the critical website *The Remnant* on June 19, 2015, titled "Why I'm Disregarding *Laudato Si* and You Should Too." In this article, he states: "First of all, what does 'accepting the world as a sacrament of communion' mean? Like all post-conciliar encyclicals, this one is heavy on nonsensical ambiguous language. We know as Catholics that there are only seven sacraments instituted by Christ Our Lord and 'the world' is not one of them. Further, the sacrament of Holy Communion is not defined as 'sharing with God and our neighbors on a global scale.' However, even if it were, what exactly are we supposed to be sharing with God and our neighbors? We aren't told. Who knows!? That is what keeps the Neo-Catholics in business isn't it? The pope provides the nonsensical ambiguity and the Neo-Catholics 'interpret' it for us and tell us what it means."

24. See the deconstruction of Jesus Christ's injunction to "render unto Caesar what is Caesar's" (Luke 20:21–25) in Barr, "Render Unto Caesar."

25. One classical example is George Weigel's deconstruction of the social doctrine tenets in Benedict XVI's last encyclical, in Weigel's essay "*Caritas in Veritate* in Gold and Red."

26. I comment on this error with more detail in my article "*Sola Traditio*."

holier! I try to change myself whenever I resist sin. That has nothing to do with this church teaching I have problems with."[27]

To this I reply: It is good and holy to keep oneself from sinning, but one must also be on guard against that which one does not believe to be a sin, yet actually is. If someone only tries to convert away from the sins one already understands as sinful (i.e., if one only tries to change that which one already wants to change) then that is not a real *metanoia*: this person already has his mind set on changing that sinful part of his. But true *metanoia* means change of mind, as we have already seen. The true struggle lies in changing those parts that *we think need no changing*. True conversion means a complete inner transformation, a perfect alignment with God's truth and will. We cannot do that if we only seek to transform according to our own perceptions of what must change and not beyond that. We must bear in mind that God is an Other, different from ourselves. If, regarding conversion, we see him always validating us and not unsettling us, then it's our own voice we are hearing, not his.

The second objection usually goes like this: "I gave Pope Francis the benefit of the doubt until a certain point, but eventually snapped.[28] Now I have taken the red pill[29] and can see clearly."[30]

This implies one tried a *metanoia*, but found it impossible. Again, this is not a true *metanoia*. When this person says he gave Pope Francis the benefit of the doubt, what he means is that he tried to square Francis's pontificate into his preexistent frame of thought and found he could not. He was unsuccessful, and it is not surprising. It is true that *Amoris Laetitia* does indeed change the discipline regarding sacramental access to the divorced and remarried.[31] The problem is that, when faced with this realization, the person came to the conclusion that the problem was

---

27. This reasoning is strongly implied whenever commentators claim that the pope is always "attacking good, faithful Catholics." See, for example: Reno, "A Failing Papacy"; Lawler, "Pope Francis Has Become a Source of Division."

28. A paradigmatic example is Phil Lawler's description of his spiritual journey under Pope Francis in the article "This Disastrous Papacy."

29. This is a pop culture reference, often used in social media, that eventually took on a life of its own. In the movie *The Matrix*, taking the "red pill" means waking up from an illusory and comfortable world and facing reality as it really is.

30. Another paradigmatic example is Taylor Marshall's video, "Red Pilled on Pope Francis," with Tim Gordon and Patrick Coffin.

31. NB: From now on I use the word "remarried" as a way to allow brevity in the discussion. Obviously, the church does not believe that a person can remarry after a divorce while his/her spouse is still alive. As a Catholic, I assent to this.

with Francis and not with himself. He struggled to convince himself that *Amoris Laetitia* did not change sacramental discipline, but could not, because that is not true. He then conceded that *Amoris Laetitia* does indeed change discipline, but he did not concede that this change of discipline is orthodox.

In this sense, he came close to *metanoia*, but did not undergo the final step. Rather, he saw the leap of faith and turned back. Tragically, the end result is just the same as if he did not try it in the first place. There was no *metanoia* in his mind, and he joined the company of those who dissented from day one.

※ ※ ※

So, should we just accept uncritically whatever it is the church teaches? Is this anti-intellectualism not foreign to Catholic tradition and thought? Of course it is. But, as G.K. Chesterton is said to have once remarked, when we go to church "we take off our hats, but not our heads";[32] and again, "We do not really want a religion that is right where we are right. What we want is a religion that is right where we are wrong."[33]

Catholic philosophy does not think the mind lies in the brain, but in the heart. *Metanoia* as a change of mind is, above all, a change of attitude. It demands humility. It behooves us to admit that we do not possess all the answers, to acknowledge that sin darkens the intellect, to confess that our understanding is always insufficient to encompass all truth.

This is not anti-intellectualism; it is actually the foundation of sound intellectuality. Only by knowing this can we go forth in search of the truth instead of keeping ourselves stagnant in our own opinions. For example, let us take science, one of the greatest intellectual endeavors of the human mind. There is a difference between science *per se* and scientism. Scientism (or scientific positivism) is the notion that "the only true or positive knowledge is knowledge based on observed facts gained through scientific investigation."[34] Those who adhere to this philosophy usually disregard theology, because theology is not a natural science. In doing so, they are actually despising a very interesting body of thought.

32. Poupard, "Christ and Science," 492.
33. Chesterton, *Catholic Church and Conversion*, chap. 5.
34. Nelson, "Positivism," 1437. For a practical example, see the debate between William Lane Craig and Peter Atkins, held at the Carter Presidential Center, Atlanta, Georgia, USA, in 1998. In this debate, Atkins argues we can know everything through science (Ochabski, "Dr. William Lane Craig vs. Dr. Peter Atkins Highlight").

We usually hear their voices dripping with arrogance, pride, and lack of humility.

On the other hand, if we look at actual scientific publications, we see how scientists usually do not overplay their hands (or rather, their minds). Making definitive conclusions is frowned upon. Rather, scientists usually temper their articles with expressions like "more studies are needed." They are prudent and humble. They acknowledge the limitations of their studies, their methodologies, their circumstances, their minds.

We do not know how a subatomic particle can behave as a wave and as a particle at the same time. Yet rejecting quantum physics is anti-intellectualism and accepting it is intellectualism. We do not know how it is possible, but we see the evidence and just admit that reality is greater than what we can conceive. We do not try to force reality into our minds, but humbly own up to our limits and do our best.

If we do this with nature, how much more should we do this with the ineffable mystery at the root of our religion: God, the Most High, the unknowable? If we see ourselves disagreeing with the magisterium, we should take it as our default position that we are in the wrong and the magisterium in the right. Of course, to do this we must have a different attitude. We must undergo a *metanoia*: we must try to change ourselves into the image and likeness of God, through the church's guidance, and not to try to change the church into our own image and likeness. Otherwise we kill any prospect of conversion.

This is the most common of sins regarding the church: the idea that the church should change to fit us and not the other way around. It is the sin of thinking we know better. The sin of not conforming to the teachings we disagree with. It is the sin of the progressives and the conservatives, the sin of the modernists and the ultratraditionalists, the sin of the apologists and the common folk.

But if the church is to be the salt of the earth, then it cannot lose its flavor.[35] If it is to help men convert, it cannot be subject to popular vote. If it is meant to proclaim eternal truths, it cannot just change according to everyone's opinions. In short, as G.K. Chesterton once more says, "We do not want . . . a Church that will move with the world. We want a Church that will move the world."[36]

✻✻✻

35. Matt 5:13.
36. Ward, *Gilbert Keith Chesterton*.

Introduction

The pope is being severely attacked by once-faithful Catholic media. He is being accused of being heterodox, if not outright heretical—something that many pious theologians only considered as a very remote possibility (when not an ontological impossibility) in the context of theoretical theological debates.[37] The critics bring up obscure cases of heterodox popes,[38] dug up from Protestant textbooks[39] and other anti-Catholic sources.[40] All the while, they are conveniently forgetting essential nuances, such as the exceptional character of those cases, and how much more common it is for those who condemned popes as heretics to end up on the wrong side of the doctrinal debate. Every single argument formulated by the critics of Francis ends up undermining the primacy of Peter, one of the best established doctrines and most foundational principles of Catholicism, for therein lies the unity of the church.[41] All of this creates great scandal

---

37. The most emblematic case is St. Cardinal Robert Bellarmine's affirmative answer to the question of whether a heretical pope can be deposed. According to this doctor of the church, a heretical pope would automatically be deposed, since a manifest heretic ceases to be a member of the church and, therefore, loses his office and jurisdiction (Bellarmine, "On the Roman Pontiff"). This ignores how St. Bellarmine explored this question in the context of theoretical speculation. He was examining five different opinions on this matter, and the idea that a heretical pope automatically loses his office is the fifth opinion. The saint, however, personally subscribed to the first opinion, that a pope could not be a heretic and, therefore, lose his office because of heresy. He calls this opinion "probable" and defends it elsewhere. However, since this first opinion was "not certain," he proceeded to evaluate the other opinions, which he could only do if he took the existence of a heretical pope for granted. It is only in this context that he later calls the fifth opinion "most certain."

38. In Buscemi et al., "Open Letter to the Bishops of the Catholic Church," a group of Catholic theologians formally accused Pope Francis of heresy because of *Amoris Laetitia*, among other things. They invoked the precedent of the allegedly heretical Pope Honorius to sustain their thesis: "The situation of a pope falling into heresy has long been a subject of discussion by Catholic theologians. This situation was brought into prominence after the ecumenical Third Council of Constantinople anathematized the Monothelite heresy in 681, and posthumously anathematized Pope Honorius for his support of this heresy; this condemnation of Honorius as a heretic was repeated by Pope St. Leo II when he ratified the acts of that Council."

39. Harris, *Fundamental Protestant Doctrines*, vol. 2, pg. 13: "Honorius was a heretic according to Roman Catholic standards and was condemned by church councils and popes for 800 years. Such facts are not known to most Protestants as they arise from the technical study of history. They naturally are not publicized by Roman Catholics. But facts they are. And they entirely disprove the papal claims." This claim is quoted in Loraine Boettner's later influential work, *Roman Catholicism*.

40. Some of these polemicists are listed in Spencer, "The Truth about Pope Honorius."

41. Vatican I, *Pastor Aeternus*: "In order, then, that the episcopal office should be

among Catholics and non-Catholics alike, pushing both away from full communion with the Vicar of Christ. For why should they be Catholic, if they cannot put their trust in the church, but only in the opinions of learned men?

These are the stakes today. So, before siding with the critics, one must answer this question honestly and decisively: "What if they are wrong? What if the pope is right instead?" Isn't the price to be paid so high that it should demand an absolute certainty, without any doubts whatsoever? Are we really that sure? Should we not explore and exhaust every possible venue to reconcile the pope with orthodoxy before undergoing this path?

Maybe this is not the time to side with those criticizing the pope. Maybe this is the time for *metanoia*. In fact, it is always time for *metanoia*. Let us take this golden opportunity. The time is ripe. Let us try to change our minds to receive the teachings of Pope Francis, even if they seem strange at first.

This is by no means meant to be an instantaneous process, successful at first try. Nevertheless, as Pope Francis teaches us, conversion begins with taking a first step. This first step should be a change of mind, through a change of heart. A humble and contrite heart God does not refuse.[42] Let us let ourselves be guided by the church, instead of seeing it as an ideological battlefield where we must fight and lobby for a church more in conformity with our own immovable ideas. Let us open our minds and hearts to *metanoia* of the mind, so that *metanoia* of our whole being may naturally follow. Let us not be the cattle of Xenophanes, but the flock of the good shepherd, the one who instituted Peter as his vicar. We have already seen how this can be achieved: by praying, with Jesus and Mary, "Thy will be done, o Lord, not mine."

This is what I propose to you today. Most especially, this is what I propose to you in this book. If I was successful in opening up your mind and heart, I will now proceed to present my arguments as to why I think Pope Francis and *Amoris Laetitia* are both orthodox.

---

one and undivided and that, by the union of the clergy, the whole multitude of believers should be held together in the unity of faith and communion, he set blessed Peter over the rest of the apostles and instituted in him the permanent principle of both unities and their visible foundation."

42. Ps 50:19.

Section I

SOME INTRODUCTORY REMARKS

Chapter 1

Is *Amoris Laetitia* Magisterial?

The Objections

The *Catechism of the Catholic Church* (CCC) defines the magisterium as follows (emphasis from now on is always mine):

> "The task of giving an *authentic interpretation of the Word of God*, whether in its written form or *in the form of Tradition*, has been entrusted to the living teaching office of the Church *alone*. Its authority in this matter is exercised in *the name of Jesus Christ.*" This means that the task of interpretation has been entrusted to the bishops in communion with the successor of Peter, *the Bishop of Rome*.[1]

Papal critics are very quick to point out that the subsequent paragraph in the *Catechism* declares that 1) the magisterium is not superior to the word of God, but rather its servant; and 2) that it teaches only what has been handed on to it.[2] Since *Amoris Laetitia* would allegedly contradict the word of God, or since it would allegedly be a novelty in rupture with what was previously held, then it could not possibly be magisterial.[3]

Of course, this objection only stands if *Amoris Laetitia* is indeed contradictory and discontinuous with previous doctrine, something I

---

1. *CCC* 85.
2. *CCC* 86.
3. See Skojec, "Is *Amoris Laetitia* an Expression of the Ordinary and Universal Magisterium?"

will try to refute in the course of this book. If *Amoris Laetitia* is orthodox, then we cannot say it is not magisterial on the basis of its heterodoxy. Nevertheless, the argument around *Amoris Laetitia*'s alleged heterodoxy is not the only one being advanced to defend the idea that this document is not magisterial. Many authors have set out to write pieces proving this.[4] As a side note, many of these authors were against *Amoris Laetitia*'s change of sacramental discipline in the first place,[5] raising the question of the possibility of bias when they wrote those pieces.

The objections laid out against the magisterial status of *Amoris Laetitia* are usually repetitions of the three arguments expounded by Cardinal Raymond Burke in an article written to the online news site *National Catholic Register* soon after the document's publication. In this article, the cardinal says, "Pope Francis makes clear, *from the beginning,* that the post-synodal apostolic exhortation is not an act of the magisterium."[6]

What does "from the beginning" mean? Please note that the cardinal is referencing to *Amoris Laetitia (AL)* 3, where the pope says:

> I would make it clear that not all discussions of doctrinal, moral or pastoral issues need to be settled by interventions of the magisterium. Unity of teaching and practice is certainly necessary in the Church, but this does not preclude various ways of interpreting some aspects of that teaching or drawing certain consequences from it.

I really think it is incorrect to suggest that *Amoris Laetitia* is not magisterial because of this quote. Pope Francis is explaining that not all discussions need to be settled by interventions of the magisterium,[7] but that does not mean that the *exhortation itself* is not magisterial.[8] The document is not hinting at being self-referential in this paragraph.

---

4. See, again, Skojec, "Is *Amoris Laetitia* an Expression of the Ordinary and Universal Magisterium?"

5. See Skojec, "The Dictator of the Vatican."

6. Burke, "'*Amoris Laetitia*' and the Constant Teaching and Practice of the Church."

7. It must be noted that the expression "not settled by the magisterium" may mean something different. Papal critics have put their emphasis on the word "magisterium," but the emphasis might also be placed in the word "settled," as in "non-definitive." See next footnote.

8. Ryan, "Weakness, and Wounded and Troubled Love," 145: "Finally, the allocution reflects the Pope's role as teacher and pastor. At the least, it is an expression of authentic magisterium. In some areas, it is both authoritative and definitive (e.g., sacramentality of marriage, the Christ-event and the scope of divine mercy). Other issues, such as those addressed in chapter 8, are authoritative but not definitive. They

For example, if a firm issues an official memo, stamped with the company logo and signed by the board, with instructions detailing how the decision-making at the lower-levels need not be micromanaged by official acts from the supervisors, does that mean that the memo itself is not official? The answer would obviously be negative. Suggesting otherwise would mean that the company could never delegate, for every official act of delegation would result in the act itself not being official. This would lead to an absurd burden on the board, who would need, by definition, to be involved in every decision at every level—an intolerable casuistry.

Returning to Cardinal Burke's article, he gives two more reasons to not consider the document magisterial. First, he claims that the apostolic exhortation was merely a "reflection of the Holy Father on the work of the last two sessions of the Synod of Bishops." In other words, what "he personally believes is the will of Christ to the Church."[9] The cardinal justifies his reasoning by mentioning this quote from the document:

> I understand those who prefer a more rigorous pastoral care which leaves no room for confusion. *But I sincerely believe* that Jesus wants a Church attentive to the goodness which the Holy Spirit sows in the midst of human weakness, a Mother who, while clearly expressing her objective teaching, "always does what good she can, even if in the process her shoes get soiled by the mud of the street."[10]

Since the Holy Father has used the wording "I sincerely believe . . . ," he would be talking in his personal capacity as a pastor and, therefore, would not "intend to impose his point of view, nor to condemn those who insist on what he calls 'a more rigorous pastoral care.'"[11]

Of course, we are not talking about a personal interview with the pope for a television network, or about a book published by the pontiff as a private theologian. For example, Benedict XVI cautions us that his christological trilogy *Jesus of Nazareth* "is in no way an exercise of the magisterium."[12] We have no such indication from Pope Francis as relating to *Amoris Laetitia*. On the contrary, the Holy Father used his capacity as

---

are, as the Pope says, open to further dialogue, hence, not settled by the magisterium."

9. Burke, "'*Amoris Laetitia*' and the Constant Teaching and Practice of the Church."

10. *AL* 308.

11. Burke, "'*Amoris Laetitia*' and the Constant Teaching and Practice of the Church."

12. Benedict XVI, *Jesus of Nazareth*, xxiii.

the successor of Peter to promulgate an apostolic exhortation, which by itself is an expression of the magisterium.[13] Cardinal Schönborn, who presented the exhortation to the public (see chapter 5), answers in an interview, "It is obvious that this is an act of the magisterium: it is an Apostolic Exhortation."[14] Pope Francis also used his papal authority to publish this document in the *Acta Apostolicae Sedis* (*AAS*), where the official acts of the Holy See are published.[15] It is very hard to claim that the pope was acting in his private capacity here, and not as a successor of Peter.

On the other hand, if saying "I believe" turns an official papal document into a personal opinion, then what to say about Pope St. Paul VI, when he wrote in *Humanae Vitae*: "*We believe* that our contemporaries are particularly capable of seeing that this teaching [the immorality of recourse to artificial contraception] is in harmony with human reason"?[16] What if someone postulated that Paul VI was only expressing his personal opinion here? That he did not mean to impose his point of view that this Catholic doctrine is compatible with human reason? And that therefore, if one deemed this doctrine to be incompatible with human reason, one would be free to reject it? This would not be an accurate reading. Nor would it be fair to reject the authoritativeness of the whole document and of its major decisions because of an isolated snippet like this. The same holds true for *Amoris Laetitia*.

The final argument given by Cardinal Burke is this: "The personal, that is, non-magisterial, nature of the document is also evident in the fact that the references cited are principally the final report of the 2015 session of the Synod of Bishops and the addresses and homilies of Pope Francis himself. There is no consistent effort to relate the text, in general, or these citations to the magisterium, the fathers of the church and other

---

13. Morrisey, "Apostolic Exhortation," 586: "Although not juridically binding, [apostolic exhortations] are a *significant expression of the magisterium* of the Church, and are morally persuasive and quite influential because they are frequently the product of consensus." See also Travers, "*Amoris Laetitia* and Canon 915," 394: "Apostolic exhortations, like encyclicals, are normally regarded as some of the most important instruments for exercise by the Pope of the ordinary authentic Magisterium." Contrast this with Christopher Altieri's objection ("From What, Precisely, Are *Amoris Laetitia* 'Dissenters' Dissenting?"): "A post-Synodal Exhortation is neither *a formal teaching document* nor a governing instrument of any kind."

14. Schönborn, "Conversation with Cardinal Schönborn."

15. Pius X, *Promulgandi pontificias Constitutiones*.

16. Paul VI, *Humanae Vitae*, 12.

proven authors."[17] This is also incorrect, for a variety of reasons. First, a synod of bishops "exercises a consultative role, offering information and counsel to the Roman Pontiff on various ecclesial questions."[18] So, obviously, a *post-synodal* apostolic exhortation will inevitably be based on the insights given by the *synod* of bishops. It seems an odd suggestion to say that referencing mainly the final report of the synod makes it a personal opinion.[19] Secondly, a synod of bishops is not devoid of magisterial authority.[20] Nor, for that matter, are the homilies of the Vicar of Christ,[21] which should be taken as an effort to relate the text with the magisterium.

Even if we do dismiss the synod's conclusions or the pope's homilies and addresses, it is not true that Francis does not try to relate the text or citations to the magisterium. The whole document is filled with references to other magisterial acts. We must remember that *Amoris Laetitia* is not limited to its eighth chapter, where the change of sacramental discipline is instituted. However, even if we only take into consideration this polemical eighth chapter, Francis quotes *Familiaris Consortio* thrice[22] (an apostolic exhortation that many papal critics assume as magisterial, in order to set it at odds against *Amoris Laetitia*) and the *Catechism*

17. Burke, "'*Amoris Laetitia*' and the Constant Teaching and Practice of the Church."

18. Francis, *Episcopalis Communio*, 3.

19. In this regard, it is worth mentioning that, in the aforementioned interview with *La Civiltà Cattolica*, Cardinal Schönborn says, after answering that *Amoris Laetitia* is magisterial: "It is clear that the Pope is exercising here his role of pastor, of master and teacher of the faith, after having benefited from the consultation of the two Synods." See also Travers, "*Amoris Laetitia* and Canon 915", 394: "[AL Chapter Eight] is an exercise by Pope Francis of the ordinary authentic Magisterium. It is an Apostolic Exhortation that he issued in the wake of two assemblies of the Synod of Bishops, which had exhaustively discussed and argued the issues at hand."

20. After all, the synod was composed by bishops, and if their final report was taken into account by the pope's apostolic exhortation, then surely they were in communion with him. See *CCC* 100: "The task of interpreting the Word of God authentically has been entrusted solely to the *Magisterium of the Church*, that is, to the Pope and to the *bishops in communion with him*."

21. See Peters, "A Non-Magisterial Magisterial Statement?": "Popes and bishops, addressing faith and morals, in public statements made during a constitutive part of a liturgy (see the definition of a 'homily' in Canon 767), are, I think, engaged in a magisterial act." It is interesting that Dr. Peters would later on take a critical stance towards *AL* and (according to a reply to him made by Roberto de Mattei regarding the application of this document) take a "minimalist conception of the Magisterium of the Church."

22. See *AL* 295n323, 298n329, 300.

twice.[23] It is noteworthy that these references to the *Catechism* are not mere accessories, but actually play a pivotal role in grounding Francis's sacramental discipline, as we shall see in chapters 4 and 7 of this book.

Nor can we ignore the Holy Father's consistent effort to relate this text to at least one "proven author," since he steadily bases his controversial eighth chapter on St. Thomas Aquinas's theology[24] (besides also quoting Augustine,[25] a father of the church). As Fr. Thomas Ryan, a theologian from the University of Notre Dame Australia, says: "[*Amoris Laetitia*] reflects the blending of the virtue ethics of Aquinas with the Ignatian tradition of the discernment of conscience."[26] A very interesting and comprehensive explanation of the thomistic roots behind the theology of *Amoris Laetitia* can be found in Stephen Walford's book *Pope Francis, the Family, and Divorce*.[27]

❖ ❖ ❖

Amoris Laetitia's *Magisterial Weight*

Nevertheless, even after addressing the main objections to the exhortation's magisterial value, the question still remains: is *Amoris Laetitia* magisterial?

Answering this question is a bit tricky, not because it is difficult *per se* to prove that *Amoris Laetitia* is magisterial, but because it is very difficult sometimes, even for theologians, to reach a consensus on the authoritativeness of many acts of the magisterium. Even if a pope tries to teach in a definitive way, theologians will sometimes argue on whether he

---

23. Both in *AL* 302.

24. See *AL* 301, 304. See also Buttiglione, *Risposte Amichevoli*, 124: "The best way to get out of a simple ethics of the norm is the one from St. Thomas Aquinas. Reason must command the soul, but in a way that is political, not despotic. Reason must, in a sense, not force, but persuade the passions to accept its directions, and can do so because passions are fundamentally oriented towards the good. Reason desires the full self-realization of the person, and this self-realization includes, by principle, the orderly satisfaction of human passions. St. Thomas therefore develops an ethics of virtue. Virtue is the habit of tending towards good through action." (My translation from the original Italian.)

25. See *AL* 306.

26. Ryan, "Weakness, and Wounded and Troubled Love," 140. See also 133–34.

27. Walford, *Pope Francis, the Family, and Divorce*, 90–94.

was actually infallible or not if the formula the pope employed was not *ex cathedra*.[28]

However, we must set out to answer this question. First of all, it is important to note that there are many levels of magisterial teachings, each one with a different level of authority:[29]

- Extraordinary magisterium: teachings by a pope (when speaking *ex cathedra*) or by an ecumenical council. These teachings enjoy an infallible degree of certitude.
- Ordinary and universal magisterium: teachings of the bishops (including the pope), dispersed throughout the world, but in moral unanimity. These teachings are also infallible.
- Ordinary magisterium (not to be confused with the ordinary and universal magisterium): teachings by individual bishops or popes. These teachings are not infallible, but are nevertheless authoritative.

When I claim that *Amoris Laetitia* is magisterial, I am not claiming it is infallible. In fact, I am not aware of anyone arguing that this exhortation belongs to the extraordinary magisterium, or even to the ordinary and universal magisterium (which would make it infallible). I do argue, however, along several theologians and commentators,[30] that *Amoris*

---

28. As an example, many articles were published in reply to Pope St. John Paul II's *Ordinatio Sacerdotalis*, wherein the Holy Father proclaimed: "Wherefore, in order that all doubt may be removed regarding a matter of great importance, a matter which pertains to the church's divine constitution itself, in virtue of my ministry of confirming the brethren I declare that the church has no authority whatsoever to confer priestly ordination on women and that this judgment is to be definitively held by all the church's faithful." This clear teaching against the possibility of ordination of women priests, that Pope Francis himself considered to be infallibly taught in a plane interview on November 1, 2016, has been questioned for not using the adequate phraseology to be considered infallible. See Gaillardetz, "Infallibility and the Ordination of Women," 3–24. (NB: This is just an example to prove my point; I assent to and agree with the teachings of the church that it cannot possibly ever ordain women as priests.)

29. Adapted from a table in Sheehan, *Apologetics and Catholic Doctrine*, 206.

30. See Pié-Ninot, "L'Ultima Parola." See also Travers, "*Amoris Laetitia* and Canon 915," 394: "Apostolic exhortations, like encyclicals, are normally regarded as some of the most important instruments for exercise by the Pope of the *ordinary* authentic Magisterium." Guerra López too refers to *AL* as a part of the ordinary magisterium in López, "Entender a Wojtyla," 42. In fact, the conclusion that *AL* belongs to the ordinary magisterium of Pope Francis is confirmed even by papal critic Roberto de Mattei in his essay "A Response to Edward Peters on the Buenos Aires Letter & Authentic Magisterium."

Laetitia belongs to the ordinary magisterium of Pope Francis, making it authoritative, even if not infallible.

To better understand the different levels of the magisterium (and how the faithful should respond to each one of them), we should turn to two official documents published by then-Cardinal Joseph Ratzinger[31] as prefect for the Congregation for the Doctrine of the Faith (CDF):

1. the instruction *Donum Veritatis* (*DV*) on the ecclesial vocation of the theologian;
2. the *Doctrinal Commentary on the Concluding Formula of the Professio fidei* (*DCPF*).

We will come back to these two documents repeatedly in the course of this chapter and the next. Regarding the ordinary magisterium of the pope, *Donum Veritatis* says:

> *Divine assistance is also given* to the successors of the apostles teaching in communion with the successor of Peter, and in a particular way, *to the Roman Pontiff* as Pastor of the whole Church, when exercising their ordinary Magisterium, *even should this not issue in an infallible definition or in a "definitive" pronouncement* but in the proposal of some teaching which leads to a better understanding of Revelation in matters of faith and morals and to moral directives derived from such teaching.[32]

In other words, just because a teaching has not been expressed in an infallible way, this does not mean that it is not magisterial or devoid of divine assistance. In his encyclical *Humani Generis*, Venerable Pope Pius XII linked the "ordinary teaching authority" of the pope to Jesus's saying: "He who heareth you, heareth Me."[33] When a pope is proposing teachings in matters of faith and morals, he is exercising his ordinary magisterium. The *Doctrinal Commentary on the Profession of the Faith* also affirms this definition.[34]

---

31. Pope Benedict XVI's birth name.
32. *DV* 17.
33. Luke 10:16. See Pius XII, *Humani Generis*, 20.
34. *DCPF*, 10: "To this paragraph belong all those teachings—on faith and morals—presented as true or at least as sure, *even if they have not been defined with a solemn judgment or proposed as definitive* by the ordinary and universal Magisterium. Such teachings are, however, an authentic expression of the ordinary Magisterium of the Roman Pontiff."

That *Amoris Laetitia* is proposing teachings on faith and morals is self-evident from a plain reading of the text. For example, when Francis states that it cannot be said that all divorced and remarried people are in a state of mortal sin and deprived of sanctifying grace,[35] is it not a teaching on faith? When the pontiff explains that a negative judgment about an objective situation does not imply a judgment about the imputability or culpability of the person involved,[36] is it not a teaching on morals? Furthermore, these teachings do indeed lead to a better understanding of revelation, for they rightly develop the teaching of mitigating circumstances, already inscribed in the *Catechism* and embryonically present since the beginning of the church in the age-old tradition of not guessing whether a soul has been damned or not based solely on its external acts.

Of course, some may reply that *Amoris Laetitia* is not a teaching document, but a pastoral one. Or that, even if *Amoris Laetitia* may contain some teachings on faith and morals, the extension of communion to some divorced and remarried couples is a matter of discipline, not teaching. Thus, this sacramental discipline would not be magisterial on those grounds.

However, the CDF documents do not allow for this reading. In *Donum Veritatis* 17, again, we can see that divine assistance is granted to the Holy Father, not just when he proposes teachings, but also in the "moral directives derived from such teachings." Later on, the same paragraph will read: "magisterial decisions in matters of discipline, even if they are not guaranteed by the charism of infallibility, are not without divine assistance." From this, we can reach two conclusions:

1. Matters of discipline can indeed be decided in a magisterial way (*Donum Veritatis* uses the expression "magisterial decisions in matters of discipline").

2. Matters of discipline decided by the pope *also* receive divine assistance.

❃❃❃

---

35. *AL* 301.
36. *AL* 302.

External Evidence

There is even more indirect evidence that *Amoris Laetitia* is magisterial. Some months after its publication, and given its reception, Pope Francis attempted to clarify the meaning of his apostolic exhortation. He ordered the publication of a letter in the *AAS*, addressed to the Buenos Aires bishops, supporting their criteria on the implementation of *Amoris Laetitia*. In this letter, Francis contradicts the notion that the apostolic exhortation is just his personal opinion: "I would like to recall that *Amoris Laetitia* was the fruit of the work and prayer of the whole church, with the mediation of two Synods and the Pope."[37] He states that the Buenos Aires criteria are the only possible interpretation for *Amoris Laetitia*. We will come back to this in later chapters.

The publication of both the Buenos Aires criteria and the papal letter supporting them in the *AAS* was accompanied by a rescript by the Secretary of State, Cardinal Pietro Parolin, in which it is noted that the pope decreed that these two documents should be promulgated as "authentic Magisterium."[38] This would be confirmed, later on, by Cardinal Francesco Coccopalmerio, president of the Pontifical Council for Legislative Texts (PCLT), who affirmed: "The fact that the pope requested that his letter and the interpretations of the Buenos Aires bishops be published in the *AAS* means that His Holiness has given these documents a particular qualification that elevates them to the level of being *official teachings of the church*. . . . Thus together the two documents became the Holy Father's *authentic magisterium* for the whole church."[39]

It would be difficult to argue that these two documents are magisterial interpretations of a non-magisterial exhortation. But even if we did make such a wild claim, it would still support my case, since the Buenos Aires criteria confirm Pope Francis's disciplinary change. So, even if we concede that *Amoris Laetitia* is not magisterial (something I do not concede, given everything previously explained) the Buenos Aires criteria

---

37. *AAS* 108 (2016), no. 10, 1071–1072.
38. *AAS* 108 (2016), no. 10, 1074.
39. Wooden, "Pope's Letter to Argentine Bishops on 'Amoris Laetitia' Part of Official Record.". The Latin word *authenticum* may be translated as "authoritative," and that is usually the connotation behind the expression "authentic magisterium." See Joseph, "The Catholic Magisterium," 50.

would still be magisterial.⁴⁰ I sincerely do not believe papal critics would be happy with such an arrangement.

Of course, if it is argued that the Buenos Aires criteria and the papal letter supporting them are both magisterial, what can be said about the apostolic exhortation[41] they refer to, also published in the *AAS*?[42] Instead of multiplying unneeded explanations, we should just conclude what is staring us in the face: *Amoris Laetitia* is, indeed, magisterial. In fact, this has been confirmed by Pope Francis himself. During his 2019 apostolic visit to southeast Asia, Pope Francis met a group of forty-eight Jesuits from the region. When asked during this meeting about how to behave pastorally towards the divorced and remarried Catholics in their communities, Pope Francis replied: "*according to the Magisterium of the Church as in the eighth chapter of Amoris Laetitia, that is, journey, accompany, and discern to find solutions.*"[43]

❦ ❦ ❦

Since most of the evidence seems overwhelmingly to point in the direction of *Amoris Laetitia* being part of Pope Francis's ordinary magisterium, and since the objections to this assertion do not seem to hold up to scrutiny, I think we cannot evade the conclusion that *Amoris Laetitia* is, indeed, magisterial. Now, we must go one step further: if *Amoris Laetitia* is magisterial, what is the proper response the faithful should give to it? I will try to answer that question in my next chapter.

---

40. See Fernández, "El capítulo VIII de Amoris Laetitia," 452: "One may ask whether the Pope can clarify his intentions through a letter to a group of bishops. But this has happened before. To give an example, let us remember an incident involving the interpretation of Vatican I. The German bishops answered Chancellor Bismark, who maintained that the council had defined a Roman centralism that would debilitate episcopal authority. With their answer, the bishops rejected this interpretation of the council. Pius IX endorsed the interpretation of these bishops with a letter (May 3, 1875) and with an audience on May 15, 1875 (DH 3112–17). This letter from Pius IX to the German bishops is cited in a note in *Lumen Gentium* 27, its hermeneutic authority being thus confirmed." (My translation from the original Spanish.)

41. I am again reminded of Morrisey's entry on "Apostolic exhortation" in the *Catholic Encyclopedia*, where it explicitly says that apostolic exhortations are "a significant expression of the magisterium of the Church."

42. See *AAS* 108 (2016), no. 4, 311–446.

43. *La Civiltà Cattolica*, "Our Little Path."

Chapter 2

The Question of Assent

Amoris Laetitia's critics often complain that papal apologists do not engage their concerns and arguments, but rather shift the discussion to a game of "Simon [Peter] says."[1] In other words, those defending Pope Francis would usually fall back on arguments based on authority: *Amoris Laetitia* is orthodox because the pope said so. *Roma locuta est, causa finita est.*[2]

I will try to avoid this mistake, and will spend the remainder of my book presenting a rational response to common objections to *Amoris Laetitia*'s orthodoxy. After all, a theistic apologist would be very ineffective if he just said to an atheist, "This is true because God says so." Same for a Christian apologist who would say to the atheist, "This is true because the Bible says so."

However, an important distinction bears emphasis: we are not dealing with atheists. We are dealing with Catholics. We are talking about Catholics who have, for years, defended the primacy of Peter with a passion until they tripped on the stumbling block of Francis's pontificate.[3]

---

1. As a paradigmatic example, see the essay by Ed Faust, "Because I said so."

2. "Rome has spoken, the discussion is over": paraphrase from St. Augustine's Sermon 131, 10. This sentence has been used for centuries by Catholic apologists in support of the papacy.

3. Contrast, for example, Taylor Marshall's tone in his chapter "The Pope as the King's Royal Steward" (Marshall, *Crucified Rabbi*, 44–47), with his podcast "Red-Pilled on Pope Francis."

So appeals to papal authority are not (or should not) be strange to them, or easily dismissed.[4]

These appeals become even more urgent, because the attempts to justify dissent from *Amoris Laetitia* have led to the dissemination of many erroneous ideas regarding how Catholics should assent to papal teachings (ideas that would be considered appalling before Francis was elected). In their zeal to protect the Catholic doctrine on the indissolubility of marriage, many Catholics are now throwing the equally important doctrine of papal primacy under the bus. The propagation of ways of thinking completely alien (or rather, antithetical) to a Catholic perspective on the papacy is troubling and needs to be addressed.

In this context, I would like to devote this chapter to the topic of how a Catholic should assent to papal teachings, and if he is allowed to dissent from those teachings based on arguments commonly used against Pope Francis. I will flesh out these arguments and try to explain, from sound doctrine, why I think they are wrong.

❊❊❊

Following Christ without Following His Vicar

"I follow Jesus, not the Pope" has become a common slogan in Catholic social media since Francis's election. Supposedly, Francis is contradicting Jesus's clear teaching on the indissolubility of marriage. Jesus's authority trumps Francis's; so if we have a conflict between them, Jesus is the one we should choose.[5]

---

4. NB: Naturally, this only works if one recognizes the authority of Pope Francis as a successor of Peter (something the "recognize and resist" faction does, given their name). For the purpose of this book, I will assume the legitimacy of Pope Francis's election as a given. Refuting sedevacantist arguments goes beyond the scope intended for this book, and the reader can find many good resources on that topic elsewhere. Interestingly, a good refutation can be found on leading "recognize and resist" site *One Peter Five*: the validity of a pope's election is a matter of infallible certainty, as long as the results of this election are peacefully and universally accepted at the moment they are known to the whole church. See Siscoe, "Dogmatic Fact." Regarding conspiracy theories about the invalidity of Benedict XVI's resignation (on the basis that it was not free), I recommend my three-part series "Was Pope Benedict forced to resign?"

5. See Mallett, "On Vatican Funkiness": "Even if a pope were to deny Jesus Christ, we ought to hold fast to Sacred Tradition and remain faithful to Jesus unto death. Indeed St. John did not 'blindly follow' the first pope into his denial. . . . This is what I intend to do, by God's grace, even should a pope deny Christ himself. My faith is not

The problem with this seemingly impeccable logic is that it assumes the conflict exists. This is a personal interpretation of the papal critic, yet he assumes that his interpretation is the correct one.[6] The existence of a contradiction between the two seems so obvious to him that he does not seem to entertain the possibility that this contradiction might not exist. However, Catholic theology has always been nuanced enough to see beyond contradictions that seem evident on the surface, but are actually not there.[7]

Take scripture, for instance. I have said elsewhere[8] that the Protestant has a point that some Catholic practices (veneration of images, for example) seem, on the surface, to blatantly contradict scripture. Since we have shown in the previous chapter that the magisterium is not superior to the word of God,[9] and since the word of God exists in written form as scripture,[10] a Protestant might feel justified in claiming that we should choose scripture over the pope. However, we know this would be an erroneous interpretation, since Catholicism explicitly rejects *Sola Scriptura*.[11]

Nor can the papal critic evade the problem by claiming that he is defending tradition, not scripture. Tradition is another form of the word of God,[12] so if the above is true for scripture, it also holds for tradition. Also, it should be remembered that many (if not most) heresies in church history were not considered novelties by their adherents, but rather were viewed as a return to a more primeval Christianity, more pristine and closer to its first-century source, before (papal) traditions of men caused

---

in Peter, but Jesus. I follow Christ, not a man." Granted, Mallet goes on to affirm he will not break communion with the Pope; but he does not do so by assenting to the things he finds "confusing," but by separating the pope from the office of the papacy. Also see Steve Skojec's tweet from December 17, 2016: "We worship Christ, not the pope. @Pontifex is fomenting doctrinal error and souls are at stake."

6. I tackle this argument in another article, "Following Christ, but Not His Vicar."

7. The Christological debates about Jesus's nature in the first millennium seem to me to be a perfect example of this. Jesus is both fully man and fully God, even if our limited conceptions would, at first, assume that there is something contradictory between these two statements. For more on this, see my article "The Crucified Church: Tensions with the Flavor of the Gospel."

8. I again refer the reader to my article "*Sola Traditio*."

9. CCC 85.

10. CCC 81.

11. CCC 82.

12. CCC 85.

Christianity to morph into something completely irreconcilable with what it originally was.[13]

In fact, if we look up the etymology of the word "heresy," we see that it means "a choice."[14] What choice? The choice between two parts of doctrine, seemingly in tension with one another, and which are reconciled by doing away with one of them. Rocco Buttiglione, a member of the Pontifical Academy of Social Sciences, cites Aquinas when he says, "The contrary of an error is not truth, but the diametrically opposite error. The truth is always the middle term between two errors: in [the case of *Amoris Laetitia*], between laxism and rigorism; or, if you will, between Molinism and Jansenism."[15]

I am not suggesting that those who do not agree with Pope Francis deserve the label of heretic. That is a very serious charge that I do not have the authority to make. I do need to caution them, however, as to how similar their thought process has come with those who historically found themselves on the wrong side of doctrinal disputes. As Buttiglione once more says, "There are very few popes in the history of the Church who can be suspected of being heretics. Nevertheless, it is certain that all heretics have claimed that the popes of their time were heretics."[16]

Those who say "I follow Jesus, not the pope" are separating that which cannot be separated. As far as teachings are concerned, there is no difference between following Jesus and the pope, since the pope is the *Vicar of Christ* (meaning the pope exercises a *vicarious* function, in the name of Jesus, as the visible head of the church). In fact, separating both can actually be considered "diabolical," if we again consider the literal etymology of this word, "to divide."[17]

---

13. This idea has been explored with significantly more detail in my article "When Heresy pretends to be Tradition."

14. Wilhelm, "Heresy": "The term heresy connotes, etymologically, both a choice and the thing chosen, the meaning being, however, narrowed to the selection of religious or political doctrines."

15. Buttiglione, *Risposte amichevoli*, 156. See also Belloc, *The Great Heresies*, 7–8: "Heresy is the dislocation of some complete and self-supporting scheme by the introduction of a novel denial of some essential part therein. . . . Heresy means, then, the warping of a system by 'Exception': by 'Picking out' one part of the structure and implies that the scheme is marred by taking away one part of it, denying one part of it, and either leaving the void unfilled or filling it with some new affirmation."

16. Buttiglione, *Risposte amichevoli*, 113.

17. In this sense, *diabolus* is in opposition to *symbolus*. A symbol (here meaning the creed, e.g., the Niceno-Constantinopolitan Symbol) means "to join together."

That we cannot separate our loyalty to Jesus from our loyalty to the pope is expressed in a sublime way by Pius XII, in his defense of an unbroken tradition going back to apostolic times.

> Since He [Jesus] was all wise He could not leave the body of the Church He had founded as a human society without a visible head. Nor against this may one argue that the primacy of jurisdiction established in the Church gives such a Mystical Body two heads. For Peter in view of his primacy is only Christ's Vicar; so that there is only one chief Head of this Body, namely Christ, who never ceases Himself to guide the Church invisibly, though at the same time He rules it visibly, through him who is His representative on earth. After His glorious Ascension into Heaven this Church rested not on Him alone, but on Peter, too, its visible foundation stone. That Christ and His Vicar constitute one only Head is the solemn teaching of Our predecessor of immortal memory Boniface VIII in the Apostolic Letter *Unam Sanctam*; and his successors have never ceased to repeat the same.
>
> *They, therefore, walk in the path of dangerous error who believe that they can accept Christ as the Head of the Church, while not adhering loyally to His Vicar on earth.* They have taken away the visible head, broken the visible bonds of unity and left the Mystical Body of the Redeemer so obscured and so maimed, that those who are seeking the haven of eternal salvation can neither see it nor find it.[18]

A proper Catholic understanding of the papacy would never rest on such an anti-Catholic proposition as "I follow Jesus, not the pope." Catholic theology is deeply influenced by the concept of filial devotion to the pope. Catholics understand that Jesus Christ gave the keys of heaven and earth (and, consequently, the power to bind and loose) to St. Peter,[19] who then passed it on to his successors through an unbroken line right up to Francis. Additionally, Jesus Christ prayed for Peter's faith: "And the Lord said: Simon, Simon, behold Satan hath desired to have you, that he may sift you as wheat: But I have prayed for thee, that thy faith fail not:

Catholics gather under the mantle of a creed, encouraging unity and eschewing division. Joseph Ratzinger has a beautiful explanation on the original definition of the word "symbol" as an object split in half, in which two people (each with a half) could recognize each other if their halves matched (see Benedict XVI, *Introduction to Christianity*, 97).

18. Pius XII, *Mystici Corporis Christi*, 40–41.
19. Matt 16:18.

and thou, being once converted, confirm thy brethren."[20] We know this prayer to be extremely powerful, for the First Vatican Council grounds its definition of papal infallibility precisely on this prayer.[21]

This is pivotal for our Catholic faith and cannot be so easily dismissed. Peter's primacy and authority come from Jesus Himself. If I may be so bold, let me quote scripture by saying, "What God has joined together, let no man put asunder."[22] It is paradoxical to defend this biblical quote on marriage, and then try to separate what God himself has authoritatively bound together: Peter's authority and Jesus's truth.

❖ ❖ ❖

Justifying Dissent from Non-infallible Teachings

Another common argument goes like this: "*Amoris Laetitia* is not infallible, so a Catholic does not need to assent to it."[23] Sometimes, the person wielding this argument will go as far as saying that, if *Amoris Laetitia* is not infallible, then it is fallible.[24] However, I am not aware of any magisterial teaching justifying the allegedly "implied" conclusion that non-infallible statements are by definition fallible. At most, *Donum Veritatis* mentions that there may be "deficiencies" in those statements,[25] but deficiencies do not necessarily entail grave error, and can actually refer to statements that may be developed or complemented later on.[26] This reading would

20. Luke 22:31–32.
21. Vatican I, *Pastor Aeternus*, 6.
22. Mark 10:9.
23. Philosopher Joseph Seifert, for example, is quoted (Seifert, "Famed Catholic Philosopher") as having said, in the context of the *AL* debate: "Someone could ask me how I, a wretched lay person, can criticize the Pope. I respond: the Pope is not infallible if he does not speak *ex cathedra*."
24. See for example Hoffan, "Cardinal Burke's critics fall into serious errors."
25. *DV* 24: "When it comes to the question of interventions in the prudential order, it could happen that some Magisterial documents might not be free from all deficiencies. Bishops and their advisors have not always taken into immediate consideration every aspect or the entire complexity of a question. *But it would be contrary to the truth, if, proceeding from some particular cases, one were to conclude that the Church's Magisterium can be habitually mistaken in its prudential judgments, or that it does not enjoy divine assistance in the integral exercise of its mission.*"
26. *DV* 24: "Some judgments of the Magisterium could be justified at the time in which they were made, because while the pronouncements contained true assertions and others which were not sure, both types were inextricably connected. Only time

be consistent with the rest of the paragraph where these "deficiencies" are mentioned, since *Donum Veritatis* also references magisterial teachings "not *per se* irreformable" and magisterial interventions in questions that involve "certain contingent and conjectural elements."[27] Either way, the question of whether papal non-infallible teachings can err is a matter that remains under discussion among theologians, even if it can be argued that the term "non-infallible" is "unhelpful"[28] given the connotations it evokes.

Whatever one's opinions on this regard may be, one thing is certain. Catholics are required to assent to more than simply *ex cathedra* teachings.[29] The church has spoken numerous times against this way of thinking, since at least the nineteenth century.[30] It became settled at Vatican II, which affirmed, in its dogmatic Constitution *Lumen Gentium* (*LG*),

---

has permitted discernment and, after deeper study, the attainment of true doctrinal progress."

27. Sheehan, *Apologetics and Catholic Doctrine*, 208, refers to these non-infallible teachings as "provisional."

28. Joseph, "The Catholic Magisterium": "I have deliberately avoided that singularly unhelpful word, 'non-infallible.' *Lumen Gentium* refers to the '*authenticum Magisterium*.' The Latin word '*authenticum*' may be translated as 'authoritative.'" See also Sheehan, *Apologetics and Catholic Doctrine*, 208: "We sometimes hear that 'the Church has admitted her teaching was wrong' or 'the Church has changed her teaching.' From what we have discussed above, it is clear that no infallibly-taught teaching could be wrong or overturned. Provisional teaching could be revised, but this is not usually what people have in mind."

29. CCC 892.

30. Pope Pius IX, the pope who presided over the First Vatican Council, condemned as erroneous the proposition that "the obligation by which Catholic teachers and authors are strictly bound is confined to those things only which are proposed to universal belief as dogmas of faith by the infallible judgment of the Church" (*Syllabus of Errors*, 22).

Another example is Leo XIII, *Sapientiae Christianae*, 24: "In defining the limits of the obedience owed to the pastors of souls, but most of all to the authority of the Roman Pontiff, *it must not be supposed that it is only to be yielded in relation to dogmas* of which the obstinate denial cannot be disjoined from the crime of heresy. Nay, further, it is not enough sincerely and firmly to assent to doctrines which, though not defined by any solemn pronouncement of the Church, are by her proposed to belief, as divinely revealed, in her common and universal teaching, and which the Vatican Council declared are to be believed 'with Catholic and divine faith.' *But this likewise must be reckoned amongst the duties of Christians, that they allow themselves to be ruled and directed by the authority and leadership of bishops, and, above all, of the apostolic see.*"

See also Pius XI, *Casti Conubii*, 104: "*For it is quite foreign to everyone bearing the name of a Christian* to trust his own mental powers with such pride as to agree only with those things which he can examine from their inner nature, and to imagine that

The Question of Assent

> This *religious submission of mind and will* must be shown in a special way to the authentic magisterium of the Roman Pontiff, *even when he is not speaking ex cathedra*; that is, it must be shown in such a way that his supreme magisterium is acknowledged with reverence, the judgments made by him are sincerely adhered to, according to his manifest mind and will.[31]

The two CDF documents I mentioned in the previous chapter reinforce *Lumen Gentium*. In the "Commentary on the Profession of the Faith," we can read:

> The third proposition of the *Professio fidei* states: "Moreover, I adhere with *religious submission of will and intellect* to the teachings which either the Roman Pontiff or the College of Bishops enunciate when they exercise their authentic Magisterium, *even if they do not intend to proclaim these teachings by a definitive act.*" To this paragraph belong all those teachings on faith and morals—presented as true or at least as sure, *even if they have not been defined with a solemn judgment or proposed as definitive by the ordinary and universal Magisterium. Such teachings are, however, an authentic expression of the ordinary Magisterium of the Roman Pontiff* or of the College of Bishops and therefore *require religious submission of will and intellect.*[32]

In summary, the authentic expressions of the ordinary magisterium of the pope require "religious submission of will and intellect."[33] What does

---

the Church, sent by God to teach and guide all nations, is not conversant with present affairs and circumstances; or even *that they must obey only in those matters which she has decreed by solemn definition as though her other decisions might be presumed to be false or putting forward insufficient motive for truth and honesty.* Quite to the contrary, *a characteristic of all true followers of Christ, lettered or unlettered, is to suffer themselves to be guided and led in all things that touch upon faith or morals by the Holy Church of God through its Supreme Pastor the Roman Pontiff*, who is himself guided by Jesus Christ Our Lord."

See also John Paul II, "Audience for March 24, 1993": "*Alongside this infallibility of the ex cathedra definitions*, there is the charism of assistance to the Holy Spirit, granted to Peter and his successors *so that they do not err in matters of faith and morals* and instead give good illumination to the Christian people. *This charisma is not limited to exceptional cases, but embraces in various degrees the whole exercise of the magisterium.*"

31. *LG* 25.
32. *DCPF* 10.
33. See Odero, "Introduction to Theology," 32n45: "It should be noted that the teachings of the ordinary Magisterium of the pope or the college of bishops that are not intended as definitions of faith are Catholic truths, but not truths of faith. Nevertheless,

this term mean? *Donum Veritatis* gives us some clues, all the while agreeing with what was said earlier:

> When the Magisterium, *not intending to act "definitively,"* teaches a doctrine to aid a better understanding of Revelation and make explicit its contents, or to recall how some teaching is in conformity with the truths of faith, or finally to guard against ideas that are incompatible with these truths, the response called for is that of the *religious submission of will and intellect. This kind of response cannot be simply exterior or disciplinary but must be understood within the logic of faith and under the impulse of obedience to the faith.*[34]

In short, not only is the faithful bound to submit to the ordinary magisterium of the pope, even when he is not teaching infallibly, this submission should also not be merely exterior, but surge from an internal adherence of the faithful, both of mind and of will, in a way inextricably linked to the wholeness of his faith.[35]

Since the eighth chapter of *Amoris Laetitia* is part of the ordinary magisterium of Pope Francis, this is the level of submission that must be accorded to it by the faithful. This has been corroborated by Salvador Pié-Ninot, a professor of fundamental theology and ecclesiology, in an article to *l'Osservatore Romano*, drawing from this very same paragraph of *Donum Veritatis*.[36]

✺ ✺ ✺

Interpreting the Magisterium against the Will of the Pope

Some critics will circumvent this difficulty by interpreting magisterial teachings in a way that is compatible with their idea of tradition. If they

---

'while the assent of faith is not required, a religious submission of intellect and will' should be accorded to them." See also Joseph, "The Catholic Magisterium."

34. *DV* 23.

35. Belmont, "God's Church," 439: "Regarding the doctrinal and moral decisions of the ordinary Magisterium of the Roman Pontiff and of the Bishops in the exercise of their authentic Magisterium, external silence is not sufficient. One has 'to adhere to it with a ready and respectful allegiance of mind.'"

36. Pié-Ninot, "L'Ultima Parola": "Please notice how this precise description must be realized in *Amoris Laetitia*, and therefore, 'the willingness to submit loyally to the teaching of the Magisterium on matters *per se* not irreformable must be the rule," (My translation from the original Italian.)

can find a way to do this, they can claim to be faithful to the magisterium, even if they are going against the intended meaning of the text. A glaring example of this can be seen with some who disagree with Francis's sacramental discipline regarding communion for the divorced and remarried. They will claim that *Amoris Laetitia* is ambiguous in this regard (it is not, as we shall see in later chapters) and so, it can be interpreted in an "orthodox" way. "Orthodox" here means the previous discipline, which they consider to be the only one compatible with Catholicism.[37] Some may even go as far as admitting that it does not matter if an interpretation is in conformity with the pope's presumed intentions.[38]

The problem with this reasoning is that magisterial teachings should not and cannot be interpreted by separating them from the magisterial teacher that issued them. *Lumen Gentium* is quite clear that the authentic magisterium of the Roman Pontiff should be "adhered to, *according to his manifest mind and will.*"[39] It goes on to explain that we can know the pope's mind and will "from the character of the documents, from his frequent repetition of the same doctrine, or from his manner of speaking." Also, the *Doctrinal Commentary on the Profession of the Faith* further clarifies:

> One can point in general to teachings set forth by the authentic ordinary Magisterium in a non-definitive way, which require degrees of adherence differentiated according to the mind and the will manifested; this is shown especially by the nature of the documents, by the frequent repetition of the same doctrine, or by the tenor of the verbal expression.[40]

I will dedicate chapters 4 and 5 of this book to figuring out the manifest mind and will of Pope Francis on this matter. For now, it suffices to say that any interpretation of *Amoris Laetitia* that does not take into account Francis's own opinions cannot be deemed a proper submission of mind and will, as required by *Lumen Gentium*.

---

37. See Montagna, "JPII Institute Profs Dismissed"; Gagliarducci, "Interpreting Amoris Laetitia"; Brugger, "A Tale of Two Interpretations of '*Amoris Laetitia*'"; Pope, "The Ambiguities of *Amoris Laetitia*."

38. Brockhaus, "A Catholic 'Paradigm Shift' Would Be Corruption." See also Lawler, "Three Things the Pope Can't Say": "The Pope cannot teach authoritatively by dropping hints. . . . But what the Pope had in mind does not carry the same weight as what the Pope actually wrote."

39. *LG* 25.

40. *DCPF* 11.

Setting Papal Discipline against Doctrine

Another objection may be that we are dealing with a change of sacramental discipline, not doctrine.[41] So a Catholic would not need to submit to the pope's pastoral approach, since submission need only be given to doctrinal teachings on faith and morals.

I do not wish to be ultramontane and claim that a Catholic needs to give religious submission of mind and will to every disciplinary and pastoral decision taken by the pope and bishops.[42] I do think that prudential judgment can be legitimately exercised here by the faithful. I also believe it is lawful for a Catholic to present his concerns to the hierarchy, as long as he does it respectfully and acknowledging the authority of the pope and bishops to make the final decision, whatever it may be.[43]

But many papal critics have crossed that line already. They do not simply postulate that they find *Amoris Laetitia* to be imprudent or careless: they actually assert that it is illegitimate and erroneous.[44] They will

---

41. "Brother André Marie" writes in "*Amoris Laetitia* and the 'Authentic Magisterium'": "The defenders of *Amoris Laetitia*, including the Holy Father's official and unofficial spokesmen in the episcopacy, have stated that the document represents no change to doctrine, but merely a different pastoral or disciplinary approach.... I say this because, by its very nature, something that belongs to the 'authentic Magisterium' is and must be a matter of faith or morals, not merely a matter of sacramental discipline or pastoral practice. Which means that in Chapter eight of *Amoris*, in the Buenos Aires guidelines, and in the Pope's letter to the Bishops of Buenos Aires, we are confronted with a body of propositions that have long been defended as merely pastoral and representing no change in doctrine being elevated to a magisterial category that is strictly doctrinal in nature." ... This leads the confused student of all this to ask some troubling questions. Do we have here a pastoral discipline that contradicts law and a doctrine that is not doctrine?"

42. Joseph, "The Catholic Magisterium": "'Decisions of the Magisterium in matters of discipline, even though they do not enjoy the charism of infallibility, are not therefore devoid of divine assistance, but call for the adherence of Christ's faithful' (no. 17). Such adherence requires obedience, but not necessarily agreement with the point of discipline."

43. Sheehan, *Apologetics and Catholic Doctrine*, 209: "We are not bound to agree with the legislation [i.e., discipline], but we must always observe it and respect it, and speak of it respectfully, even if we hope for a change in some point."

44. See again the previously-mentioned "Open Letter to the Bishops of the Catholic Church," wherein a group of Catholic theologians formally accused Pope Francis of heresy on account of *Amoris Laetitia*.

postulate that this discipline violates perennial and definitive church teaching. They use their disagreement to foster divisions that significantly harm the unity of the church under the Roman Pontiff. In doing so, they are constraining the pope's authority regarding church discipline in ways simply incompatible with a Catholic understanding of papal primacy.[45] In fact, this contradicts the *infallible* teachings of the First Vatican Council:

> *Hence We teach and declare* that by the appointment of our Lord the Roman Church possesses a sovereignty of ordinary power over all other Churches, and that this power of jurisdiction of the Roman Pontiff, which is truly episcopal, is immediate; to which all, of whatsoever rite and dignity, *both pastors and faithful, both individually and collectively, are bound*, by their duty of hierarchical subordination and true obedience, *to submit, not only in matters which belong to faith and morals, but also in those that appertain to the discipline and government of the Church throughout the world*; so that the Church of Christ may be one flock under one supreme Pastor, through the preservation of unity, both of communion and of profession of the same faith, with the Roman Pontiff. *This is the teaching of Catholic truth, from which no one can deviate without loss of faith and of salvation....*
>
> If then any shall say that the Roman Pontiff has the office merely of inspection or direction, and not full and supreme power of jurisdiction over the universal Church, *not only in things which belong to faith and morals, but also in those things which relate to the discipline and government of the Church spread throughout the world . . . let him be anathema.*[46]

Even before this council, Pope Pius VI had already condemned the proposition that the church could establish a discipline that would be dangerous, harmful or leading to materialism as "false, rash, scandalous, dangerous, offensive to pious ears, injurious to the church and to the Spirit of God by whom it is guided, at least erroneous."[47] This wording seems to be echoed in more recent times in the aforementioned *CDF Commentary on the Profession of the Faith*:

---

45. Regarding changes in the legislation of the church (in this case, discipline), see Sheehan, *Apologetics and Catholic Doctrine*, 209: "If the Supreme Pontiff declares that the Church has no intention of changing something, a good Catholic will not foment division and discontent by prolonging the debate."

46. Vatican I, *Pastor Aeternus*, chap. 3.

47. Pius VI, *Auctorem Fidei*, 1578.

A proposition contrary to these doctrines can be qualified as erroneous or, *in the case of teachings of the prudential order, as rash or dangerous* and therefore 'tuto doceri non potest.'[48]

I have already established, in my previous chapter, that matters of discipline could also be a part of a pope's magisterium, so that they are not without divine assistance, and that they require the adherence of the faithful.[49] Wielding the term "discipline" as a way to justify dissent is simply foreign to a proper Catholic understanding of papal primacy.

❋❋❋

The One Single Legitimate Exception, and Why It Does Not Apply

Regarding dissent, it seems like the church allows only one possible exception: the case of the theologian, as explained in *Donum Veritatis*. In this document, the CDF accepts that "the theologian . . . might have serious difficulties, for reasons which appear to him well-founded, in accepting a non-irreformable magisterial teaching."[50] This may give rise to "tensions" between the theologian and the magisterium that may actually "become a dynamic factor, a stimulus to both the magisterium and theologians to fulfill their respective roles while practicing dialogue."[51]

This concession, however, does not give *carte blanche* for a theologian to act as he pleases. First of all, the theologian is urged, first and foremost, to conform his mind with the church and loyally accept the teaching of the magisterium as it is presented.[52] If, however, despite a loyal effort on the theologian's part, the difficulties persist, then *Donum Veritatis* instructs:

---

48. DCPF 10.
49. *DV* 17.
50. *DV* 28.
51. *DV* 25.

52. *DV* 29. See also *DV* 28: "Such a disagreement could not be justified if it were based solely upon the fact that the validity of the given teaching is not evident or upon the opinion that the opposite position would be the more probable. Nor, furthermore, would the judgment of the subjective conscience of the theologian justify it because conscience does not constitute an autonomous and exclusive authority for deciding the truth of a doctrine."

> Even if the doctrine of the faith is not in question, *the theologian will not present his own opinions or divergent hypotheses as though they were non-arguable conclusions*. Respect for the truth as well as for the People of God requires this discretion (cf. Rom 14:1–15; 1 Cor 8, 10:23–33). For the same reasons, the theologian *will refrain from giving untimely public expression* to them. . . .
>
> In cases like these, the theologian should avoid turning to the *"mass media,"* but have recourse to the responsible authority, for it is not by seeking to exert the pressure of public opinion that one contributes to the clarification of doctrinal issues and renders service to the truth.[53]

This contrasts dramatically with the *modus operandi* of the most vocal papal critics, some of whom are prominent theologians. Usually they voice their contrary opinions in the loudest way possible, publishing articles and interviews in sympathetic Catholic news media[54] or signing petitions that they then make public.[55] Sometimes, they go so far as to say they will "correct" the pope if he does not yield to their theological concerns.[56] Other times, they actually and publicly "correct" the Holy Father.[57] There have even been some theologians that accused the pope, both formally[58] and informally,[59] of being a heretic: a rash accusation they have no authority to make.[60] All of this goes way beyond the concession the church allows for dissent from the pope's magisterium.

❊ ❊ ❊

Having said that, it seems like the papal critic is in a very dire situation. Let us recapitulate:

---

53. *DV* 27, 30. See also Pié-Ninot, "L'Ultima Parola": "This cannot become—as some have done, surely in good faith—an opportunity to manifest a certain dissent in the form of public criticisms, with the purpose of refutation" (my translation from the original Italian).

54. See, for example, Seifert, "The Church After *Amoris Laetitia*."

55. McElwee, "Signers of Document Critiquing 'Amoris Laetitia' Revealed."

56. See Pentin, "Cardinal Burke on *Amoris Laetitia Dubia*: 'Tremendous Division' Warrants Action."

57. See "*Correctio Filialis.*"

58. See the aforementioned "Open Letter to the Bishops of the Catholic Church."

59. Catholic News Agency, "Retired Archbishop Disciplined after Calling Pope Francis a 'Heretic.'"

60. *Code of Canon Law*, c. 1404: "The First See is judged by no one."

1. *Amoris Laetitia* is part of the ordinary magisterium of Pope Francis.
2. The ordinary magisterium of the pope must be interpreted according to the pontiff's manifest mind and will.
3. The faithful should give religious submission of mind and will to the magisterium of the pope, even if he is not being infallible.
4. Even *Amoris Laetitia*'s sacramental discipline is a "magisterial decision in matters of discipline," and is not without divine assistance.
5. It is rash and dangerous to criticize the pope's magisterium, even in prudential matters.

Having acknowledged this, the Catholics in this situation may proceed in two ways: either refuse to listen, and turn to dissenting authors in search of arguments to validate their stance; or accept that something is amiss with their own approach. In the latter case, I suggest re-reading my appeal in the introduction of this book, so that the readers might also consider that the problem may lie with their own perception and consider changing their opinion on the matter: in short, a *metanoia* of the mind.

Nevertheless, even if the readers may accept this, it does not necessarily follow that they will immediately be able to agree with everything issuing from Francis's ordinary magisterium (in particular, with *Amoris Laetitia*). There has been so much disinformation being spread by apparently reliable sources, both before and after Francis's election, that a person might find it difficult to understand how it is possible to reconcile *Amoris Laetitia* with orthodoxy. The remainder of this book aims at providing a satisfactory rational response to those people, so that they may be able to successfully resolve the cognitive tensions that this apostolic exhortation might exert on them.

But for someone to know how to properly assent to *Amoris Laetitia*, one must know what it actually means. The next section will try to give the most accurate interpretation of this document on the polemical change of sacramental discipline.

Section II

CLARIFYING *AMORIS LAETITIA*

CHAPTER 3

The "Multiple Interpretations" Objection

IN ORDER TO SUBMIT to a papal teaching, we must understand the teaching. But some critics will object that there are too many interpretations on how to implement *Amoris Laetitia*'s sacramental discipline.[1] Can divorced and remarried people receive communion or not? If so, in what circumstances? Since *Amoris Laetitia* is not "clear" on this (so they argue), it is impossible to know which interpretation is correct. Therefore, it is impossible to give a proper assent to the pope.[2]

I must caution against this argumentative strategy. If we turn to other areas of knowledge, the existence of multiple interpretations does not in itself stop people from picking one side based on the evidence they find. Otherwise, who could withstand the intellectual paralysis that would ensue? Is there any topic where universal agreement has ever been achieved? Even solidly well-established facts have some detractors. The very existence of minority opinions does not in itself refute the more demonstrable and cogent ones. If a theory wishes to be taken seriously, it does not suffice that it exists alongside others: it must prove itself.

It is impressive how the most somber warnings against this kind of reasoning actually came from the previous pontificate. Pope Benedict XVI dedicated his years as pontiff to fighting what he perceived to be a "dictatorship of relativism."[3] Relativism is defined as the philosophy

1. Melina, "Le Sfide di Amoris laetitia," 233–50.
2. Altieri, "From What, Precisely, Are Amoris Laetitia 'Dissenters' Dissenting?"
3. Joseph Ratzinger popularized this term in the homily he gave for the Mass *Pro Eligendo Romano Pontifice*, preached right before the conclave that would have him elected. This homily would become programmatic of his pontificate.

where the "existence of one valid truth for all" cannot be affirmed.[4] Theologically speaking, relativism is the notion that we "can never grasp ultimate truth in itself, but only its appearance in our way of perceiving through different 'lenses.'"[5] Relativism "does not recognize anything as definitive."[6]

Against this relativism, Benedict proposed an honest and unprejudiced search for truth, wherever it might lead us. In fact, he even adopted *Cooperatores Veritatis*[7] as his papal motto. For Benedict, "Truth, by enabling men and women to let go of their subjective opinions and impressions, allows them to move beyond cultural and historical limitations and to come together in the assessment of the value and substance of things."[8]

In this sense, we must be moved by this spirit in assessing the substance of any interpretation of *Amoris Laetitia* presented to us. We cannot look at the alleged multiplicity of interpretations and claim it is impossible to find the true meaning of the text based on that multiplicity alone.

❖❖❖

So, the next question is: how do we know if a given interpretation is cogent or not? The answer is this: the more cogent a given interpretation is, the more it will conform to the pope's "manifest mind and will." Again, this is how *Lumen Gentium* 25 tells us we should adhere to the pope's magisterium. Even on purely secular grounds, the correct interpretation of a text belongs to its author.

One can then object that Francis's interpretation is that there should be multiple interpretations. This is usually done by quoting the introduction of the exhortation:

> I would make it clear that not all discussions of doctrinal, moral or pastoral issues need to be settled by interventions of the magisterium. Unity of teaching and practice is certainly necessary in the Church, but this *does not preclude various ways of*

---

4. Ratzinger, "Relativism: The Central Problem."
5. Ratzinger, "Relativism: The Central Problem."
6. Ratzinger, "Homily for the Mass *Pro Eligendo Romano Pontifice*."
7. Translation: "Cooperators with the truth."
8. Benedict XVI, *Caritas in Veritate*, 4.

interpreting some aspects of that teaching or drawing certain consequences from it.⁹

However, we must remember, as I explained in chapter 1, that this quote is not self-referential. Francis is not saying that *Amoris Laetitia* itself has many possible interpretations. Rather, he is giving us the correct interpretation for *Amoris Laetitia*: that not everything needs to be settled by interventions from the magisterium. He is giving leeway for Catholics in the field to be able to account for every possible situation they encounter around the world. If we continue reading into the polemical eighth chapter, we clearly see this is what he is referring to:

> *If we consider the immense variety of concrete situations such as those I have mentioned*, it is understandable that neither the Synod nor this Exhortation could be expected to provide a new set of general rules, canonical in nature and applicable to all cases. *What is possible is simply a renewed encouragement to undertake a responsible personal and pastoral discernment of particular cases.* . . . It is true that general rules set forth a good which can never be disregarded or neglected, but in their formulation *they cannot provide absolutely for all particular situations.*¹⁰

In other words, Pope Francis does not assume (as any person with good sense would not) that any singular document, no matter how thorough or detailed, can ever encompass all possible situations in the real world. The Holy Father circumvents this by giving enough latitude of action for an orthodox pastor with good discernment to accompany any divorced and remarried person, whatever his or her situation.

Also, we must bear in mind that synodality has been a hallmark of Pope Francis's pontificate, and a topic close to his heart.¹¹ It is quite possible that Pope Francis has seen *Amoris Laetitia* (and its practical implementation) as an opportunity for synodality, and really does intend local churches, communities, and pastors to exercise pastorally-oriented discernment¹² that he does not want to make too definitive. After all, apostolic exhortations have an exhortative, not legally binding, nature.¹³

---

9. *AL* 3.
10. *AL* 300, 304.
11. Mares, "Pope Francis: Synodality Is What the Lord Expects of the Church."
12. See Walford, *Pope Francis, the Family, and Divorce*, 154–55.
13. Morrisey, "Apostolic Exhortation": "Although not juridically binding, [apostolic exhortations] are a significant expression of the magisterium of the Church, and

However, even if Pope Francis may tolerate a certain diversity in practice, he certainly expects this diversity to fall within a particular range. Certainly, there are different ways of receiving this exhortation, but they can never deny its fundamental content.[14]

Let us read the introduction of the apostolic exhortation[15] once again. Francis indeed says there can be "various ways of interpreting *some* aspects of teaching" (I emphasize the word "some"), but also that "unity of teaching and practice is certainly *necessary* in the Church" (I emphasize the word "necessary"). In short, this quote allows for some diversity, but not in a way that hinders church unity, even in practical matters. In this regard, theologian Salvador Pié-Ninot, basing himself precisely on *AL* 3, argues that even if there can be a "plurality on the practical level," this same plurality cannot be of a "relativist" or "purely subjective" kind.[16] This "applied practical plurality cannot become . . . an opportunity to manifest a certain dissent in the form of public criticisms, with the purpose of refuting" *Amoris Laetitia*'s sacramental discipline.[17]

How can we walk this very thin line between the plurality allowed by Francis and subjectivism/relativism? I believe the answer can be found by looking towards Peter.[18] After all, Francis has also been clear that synodality always acts *cum Petro et sub Petro*,[19] and that this is not a limitation of freedom but a guarantee of unity.[20] In this sense, we should

---

are morally persuasive and quite influential because they are frequently the product of consensus."

14. Passos, "Reception of the Post-Synodal." See also Ivereigh, *The Wounded Shepherd*, 264: "As Francis had made clear in *Evangelii Gaudium*, local bishops needed freedom to be able to respond to their own challenges without being straitjacketed by Roman centralism. But latitude in implementation wasn't the same as pluralism of interpretation: the Gospel needed to be inculturated, not cherry-picked."

15. *AL* 3.

16. Pié-Ninot, "L'Ultima Parola."

17. Pié-Ninot, "L'Ultima Parola."

18. Pié-Ninot, "L'Ultima Parola": "We need to bear in mind that in the Catholic faith, the confrontation with the Magisterium (in this case, papal) is a dissenting theological interpretation, not a mere conflict between two opinions, since the Magisterium of the Pope is not just any theological opinion, but is born of a witness of faith as an 'authentic interpreter of the Word of God' (*DV*, 13)."

19. Latin for "with Peter and under Peter."

20. Francis, "Ceremony Commemorating the 50th Anniversary."

try to ascertain the pontiff's opinion, even in matters where he allows some diversity.[21]

In this regard, it is noteworthy how Francis has used his official capacity to back up only one interpretation. When he published the Buenos Aires bishops' criteria in the *AAS*, he attached to them a letter where he wrote, "There are no other interpretations."[22] Because of this, it is difficult to substantiate the argument that Pope Francis has not made his intended meaning clear.[23] Even if Francis may be willing, in the interest of synodality and pastoral care, to allow the implementation of other interpretations, he has indeed clarified in an official way the meaning he prefers.

So we must now undertake the next step. We must consider each interpretation on its own and evaluate how much it matches up to the pope's manifest mind and will. This may seem like a daunting task, especially since we have been talking about "multiple interpretations" until now. But how many interpretations are out there exactly? The conclusion I have reached after years of debate is that there are actually only two or three main interpretations.[24] I will proceed to expound on each one of them.

---

21. See Passos, "Reception of the Post-Synodal": "Francis warns that not everything can be settled by the Magisterium, and that there are different ways of interpreting doctrine: he indicates that each local situation must have inculturated solutions in harmony with the local traditions and challenges.... However, we must search for some fundamental criteria so as to receive the Pope's orientations without betraying or misrepresenting what he actually intended to say" (my translation from the original Portuguese).

22. *AAS* 108 (2016), no. 10, 1071–1072.

23. See Fernández, "El capítulo VIII de *Amoris Laetitia*": in a very aptly-named section called "No hay otras interpretaciones" ("There are no other interpretations"), Archbishop Fernández says, "If we are interested in knowing how the Pope himself interprets what he has written, the answer is very explicit in his commentary on the guidelines by the Bishops of the Buenos Aires Region." See also López, "Para Comprender Amoris Laetitia," 442: "After this declaration of the Pope, it is impossible to argue that the access to the sacraments is completely forbidden" (my translation from the original Spanish).

24. The three interpretations I am going to explore roughly mirror the ones expounded by Buttiglione, *Risposte Amichevoli*, 74–77. See also Brugger, "A Tale of Two Interpretations of *Amoris Laetitia*."

Interpretation One—*Amoris Laetitia* Does Not Change Previous Sacramental Discipline

According to this interpretation, *Amoris Laetitia* simply reasserts the sacramental discipline previously defined by Pope St. John Paul II in *Familiaris Consortio (FC)*.[25] Put simply, this means that no civilly remarried person can receive the Eucharist unless he or she abides by total continence.

A note about the supporters of this theory: People included in this group are, as always, extremely heterogeneous. There are many who espouse this view and who honestly believe it is the best interpretation for *Amoris Laetitia*. They do not use this interpretation as a way to resist the pope's reforms.[26] Their input is valid and can help enrich this debate.

Still, this interpretation has also been advanced by some Catholics who oppose the widening of access to the Eucharist beyond the limits set forth by *Familiaris Consortio*, whether the pope promulgates it or not.[27] Interestingly, the latter may sometimes also be the ones advancing the "multiple interpretation" objection. According to my experience, this may be done in two possible ways:

1. By asserting the existence of multiple possible interpretations and then proceeding to argue that Interpretation One is just one more among them.[28] However, since Interpretation One is the only one that—so it is claimed—is compatible with orthodoxy, then this is the only one we should follow.[29] In this way, the discussion on whether

---

25. This seems to be the interpretation advocated by Granados et al., *Accompanying, Discerning, Integrating*.

26. Two cases come to mind: Fastiggi, "Responding to the Five Dubia from *Amoris Laetitia* itself"; and Matthew Schneider, "Does the Text of *Amoris Laetitia* Allow Communion for the Divorced and Remarried?"

27. Müller, "Development, or Corruption?" See especially: "Recently groups of bishops or individual episcopal conferences have issued directives concerning the reception of the sacraments. For these statements to be orthodox, it is not enough that they declare their conformity with the pope's presumed intentions in *Amoris Laetitia*. They are orthodox only if they agree with the words of Christ preserved in the deposit of faith. Similarly, when cardinals, bishops, priests, and laity ask the pope for clarity on these matters, what they request is not a clarification of the pope's opinion. What they seek is clarity regarding the continuity of the pope's teaching in *Amoris Laetitia* with the rest of tradition."

28. Montagna, "JPII Institute Profs Dismissed for Interpreting Francis in Line with Tradition?"

29. Montagna, "JPII Institute Profs Dismissed for Interpreting Francis in Line with

Interpretation One is cogent or not is averted, and this viewpoint is insisted on as the only legitimate one, even if the starting point was the possibility of many interpretations.[30]

2. The existence of multiple interpretations can be used to corroborate the idea that *Amoris Laetitia* is "ambiguous" and "confusing."[31] This can then be contrasted with the "clear" definition from *Familiaris*.[32] Since one is ambiguous and the other is clear, we should follow the latter, for we will be on more solid ground by doing so.[33]

Unfortunately, both of these tactics are based on assumptions: They assume that only this interpretation is orthodox. They assume that *Amoris Laetitia* is ambiguous. But, above all, they assume that there are many possible interpretations. I will focus the rest of this book in refuting all these assumptions.

More importantly, this reasoning is not useful for determining which interpretation is the likeliest. These are, ultimately, relativistic arguments, based on the notion that it is impossible to know what the correct interpretation is, in itself. In other words, the correct interpretation would be reached, not through the text itself (i.e. the more cogent interpretation), but from modifiers external to the text: "the correct interpretation is the one which is orthodox" or "the one which is clear." These same modifiers can then be used to undercut competing interpretations. If only one interpretation is "orthodox," "consistent with tradition," and "clear," the others are labeled as "heretical," "ambiguous," "confusing," and should be discarded for this very same reason. The person advancing this argument will judge by himself which interpretation is orthodox and heterodox, clear or ambiguous. By following this faulty logic, some Catholics may

---

Tradition?"

30. Gagliarducci, "Interpreting *Amoris Laetitia* 'through the Lens of Catholic Tradition.'"

31. Longley, "*Amoris Laetitia*: Pope Francis Has Created Confusion Where We Needed Clarity." See also Scanlon, "Flawed Strategy Behind *Amoris Laetitia*."

32. Longley, "Amoris Laetitia: Pope Francis Has Created Confusion Where We Needed Clarity."

33. See Melina, "Le Sfide di Amoris laetitia": "Given the amount of divergent and conflicting interpretations, it is difficult to deny that *Amoris Laetitia* is not a profoundly ambivalent text in this decisive point. The current Church discipline . . . is clearly taught by St. John Paul II in *Familiaris Consortio* 84. . . . In no part of Francis's post-synodal exhortation is it explicitly affirmed that we can introduce a contrary practice." (My translation from the original Italian.)

end up rejecting a cogent interpretation, even if sanctioned by the pope, and subscribing instead to an interpretation that is actually less probable.

This reasoning may even be used to claim that the interpretation favored by the pope himself is heterodox. Such is not the case, as the rest of this book will try to demonstrate. Nevertheless, given what I explained in chapter 2, asserting that the pope is advancing heterodoxy in an official magisterial document is a very serious charge, which should not be undertaken lightly.

Interpretation Two—Amoris Laetitia *Now Allows for Communion to the Divorced and Remarried with Mitigating Circumstances Reducing Culpability*

This is the interpretation I believe is more in line with the pope's manifest mind and will, and I will spend the next two chapters explaining why I believe so. This interpretation seems to find adherents in liberal quarters who think this sacramental discipline is closer to their position than the previous, more restrictive one. However, it must be noted that many do not view this interpretation as completely compatible with what they want,[34] but simply as an intermediary step conducive to the complete fulfillment of their ideal church.[35] Papal critics will point this out as proof

---

34. This seems to be the interpretation from Irrazabal, "*Amoris Laetitia* y los divorciados." While the theologian clearly affirms that Interpretation Two is the one closer to the pope's mind and will, he also criticizes it as "argumentatively weak": "We have to admit, however, that *AL* also bears a certain involution, inasmuch as it re-centers the topic in the scheme of the objective law and the subjective culpability. The text seems to suppose in general that those who act as best as they can, given their difficult situations and their own moral capabilities, even without fulfilling the law, still objectively sin, even if their responsibility is attenuated according to the case in question. . . . In the case of a divorced person that lives in a consolidated second union, would it make a difference if his pastor warned him that he is in sin, and that his new union is not according to the will of God, even if he is not completely culpable; or on the other hand, if the pastor would recognize the objective value of his life decision? One would expect that a document so centered on mercy would value the last possibility. . . . Unfortunately, in a contradictory way, *AL* assumes a very distinct path: it starts with the premise that all irregular situations are sinful from an objective point of view, even if the sin is not mortal given mitigating circumstances." (My translation from the original Spanish.)

35. *Focus News*, "Is *Amoris Laetitia* Good News?": "While *Amoris Laetitia* did not go far enough in creating a more inclusive church, it did re-orient Catholics, after a long period of Vatican II retrenchment, toward a more vibrant understanding of discernment, the primacy of conscience, the internal forum and accompaniment." See

The "Multiple Interpretations" Objection

of the need to resist,[36] but fail to understand that, by grounding itself firmly in orthodox principles, *Amoris Laetitia* has shielded itself against slippery slopes such as these. The main problem for those papal critics is that they do not see *Amoris Laetitia* as based on orthodox principles to begin with, so this reassurance is lost on them.

On the other hand, the supporters of Interpretation Two are not only liberals, but also (and most especially) Catholics who cannot be squared with any ideological label.[37] They transcend the "liberal-conservative" divide by following doctrine consistently. They are guided, not by ulterior agendas, but by faithfulness to the pope's teachings on matters of faith and morals, regardless of political allegiances.

If I may be so bold, I would like to give my individual experience as well. Before Francis, I was against giving communion to divorced and remarried people who did not abide by total continence, because I assented to *Familiaris Consortio*. After *Amoris Laetitia*'s publication, however, I read the document with the express intent of knowing the pope's manifest will, with a mind open to the possibility that I might need to revise my opinions on the matter. Having discovered that the discipline had indeed changed, and having recognized the orthodoxy of the doctrine underlying this new discipline, I submitted to it. This is by no means an isolated account, but has been mirrored by many Catholics who I met along the way and who have reached the same conclusion as I did: Interpretation Two is the most cogent one.

Interpretation Three—Amoris Laetitia Now Allows for Communion to Divorced and Remarried People Who Do Not Fulfill the Conditions Delineated in the Previous Interpretations

By definition, this category will encompass a wide variety of different interpretations, as long as they are more permissive than Interpretations

---

also FutureChurch, "FutureChurch Calls on Bishops to Implement *Amoris Laetitia*": "While there are many areas of *Amoris Laetitia* that need further development, this apostolic exhortation could, over time, have far reaching implications for all of the people of God, whether gay or straight, male or female, married or divorced."

36. Brugger, "A Tale of Two Interpretations of *Amoris Laetitia*."

37. This heterogeneous group includes (but is not limited to): Cristoph Schönborn, Victor Fernández, Patrick Travers, Paul Keller, Rocco Buttiglione, Guerra López, Stephen Walford, Mike Lewis, and Austen Ivereigh, among many others.

One and Two. Also, we cannot forget that *Amoris Laetitia*, and the synods from whence it emerged, are inserted into a decades-long discussion on the subject, dating back at least to the 1980s.[38] Some of these proposals were indeed discussed before, during, and after the synods. The most widely known is Cardinal Walter Kasper's proposal of a "penitential path," whereby a divorced and remarried person could be admitted to communion after a period of time, if that person had indeed repented of the failure of his or her first marriage, had found it impossible to turn back to the original situation, and was indeed committed to doing his or her best to live up the Catholic faith in spite of these limitations.[39] Another approach would be the age-old practice of the Eastern Orthodox churches, founded on the principles of *oikonomia*[40] and *epikeia*.[41]

However, these proposals (along with other more permissive approaches) did not seem to take hold during the synods.[42] According to some accounts, Cardinal Kasper himself, recognizing the controversial character of his proposal, joined together with other cardinals (belonging to what could be termed a more "conservative" persuasion) to try to achieve a middle-ground solution.[43] Some people involved also recount

---

38. Williams, "When Ratzinger Said No."

39. See *Inside The Vatican*, "Cardinal Kasper's Proposal."

40. As Cardinal Kasper would explain in a May 7, 2014, interview with *Commonweal*, "The Orthodox have the principle of *oikonomia*, which allows them in concrete cases to dispense, as Catholics would say, the first marriage and to permit a second in the church. But they do not consider the second marriage a sacrament. That's important. They make that distinction."

41. Fox, "Natural Law": "When the law of the legislator is not in harmony with the dictates of the natural law, equity (*æquitas, epikeia*) demands that it be set aside or corrected. St. Thomas explains the lawfulness of this procedure. Because human actions, which are the subject of laws, are individual and innumerable, it is not possible to establish any law that may not sometimes work out unjustly. Legislators, however, in passing laws attend to what commonly happens, though to apply the common rule will sometimes work injustice and defeat the intention of the law itself. In such cases it is bad to follow the law; it is good to set aside its letter and follow the dictates of justice and the common good."

42. Ivereigh, *The Wounded Shepherd*, 253, 272: "Yet, very few were persuaded by Kasper's proposal of a penitential path on the Orthodox church model, which allowed for the blessing of a new union, following a recognition of failure.... *A middle way was beginning to emerge*. Only a few now continued to advocate Kasper's Orthodox-style penitential route back to the sacraments.... Between these positions, most delegates were looking for a solution that would retain the general norm but allow greater pastoral flexibility in its application."

43. Ivereigh, *The Wounded Shepherd*, 273: "The eleventh-hour breakthrough came

that such a middle-ground solution was also what Pope Francis intended all along, eschewing the permissive proposals[44] as well as the restrictive ones. Archbishop Victor Fernández, who helped draft *Amoris Laetitia*, recounts, "The Pope, faithful to the real and limited possibilities allowed by the Synod—and also against the proposals of progressive moralists—decided to keep the distinction between objective sin and subjective guilt."[45]

Cardinal Kasper himself, in an interview after the exhortation's publication, affirmed that the Catholic faithful indeed "understand *Amoris Laetitia*."[46] Speaking of the controversial sacramental discipline, Kasper

---

from a most unlikely place: the single German-language group, Germanicus, moderated by Cardinal Christoph Schönborn and packed with heavyweights on both sides of the argument, including Kasper, Marx, and Müller. Despite their historic disagreements, they united in irritation at Pell's remarks to *Le Figaro* that the synod's battle over Communion came down to a duel between Ratzingerians and Kasperites. To show that theological consensus was possible, the Germans invited a learned eight-hundred-year-old to join the discussion. 'When Cardinal Kasper and Cardinal Müller and Cardinal Schönborn are all talking about Saint Thomas [Aquinas], that is very interesting!' Marx later told journalists."

44. Ivereigh, *The Wounded Shepherd*, 252: "Francis asked another German, the octogenarian theologian and cardinal Walter Kasper, to address the entire College of Cardinals in February 2014 as a prelude to the synod in October . . . leading nervous conservatives to assume at once that Francis was siding with 'the liberals.' But that was to misread him. Francis's aim throughout, but especially at this pre-synod stage, was to create the conditions for an authentic discernment." See also p. 366: "The 'liberal' lobbying was confirmed both by Archbishop Victor Fernández, who helped draft *Amoris*, as well as by Cardinal Schönborn. 'I was so relieved and glad that Pope Francis stood clear on this,' Schönborn said in Limerick. 'The canonical dispositions are clear and need no supplement.'" And see also Bordeyne, "Divorcés remariés": "Before the Synod, certain theologians proposed the application of the Eastern Orthodox's practice, which would allow, in the case of a second union, a return to Communion after a very precise, almost automatic process. The Pope refuses all automatism." (My translation from the original French.)

45. Fernández, "El capítulo VIII de *Amoris Laetitia*," 457. See also Walford, *Pope Francis, the Family, and Divorce*, 20–24.

46. Gisotti, "Kasper: the faithful understand *Amoris Laetitia*": "The Council of Trent says that in the case in which there is no grave sin, but venial, the Eucharist removes that sin. Sin is a complex term. It not only includes an objective principle, but there is also the intention, the person's conscience. And this needs to be examined in the internal forum—in the Sacrament of Reconciliation—if there is truly a grave sin, or perhaps a venial sin, or perhaps nothing. If it is only a venial sin, the person can be absolved and admitted to the Sacrament of the Eucharist. This already corresponds with the doctrine of Pope John Paul II and, in this sense, Pope Francis is in complete continuity with the direction opened by preceding Popes."

makes the distinction between grave sin and venial sin—a distinction not present in his initial proposal, and on which Interpretation Two rests, as we shall see later.

Another way to advance a more permissive interpretation of *Amoris Laetitia* would be to argue a creative role for conscience, according to which the divorced and remarried person could discern to be in a virtuous relationship, willed by God, and indistinguishable from a Catholic marriage. While some theologians of a more liberal streak may advocate this position, I have found that most actually understand how *Amoris Laetitia* does not stretch so far. This is why they usually say that *Amoris Laetitia* is a "positive step"[47] in the right direction, while remaining critical of the present arrangement.[48]

In this sense, I find it interesting that this "creative conscience" interpretation usually does not seem to sprout from liberal sectors, but rather from conservative ones. This is the interpretation conservatives fear the most, and so they use it to show how *Amoris Laetitia* is a dangerous document.[49]

Nevertheless, this interpretation also blatantly contradicts *Amoris Laetitia* (as I will explain in chapter 6). It is, therefore, extremely paradoxical and counterproductive that papal critics will not (as they would have done in their apologetics in previous pontificates) simply refute this interpretation, so that *Amoris Laetitia* cannot be hijacked to advance heterodoxy. This is a *faux-pas* in every way equivalent to their undermining of the authoritativeness of the pope's magisterium (see chapter 2): a strategy that, in the long run, will probably be more beneficial to the liberal side than to theirs.

---

47. We Are Church Ireland, "Irish reform group welcomes exhortation": "Overall this is a positive step forward by Pope Francis especially on his emphasis on the overarching importance of Mercy and compassion in the Church." But also: "While its pastoral outlook and its emphasis on the 'logic of mercy' are very welcome we are disappointed that there are no positive changes for the many divorced and civilly remarried Catholics who are in second relationships."

48. Irrazabal, "*Amoris Laetitia* y los divorciados."

49. A paradigmatic example is the fifth allegedly heretical *Amoris Laetitia* proposition "corrected" by the authors of the *Correctio Filialis*: "Conscience can truly and rightly judge that sexual acts between persons who have contracted a civil marriage with each other, although one or both of them is sacramentally married to another person, can sometimes be morally right or requested or even commanded by God." The authors argue, correctly, that this statement is incompatible with Catholic doctrine, but they also argue, incorrectly, that *Amoris Laetitia* subscribes to this statement.

The "Multiple Interpretations" Objection

❖❖❖

The Bishops' Guidelines

What I said about the supporters of these three interpretations comes from my three-year experience in online debates with all sorts of Catholics from every possible ideological quadrant. Nevertheless, it must also be said that the "multiple interpretation" objection does not limit itself to the diversity of opinions found in Catholic social media and forums. Papal critics will often point out that the disagreement happens at the highest echelons, namely at the epicoscopal level. Bishops from different regions and countries would interpret *Amoris Laetitia* in different ways and, by extension, would implement it differently. These papal critics will point out that a divorced and remarried person might be forbidden to take communion in Poland, and then cross the border and receive it in Germany.[50]

First of all, as I have said earlier, some diversity is indeed willed by Pope Francis. Also, this practical heterogeneity is not without precedent as far as sacraments are concerned. For example, a sinner (not necessarily a divorced and remarried person but, let us say, a porn addict) may confess his sins in a parish and be denied absolution, and then go to another parish and receive it from another priest. This heterogeneity is inextricably linked to the complexity of reality and to the diversity of reasoning among human beings (including clergy). It would be very hard to use this heterogeneity as an argument for limiting each priest's capacity to discern each situation coming before him as he sees fit.

Still, let us take this objection as valid and ask ourselves: are there so many different practical implementations of *Amoris Laetitia* on the

---

50. Hort, "Leitartikel: Faktisches Schisma": "When he—together with the bishop of Gozo—now instructs the pastors of his own small island state that every remarried divorcee may deal himself with the dear God as to whether he may go to Communion (see page 5 [of *Die Tagespost*]), then that means very clearly that each local church may now do as it pleases. The furrow grows deeper. *Florence against Rome, Poland against Argentina, Malta against Milan.* That is what one calls a *de facto* schism." (Translation from the original German by Maike Hickson from *One Peter Five.*) See also the letter from Cardinal Carlo Caffarra (Pentin, "Full Text of *Dubia* Cardinals' Letter Asking Pope for an Audience"): "And so it is happening — how painful it is to see this! — *that what is sin in Poland is good in Germany, that what is prohibited in the archdiocese of Philadelphia is permitted in Malta.* And so on. One is reminded of the bitter observation of B. Pascal: 'Justice on this side of the Pyrenees, injustice on the other; justice on the left bank of the river, injustice on the right bank.'"

ground? Of course, it would be too tedious (and occupy a significant part of this book) to make an exposition on every single approved episcopal guideline around the world. I do not think that is necessary, though. According to my personal experience, most papal critics use only four of these bishops' guidelines to make their point.[51] So these four cases could be considered as paradigmatic and representative, even if not all-inclusive. In this sense, it would be instructive to examine those four guidelines with more detail to see if a discernible pattern begins to emerge. They are

1. the Polish Bishops' Conference document "Pastoral Guidelines for the Exhortation *Amoris Laetitia*";
2. the statement "The joy of love experienced by families is also the joy of the Church" from the German Bishops' Conference;
3. the "Criteria for the application of Chapter 8 of *Amoris Laetitia*," by the Archdiocese of Malta and the Diocese of Gozo;
4. and the "Basic criteria for the application of Chapter 8 of the *Amoris Laetitia*," by the Bishops of the Pastoral Region of Buenos Aires.

The papal critic will use the Polish guidelines as a benchmark of orthodoxy, since they allegedly do not allow communion for the divorced and remarried. The German, Maltese, and Buenos Aires[52] criteria, on the other hand, are contrasted to the Polish guidelines, as proof of the diversity of implementations and, therefore, of *Amoris Laetitia*'s ambiguity.[53]

   51. Interestingly, my experience is that papal critics in social media seldom use the Philadelphia guidelines to make their case. They prefer to use the Polish guidelines, which, as we shall see, do not support their point, whereas the ones from Philadelphia explicitly reject the possibility of Communion for the divorced and remarried who do not live "as brother and sister." See Chaput, "Pastoral Guidelines," 4: "What of Communion? Every Catholic, not only the divorced and civilly-remarried, must sacramentally confess all serious sins of which he or she is aware, with a firm purpose to change, before receiving the Eucharist. In some cases, the subjective responsibility of the person for a past action may be diminished. But the person must still repent and renounce the sin, with a firm purpose of amendment. . . . Undertaking to live as brother and sister is necessary for the divorced and civilly-remarried to receive reconciliation in the Sacrament of Penance, which could then open the way to the Eucharist."
   52. Just as an interesting sidenote, my personal experience is that the Buenos Aires criteria have been used fewer times as an example since the pope has explicitly supported them by publishing them in the *AAS*. Now, only the ones from Malta and Germany are mentioned by many papal critics as examples of heterogeneity in the church, and the Buenos Aires criteria's existence is simply ignored.
   53. Mazurczak, "Polish Bishops' *Amoris Laetitia* Guidelines Stress Discernment and Compassion."

Yet, this leads to the question: are these four implementations so diverse as the papal critics make them out to be? An attentive reading will show us this is not the case.

The Polish guidelines do not forbid giving communion to divorced and remarried people. In fact, they are completely silent on the matter. Of course, one may argue that, absent an explicit abrogation of *Familiaris Consortio*, its discipline still applies. But one may also argue that a Polish priest who gives communion to a divorced and remarried person in the terms delineated by *Amoris Laetitia* is not being disobedient to his bishop, while being faithful to the pope.

As far as the other guidelines go, they are not so different. They all allow divorced and remarried people with mitigating circumstances to receive communion. By doing so, they distance themselves from Interpretation One:

- Buenos Aires criteria: "If it is recognized that, in a specific case, there are limitations that mitigate liability and guilt, particularly when a person considers that he would fall on a further fault damaging the children of the new union, *Amoris Laetitia* opens the possibility of access to the sacraments of Reconciliation and the Eucharist."

- German statement: "*Amoris laetitia* opens up the possibility to receive the sacraments of Reconciliation and the Eucharist. . . . It becomes clear what the Pope means in this context by discerning when he states in *Amoris laetitia*: 'The Church possesses a solid body of reflection concerning mitigating factors and situations. Hence it can no longer simply be said that all those in any "irregular" situation are living in a state of mortal sin and are deprived of sanctifying grace.'"

- Maltese criteria: "If, as a result of the process of discernment, undertaken with 'humility, discretion, and love for the Church and her teaching, in a sincere search for God's will and a desire to make a more perfect response to it' (*AL* 300), a separated or divorced person who is living in a new relationship manages, with an informed and enlightened conscience, to acknowledge and believe that he or she are at peace with God, he or she cannot be precluded from participating in the sacraments of Reconciliation and the Eucharist."

However, all of these three episcopal bodies do not wish to open the Eucharistic floodgates to anyone in an irregular situation who requests communion. Rather, all of them mention the teaching on mitigating circumstances on which Interpretation Two is built. In so doing, they seem to side with this interpretation and not with the expansive version of Interpretation Three that papal critics so fear:

- Buenos Aires criteria: "First of all we remember that it is not convenient to speak of 'permits' to access the sacraments, but of a process of discernment accompanied by a pastor. . . . This path does not necessarily end in the sacraments. . . . We must avoid understanding this possibility as an unrestricted access to the sacraments, or as if any situation justified it. What is proposed is a discernment that adequately distinguishes each case."

- German statement: "*Amoris laetitia* does not offer a general rule with regard to this matter, and it does not provide an automatic mechanism to admit all those who are divorced and civilly remarried to the sacraments. . . . Not all faithful whose marriages have broken down and are divorced and civilly remarried can receive the sacraments without discernment. . . . Such a spiritual process, which is always concerned about integrating, does not always conclude with the receipt of the sacraments of Reconciliation and the Eucharist."

- Maltese criteria: "Throughout the discernment process, we need to weigh the moral responsibility in particular situations, with due consideration to the conditioning restraints and attenuating circumstances. . . . Throughout this process, our role is not simply that of granting permission for these people to receive the sacraments, or to offer 'easy recipes' (see *AL* 298), or to substitute their conscience."

In fact, both Interpretations One and Three are made less plausible, since both the German and the Maltese documents explicitly mention the need to avoid falling into the two extremes of excess rigor and excess laxity. Germans, Maltese, and Argentines seem to be in agreement with Interpretation Two. The Polish did not make an official pronouncement on any of the interpretations. So, it seems like *Amoris Laetitia* is actually being implemented very consistently and, as I wish to prove in my next chapter, in accordance with the pope's manifest mind and will.

❖ ❖ ❖

The "Multiple Interpretations" Objection

At the end of this chapter, I hope to have shown that the "multiple interpretations" objection is not sound. There are many interpretations, indeed, but this does not mean that they enjoy the same degree of certitude. As this book unfolds, an interpretation seems to be emerging, more likely and cogent than the others.

Yet, as I said before, Pope Francis may still allow some diversity of implementation beyond what he originally envisioned, out of synodal and pastoral concerns. Some may find this troublesome, fearing that this decentralization may unnecessarily risk the implementation of heterodox interpretations on the ground. But this decentralization does not apply to doctrine, at least not in the sense of creating "disunity" in terms of interpreting "truth." Francis's idea of decentralization does not mean that the truths of the faith can be changed. Employing decentralization is *structural*, not *doctrinal*. Decentralization is Francis's preferred pastoral governance approach, because it enables him to effectively listen to the voice of the people of God and get their input and feedback. With this decentralization, Francis can place greater emphasis on synodality, discerning, accompanying, and evangelizing.[54] However, this is not the same as "nationalizing" morality or relativizing truth. If Peter sees fit to decentralize his responsibilities, he can. We believe that Truth himself gave the keys to Peter. We have nothing to fear, as long as this decentralization is done with and under Peter.[55]

Having said that, how do we know which interpretation is the one more in accordance with the pope's manifest mind and will? Throughout this chapter, I have already provided a glimpse regarding which interpretation I consider more sound. Even so, to answer this question appropriately, we should read *Amoris Laetitia* carefully. I sincerely believe the answers are in the text itself. It is necessary to do a proper exegesis of this document. This is what I set out to do in my next chapter.

---

54. Domingues, "Pope Francis's Decentralization."
55. Domingues, "Pope Francis's Decentralization."

Chapter 4

Who Is Allowed to Receive Communion?

In this chapter I will try to interpret *Amoris Laetitia*'s contentious sacramental discipline by focusing on the apostolic exhortation's wording. In short, I will try to draw conclusions from the text itself, and from nothing else. In the next chapter, I will use other documents and facts as a source for external validation of the conclusions drawn here. For now, let us try to answer the question: who does *Amoris Laetitia* allow to receive communion, and in what circumstances? In order to answer this question, we need to break it up into smaller questions:

❖❖❖

Question One—Does Amoris Laetitia *Allow Civilly Remarried People to Receive Communion or Not?*

The answer to this question can be found in the footnote at the core of the whole controversy:

> In certain cases, this can include the help of the sacraments. Hence, "I want to remind priests that the confessional must not be a torture chamber, but rather an encounter with the Lord's mercy" (*Apostolic Exhortation Evangelii Gaudium* [24 November 2013], 44: *AAS* 105 [2013], 1038). I would also point out that the Eucharist "is not a prize for the perfect, but a powerful medicine and nourishment for the weak."[1]

1. *AL* n351.

Who Is Allowed to Receive Communion?

Here, Pope Francis specifically states that the help of the sacraments may be considered. Although he does not specify which sacraments he is referring to, it is strongly implied by the two subsequent sentences that he means the sacraments of Reconciliation and Eucharist. Otherwise the rest of the footnote would not make any sense, since it would be very oddly compartmentalized.

So Francis wants pastors to consider the possibility of the sacraments, namely the Eucharist. To whom does he open this possibility? Footnote 351 refers to paragraph 305, and the exhortation has been delving on the topic of divorced and remarried Catholics since at least #298.

So we can conclude that Pope Francis opens the possibility of the Eucharist to (at least some) people who are civilly remarried.[2]

❊ ❊ ❊

Question Two—Does Amoris Laetitia *Allow Communion for* Every *Divorced and Remarried Person?*

I think the answer to this question is found in footnote 351 itself. The footnote starts with "*in certain cases*, this can include the help of the sacraments." By definition, this wording excludes some cases.[3] Commenting on the same passage, Rocco Buttiglione agrees with this interpretation: "It is not said that the divorced and remarried have the right, like all faithful Catholics in the same situation, to receive the Eucharist. It

---

2. López, "Para Comprender *Amoris Laetitia*," 436: "Ask if it is possible now to grant absolution in the sacrament of Penance and, consequently, admit to the Holy Eucharist a person who, being united by a valid matrimonial tie, lives 'more uxorio' with another one. The answer is clear. I think that in some occasions it is possible and in other occasions no." See also Almeida, "*Amoris Laetitia*—reflexões," 376: "In footnote 351 . . . Francis clearly opens the possibility of Reconciliation and Eucharist to the civilly remarried who undertake a path of accompaniment and discernment" (my translation from the original Portuguese). See also Fernández, "El capítulo VIII de *Amoris Laetitia*," 452: "Therefore, there can be a path of discernment open to the possibility of receiving the Eucharist." This is even confirmed by papal critic Josef Seifert, who, when asked in an interview for *One Peter Five* if he had "any doubt left as to whether Pope Francis intends to allow some 'remarried' divorcees access to the Sacraments," replied, "No doubt about that." (Seifert, "The Church After Amoris Laetitia.")

3. *AL* 298, for example, seems to imply that those who have recently entered a new union are not considered for this discernment path. This opinion is shared by Fernández, "El capítulo VIII de *Amoris Laetitia*," 464.

is said that the priest can ('can,' not 'must') in some cases, that is, by way of exception, admit them to the Eucharist."[4]

On the other hand, the main topic of *Amoris Laetitia*'s eighth chapter (where the footnote is located) is discernment. If *Amoris Laetitia* simply opened up the possibility to any civilly remarried person who sought it, why spend so much time talking about discernment at all? In his essay on the matter, theologian Thomas Ryan says: "Clearly, the Pope is not giving a blanket permission for those divorced and remarried *extra-ecclesia* to receive Holy Communion. Such a step can only be the result of a personal discernment before God, made within the internal forum, within an ecclesial setting (with one's pastor or spiritual guide) and put into practice with humility and discretion."[5]

Nevertheless, is there actual textual evidence supporting the claim that the exhortation does not simply open access to the Eucharist to every single divorced and remarried person? Let us read #300:

> These attitudes are essential for avoiding the grave danger of misunderstandings, such as the notion that any priest can quickly grant "exceptions," or that some people can obtain sacramental privileges in exchange for favours.[6]

Amoris Laetitia does not give *carte blanche* for a priest to grant exceptions or sacramental privileges at will. According to the pope himself, that would be a "grave misunderstanding." In fact, according to Fr. Ryan, "granting permissions" would actually "distort the purpose of discernment," since it would "ultimately keep people in a state of dependency and deprive them of their right to respond to God with deepening insight and love as mature adults."[7]

❋❋❋

4. Buttiglione, *Risposte Amichevoli*, 155–56. See also pp. 37 and 40.
5. Ryan, "Weakness, and Wounded and Troubled Love," 143.
6. *AL* 300.
7. Ryan, "Weakness, and Wounded and Troubled Love," 144. In the same vein, see Almeida, "*Amoris Laetitia*—reflexões," 383: "The real challenge is to accompany and discern. The 'cool' pastor may actually not be merciful, but only lazy, when he dispenses the remarried Catholic from a long process of accompaniment and discernment. That's a lot of work! Many will prefer the old practice of simply 'allowing' communion. Worse still, if they use *Amoris Laetitia* as an excuse for that. . . . Easy solutions do not help people to commit with the Church, but only turn the Church into a mere service provider company. . . . So it is clear that this proposal is not for everyone."

Question Three—Does a Divorced and Remarried Person Need to Live "as Brother and Sister" to Receive Communion?

Since not all divorced and remarried couples may partake of the Eucharist, it may be argued that the only ones who can do it are the ones already covered by the previous sacramental discipline, as defined by *Familiaris Consortio* 84. In other words, these would be couples who would cease to live *more uxorio* (i.e., stop having intercourse) and live instead as "brother and sister" (this is Interpretation One explored in the previous chapter).

I argue that *Amoris Laetitia* does not restrict itself to such cases for two reasons. First of all, some civilly remarried couples may try to stop living *more uxorio*, but often relapse into temptation. This is common for every sin, let alone every sin of the flesh. For these cases, Francis explains:

> Perhaps out of a certain scrupulosity, concealed beneath a zeal for fidelity to the truth, some priests demand of penitents a purpose of amendment so lacking in nuance that it causes mercy to be obscured by the pursuit of a supposedly pure justice. For this reason, it is helpful to recall the teaching of Saint John Paul II, who stated that the possibility of a new fall "should not prejudice the authenticity of the resolution."[8]

One may be contrite and yet acknowledge that he will most likely sin again. Here, as with any other sin, this is not a valid reason to withhold the sacraments. In fact, Guerra López, member of the theological team of CELAM,[9] highlights how this praxis is *not* a "kind of undue complacency towards a particular sin, or a kind of 'permission' to keep living in habitual sin."[10]

However, there is more to it. What about the civilly remarried who do not stop living *more uxorio*, not by trying and failing, but because there is an impediment to such a resolution in the first place? For example, the

---

8. AL 364.

9. Latin-American Episcopal Conference.

10. López, "Entender a Wojtyla," 49: "This statement does not consist in any kind of undue complacency with a habitual sin, or a kind of 'permission' to keep living in habitual sin. It means that the pastor should respect what a sincere conscience can discover about the limits of its situation. And, from this limited reality, undertake a path. Recognizing the limits, the person is disposed to try to overcome them, but will do so in the measure of his real possibilities. This is why, as is well known, even if the possibility of a new relapse is foreseeable, this should not prejudice the authenticity of the purpose of amendment on the part of the penitent."

Holy Father mentions a situation "where, for serious reasons, such as the children's upbringing, a man and woman cannot satisfy the obligation to separate"[11] and where "if certain expressions of intimacy are lacking . . . faithfulness is endangered and the good of the children suffers."[12] In these cases, another much-disputed quote comes into play:

> Yet conscience can do more than recognize that a given situation does not correspond objectively to the overall demands of the Gospel. It can also recognize with sincerity and honesty what for now is the most generous response which can be given to God, and come to see with a certain moral security that it is what God himself is asking amid the concrete complexity of one's limits, *while yet not fully the objective ideal*.[13]

Let me highlight "while yet not fully the objective ideal." In certain situations where the new union cannot be legitimately regularized, this "objective ideal" would be living as brother and sister. Does this mean that people who do not fully realize this objective ideal can receive communion?[14]

❊❊❊

Question Four—In What Circumstances Is a Civilly Remarried Person Allowed To Receive Communion?

Since it was in #303 that Pope Francis mentions not fulfilling the objective ideal, let us contextualize by reading the beginning of that paragraph:

> *Recognizing the influence of such concrete factors*, we can add that *individual conscience* needs to be better incorporated into the Church's praxis in certain situations which do not objectively embody our understanding of marriage.

Previously, we saw that conscience determines what the most generous response is, even if it is not yet the fully objective ideal. This same conscience needs to be "better incorporated into the Church's praxis." How? By "recognizing the influence of such concrete factors."

---

11. *AL* 298.
12. *AL* 329, referring back to the same paragraph 298.
13. *AL* 303.
14. Rocco Buttiglione seems to give a qualified affirmative answer to this question, in certain circumstances. See *Risposte amichevoli*, 172.

Who Is Allowed to Receive Communion?

What "concrete factors" are these? This directs us to the previous couple of paragraphs, which in fact deal solely with those "concrete factors":

> The Church possesses a solid body of reflection concerning mitigating factors and situations. Hence it can no longer simply be said that all those in any "irregular" situation are living in a state of mortal sin and are deprived of sanctifying grace.[15]

The church teaches that these mitigating factors may reduce culpability in such a way that a sin with grave matter is not a mortal sin. This is doctrinally sound (as seen in chapter 7 of this book). It is also doctrinally sound to state that a person can receive communion if he or she is not in mortal sin (again, I will explain this with more detail in chapter 7 of this book). Pope Francis would only incur heresy if he stated the opposite, allowing people in mortal sin to receive communion.[16]

Pope Francis brings up the church's "solid body of reflection concerning mitigating factors" *explicitly to prevent the notion that* "the demands of the Gospel are in any way being compromised."[17] It is wrong to oppose those two parts of Catholic doctrine, as if discerning the mitigating factors would somehow detract from the demands of the gospel regarding marriage. The pope specifically tells us here that they are not mutually exclusive. In fact, it is by remembering Catholic doctrine on mitigating factors that we can apply his pastoral principles without compromising the gospel.

Is this what Francis is referring to in footnote 351, where he allows communion for the divorced and remarried? Some may argue that the Holy Father does not specifically say that these mitigating factors should have an impact on sacramental discipline, only on pastoral accompaniment.

Such an objection, however, can only be sustained if we do a fragmented reading of the document. Paragraphs 300 to 303 revolve around mitigating factors. And footnote 351, opening the possibility of communion, refers back to this part in #305:

> *Because of forms of conditioning and mitigating factors*, it is possible that in an objective situation of sin—which may not

---

15. *AL* 301.

16. López, "Para comprender *Amoris Laetitia*," 437: "The impossibility to receive the Eucharist in mortal sin is of the doctrinal order, not merely disciplinary."

17. *AL* 301.

be subjectively culpable, or fully such—*a person can be living in God's grace, can love and can also grow in the life of grace and charity, while receiving the Church's help to this end.*[18]

This ties very nicely with the preceding paragraphs. Hence, the permissibility of communion to some who have divorced and civilly remarried, per footnote 351, has everything to do with mitigating factors diminishing subjective culpability, so that the person can "live in God's grace" (i.e., not be in mortal sin).[19]

In fact, this interpretation is even confirmed elsewhere in the text:

> What is possible is simply a renewed encouragement to undertake a responsible personal and pastoral discernment of particular cases, one which would recognize that, *since "the degree of responsibility is not equal in all cases,"* the *consequences* or effects of a rule *need not necessarily always be the same.*[20]

In other words, by undertaking a "discernment of particular cases," recognizing the "responsibility" (i.e., culpability) in each case, we can establish the "consequences" for each individual situation. What is the scope of these "consequences"? The aforementioned paragraph contains a footnote:

> This is also the case with regard to *sacramental discipline*, since discernment can recognize that in a particular situation no grave fault exists.[21]

In short, the consequences drawn from this discernment also include "sacramental discipline." It seems that the document is actually quite clear.[22] The Eucharist may be given to those in irregular situations who,

---

18. *AL* 305.

19. Ryan, "Weakness, and wounded, and troubled love," 143: "While, in chapter 8, there is no explicit mention of reception of 'Holy Communion', it is implied in the wording of this footnote.... What the Pope implies in this footnote is fully consistent with his whole argument about the levels or absence of culpability, even in objectively grave situations."

20. *AL* 300.

21. *AL* 335.

22. López, "Para comprender *Amoris Laetitia*," 436: "Ask if it is possible now to grant absolution in the sacrament of Penance and, consequently, admit to the Holy Eucharist a person who, being united by a valid matrimonial tie, lives '*more uxorio*' with another one. *The answer is clear.* I think that in some occasions it is possible and in other occasions no. *It will all depend on whether there is an authentic moral sin, or if there are mitigating factors* that will make it a sin not of this nature. It is worth

on account of mitigating factors diminishing subjective culpability, are not in a state of mortal sin.

❊❊❊

Question Five—Is This Arrangement Definitive?

Should the priest grant communion to a divorced and remarried person in such circumstances at all times? Of course, since Pope Francis wants to give enough latitude of action for a priest to deal with any given sinner in any given situation, he could never create a rigid timetable according to which it would be permissible to grant communion during an arbitrarily-defined period of time, and not outside it.

However, it also seems clear that the Holy Father does not want this arrangement to be definitive, but only to act as a temporary step to allow the divorced and remarried person to receive sacramental grace to help him or her attain the objective ideal. Let us recall #303, but this time read it until its end:

> In any event, let us recall that this discernment is dynamic; it must remain ever open to new stages of growth and to new decisions which can enable the ideal to be more fully realized.

This interpretation is reinforced by the fact that *Amoris Laetita* had set a context prior to this, saying:

> All these situations require a constructive response seeking to transform them into *opportunities that can lead to the full reality of marriage and family in conformity with the Gospel.* These couples need to be welcomed and guided patiently and discreetly.... Along these lines, Saint John Paul II proposed the so-called "law of gradualness" in the knowledge that the human being "knows, loves, and accomplishes moral good by different stages of growth." This is not a "gradualness of law" but rather a gradualness in the prudential exercise of free acts on the part

---

remembering that mortal sin requires three elements in a human act: grave matter, full knowledge, and deliberate consent. Grave matter alone does not constitute a mortal sin." Finally, see also Buttiglione, *Risposte amichevoli*, 152: "The considerations of *Amoris Laetitia* are *clearly* inserted precisely on the sphere of *subjective mitigating circumstances*."

of *subjects who are not in a position to understand, appreciate, or fully carry out the objective demands of the law.*[23]

"Subjects who are not in position to understand, appreciate, or fully carry out the objective demands of the law" seem to be the ones who have mitigating factors interfering with full knowledge and full consent. We already established that those are the ones considered for communion. These people "require a constructive response seeking to transform them into opportunities that can lead to the full reality of marriage and family in conformity with the Gospel." This is the goal.[24]

Nevertheless, it might just happen that such opportunities might never come. The pace of the individual in question must be respected: according to the situation, this next step might never come to fruition. In this sense, the sacramental provisions of *Amoris Laetitia* should be *preferably* a provisional situation that should *ideally* lead to a stage more in line with the church's teaching.[25] The spiritual journey should be *open* to new stages of growth, and these opportunities should be taken as soon as they manifest themselves.

❊❊❊

23. AL 294–95.

24. Travers, "*Amoris Laetitia* and Canon 915," 376: "Throughout this process of discernment, this person must remain open to future developments that will make possible a more complete response to the demands of the Gospel. The access of that person to the Sacraments, particularly Holy Communion, does not, however, need to await those developments and that response." See also Buttiglione, *Risposte amichevoli*, 172: "It is possible that the sinner is not in a stage where he can realize this detachment and reconquer his own sovereignty in an immediate way. . . . He must strive, so as to keep the resolution to leave the situation of sin."

25. In his interview with *La Civiltà Cattolica* ("A Conversation with Cardinal Schönborn on '*Amoris Laetitia*'"), Cardinal Schönborn was asked whether the pope is referring to those who do not succeed in objectively realizing our concept of marriage and in transforming their way of life in accordance with this requirement. The Cardinal answered, "Yes, certainly! In his great experience of accompanying people spiritually, when the Holy Father speaks of 'objective situations of sin,' he does not stop short at the kinds of cases that are specified in nr. 84 of *Familiaris consortio*. He refers in a broader way to 'certain situations which do not objectively embody our understanding of marriage. Every effort should be made to encourage the development of an enlightened conscience' while 'recognizing the influence of concrete factors' (AL 303)."

Provisional Conclusions

From this exegesis of the eighth chapter of *Amoris Laetitia*, specifically the controversial paragraphs and their immediate context, we have arrived at the following conclusions:

1. *Amoris Laetitia* opens the possibility of communion to some divorced and remarried people (footnote 351),
2. though not all (footnote 351, #300),
3. even if those divorced and remarried people have not yet attained the fully objective ideal (#303)
4. as long as they have mitigating factors diminishing subjective culpability (#300–305)
5. so that they are not in mortal sin (#301)
6. as an ideally provisional step to help them attain the objective ideal in accordance with the gospel (#294–95, #303).

This interpretation seems to be consistent throughout the text. As far as I am aware, there is nothing in *Amoris Laetitia* contradicting it. However, here we have considered only the apostolic exhortation itself. In my next chapter, I will try to confirm the accuracy of this interpretation by validating it with other sources besides the exhortation.

Chapter 5

External Validation

IN THE PREVIOUS CHAPTER, I tried to interpret *Amoris Laetitia* by limiting myself to the exhortation's own words. But is there a way to validate the cogency of this interpretation? That is, is this interpretation compatible with the pope's manifest mind and will?

How can we know what the pontiff's mind and will on the matter are? When *Lumen Gentium* defines the submission Catholics owe to the pope's ordinary magisterium, it also clarifies: "His [the pope's] mind and will in the matter may be known either from the character of the documents, from his frequent repetition of the same doctrine, or from his manner of speaking."[1]

In this sense, I believe the strongest indicator of Pope Francis's mind and will on this matter is the support he gave to the Buenos Aires criteria.

The Buenos Aires Criteria

Given *Amoris Laetitia*'s mixed reception among the faithful, Francis found it necessary to clarify what he meant. The bishops of the Buenos Aires Pastoral Region had previously written a set of criteria on how to implement the exhortation. The pope then ordered these criteria to be published, first on the Vatican website, and later in the *Acta Apostolicae Sedes*. This publication was accompanied by a letter, penned by the pope himself, where he states:

---

1. *LG* 25.

> The writing is very good and explicitly the meaning of chapter VIII of Amoris Laetitia. *There are no other interpretations.*[2]

This is very strongly worded. I believe that if we want to take the pope's mind and will into consideration, we cannot avoid the clear and strong position he has taken with these official acts.

In fact, the pope is not alone in this clarification. Archbishop Victor Fernández, who helped draft *Amoris Laetitia*,[3] wrote an essay about this exhortation's eighth chapter. In a very aptly named section, "No Hay Otras Interpretaciones" ("There are no other interpretations"), the archbishop postulates:

> *If one is interested in knowing how the Pope himself interprets what he has written, the answer is very explicit in his commentary on the guidelines by the bishops of the Buenos Aires Region.* . . . Francis has immediately sent a formal letter saying that "the writing is very good and thoroughly explains the meaning of Chapter VIII." But it is also important to note that he adds: "There are no other interpretations." *Consequently, it is not necessary to wait for any other answer from the Pope on this matter.* . . . Evidently, a letter from the Pope does not possess the same value as an encyclical. But, as we shall see, *it can have a decisive practical importance in explaining the correct interpretation of a text of greater value.* If the Pope received the charism, unique in the Church, to provide the correct interpretation of the divine Word—the charism of Peter to bind and loose, and confirm his brothers in the faith—*this cannot exclude his capacity to interpret the documents that he himself has written.*[4]

---

2. *AAS* 108 (2016), no. 10, 1071–1072.

3. Ivereigh, "*Wounded Shepherd*," 366. See also Pentin, "Archbishop Fernández Defends '*Amoris Laetitia*' From Its Critics."

4. Fernández, "El capítulo VIII de *Amoris Laetitia*," 451–52. See also López, "Para Comprender *Amoris Laetitia*," 442: "This position of the bishops from the Buenos Aires region has been personally commented by Pope Francis in the following way: 'The writing is very good and thoroughly explains the meaning of Chapter VIII of *Amoris Laetitia*. There are no other interpretations.' After this declaration from Pope Francis, it is impossible to argue that the access to the sacraments is absolutely forbidden to all people living in a situation of sin with grave matter. Each situation must be ascertained on a case by case basis, and absolution and the eucharist must be withheld only if the person is unrepentant of mortal sin." See also Travers, "*Amoris Laetitia* and Canon 915," 382: "This possibility [that Pope Francis did not intend a major change in sacramental discipline] was decisively put to rest by the letter of September 5, 2016, from Pope Francis to Bishop Sergio Alfredo Penoy, Delegate of the Bishops of the Buenos Aires Pastoral Region of Argentina"

Bishop Juan Ignacio Arrieta, a Senior Vatican canonist from the Pontifical Council for Legislative Texts (PCLT), also said in an interview to the *National Catholic Register* that "the Pope's decision" to publish this letter of support for the Buenos Aires criteria "is a 'polite way' to handle the contentious issue of admitting some civilly remarried divorcees to the sacraments."[5] Similar comments would be issued by Cardinal Pietro Parolin, Secretary of State, and Cardinal Francesco Coccopalmerio, president of the PCLT (see chapter 1 of this book).

In conclusion, if we are to read the apostolic exhortation according to the pope's manifest mind and will, we must necessarily take into consideration the Buenos Aires criteria. Let us then compare the provisional conclusions I drew in my previous chapter and see if they match what the Buenos Aires criteria say:

Table 1. *External validation using the Buenos Aires criteria*

	Provisional conclusions	Buenos Aires criteria[6]
1	*Amoris Laetitia* opens the possibility of Communion to some divorced and remarried people . . .	"*Amoris Laetitia* opens the possibility of access to the sacraments of Reconciliation and the Eucharist."
2	. . . though not for all people . . .	"First of all we remember that it is not convenient to speak of 'permits' to access the sacraments, but of a process of discernment accompanied by a pastor. . . . This path does not necessarily end in the sacraments. . . . We must avoid understanding this possibility as an unrestricted access to the sacraments, or as if any situation justified it. What is proposed is a discernment that adequately distinguishes each case."
3	. . . even if those divorced and remarried people have not yet attained the fully objective ideal . . .	"When the concrete circumstances of a couple make it feasible, especially when both are Christian with a path of faith, the commitment to live in continence can be proposed. *Amoris Laetitia* does not ignore the difficulties of this option and leaves open the possibility of accessing the sacrament of Reconciliation when that purpose is failed."

5. Pentin, "Archbishop Fernández Defends '*Amoris Laetitia*' From Its Critics."

6. Bishops of the Pastoral Region of Buenos Aires, "Carta del Santo Padre Francisco."

4	... as long as they have mitigating factors diminishing subjective culpability ...	"If it is recognized that, in a specific case, there are limitations that mitigate liability and guilt, particularly when a person considers that he would fall on a further fault damaging the children of the new union, *Amoris Laetitia* opens the possibility of access to the sacraments of Reconciliation and the Eucharist."
5	... so that they are not in mortal sin ...	"These [the sacraments of Reconciliation and the Eucharist], in turn, dispose the person to continue maturing and growing with the strength of grace."[7]
6	... as an ideally provisional step to help them grow into achieving the objective ideal in accordance with the Gospel.	"These [the sacraments of Reconciliation and the Eucharist], in turn, dispose the person to continue maturing and growing with the strength of grace.... Discernment is not closed, because 'it is dynamic and must always remain open to new stages of growth and new decisions that allow the ideal to be fulfilled more fully,' according to the 'law of graduality' and trusting in the help of grace."

In short, every single one of the provisional conclusions matches with the Buenos Aires interpretation. Therefore, we can only conclude that this is a valid interpretation for *Amoris Laetitia*.

❖❖❖

Additional Evidence

However, the Buenos Aires criteria are not the only source of evidence on how to interpret *Amoris Laetitia*. Other pontifical interventions can be invoked to strengthen our position.

A few days after the publication of his apostolic exhortation, Pope Francis gave an interview during his return flight from his visit to the Greek island of Lesbos. In this interview, Francis was asked by Frank Rocca, correspondent of the *Wall Street Journal*, if there were new, concrete possibilities for eucharistic access to the divorced and remarried that did not exist before the publication of the exhortation. The pope replied:

---

7. This is implied, since a person in a state of mortal sin is deprived of sanctifying grace. See O'Neil, "Sin"; *AL* 301.

> *I could say "yes" and leave it at that.* But that would be too brief a response. I recommend that all of you read the presentation made by Cardinal Schönborn, a great theologian. He is a member of the Congregation for the Doctrine of the Faith and he knows the Church's teaching very well. Your question will find its answer in that presentation. Thank you.[8]

Please note the Holy Father said "yes." Yes, there are new, concrete possibilities that did not exist before *Amoris Laetitia*. If the answer were not "yes," why would he say: "I could say 'yes' and leave it at that"? The reason the pontiff does not "leave it at that" is because that "would be too brief a response," not that it would be an incorrect response. Francis correctly notes that this is a complex issue that cannot be resolved with a simple yes/no answer with a very brief explanation in an airplane interview. Still, we cannot evade the fact that he answered in the affirmative.

Francis then refers us to the presentation made by Cardinal Schönborn at the press conference where *Amoris Laetitia* was presented a few days earlier. In this presentation, the cardinal makes a general commentary on the full exhortation, giving us a more holistic outlook of the pope's vision. This is consistent with Francis's answer in the in-flight interview, in that there should be no brief answers. The pope does not wish the fullness of his document to be overshadowed by polemics over a single footnote. In fact, he laments this on a subsequent answer during the same plane interview:

> Look, one of the recent Popes, speaking about the Council, said that there were two Councils: Vatican II, which took place in Saint Peter's Basilica, and another Council which took place in the media. When I called the first Synod, the most [sic] of the media were concerned with one question: Will the divorced and remarried be able to receive communion? Since I am not a saint, this was somewhat annoying to me, and even made me a bit sad. Because I think: those media that say all these things, don't they realize that that is not the important issue? Don't they realize that the family, all over the world, is in crisis? And the family is the basis of society! Don't they realize that young people don't want to get married? Don't they realize that the declining birth rate in Europe is enough to make us weep? Don't they realize that the shortage of jobs and employment opportunities is forcing fathers and mothers to take two jobs and children to grow

---

8. Francis, "In-flight Press Conference from Lesbos to Rome."

up by themselves and not learn how to talk with their mothers and fathers? These are the big issues![9]

This frustration about an inappropriate focus on the controversial eighth chapter is also repeated elsewhere.[10] Archbishop Victor Fernández confirms it in his essay:

> Even if the question of whether some divorced and remarried people might gain access to communion has generated much turmoil, the Pope has tried—unsuccessfully—to ensure that this step is taken in a discreet way. Therefore, after developing the principles underlying this decision in the body of the document, he made it explicit in a footnote. This choice is understandable, because what Francis considers "central" are the other chapters of *Amoris Laetitia*, dedicated to love, where he proposed a beautiful task of stimulating "a growth, a consolidation, and a deepening of conjugal and familiar love" (AL 89).[11]

Unfortunately, since both Pope Francis and *Amoris Laetitia* are being criticized as heterodox on account of chapter 8, any apologetics effort will inevitably focus on this controversial chapter. That is the purpose of this book. Yet, if one seeks to obey the pope's manifest mind and will on the matter, one must not limit oneself to reading literature about the controversy, but must read *Amoris Laetitia* from beginning to end to contextualize the polemical sections.[12]

So, let us return to the question of communion to the divorced and remarried. Francis referred us to Cardinal Schönborn's presentation. In this presentation, we can read:

> Naturally this poses the question: what does the Pope say in relation to access to the sacraments for people who live in

---

9. Francis, "In-flight Press Conference from Lesbos to Rome."

10. In the preface he wrote to Stephen Walford's book, *Pope Francis, the Family, and Divorce,* on pg. 207, the Holy Father said: "The Exhortation *Amoris Laetitia* is a unified whole, which means that, in order to understand its message, it must be read in its entirety and from the beginning. This is because there is a development both of theological reflection and on the way in which problems are approached.... If the Exhortation is not read in its entirety and in the order it is written, it will either not be understood or it will be distorted."

11. Fernández, "El capítulo VIII de Amoris Laetitia," 467.

12. Even if it does not replace the reading of the exhortation in its entirety, a magnificent summary of the full document can be found in the second chapter of Stephen Walford's book, *Pope Francis, the Family, and Divorce,* titled "*Amoris Laetitia*: the family journeying towards God," pp. 29–51.

> "irregular" situations? ... In the sense of this "via caritatis" (*AL* 306), the Pope affirms, in a humble and simple manner, in a note (351) *that the help of the sacraments may also be given "in certain cases"*. But for this purpose he does not offer us case studies or recipes, but instead simply reminds us of two of his famous phrases: "I want to remind priests that the confessional should not be a torture chamber but rather an encounter with the Lord's mercy" (*EG* 44), and the Eucharist "is not a prize for the perfect but a powerful medicine and nourishment for the weak" (*EG* 47).[13]

It seems like Cardinal Schönborn's presentation mentions the possibility of the help of the sacraments. This is consistent with our interpretation. Later on, Cardinal Schönborn would give an interview to the English Edition of *La Civiltà Cattolica*, where he would explain this sacramental discipline with more detail:

> On the level of praxis, in view of the difficult situations and the wounded families, the Holy Father has written that all that is possible is a new encouragement to undertake a responsible personal and pastoral discernment of the specific cases. This must recognize that "since 'the degree of responsibility is not equal in all cases,' the consequences or effects of a rule need not necessarily always be the same" (*AL* 300). He adds, *very clearly and without ambiguity*, that this discernment also concerns "*sacramental discipline*, since discernment can recognize that in a particular situation no grave fault exists" (*AL*, footnote 336).... There is an evolution, clearly expressed by Pope Francis, in the Church's perception of the elements that condition and that mitigate, elements that are specific to our own epoch. "The Church possesses a solid body of reflection concerning mitigating factors and situations. Hence it can no longer simply be said that those in any 'irregular' situation are living in a state of mortal sin and are deprived of sanctifying grace. More is involved here than mere ignorance of the rule. A subject may know full well the rule, yet have great difficulty in understanding 'its inherent values,' or be in a concrete situation which does not allow him or her to decide differently and act otherwise without further sin. As the Synod Fathers put it, 'factors may exist which limit the ability to make a decision'" (*AL* 301).[14]

---

13. Holy See Press Office, "Presentation of the Post-Synodal Apostolic Exhortation *Amoris Laetitia.*"

14. Schönborn, "Conversation with Cardinal Schönborn."

There is even more evidence, however. In a 2019 meeting with a group of Jesuits in his papal visit to Romania, Pope Francis further elucidated *Amoris Laetitia*'s sacramental discipline:

> That point at which *Amoris Laetitia* speaks of the integration of divorcees, *eventually opening up to the possibility of the sacraments*, was developed according to the most classical morals of St. Thomas, the most orthodox, not the decadent casuistry of "one can or one cannot."[15]

It can be argued that the magisterial weight of these off-the-cuff remarks (both the 2016 plane interview and the 2019 meeting with the Jesuits) is low, when compared with official papal pronouncements. However, this objection does not hold, for two reasons. First, their magisterial weight might be low, but it is not necessarily null. Second, we are not trying to establish that these comments are magisterial: rather we are using them to ascertain what the manifest mind and will of the pope is on this issue. *Amoris Laetitia* is what is to be considered a part of Francis's authentic magisterium (as per chapter 1) and we can accurately interpret it by looking at the pope's manner of speaking and to his frequent repetition of what he intends.[16] By doing this we can see that Pope Francis does indeed wish a bigger opening for the divorced and civilly remarried to access communion. Therefore, *Amoris Laetitia* should be read bearing this in mind.

❊❊❊

One final clue is given through an uncommon venue. Since the publication of the exhortation, notable apologist Stephen Walford has taken up the task of defending Pope Francis against his detractors. In 2018, Walford published a book on this matter, titled *Pope Francis, the Family and Divorce*. Walford asked the Holy Father to write a preface for the book, and he accepted. In this papal letter, we can read:

> Over the course of the Exhortation, current and concrete problems are dealt with: the family in today's world, the education of children, marriage preparation, families in difficulty, and so on; *these are treated with a hermeneutic that comes from the whole document which is the magisterial hermeneutic of the Church, always in continuity (without ruptures), yet always maturing*. In

---

15. Esteves, "Church Wounded by Internal Tensions, Pope Tells Jesuits in Romania."
16. *LG* 25.

this regard, Stephen Walford mentions Saint Vincent of Lérins in his *Commonitorium Primum*: "ut annis scilicet consolidetur, diatetur tempore, sublimetur aetate." With respect to the problems that involve ethical situations, the Exhortation follows the classical doctrine of Saint Thomas Aquinas. *I feel certain that this book will be helpful to families. I pray for this.*[17]

Papal critics have tried to invoke all kinds of objections, namely speculating about whether Francis had read the full book or not.[18] Yet, the rarity with which a successor of Peter allows himself to write a preface for a layman's book should give us pause (especially a book written about a controversy at the root of many of the attacks against the pope). Also, Francis is sufficiently familiar with the book to know that Walford mentions St. Vincent de Lérins.

Here too, we can catch another glimpse at how the pope manifests his mind and will regarding *Amoris Laetitia*. The document should be read with a hermeneutic of continuity (therefore eschewing the interpretation that *Amoris Laetitia* opens up an indiscriminate access to all divorced and remarried, even the impenitent ones) but also always maturing (which would not be mentioned if there was no development in *Amoris Laetitia* from previous practice). I will dedicate section III of this book to try to show how the correct interpretation of the document is actually in continuity with previous magisterial pronouncements on this matter.

Also, it is worth mentioning that the preface's last sentence seems like an endorsement of the book (as if writing a preface for it was not proof enough). And Walford's book postulates the interpretation we have explored so far:

> Pope Francis has in fact altered sacramental discipline for the divorced and civilly remarried. *He is quite clear stating that for souls not in a subjective state of mortal sin*, with a sincere desire to respond to grace, *they can benefit from receiving absolution in Confession and the Holy Eucharist at Mass*, as long as this is done in *a discreet way that avoids scandal* for the faith community.[19]

All of this supports even further the evidence in favor of the interpretation we have been exploring so far: the sacramental discipline has been

---

17. Walford, *Pope Francis, the Family, and Divorce*, 207.
18. O'Reilly, "Pope Francis, the Open Letter, and the Pesky Preface."
19. Walford, *Pope Francis, the Family, and Divorce*, 61.

altered in order to allow communion to divorced and remarried people who, on account of mitigating circumstances diminishing some of their culpability, are not in mortal sin. All evidence seems to point to this being the pope's manifest mind and will for the exhortation, and no evidence to the contrary seems to emerge.

CHAPTER 6

Misinterpretations

IN MY ANALYSIS, I have tried to understand the pope's mind and will as to how the exhortation should be implemented. I tried to do so both by studying the wording of the text, taking it at face value, and by collecting information from the pope's manner of speaking in other contexts. I validated this interpretation, both internally and externally.

In this chapter, I would like to address some mistaken readings of the document that do not hold up to the same scrutiny. These errors are commonly thrown around in social media as if they were certain and correct explanations for *Amoris Laetitia*, but they conflict both with the text itself and with the interpretation I have provided earlier.

Paradoxically, even if these misinterpretations lean on the liberal side, they are usually advanced by conservative papal critics.[1] They are presented as possible readings of the exhortation, not because the interlocutors agree with them, but quite the opposite: they are used as a way to prove the heterodoxy of the document, or that it can lead to heterodoxy. In so doing, these critics (either willingly or unwillingly) delegitimize a magisterial document by setting up a heterodox straw man.

Nevertheless, as I said, those erroneous readings conflict with other parts of *Amoris Laetitia*. So, when we encounter such conflicts, we may proceed in two ways: 1) either we take the path of the Bible-debunking atheist and claim that conflicting accounts are proof of lack of clarity (and therefore, authority) of the document; or 2) we take the path of the exegete

---

1. Most of the misinterpretations I am going to explore here can be found in the so-called "Filial Correction" (*Correctio filialis de haeresibus propagatis*) from sixty-two clergy and lay scholars, accusing the pope of propagating seven heretical propositions.

and set ourselves to find out what the author meant when he wrote those words, charitably assuming he was probably not being incoherent, and rejecting conclusions leading to unnecessary internal conflicts. I will take the second approach here, and proceed with a refutation of these errors.

❁❁❁

That Amoris Laetitia *Endangers Church Teaching on the Indissolubility of Marriage*[2]

Asserting that marriage is not indissoluble, or that divorce is justifiable, conflicts with so many parts of *Amoris Laetitia* (especially in the chapters preceding the eighth), that listing them all would make this book too long. A single quote will suffice to prove the wrongness of this interpretation:

> The Christian community's care of such persons [the divorced] *is not to be considered a weakening of its faith and testimony to the indissolubility of marriage*; rather, such care is a particular expression of its charity.[3]

Ergo, *Amoris Laetitia*'s sacramental provisions can never be interpreted in a way that weakens the church's faith and testimony to the indissolubility of marriage.[4] Doing so is clearly going against the pope's manifest will.

---

2. As an example, see Brugger, "Five Serious Problems with Chapter 8 of *Amoris Laetitia*": "If a green light were given to invalidly married persons to receive Holy Communion—and we know that the civil marriages of Catholics are invalid because at very least they lack proper form—if priests give this green light (which would constitute an ecclesial act), this would teach that marriage is not indissoluble. How could it be indissoluble if the Church says that second unions are valid? The acts of the Church's pastors will undermine the revealed truth of the indissolubility of marriage." See also Schneider, "Important: Bishop Athanasius Schneider interview with *Rorate Caeli*": "The Buenos Aires bishops' instructions do not express directly a heresy. Yet they allow, in individual cases, 'divorced and remarried' people to receive Holy Communion in spite of the fact that they do not want to stop sexual relationships with their non-conjugal partner. In this case the mentioned pastoral instructions deny in practice, and hence indirectly, the Divinely revealed truth of the indissolubility of marriage."

3. *AL* 243.

4. This is validated by many theologians. As an example, see Buttiglione, *Risposte amichevoli*, 44: "There is no change in the theology of matrimony. The matrimony remains indissoluble, extra-marital sexual acts remain comdemned."

See also Cristoph Schönborn's interview in *La Civiltà Cattolica* on March 1, 2017:

Since many of the passages where Francis reaffirms the church's perennial teaching on the indissolubility of marriage[5] are in chapters preceding number eight, this may also explain the Holy Father's exasperation with people not reading the document in its entirety and out of the order it was written (as I mentioned in my previous chapter). If a reader, eager to read the polemical parts, jumps directly to the exhortation's eighth chapter, he will lose all the contextualization the pontiff has made regarding the sacredness of marriage, making him more prone to accept the false notion that the pope does not believe in its indissolubility.

❖❖❖

That Amoris Laetitia *Asserts Divorce and Remarriage Can Be Good or Justifiable Sometimes*[6]

This position completely misses the mark of what *Amoris Laetitia* is trying to do. As I have already established, the exhortation deals with mitigating factors diminishing subjective culpability. There can be no culpability (even if diminished) in something that is not wrong. So, living *more uxorio* in a divorce and remarriage setting must, by necessity, be wrong.

But what about textual evidence to refute this? Let us revisit the paragraph where the notorious footnote allowing communion is located:

> Because of forms of conditioning and mitigating factors, it is possible that in an *objective situation of sin*—which may not be subjectively culpable, or fully such—a person can be living in

---

"The great daring of the Pope is precisely to demonstrate that this perspective, which is capable of appreciating and is permeated by benevolence and trust, does not do any damage whatsoever to the strength of doctrine.... On the level of principles, the doctrine of marriage and the sacraments is clear. Pope Francis has newly expressed it with a great communicative clarity."

5. See, as further examples, *AL* 123, 124, 147, and 291.

6. Fifth alleged heretical proposition "corrected" by the *Correctio filialis*: "Conscience can truly and rightly judge that sexual acts between persons who have contracted a civil marriage with each other, although one or both of them is sacramentally married to another person, can sometimes be morally right or requested or even commanded by God."

God's grace, can love and can also grow in the life of grace and charity, while receiving the Church's help to this end.[7]

From this, we can see that, contrary to what many critics have been claiming, Pope Francis is indeed clear on the church's unchangeable teaching that divorce and civil remarriage is sinful. He calls it "an objective situation of sin," with no ambiguity.[8]

Furthermore, Francis echoes Pope St. John Paul II at least two times in his exhortation, highlighting how the law of gradualness does not mean gradualness of the law:[9]

> Along these lines, Saint John Paul II proposed the so-called "law of gradualness" in the knowledge that the human being "knows, loves, and accomplishes moral good by different stages of growth." *This is not a "gradualness of law."* . . . Conversation with the priest, in the internal forum, contributes to the formation of a correct judgment on what hinders the possibility of a fuller participation in the life of the Church and on what steps can foster it and make it grow. *Given that gradualness is not in the law itself* (cf. Familiaris Consortio, 34), *this discernment can never prescind from the Gospel demands of truth and charity, as proposed by the Church.*[10]

This is the framework according to which we should read the controversial footnote that extended communion for the divorced and civilly remarried in certain situations. *Amoris Laetitia* can in no way be used to claim a gradualness of the law, meaning that there are no situations in which an objective evil ceases to be so on account of these circumstances.

❊❊❊

---

7. *AL* 305.

8. See Walford, *Pope Francis, the Family, and Divorce*, 97: "It must be reaffirmed that at no time does *Amoris Laetitia* suggest that adultery is no longer wrong in certain cases, or that it possesses some moral good. What we come back to is the influences and circumstances that mitigate the guilt to such an extent that in some cases it is no longer present."

9. Walford, *Pope Francis, the Family, and Divorce*, 55. See also López, "Entender Wojtyla," 43.

10. *AL* 295, 300.

That Amoris Laetitia *Affirms That Following the Law Can Be Sinful*[11]

This is a mirrored version of the previous error, so most of what I said before also applies here. This misinterpretation is based on two *Amoris Laetitia* quotes. Both of them only lend themselves to that reading if taken out of context. The first one is:

> One thing is a second union consolidated over time, with new children, proven fidelity, generous self giving, Christian commitment, a consciousness of its irregularity and of the great difficulty of going back without feeling in conscience that one would fall into new sins.[12]

Please note that the pope never stated that the couple would fall into new sins if it regularized its situation, only that the divorced and remarried person could *feel*, in conscience, that he or she would fall into new sins. This may seem like a distinction without difference, especially since later on, the pope wishes "that individual conscience needs to be better incorporated into the Church's praxis in certain situations which do not objectively embody our understanding of marriage."[13]

However, this is not the context in which the pope said that a person could feel, in conscience, that he would fall into new sins if the situation was regularized. Francis is not talking about conscience formation yet. Rather, he is talking about not pigeonholing all divorced and civilly remarried people into "rigid classifications, leaving no room for a suitable personal and pastoral discernment."[14] The Holy Father then exemplifies this by contrasting several different situations in which the subjective culpability is clearly not the same.

> One thing is a second union consolidated over time, with new children, proven fidelity, generous self giving, Christian commitment, a consciousness of its irregularity and of the great difficulty of going back without feeling in conscience that one would fall into new sins. . . . Another thing is a new union arising from a recent divorce, with all the suffering and confusion

---

11. Fourth alleged heretical proposition "corrected" by the *Correctio filialis*: "A person is able, while he obeys a divine prohibition, to sin against God by that very act of obedience."
12. *AL* 298.
13. *AL* 303.
14. *AL* 298.

which this entails for children and entire families, or the case of someone who has consistently failed in his obligations to the family.[15]

This is the context in which the pope presents the case of someone who, in conscience, feels he would fall into new sins. It is done to contrast those two different situations. Can anyone really suggest these two are completely overlapping vis-à-vis subjective culpability? Either way, and lest there would be any doubts, after giving these examples, the pope *immediately* points out: "It must remain clear that this is not the ideal which the Gospel proposes for marriage and the family."

One other citation, however, seems to be more prone for this misinterpretation:

> A subject may . . . be in a concrete situation which does not allow him or her to act differently and decide otherwise without further sin.[16]

Again, we cannot read this in isolation from the context of the whole document. This quote is inserted in a paragraph about mitigating factors. We have already established that mitigating factors refer to subjective culpability, and there is no culpability in an act that is not evil. We have seen that the pope unambiguously describes divorce and remarriage as "objective situations of sin." And, in fact, the expression "further sin" implies that the person is entangled in a sinful situation already.

So we should read this in a way that does not create further conflicts with what has already been established earlier. Francis is not saying that following the law is sinful in itself, but that doing so could drive the person to be thrust into a position where he would be prone to further sins. This is undeniable, if we understand that a breakdown of a family (even one built on the basis of a remarriage following a divorce) will undoubtedly lead to problems where the person will probably sin (like, for instance, engaging in heated arguments with his or her partner and children). Again, this does not justify the decision, but it certainly mitigates the culpability of someone who hesitates to follow the church's directives. I refer the reader to the case-study in chapter 16 of this book, for an example of how this might play out.

❊❊❊

15. *AL* 298.
16. *AL* 301.

That Amoris Laetitia *Allows People in Mortal Sin to Receive Communion*[17]

Papal critics who claim this erroneous interpretation often conflate "mortal sin" with any sin with grave matter.[18] This is a gross misrepresentation of Catholic doctrine, as I will expound with more detail in my next chapter. For now, suffice it to say that grave matter is a *necessary*, but not *sufficient* condition for mortal sin. So, even if someone has committed a sin with grave matter (like living *more uxorio* in a remarriage setting), we are not justified in claiming that said person is necessarily in mortal sin.

We know this is where Francis is coming from, when he references this:

> The Church possesses a solid body of reflections concerning mitigating factors and situations. *Hence it can no longer simply be said that all those in any "irregular" situation are living in a state of mortal sin* and are deprived of sanctifying grace.[19]

Therefore, the exhortation's provisions do not apply to people living in a state of mortal sin.[20] I had already established this as a conclusion in chapter 4 (see provisional conclusion number five of that chapter).

---

17. See Hoffman, "Pope Praises Lisbon Guidelines That Allow Communion to Divorced and Remarried": "Such provisions would seem to contradict the clear and constant doctrine of the Catholic Church on the reception of Holy Communion. The Catholic Church, echoing the words of Christ himself, regards divorce and remarriage as an act of adultery, which is a mortal sin, one that will lead to eternal damnation if those guilty of the sin do not repent before death and receive the grace of absolution. The Church's consistent practice throughout its history is to prohibit those who are in a state of mortal sin from receiving Communion, including those divorced and invalidly remarried." This is also implied in the second alleged heretical proposition "corrected" by the *Correctio filialis*: "Christians who have obtained a civil divorce from the spouse to whom they are validly married and have contracted a civil marriage with some other person during the lifetime of their spouse, who live *more uxorio* with their civil partner, and who choose to remain in this state with full knowledge of the nature of their act and full consent of the will to that act, are not necessarily in a state of mortal sin, and can receive sanctifying grace and grow in charity." Of course, by saying that *Amoris Laetitia* subscribes to this proposition, the "correction" misses the mark. What is at stake is whether these divorced and remarried people have full knowledge and full consent to begin with."

18. Hoffman, "Pope Praises Lisbon Guidelines That Allow Communion to Divorced and Remarried."

19. *AL* 301.

20. See Buttiglione, *Risposte amichevoli*, 43–45.

In fact, the notion that Pope Francis would allow people in mortal sin to receive the Eucharist is contradicted by another excerpt:

> Those who approach the Body and Blood of Christ may not wound that same Body by creating scandalous distinctions and divisions among its members. This is what it means to "discern" the body of the Lord, to acknowledge it with faith and charity both in the sacramental signs and in the community; *those who fail to do so eat and drink judgment against themselves* (cf. v. 29). The celebration of the Eucharist thus becomes a constant summons for everyone "to examine himself or herself."[21]

Granted, when Francis mentions this, he is dealing with another set of sins: the sin of creating scandal and sowing division in the church (see chapter 8). But still, this shows how the Holy Father does indeed know that people in a state of mortal sin should not receive the Eucharist.

❊❊❊

That Amoris Laetitia *Allows Communion to Impenitent Sinners*[22]

In my provisional conclusions in chapter 4, I said that certain divorced and remarried people might receive communion even if they had not attained the objective ideal (which would be a marriage annulment or living in perfect continence). From this conclusion, many critics will probably contest *Amoris Laetitia*, on the basis that it will allow impenitent adulterers to just keep sinning while receiving the Eucharist.

This, however, comes from a simplistic worldview, whereby a sinner who gives an imperfect answer not fulfilling the objective ideal is

---

21. *AL* 186. See Buttiglione, *Risposte amichevoli*, 155–56: "The rule according to which nobody outside the grace of God can receive the Eucharist, by its own nature, does not admit exceptions. He who receives the Body and Blood of Christ in an unworthy way, eats and drinks his own condemnation."

22. See Seifert, "The Church After *Amoris Laetitia*": "From this you see that also these defenders of AL agree that AL in fact proposes to admit unrepentant adulterers and other sinners, after due discernment, to the sacraments." See also the seventh alleged heretical proposition "corrected" by the *Correctio filialis*: "Our Lord Jesus Christ wills that the Church abandon her perennial discipline of refusing the Eucharist to the divorced and remarried and of refusing absolution to the divorced and remarried who do not express contrition for their state of life and a firm purpose of amendment with regard to it."

necessarily impenitent.²³ Yet we know that impenitent sinners are not included in the exhortation's provisions.

> "*For this discernment to happen, the following conditions must necessarily be present: humility, discretion, and love for the Church and her teaching, in a sincere search for God's will and a desire to make a more perfect response to it.*" These attitudes are essential for avoiding the grave danger of misunderstandings, such as the notion that any priest can quickly grant "exceptions," or that some people can obtain sacramental privileges in exchange for favours. *When a responsible and tactful person, who does not presume to put his or her own desires ahead of the common good of the Church, meets with a pastor capable of acknowledging the seriousness of the matter before him*, there can be no risk that a specific discernment may lead people to think that the Church maintains a double standard.²⁴

Please note: for the discernment to begin, those conditions must *necessarily* be present. I notice papal critics often overlook this fundamental part of *Amoris Laetitia*. But this cannot be ignored. It is crucial for an accurate interpretation of the document. Everything in the eighth chapter hinges on this, including the footnote opening the door to the Eucharist. A person with no love for the church and its teachings is *automatically excluded* from the path of discernment and accompaniment suggested in *Amoris Laetitia* (and which could lead up to access to the sacraments). How can anyone suggest an impenitent sinner has "humility, discretion, and love for the Church and Her teaching"?

It is most likely the Holy Father is talking about people who do love the church's teachings, and who do want to live in accordance with those teachings, but feel somehow torn between two competing and mutually exclusive responsibilities: God and the church on one hand and a spouse and children on the other. In these situations, the person may feel

---

23. See Fernández, "El capítulo VIII de *Amoris Laetitia*," 455: "For that reason, it is licit to ask whether every act of *more uxorio* must always fall, in its integral sense, within the negative precept that prohibits 'fornicating.' I say 'in its integral sense,' because it is not possible to sustain that these acts are, in all cases, seriously dishonest in a subjective sense. . . . It is not easy to call 'adulteress' to a woman who has been beaten down and humiliated by her Catholic husband, and who took refuge with, and received economic and psychological help from, another man that helped her raise the children of her previous union, and with whom she bore other children, and lived with for several years."

24. *AL* 300.

unprepared to follow the fullness of the teaching of the church, even if he wants to undergo a path of conversion. *We must remember: the Holy Father does not validate this decision. It is still an* "objective situation of sin."[25] However, the subjective culpability is certainly diminished, so that we cannot really say this person is in mortal sin. If this person is not in mortal sin, he or she may receive the Eucharist, not as a "prize," but as "medicine and nourishment"[26] to be able to attain strength through sacramental grace.

We can also see that Pope Francis does not have impenitent sinners in mind in another excerpt, even if it does not relate directly to sacramental discipline:

> Naturally, *if someone flaunts an objective sin as if it were part of the Christian ideal, or wants to impose something other than what the Church teaches,* he or she can in no way presume to teach or preach to others; *this is a case of something which separates from the community* (cf. Matt 18:17). Such a person needs to listen once more to the Gospel message and its call to conversion.[27]

One may argue that this is not enough. The *Catechism* states that "among the penitent's acts, contrition occupies first place." Contrition is "sorrow of the soul and detestation for the sin committed, *together with the resolution not to sin again.*"[28] Since the people involved would be in a situation where they would not attain the objective ideal immediately, they could not have a resolution to not sin again, and therefore would be, by definition, non-contrite and impenitent. This is, however, an overly restrictive interpretation of the *Catechism*. Rocco Buttiglione, for instance, argues that the resolution to not sin again is "certainly necessary." However, this means that the sinner must have "the desire of leaving his irregular situation and strive to perform acts that will allow him to effectively leave such a situation. It is possible, however, that the sinner will not be in a stage where he can realize this detachment and reconquer his own sovereignty in an immediate way. . . . He must strive, *so as to keep the resolution,* to leave the situation of sin."[29] In other words, the resolution to not sin

---

25. *AL* 305.
26. *AL* n351.
27. *AL* 297.
28. *CCC* 1451.
29. Buttiglione, *Risposte amichevoli*, 172.

again means an "endeavor to remove, in an opportune way and timing, the objective impediments."[30]

❦ ❦ ❦

That Amoris Laetitia Says a Person's Conscience May Discern That God Wills Him to Continue in an Objectively Sinful State[31]

Those who advance this misinterpretation usually focus on this quote:

> Yet conscience can do more than recognize that a given situation does not correspond objectively to the overall demands of the Gospel. It can also recognize with sincerity and honesty what for now is the most generous response which can be given to God, and come to see with a certain moral security *that it is what God himself is asking amid the concrete complexity of one's limits,* while yet not fully the objective ideal.[32]

The most fundamental flaw in this interpretation is in assuming that "will of God" here refers to the "not yet fully objective ideal" situation (i.e., remaining in sin)[33] and not to the "most generous response that can be given to God" "for now."[34] In fact, Juliano Almeida, a theologian from

---

30. Buttiglione, *Risposte amichevoli*, 181.

31. See again the fifth alleged heretical proposition "corrected" by the *Correctio filialis*: "Conscience can truly and rightly judge that sexual acts between persons who have contracted a civil marriage with each other, although one or both of them is sacramentally married to another person, can sometimes be morally right or requested or even commanded by God."

32. *AL* 303.

33. See Seifert, "Does Pure Logic Threaten to Destroy the Entire Moral Doctrine of the Catholic Church?": "From the previous as well as from the later context it is clear that this 'will of God' here refers to continuing to live in what constitutes objectively a grave sin." See also Brugger, "Five Serious Problems with Chapter 8 of *Amoris Laetitia*": "The text places the two in direct opposition. An individual's conscience may both: [1] judge that some action does not correspond to the overall demands of the Gospel; and [2] judge that God is asking them to perform that action. In other words, God can be 'asking' someone to live in a life-state in which they are objectively violating grave matter."

34. Fernández, "El Capítulo VIII de *Amoris Laetitia*": "If the act remains objectively dishonest and does not lose its objective gravity, then it cannot possibly be 'chosen' with conviction, as if it were part of the Christian ideal. . . . Another very different

the Jesuit Faculty of Philosophy and Theology of Belo Horizonte (Brazil) brings attention to the fact that the Latin version of the text uses the word *oblationem* ("oblation"). Therefore, God is actually requesting a sacrifice: the sacrifice that is possible for the sinner as a first step towards the *objectivum exemplar* ("objective example," not "objective ideal").[35]

In other words, the will of God is not for the sin to continue, but for the sinner to give a response to God, even if this response is imperfect. This means the sinner will not become perfected instantly, but undergo a progressive path toward the Christian ideal. If this path is progressive, then the objective situation of sin may persist for some time. It is obviously the will of God, however, that the sinner should begin this path rather than stay where he is, or else he will never live a moral life.

How do we know that this is the correct interpretation for *AL* 303, and not the one done by papal critics? How do we know if the "will of God" refers to the most generous response and not to the objectively sinful situation? Because the interpretation advanced by the papal critics conflicts with what Francis said elsewhere in the document: "*any* breach of the marriage bond is *against the will of God.*"[36]

How can "any breach of the marriage bond" be against the will of God in #291 and then be considered something compatible with God's will in #303? We must charitably assume the pontiff is not contradicting himself, and therefore reject this interpretation.

❀❀❀

That Amoris Laetitia *Postulates That a Sinner May Not Have Sufficient Grace to Stop Sinning*[37]

Some papal critics will affirm that *Amoris Laetitia* is a heretical document, since it allegedly contradicts settled infallible doctrine on justification.

---

thing is to propose, as Francis does, that in a context of mitigated culpability, one seeks to respond to the will of God with a greater dedication, as far as possible in the context of that situation."

35. Almeida, "*Amoris Laetitia*—reflexões," 379 (my translation from the original Portuguese).

36. *AL* 291.

37. "See the first alleged heretical proposition "corrected" by the *Correctio filialis*: "A justified person has not the strength with God's grace to carry out the objective demands of the divine law, as though any of the commandments of God are impossible

By saying that an imperfect response, "while not yet fully the objective ideal," is "the most generous response which can be given God,"[38] the pope would allegedly be saying that God would not be granting sufficient grace for the sinner to stop sinning. This would be a contradiction of the Council of Trent.

Of course, it does not contradict Trent, but only a personal interpretation of Trent by people in modern times. According to this personal interpretation of Trent, a sinner would never sin if he really wanted to stop sinning, for God would always provide enough grace for the sinner to immediately achieve this. This wrong interpretation of Trent flies in the face of reality itself; otherwise people would not struggle with their sins. Also, it blatantly contradicts the law of gradualness I mentioned earlier, taught by St. John Paul II himself. For there can be no gradualness if grace simply immediately stopped people from sinning at all times.

Later on, in chapter 13 of this book, I will explain how *Amoris Laetitia* not only does *not* contradict Trent, but in fact complements it and harmonizes it with the realities I mentioned above. For now, suffice it to say that Francis never claims that the law cannot be followed by everyone, or that there is not enough grace available for the sinner. In fact, this actually runs counter to what Francis says, since he writes: "The law is . . . a gift for everyone, *without exception*; it can be followed with the help of grace."[39]

Shortly thereafter, we get additional clarification on this topic:

> "In considering a pastoral approach towards people who have contracted a civil marriage, who are divorced and remarried, or simply living together, the Church has the responsibility of helping them understand the divine pedagogy of grace in their lives and offering them assistance so they can reach the fullness of God's plan for them," something *which is always possible by the power of the Holy Spirit.*[40]

One variation of this objection, however, is when papal critics point out that the pope said: "If certain expressions of intimacy are lacking, it often happens that faithfulness is endangered and the good of the children

---

for the justified; or as meaning that God's grace, when it produces justification in an individual, does not invariably and of its nature produce conversion from all serious sin, or is not sufficient for conversion from all serious sin."

38. *AL* 303.
39. *AL* 295.
40. *AL* 297.

suffers."[41] This would, again, seem like a distrust in the grace of God, for it would seem like God would not give a person enough grace to be faithful to not engage in intercourse. However, it must be pointed out, Francis is not necessarily validating this idea, but simply exposing the fact that many people, who accepted the possibility of living "as brother and sister," pointed out this problem.[42] Also, he says that the faithfulness could be "endangered," not that it would be "impossible"—something that is obvious, again, if we take into account how people may struggle with sinful inclinations.

We must remember that the pope is not writing here in his own words, but rather quoting the Second Vatican Council's pastoral constitution *Gaudium et Spes*: the council mentions that, in cases "where the intimacy of married life is broken off, its faithfulness can sometimes be imperiled and its quality of fruitfulness ruined, for then the upbringing of children and the courage to accept new ones are both endangered."[43] It is noteworthy that the council does not mention them approvingly, but to warn these couples against those who would presume to offer "dishonorable solutions" to these problems (artificial contraception and abortion). Nevertheless, even if the council does not justify these solutions, it still recognizes the breaking of intimacy as a problem that couples have to deal with. In so doing, the council writes its document with the exact same wording as Francis.[44]

41. *AL* n329. See Milco, "Francis's Argentine Letter": "In some cases, the bishops suppose, abstention from sexual relations may damage the familial situation involved in the second union, or may simply be unrealistic, so that failures of chastity become subjectively inculpable (i.e., not instances of sin). In this they follow the somewhat cryptic reasoning of *Amoris Laetitia*'s infamous Footnote 329, which suggests that in some cases, when continence is practiced with the second spouse, 'faithfulness is endangered and the good of the children suffers.' (The incoherence of this reasoning has been amply discussed elsewhere.) The Church teaches and has always taught, from St. Paul to the Council of Trent and beyond, that grace strengthens and liberates us from the bonds of sin, and that while we may never, in the present life, be perfectly free from the inclination to do wrong, it is possible through grace to keep the commandments."

42. Again, see *AL* n329.

43. Vatican II, *Gaudium et Spes*, 51.

44. Some may argue that *Gaudium et Spes* is dealing here with couples with a valid Catholic marriage, not divorced and remarried couples. This is irrelevant for the following reason: The document mentions the breaking off of intimacy as an occasion of sin for these couples, regarding the temptations of abortion and artificial contraception. The same holds true for the divorced and remarried: the breaking off of intimacy leads to occasion of other sins, as explained previously. These other sins are the focus

Anyway, we have confirmation that Francis does not mean to tell us that this "endangering" of the faithfulness of the couple and the well-being of the children is meant to be understood as God not providing enough grace for the sinner to stop sinning: the preceding paragraph was the very paragraph where the Holy Father said that reaching the fullness of the Christian ideal is "always possible by the power of the Holy Spirit."[45] A single paragraph is too short a distance for the pope to forget what he previously said, and in fact should warn us that the previous paragraph should be used as context for what follows next.

❋ ❋ ❋

That Amoris Laetitia *Denies the Existence of Hell*[46]

This misinterpretation is a little off-topic, since it does not touch upon the contested sacramental discipline. Nevertheless, I thought it would be appropriate to briefly debunk it, since this book is devoted to proving the orthodoxy of *Amoris Laetitia*.

Papal critics will claim that *Amoris Laetitia* denies the existence of Hell, when it says: "No one can be condemned for ever, because that is not the logic of the Gospel."[47] Since Hell is, by definition, everlasting condemnation, then the exhortation would heretically deny the existence of Hell.

We know that Francis cannot possibly be denying the existence of Hell here, for the pope has affirmed the existence of Hell elsewhere.[48]

---

of both quotes (that living *more uxorio* in a situation of divorce and remarriage is an objective situation of sin is explained elsewhere in *Amoris Laetitia*, as I previously said).

45. *AL* 297.

46. See for example Martin, "Did Francis Formally Profess Heresy?": "Pope Francis's Apostolic Exhortation *Amoris Laetitia* appears to contain such heresy. Paragraph 297 states: 'No one can be condemned forever, because that is not the logic of the Gospel! Here I am not speaking only of the divorced and remarried, but of everyone, in whatever situation they find themselves.' According to Francis, unrepentant sinners of any kind, be they rapists, thieves, pedophiles, killers, abortionists, thugs, Mafia members, or apostates, will never be condemned eternally to the fires of hell."

47. *AL* 297.

48. Francis, "19th Memorial and Commitment Day": "And I feel that I cannot conclude without saying a word to the absent bosses today, to those absent but central figures: the men and women of the mafia. Please, change your lives, convert, stop,

Misinterpretations

So, again, we must assume the pope is not contradicting himself, and the problem may be lying in our reading of his text.

And, in fact, if we read the sentence in its full context, we can gather further information:

> "There are two ways of thinking which recur throughout the Church's history: casting off and reinstating. The Church's way, from the time of the Council of Jerusalem, has always been the way of Jesus, the way of mercy and reinstatement. . . . *The way of the Church is not to condemn anyone forever; it is to pour out the balm of God's mercy on all those who ask for it with a sincere heart.* . . . For true charity is always unmerited, unconditional, and gratuitous". Consequently, there is a need "to avoid judgments which do not take into account the complexity of various situations" and "to be attentive, by necessity, to how people experience distress because of their condition."
>
> *It is a matter of reaching out to everyone, of needing to help each person find his or her proper way of participating in the ecclesial community* and thus to experience being touched by an "unmerited, unconditional, and gratuitous" mercy. No one can be condemned for ever, because that is not the logic of the Gospel!⁴⁹

In sum, the pope is not talking about the eternal fate awaiting souls after death, but about the way the church should handle sinners while they are still alive. It is not eschatological, it is pastoral. The Holy Father contrasts two attitudes regarding the pastoral accompaniment of sinners: those who condemn forever and those who do not, extending the unmerited mercy of God to them. The pope concludes, and rightfully so, that the former do not follow the logic of the gospel. This should be understandable for those acquainted with the gospel, since Jesus never seems to condemn anyone, not even those who crucified him and whom he denounced throughout his life.⁵⁰

---

cease to do evil! We are praying for you. Convert, I ask it on my knees; it is for your own good. . . . *Convert, there is still time, so that you don't end up in hell.* That is what awaits you if you continue on this path. You had a father and a mother: think of them. Cry a little and convert."

See also Francis, "Message of His Holiness": "Yet the danger always remains that by a constant refusal to open the doors of their hearts to Christ who knocks on them in the poor, the proud, rich, and powerful will end up condemning themselves and plunging into the *eternal* abyss of solitude which is *Hell*."

49. AL 296–97.

50. Luke 23:34: "Forgive them, Father, for they know not what they are doing."

But I believe it is actually deeper than that. As philosopher Guerra López explains:

> Reason can discover a rational path by allowing itself to be informed by the faith. Thanks to this, it manages to notice what seems humanly impossible: "No one can be condemned forever". For every single human being, no matter how wounded, there is always a way.... In effect, evil never has the last word. If this fact begins by being intuited as true in the natural order by meditating on the ontological structure of evil, it is nevertheless even truer in light of the mystery of Redemption.... There is always a path to rebuild one's life after sin. In this sense, "no one can be condemned forever." Jesus offers himself as the way, the truth, and the life, at all times![51]

I do not think we can deny the catholicity of this way of thinking, under the pains of denying that a sinner can ever turn from a life of sin towards salvation.

---

51. López, "Para Comprender Amoris Laetitia," 414, 430. See also Buttiglione, *Risposte amichevoli*, 110–13.

CHAPTER 7

The Teaching on Mitigating Circumstances

As I hope to have shown in my previous chapters, *Amoris Laetitia*'s new sacramental discipline is grounded on the teaching of mitigating circumstances. This conclusion seems to be shared by a number of theologians, philosophers, and apologists.[1] In fact, the exhortation's chapter 8 has a full segment named "Mitigating factors in Pastoral Discernment," immediately preceding the one where footnote 351 is inserted. In other words, the sacramental discipline laid out in footnote 351 is to be contextualized by the teaching on mitigating factors.

If we want to understand this document, we need to become acquainted with this teaching. This doctrine is inextricably linked to the nature of sin, namely the distinction between mortal and venial sins.

Mitigating Factors and Mortal Sin

The *Catechism of the Catholic Church* affirms that, for a sin to be a mortal sin, three conditions must *necessarily* be present.[2] In other words, if just one of these conditions is absent, then the sin is not mortal in nature,

---

1. See Fernández, "El Capítulo VIII de *Amoris Laetitia*," 457–58; Travers, "*Amoris Laetitia* and Canon 915," 374–76; López, "Para Comprender *Amoris Laetitia*," 436; Buttiglione, *Risposte amichevoli*, 36, 43, 119, 139; Ryan, "Weakness, and Wounded and Troubled Love," 134–35, 143; Walford, *Pope Francis, the Family, and Divorce*, 59.

2. CCC 1857. The *Catechism* as a reference for *Amoris Laetitia*'s sacramental discipline is mentioned by Fernández, "El Capítulo VIII de *Amoris Laetitia*," 457–58, and also Buttiglione, *Risposte amichevoli*, 139.

even if the other conditions are present. These conditions are, as defined by the *Catechism*: 1) grave matter; 2) full knowledge; and 3) full consent.

Grave matter refers to the gravity of the sin. Among sins with grave matter, the *Catechism* explicitly lists the sin of adultery.[3] A person who divorces, remarries and then proceeds to have intercourse with his or her new partner commits, according to Catholic doctrine, the sin of adultery, for this contradicts Jesus Christ's commandment: "Every one that putteth away his wife, and marrieth another, committeth adultery: and he that marrieth her that is put away from her husband, committeth adultery."[4]

In short, divorced and remarried people who do not abide by total continence commit a sin with grave matter. That much is undisputed. Let me reiterate: *I completely agree and assent to the church's teaching on this point.*

However, just because we established that this situation is a sin with grave matter, we have not proven that it is a mortal sin. Two other conditions must necessarily be met—whether there was full knowledge, and whether there was full consent—and we cannot know if those conditions are fulfilled if we do not consider the particular situation of the individual sinner. For we can only know if someone acts with full knowledge and full consent if we know the sinner and his situation.

Papal critics often conflate grave matter with mortal sin.[5] "Adulterous people are in mortal sin,"[6] without any other qualifier, is a common

---

3. CCC 1858.

4. Luke 16:18.

5. Granted, this can also stem from terminological imprecisions issuing from the Church herself, as John Paul II's post-synodal apostolic exhortation *Reconciliatio et Paenitentia* admits: "Hence, in the church's doctrine and pastoral action, grave sin is in practice identified with mortal sin." However, *the same document* also makes the distinction I mentioned here: "The synod in fact not only reaffirmed the teaching of the Council of Trent concerning the existence and nature of mortal and venial sins, but it also recalled that mortal sin is sin whose object is grave matter and which is also committed with full knowledge and deliberate consent." See also Buttiglione, *Risposte amichevoli*, 151.

Papal critics will also often conflate intrinsically evil sin with mortal sin. This is also incorrect. An intrinsically evil sin is a sin that can never be justified (i.e., made virtuous) in any circumstance. However, this has to do with the objective nature of the sin, not with the state of the soul of the person committing it.

6. See, for example, Hoffman, "Pope Praises Lisbon Guidelines That Allow Communion to Divorced and Remarried": "The Catholic Church, echoing the words of Christ himself, regards divorce and remarriage as an act of adultery, which is a mortal sin, one that will lead to eternal damnation if those guilty of the sin do not repent before death and receive the grace of absolution."

argument. This is a common misunderstanding, but it goes against established doctrine: the *Catechism* itself *explicitly* says that when one disobeys the moral law in a grave matter, but without full knowledge or without complete consent, then the sin is venial, not mortal.[7]

We know this is what Pope Francis is getting at in *Amoris Laetitia*, since he states, right at the beginning of his segment on "Mitigating factors in Pastoral Discernment":

> The Church possesses a solid body of reflection concerning mitigating factors and situations. Hence it can no longer simply be said that all those in any "irregular" situation are living in a state of mortal sin and are deprived of sanctifying grace.[8]

Being in a state of mortal sin carries with it some damning consequences, like precluding the sinner from partaking of the Eucharist. Those who take communion in mortal sin eat and drink judgment against themselves.[9] Since papal critics often confuse grave matter with mortal sin, then it is unsurprising they would think that any divorced and remarried person living *more uxorio* should be barred from communion. Yet, as I explained before, this is based on a misconception, not in the actual doctrine of the church: grave matter is a necessary, but not sufficient, condition for mortal sin. All mortal sins have grave matter, but not all sins with grave matter are mortal sins.[10]

The only stipulation the church has infallibly established as excluding the sinner from communion is a state of mortal sin. As the Council of Trent says:

> If it is unbecoming for any one to approach to any of the sacred functions, unless he approach in a spirit of piety; assuredly, the more the holiness and divinity of this heavenly sacrament are understood by a Christian, the more diligently ought he to give heed that he approach not to receive it but with great reverence and holiness, especially as we read in the Apostle those words full of terror; He that eateth and drinketh unworthily, eateth and

---

7. CCC 1862. See Ryan, "Weakness, and Wounded and Troubled Love," 136: "On both scores, it could well involve fault/blame that is diminished or even removed. Consistent with these traditional principles we must be very wary of identifying the fact of objective disorder with personal culpability and of using phrases involving 'mortal sin.'"

8. *AL* 301.

9. 1 Cor 11:29.

10. López, "Para Comprender *Amoris Laetitia*," 437.

> drinketh judgment to himself. Wherefore, he who would communicate, ought to recall to mind the precept of the Apostle; *Let a man prove himself.* Now ecclesiastical usage declares that necessary proof to be, that no one, conscious to himself of mortal sin, how contrite soever he may seem to himself, ought to approach to the sacred Eucharist without previous sacramental confession. This the holy Synod hath decreed is to be invariably observed by all Christians.[11]

Any other requirements that the church may establish are based on its prudential judgment.[12] This means they are to be respected, but also that they may be overturned without any implication against the church's infallibility or reliability. For centuries, the church has imposed excommunications on certain groups and actions, and later lifted them up, according to its discernment of the particular context surrounding them.[13]

In other words, the successor of Peter may indeed have, in the past, banned the divorced and remarried living *more uxorio* from partaking in the Eucharist. Yet, this does not preclude the current pope from lifting up those limitations as he sees fit, provided the people involved are not in a state of mortal sin.

That a person not in mortal sin may receive the Eucharist is again confirmed by the *Catechism*: "As bodily nourishment restores lost

---

11. Council of Trent, "13th Session, Chapter VII."

12. See López, "Para Comprender *Amoris Laetitia*," 437: "The Eucharistic prohibition in a situation of sin with grave matter, as in Canon 915, rests in the possibility of creating scandal in the community. In other words, it is a disciplinary, not doctrinal norm, which the Pope can change (or, even without changing it, create exceptions based on the canonical principle of '*salus animarum*'). On the contrary, the impossibility of taking the Eucharist in mortal sin is of a doctrinal order, not merely disciplinary."

13. Just to name an illustrative, but by no means exhaustive example, Pope St. Pius V issued the bull *De Salute Gregis Dominici* in 1567, where he forbade everyone from participating in or attending bullfights, under pain of excommunication. *This was to be held in perpetuity.* Nevertheless, his successor Gregory XIII limited this prohibition to the clergy in his bull *Exponi*. It was Pius V's prerogative to issue this prohibition since, as pastor of souls, it was his duty to denounce "cruel and base spectacles of the devil and not of man" "removed from Christian piety and charity," as he called them. However, it was also Gregory's prerogative, as pastor of souls, to lift this ban, since the backlash from Spanish quarters demonstrated that the excommunication was being counterproductive (especially in the context of the Reformation, where support from Spanish Catholics was important). Still, what would have happened if people in that age would have analyzed this episode in the same way as papal critics do today? They would have probably lost faith in the church, given such a blatant contradiction of an allegedly perpetual sacramental discipline.

strength, so the *Eucharist strengthens our charity*, which tends to be weakened in daily life; and *this living charity wipes away venial sins*."[14] The same *Catechism*, as we already mentioned, determines that a person commits a venial sin if he does not act with full knowledge or full consent, even if the sin has grave matter.[15]

In summary, for a divorced and civilly remarried person living *more uxorio* to be in mortal sin, three conditions must be fulfilled. Grave matter is, of course, present by definition. Nevertheless, two more conditions are needed to bar the person from the Eucharist: full knowledge and full consent. Even if these do not interfere with the objective morality of the sin (the sin remains grave and immoral, regardless of circumstances),[16] they certainly may change the subjective culpability of the individual sinner. Some circumstances may diminish subjective culpability in such a way, that the sinner is not in a mortal sin and is, therefore, not precluded from the Eucharist if the church so allows. Circumstances diminishing subjective culpability are what we call "mitigating circumstances."

❖ ❖ ❖

Objective Evil vs. Subjective guilt—A Wojtylan Tradition

Before we proceed, it is important to dispel another misconception that may appear at the outset. Again, we must reiterate: considerations about mitigating circumstances do not in any way diminish or justify the objectively evil nature of sin.[17] Having intercourse with a partner from a civil remarriage after a divorce is an intrinsically evil act. *This means it*

---

14. *CCC* 1394. It is impressive how this *Catechism* passage mirrors the polemical footnote, where we are urged to consider the Eucharist a "powerful medicine and nourishment for the weak."

15. *CCC* 1862.

16. See Fernández, "El Capítulo VIII de *Amoris Laetitia*," 458: "Nevertheless, for Francis, it is not the concrete circumstances that determine the objective morality. Just because the mitigating factors diminish the culpability, this does not mean that what is objectively evil suddenly becomes objectively good." See also Almeida, "*Amoris Laetitia*—reflexões," 379: "Pope Francis never said that mitigating circumstances justify the irregular situation, only that they may allow it to be tolerated."

17. See Fernández, "El Capítulo VIII de *Amoris Laetitia*," 458; and also p. 463: "Once more, it is important to remember that this does not imply cheapening objective values."

can never be justified, whatever the situation is, whether mitigating circumstances are present or not.

This is important, because papal critics tend to accuse Francis and those faithful to him of engaging in situation ethics,[18] something condemned by the church since at least Pius XII.[19] Situation ethics means that man's internal "judgment is not measured, must not and cannot be measured, as regards its objective rectitude and truth, by any objective norm situated outside man and independent of his subjective persuasion, but is entirely self-sufficient."[20] Put simply, situation ethics means that morality depends, not on objective moral laws, but on the circumstances and how conscience judges them.

This is very different from the teaching on mitigating circumstances.[21] Contrary to situation ethics, mitigating circumstances do not change the objective nature of sin, but only the culpability of the sinner engaged in it. In fact, Pope St. John Paul II, who is usually quoted as a formidable adversary of situation ethics on account of his encyclical *Veritatis Splendor*,[22] was also the pope that codified the teaching on mitigating circumstances in the *Catechism* he promulgated. Therefore, these principles cannot contradict one another.[23]

18. See, as an example, Vennari, "Situation Ethics Enshrined."

19. This document issued from the Supreme Sacred Congregation of the Holy Office, "Instruction on 'Situation Ethics' *Contra Doctrinam*," is found in *AAS* 48 (1956), 144: "In order to safeguard the purity and intactness of Catholic doctrine, this Supreme Sacred Congregation of the Holy Office interdicts and prohibits this doctrine of 'Situation Ethics' from being taught or approved, under any name whatsoever it may be designated."

20. *AAS* 48 (1956), 144.

21. See Buttiglione, *Risposte amichevoli*, 47–48.

22. John Paul II, *Veritatis Splendor*, 32: "Once the idea of a universal truth about the good, knowable by human reason, is lost, inevitably the notion of conscience also changes. Conscience is no longer considered in its primordial reality as an act of a person's intelligence, the function of which is to apply the universal knowledge of the good in a specific situation and thus to express a judgment about the right conduct to be chosen here and now. *Instead, there is a tendency to grant to the individual conscience the prerogative of independently determining the criteria of good and evil and then acting accordingly. Such an outlook is quite congenial to an individualist ethic, wherein each individual is faced with his own truth, different from the truth of others.* Taken to its extreme consequences, this individualism leads to a denial of the very idea of human nature."

23. In chapter 12 of this book, I will explore with more detail how *Veritatis Splendor* deals with the subjective component of culpability vis-à-vis an objective situation of sin.

Take the example of another intrinsically evil act: abortion. John Paul II teaches in his encyclical *Evangelium Vitae* that abortion can never be justified in any circumstance,[24] since it is the killing of an innocent human life. However, let us consider two distinct situations: 1) a woman who gets pregnant after a one-night stand and who aborts because it would be inconvenient for her; 2) a teenage girl who gets pregnant from her abusive stepfather and who, threatened of being thrown out in the streets without money if she does not comply, is forced to abort to avoid scandal.

In both of these instances, one unborn child was killed. The child's life in the second situation is not lesser than the first child's, just because of the circumstances surrounding her conception. They were both objectively evil acts. But can anyone really claim that both women are equally culpable of this evil? In fact, can we say the teenage girl has been guilty at all, instead of her stepfather?

If we answer that both women are not culpable to the same degree, then we are acknowledging the doctrine of mitigating circumstances. This is very different from situation ethics, for situation ethics would mandate that abortion in the second situation was justified or even a moral good. This would mean that an innocent life could be killed. In fact, it could lead to a slippery slope where the first woman might rationalize her choice as a moral good, according to her conscience. But what we are arguing is not whether we are dealing with an objective evil. Such is taken as a given. Rather, what is at stake is the subjective culpability of each person involved in this objectively evil act. One person has mitigating, attenuating circumstances, and the other does not.

John Paul II acknowledged this. In the very same encyclical where he condemns abortion as an intrinsically evil act, he also says: "Decisions that go against life sometimes arise from difficult or even tragic situations of profound suffering, loneliness, a total lack of economic prospects, depression and anxiety about the future. Such circumstances can mitigate even to a notable degree subjective responsibility and the consequent

---

24. John Paul II, *Evangelium Vitae*, 62: "I declare that direct abortion, that is, *abortion willed as an end or as a means, always constitutes a grave moral disorder*, since it is the deliberate killing of an innocent human being. . . . *No circumstance, no purpose, no law whatsoever can ever make licit an act which is intrinsically illicit*, since it is contrary to the Law of God which is written in every human heart, knowable by reason itself, and proclaimed by the Church."

culpability of those who make these choices which in themselves are evil."[25] Again, we should not think that the Polish pontiff is contradicting himself, but rather that there is no contradiction between the two concepts.

In fact, the tension between objective sin and the sinner's subjectivity was a part of Karol Wojtyla's[26] thought before he ascended to the papacy. Rocco Buttiglione, one of John Paul II's disciples, explains that this pope never wanted to annul the role of the subjective conscience. "The objective side of the action decides on the goodness or gravity of the action, the subjective side of the action decides on the level of responsibility of the agent."[27] Philosopher Guerra López agrees with Buttiglione, explaining Wojtyla's understanding of reality as follows: "the objective recognition of reality implies the recognition of the objective existence of subjectivity."[28] Wojtyla does not teach a simple objectivism, but explains that "the tension between the philosophy of being [i.e., objectivism] and the philosophy of conscience [i.e., subjectivism][29] is resolved through an adequate philosophy of the human person," recognizing simultaneously that "conscience is being, and that being gives itself up to conscience."[30]

This role of conscience, unlike situation ethics, does not detract from God's sovereignty in creation. In fact, it presupposes it:

> The creative act with which man creates his own internal world of values, and also the society around him, does not take place in a vacuum, it is not an original act, it is not an act without presuppositions. It takes place on the basis of an original act of God who creates the world and creates man by providing both the world and man with a structure endowed with meaning that man must recognize and respect in order to be able to carry out his creativity.[31]

Both Rocco Buttiglione and Guerra López have written essays on the concept of "person-in-action," developed by Wojtyla, and later on taken

---

25. John Paul II, *Evangelium Vitae*, 18.
26. Pope St. John Paul II's birth name.
27. Buttiglione, *Risposte amichevoli*, 137. See also p. 50.
28. López, "Entender a Wojtyla," 38.
29. López, "Entender a Wojtyla," 43–46, explains the tensions between philosophy of being and philosophy of conscience, namely as approached by Husserl and Wojtyla.
30. López, "Entender a Wojtyla," 45.
31. Buttiglione, "L'Approccio Antropologico."

The Teaching on Mitigating Circumstances

by Francis in *Amoris Laetitia*.[32] Referencing St. John of the Cross's idea of *homo viator*,[33] Guerra López explains that Wojtyla's personalism sees human action "as a norm for a yet unfinished person, as a moral norm for the person in transit, a person-in-action, demanding great patience and tenderness, great care and respect for the most intimate dynamics of the person, a conscience that is not educated 'at once,' but is always on journey."[34] This would be how one would achieve a true "realism in ethics."[35] Buttiglione incorporates mitigating circumstances into this "realist ethics of John Paul II," which is "proper of the balance of Catholic ethics" and distinguished from the "objectivist ethics advocated by some adversaries of Pope Francis."[36]

Guerra López then goes on to explain that the "experience of a person is never an experience of a static, a-temporal or meta-historical being. On the contrary, the fundamental human experience, at the basis of all other experiences, at the root of what it means to be human, is the experience of the person under construction. This construction realizes itself through a *vertical transcendence*. In other words, the way through which freedom allows us to go beyond ourselves, *by choosing truth*."[37] Or, as Buttiglione postulates: "If no one can escape one's cross, it is also true that no story begins with the cross. It is a path. In this journey, 'time is greater than space.' In what direction is the sinner moving? Towards the house of the Father, or away from it? The direction of the movement (marked by time) counts more than the absolute distance."[38]

From this recognition, we can understand the teaching of Francis about the possibility of love, growing, and living in God's grace, even

---

32. López, "Entender a Wojtyla"; Buttiglione, "L'Approccio Antropologico."

33. i.e., "journeying man." See López, "Entender a Wojtyla," 48.

34. López, "Entender a Wojtyla," 41.

35. López, "Entender a Wojtyla," 41. See also Walford, *Pope Francis, the Family, and Divorce*, 63.

36. Buttiglione, "L'Approccio Antropologico."

37. López, "Entender a Wojtyla," 47.

38. Buttiglione, "L'Approccio Antropologico." See also Calmeyn, "Accompagnamento e legge di gradualità": "It is the classical notion of the 'path in the Good,' also called 'the law of gradualness' that allows us to understand *Amoris Laetitia*'s real contribution, and the way the document positions itself in Tradition" (translated from the original Italian). Finally see Francis, *Evangelii Gaudium*, 44: "A small step, in the midst of great human limitations, can be more pleasing to God than a life which appears outwardly in order but moves through the day without confronting great difficulties."

in an objective situation of sin. It is necessary to love and support the growth of the person-in-action.[39]

❖❖❖

The Objections[40]

When confronted with how *Amoris Laetitia* bases itself in the sound and orthodox teaching on mitigating circumstances, the papal critic will usually answer something like this: "Yes, ignorance may diminish subjective culpability; but in that case, the priest must inform the sinner of his sin, thereby dispelling his ignorance; from that point onward, this ceases to apply."[41]

This seems like an argument, but it is actually a set of two arguments melded together. In a fell swoop, the papal critic has

1. Postulated that ignorance ceases to be a mitigating circumstance simply by informing the sinner that he is sinning;
2. Very subtly swept "full consent" under the rug; only ignorance / full knowledge is being considered from that point on.

I wish now to explain why both of these arguments are wrong, by delving more deeply into the Catholic teaching of mitigating circumstances.

---

39. López, "Entender a Wojtyla," 38. According to Cardinal Schönborn ("Conversation with Cardinal Schönborn"), it is not only the person that is "in action," but the family unit too: "The Bible itself presents family life, not as an abstract ideal, but as what the Holy Father calls a 'work of craftsmanship.' . . . The Pope speaks very clearly: no family is a perfect reality, since it is made up of sinners. The family is en route. I believe that this is the bedrock of the entire document."

40. The objections mentioned here presuppose that the papal critic has correctly understood that *Amoris Laetitia* deals with mitigating circumstances. I always found it puzzling that, for example, the alleged heretical propositions "corrected" by the *Correctio filialis* specifically say that *Amoris Laetitia* is talking about sinners with full knowledge and full consent. Of course sinners in that situation are in mortal sin, but Francis is very clear that *Amoris Laetitia* deals with sinners with impaired knowledge and consent. It is bewildering to think how people could set up such an elaborate strawman, with such a precise language and such well-defined concepts, which goes so against the clear purpose of the exhortation.

41. See Brugger, "The Catholic Conscience, the Argentine Bishops, and '*Amoris Laetitia*,'" namely the section "Conscience with diminished culpability," followed by the section "Solution? To form consciences!"

Full Knowledge

If "full knowledge" is a necessary condition for mortal sin, then ignorance can act as a mitigating factor. The sin remains objectively sinful, but ignorance diminishes the culpability of the sinner, so that it is possible for him to not be in a state of mortal sin. On this point, the *Catechism* teaches:

> Mortal sin requires full knowledge.... It presupposes knowledge of the sinful character of the act, of its opposition to God's law.... Unintentional ignorance can *diminish* or even *remove the imputability of a grave offense*.[42]

Please note, unintentional ignorance can diminish or even remove the imputability of a sin with grave matter (like adultery). This is doctrine, inscribed in the *Catechism* since St. John Paul II's pontificate. It is not an innovation from Pope Francis.

Granted, the *Catechism* also states that "no one is deemed to be ignorant of the principles of the moral law, which are written in the conscience of every man."[43] However, this cannot be interpreted as meaning that ignorance cannot ever exist. Otherwise, the *Catechism* would be self-contradictory. Rather, the *Catechism* is referring here to the first principles, i.e., to sins decried in the Ten Commandments. Of course, "thou shalt not commit adultery"[44] is one of those commandments. It is written in the heart of every man and woman that adultery is sinful and wrong, and no one can be deemed ignorant of this fact.

However, sin (especially sensual sin) darkens the intellect.[45] Conscience cannot ignore the first principles, but it can err in applying them to a particular case.[46] Buttiglione masterfully draws from Thomistic theology in order to show how principles are always present in practical reason, while the *habitus* applies them into particular cases—here, the capacity to recognize the principles in the concrete situation may be faulty.[47] Put simply: even if a sinner might have written in his heart that adultery

---

42. CCC 1859–60.

43. CCC 1860.

44. Exod 20:40.

45. Council of Trent, *Catechism*, part III. See also Third Plenary Council of Baltimore, *Baltimore Catechism #3*, lesson 5, Q259, 261.

46. Buttiglione, *Risposte amichevoli*, 80.

47. Buttiglione, *Risposte amichevoli*, 77–82. I highly recommend the reading of this full section of Buttiglione's book.

is sinful, he might have difficulty in understanding why a divorce and remarriage is adulterous. This may be aggravated by cultural and educational factors, and by that particular sinner's life story and background. This is why *Amoris Laetitia* says:

> More is involved here than mere ignorance of the rule. A subject may know full well the rule, yet have great difficulty in understanding "its inherent values."[48]

So, for instance, a sinner might understand that adultery is wrong, but not understand that divorce and remarriage constitutes adultery, because such is based on the "inherent value" of the indissolubility of marriage that many people today do not comprehend. Fr. Thomas Ryan agrees that this is what is at stake here: "A person could be so inured through the influence of cultural and social factors that he or she acts from 'invincible ignorance (or error).' An individual may see nothing wrong in what he or she is doing. Or he or she may know what marriage involves speculatively but not at the level of a personally interiorised value."[49]

Understanding this "inherent value" may be even more difficult, if this sinner is living in a stable relationship that externally looks more like marriage than an affair. In this sad, hedonistic, and modernistic society, even the sinner's first spouse (the legitimate one) might think that his or her former companion is not in adultery, and may actually approve of this arrangement.[50] Extreme situations can also add to this confusion. Archbishop Victor Fernández explains: "It is not easy to call 'adulteress' to a woman who has been beaten down and humiliated by her Catholic husband, and who took refuge with, and received economic and psychological help from, another man who helped her raise the children of her previous union, and with whom she bore other children, and lived with for several years."[51]

---

48. *AL* 301.

49. Ryan, "Weakness, and Wounded and Troubled Love," 136.

50. Buttiglione, *Risposte amichevoli*, 140: "A common place of our culture is the primacy of the spontaneity of feeling over the commitment of the will assuming a duty. There is confusion between the emotional fact of getting enamored and the human act of love.... For many, the truth about marriage is not immediately evident. One gets married without knowing exactly what one is doing and what one is committing to. Then, with just as much superficiality, one divorces."

51. Fernández, "El Capítulo VIII de *Amoris Laetitia*," 455. Please bear in mind that even the church tolerates divorce in these situations (*CCC* 2383), even if it does not approve of remarriage.

We may have a glimpse at Pope Francis's thoughts on the matter from an answer he gave in a press conference during the return flight from Rio de Janeiro, on July 28, 2013:

> Cardinal Quarracino, my predecessor, used to say that as far as he was concerned, half of all marriages are null. But why did he say this? Because people get married lacking maturity, they get married without realizing that it is a life-long commitment, they get married because society tells them they have to get married. And this is where the pastoral care of marriage also comes in.[52]

Of course, the papal critic might counter-argue: if we are dealing with unintentional ignorance and no one is unable to understand the principles of the moral law, then all we should do is inform the sinner that he or she is, in fact, committing adultery.

As appealing as this might be, it is not so. It is a simplistic way of looking at reality. A person cannot be formally informed that he is sinning and, from that point on, be liable and fully culpable if he does not accept our explanation. Many papal critics seem to think this is an accurate description of reality, but the church herself has acknowledged how humanity is more complex than this.

The church has always understood the potential dilemma of informing a sinner not prepared to receive the full truth. In this case, the sinner will start formally to sin, even if the person guiding him knew he could not bear the full weight of doctrine at the time. Since our aim should be the salvation of souls and not their damnation, Catholics are urged to exercise discernment about the best timing and way to tell the truth to the sinner.

Again, this is not a modern, watered-down pastoral approach coming from a lukewarm "Church of Nice,"[53] as some critics affirm. It is actually quite traditional. It dates back to apostolic times, to St. Paul:

> And I, brethren, could not speak to you as unto spiritual, but as unto carnal. As unto little ones in Christ. I gave you milk to drink, not meat; for you were not able as yet. But neither indeed are you now able; for you are yet carnal.[54]

---

52. See also Ryan, "Weakness, and Wounded and Troubled Love," 135–36: "For instance, Roman Rota jurisprudence is almost unanimous in the view that, in contemporary Western culture, error about the permanence of marriage is deeply engrained."

53. Term coined and popularized by Michael Voris, in his 2012 video titled "Church of Nice!"

54. 1 Cor 3:1–2.

In fact, it dates to Jesus himself, for he said to his disciples: "I have yet many things to say to you: but you cannot bear them now."[55] They could only bear those teachings when the Holy Spirit descended upon them.

In his foundational book about pastoral care of the souls, Pope St. Gregory the Great instructed his priests 1,500 years ago to proceed like this:

> But some things, even though openly known, ought to be seasonably tolerated; that is, when circumstances afford no suitable opportunity for openly correcting them. For sores by being unseasonably cut are the worse enflamed and, if medicaments suit not the time, it is undoubtedly evident that they lose their medicinal function. But, while a fitting time for the correction of subordinates is being sought, the patience of the prelate is exercised under the very weight of their offenses.[56]

St. Alphonse Liguori, no moral laxist to be sure, also instructed confessors in this regard. He called this the "principle of good faith":

> If [the sinner] is inculpably ignorant of some other matter (of which he can be ignorant)—even something of the divine law, the confessor should prudently decide whether the instruction will be profitable for the penitent. If it will not be profitable, he should not make the correction, but rather leave him in good faith. The reason is: the danger of formal sin is a much more serious thing than material sin. God punishes formal sin, for that alone is what offends Him.[57]

This principle of "good faith" is echoed already in post-conciliar times, in a *Vademecum* published under Pope St. John Paul II (I will return to this *Vademecum* later, in chapter 14):

> The principle according to which it is preferable to let penitents remain in good faith in cases of error due to subjectively invincible ignorance, is certainly to be considered always valid, even in matters of conjugal chastity. And this applies whenever it is foreseen that the penitent, although oriented towards living

---

55. John 16:12.

56. Gregory the Great, *Pastoral Rule*, 2:10.

57. Liguori, "Guide for Confessors," 11–12. See also Ryan, "Weakness, and Wounded and Troubled Love," 138: "Some manualist theologians (e.g., Merkelbach, Noldin) continued the tradition from St Alphonsus. The person acting out of love when committing error (or a disordered act 'in good faith') is not just 'excused' but is good and the act itself is meritorious because it is directed towards a good end."

within the bounds of a life of faith, would not be prepared to change his own conduct, but rather would begin formally to sin.[58]

This, of course, does not mean the sinner should be deprived of the sound doctrine that will help him turn away from his sinful life. Otherwise, we would not have a law of gradualism, but an intolerable gradualism of the law, whereby some people would be forever considered unable to follow the dictates of the moral law. The idea is not to keep the sinner in a state of ignorance forever in order to protect him from formal sin. Quite the contrary, what is intended is that eventually, and as soon as possible, he will be instructed on the teachings of the church. Nevertheless, sometimes, a process of conscience formation must be undertaken before that can happen. Far from being a way to water down truth, this is a way to protect truth from being trampled by being presented in a context and timing where it will not produce its effect.

Most importantly, this shows that there is a difference between evangelizing and "notifying." If we think that a mere exposition of the church's doctrine is sufficient to dispel ignorance, regardless of pastoral sensitivities, and without any discernment towards the characteristics of the sinner before us (or any consideration on whether he will be saved or condemned by our actions), then we are not acting in a Catholic or even traditional way. Understanding does not mean accepting or rejecting: it means to discern.[59] This is how Catholics are called to form consciences.

The rediscovery of the proper way to evangelize is, in fact, a major overtone of Francis's pontificate.[60] People concerned with the growing secularization of our society would do well to heed His Holiness's counsels.

※※※

Full Consent

Even if the papal critic seems to focus solely on the ignorance of the sinner, the truth is that this is mostly a red herring. *Amoris Laetitia* does

---

58. Pontifical Council for the Family, "Vademecum," section 3, para. 8.

59. Buttiglione, *Risposte amichevoli,* 138. See also Fernández, "El Capítulo VIII de Amoris Laetitia," 455–56.

60. See Francis, *Evangelii Gaudium.*

not talk too much about ignorance. To the contrary, it is usually Francis's detractors who do talk about ignorance. For years, many of them have decried the watering down of doctrine by the clergy as the main factor for the current church crisis.[61] Therefore, it is hardly surprising they would think that the only mitigating circumstance is ignorance, and that ignorance can easily be overcome by strong doctrinal statements.

By doing this, the papal critic is interpreting *Amoris Laetitia* through the prism of his own concerns and biases. This is, however, not consistent with how the apostolic exhortation tackles the issue. Even if Francis grounds his sacramental discipline on the teaching of mitigating circumstances, the truth is that he does not delve too much on the "full knowledge" side of the equation, but rather on "full consent." In fact, the only part of *Amoris Laetitia* in which Francis mentions impaired knowledge and ignorance is one sole sentence, which I quoted above. While Francis dedicates half a sentence to "full knowledge," he develops the concept of "full consent" throughout almost two paragraphs.

Thus, when the papal critic says that mitigating circumstances do not apply because all that is needed to overcome ignorance is to instruct the sinner, he is disregarding the most important foundation for the new sacramental discipline: consent.

The critic does this because he does not think full consent is impaired in most situations.[62] I theorize that many are influenced by a libertarian outlook, where the only way to coerce someone is through physical violence.[63] However, libertarianism is a post-Enlightenment philosophy, and we wish to focus our attention into what Catholicism actually teaches. If we look at doctrine, we notice that orthodoxy takes a much broader approach to the question of impaired consent than the

---

61. See again Michael Voris's video "The Church of Nice!"

62. See for example Arntz, "Guest Op-Ed: *Amoris Laetitia* and the New Church of Francis": "Furthermore, it is extremely rare to enter a second union without full consent; the only kind of sexual union that does not have full consent is considered rape. Very few actually enter into a union that would be considered rape. In this case of this man, unless he were pressured by the woman, he is consenting to marry her, which means that he is not actually marrying her under any '[mitigating] conditions.'"

63. Rothbard, *War, Peace, and the State*, 116: "No one may threaten or commit violence ('aggress') against another man's person or property. Violence may be employed only against the man who commits such violence; that is, only defensively against the aggressive violence of another. In short, no violence may be employed against a nonaggressor. Here is the fundamental rule from which can be deduced the entire corpus of libertarian theory."

reductionist view limited to the non-aggression principle. After all, sin not only darkens the intellect, it also weakens the will.[64]

Returning to the *Catechism*'s section on mortal sin, and reading what it has to say about full consent, we can see that "the promptings of feelings and passions can also diminish the voluntary and free character of the offense, as can external pressures or pathological disorders."[65] In the *Catechism*'s section on freedom, we can read that imputability and responsibility for an action can be diminished or even nullified, not only by ignorance, but also by "inadvertence, duress, fear, habit, inordinate attachments, and other psychological or social factors."[66] A man is only responsible for his acts to the extent that they are voluntary,[67] i.e., done with full and free consent.[68] Full consent must always implicate the will.[69]

Please note that what was said above refers to "responsibility for an action." There is no qualifier for what that action might be. *Any* action is encompassed in this reasoning, including intrinsically evil acts like adultery. However, sins of the flesh, being driven by passions and concupiscence, are particularly prone to this.[70] In fact, there is precedent in the *Catechism* for evaluating mitigating circumstances impairing full consent for another intrinsically evil act of a sexual nature: masturbation.

---

64. Council of Trent, *Catechism*, part IV. See also *Baltimore Catechism #3*, lesson 5, Q259.

65. *CCC* 1860.

66. *CCC* 1735.

67. *CCC* 1734.

68. See also Francis, *Amoris Laetitia*, 273, on the topic of drug abuse: "A distinction is not always adequately drawn between 'voluntary' and 'free' acts. A person may clearly and willingly desire something evil, but do so as the result of an irresistible passion or a poor upbringing. In such cases, while the decision is voluntary, inasmuch as it does not run counter to the inclination of their desire, it is not free, since it is practically impossible for them not to choose that evil. We see this in the case of compulsive drug addicts. When they want a fix, they want it completely, yet they are so conditioned that at that moment no other decision is possible. Their decision is voluntary but not free."

69. Buttiglione, *Risposte amichevoli*, 140: "Full consent is a factor that implicates the will. There can arise situations where the person can, knowing whether some actions are good or evil, be overwhelmed by uncontrollable emotions."

70. Congregation for the Doctrine of the Faith, *Persona Humana*, X: "It is true that in sins of the sexual order, in view of their kind and their causes, it more easily happens that free consent is not fully given; this is a fact which calls for caution in all judgment as to the subject's responsibility."

> Both the Magisterium of the Church, in the course of a constant tradition, and the moral sense of the faithful have been in no doubt and have firmly maintained that masturbation is an intrinsically and gravely disordered action. . . . *To form an equitable judgment about the subjects' moral responsibility and to guide pastoral action, one must take into account the affective immaturity, force of acquired habit, conditions of anxiety or other psychological or social factors that lessen, if not even reduce to a minimum, moral culpability.*[71]

In other words, the same paragraph of the *Catechism* acknowledges that masturbation is intrinsically evil, but also that mitigating circumstances (even immaturity, habit, or anxiety) may impair full consent in order to lessen the moral culpability of the same act. These are not contradictory statements.

Is this important to interpret *Amoris Laetitia*? We cannot pretend otherwise, for these sections of the *Catechism* that I mentioned here are, in fact, *explicitly quoted* in the *Amoris Laetitia* section about mitigating factors in pastoral discernment.[72] I remind the reader, this pastoral discernment on mitigating factors is precisely where the pontiff's sacramental discipline rests. *In other words, these parts of the* Catechism *are key to interpreting Francis's manifest mind and will on this issue.*

Pope Francis is not producing some new doctrine; he is simply extending a preexisting doctrine to another set of sins, previously excluded from this pastoral logic by the church's prudential judgment. Far from creating a special situation for the divorced and remarried, *Amoris Laetitia* is simply applying the general rule that was previously applied to all other penitents.[73] It is in the church's power to do this, as it does not contradict any definitively defined doctrine (as I will explain with more detail in the next section of this book).

❊❊❊

---

71. CCC 2352.

72. AL 302.

73. Buttiglione, *Risposte amichevoli*, 37, 68, 146. See also pp. 144–45: "Before, the divorced and remarried were sinners of a particular kind, almost excommunicated (even if not formally excommunicated, they could not partake of Communion unless they lived 'as brothers and sisters'). Now, they have become ordinary sinners."

The "Retrospective vs. Prospective" Objection

Some critics, who actually understand the doctrinal core of *Amoris Laetitia*, will claim that the teaching on mitigating circumstances is being misapplied here. As I said before in chapter 4, the "while not yet the fully objective ideal" wording implies that the sinful behavior might persist for some time, while the pastor tries to bring the sinner back into full communion with the church. According to these critics, this is wrong because mitigating circumstances only apply retroactively.[74]

In other words, "mitigating circumstances" are useful guides for a sinner to perform a conscience exam *after* the sin has been committed. If, after this conscience exam, the sinner determines he had no full consent while performing the sin, he is not in mortal sin and can receive communion. This is very different—so it is argued—from someone saying "I have mitigating circumstances, so I have permission to sin in the future." This would open the Eucharist to impenitent sinners, who have no firm resolution to not sin again.

I believe this is a warped version of what Pope Francis intends to implement. As I explained in chapter 6, it is a misinterpretation to claim that communion should be given to impenitent sinners. Francis is quite clear that this process of pastoral discernment is open only to people with "humility, discretion, and love for the Church and her teaching, in a sincere search for God's will and a desire to make a more perfect response to it."[75] This is *not* a description of an impenitent sinner. Nor can we say this person has no firm resolution to not sin again, because mitigating circumstances are encumbering such resolution: "the possibility of a new fall should not prejudice the authenticity of the resolution."[76]

---

74. As an example, see Brugger, "Five Serious Problems with Chapter 8 of *Amoris Laetitia*": "Catholic moral theology has spoken about the importance of pastors being sensitive to factors limiting a penitent's subjective guilt in order to help penitents assess their true guilt retrospectively, i.e., to help them look at what they've already done to assist them to judge rightly about their culpability, so they can repent and be forgiven and deal with those factors and begin freely to choose rightly. Chapter 8 introduces a significant change in the role that mitigating factors play in pastoral care. Pastors are directed to assess subjective culpability as a way of 'discerning' what kinds of ecclesial participation, including sacramental participation, are appropriate for people who are going forth from the confessional. It focuses on assessing mitigated guilt for directing prospective action leaving in place the factors that mitigate guilt, so people may continue to sin without ever becoming responsible enough to sin mortally."

75. *AL* 300.

76. *AL* n364.

In light of this, we should stop thinking about sinners who self-justify themselves as "I have mitigating circumstances, so I have permission to sin in the future," since those are excluded from the discernment process as laid out by #300. On the contrary, we should start thinking instead about sinners who worry, "I have mitigating circumstances that will not disappear in the foreseeable future. I do not want to sin, but need grace to help me with this situation; the sacraments would help."

Still, the question remains: can mitigating circumstances really be applied to future sins? Please note there is nothing in the *Catechism* stating otherwise. The *Catechism* says that full consent may be impaired by passions, fear, habit, duress, inordinate attachments, and many other factors. These circumstances do not cease just because the person has already sinned. In fact, these are situations where the sinner finds himself, and may persist for an indeterminate amount of time, making the sinning behavior more likely, and therefore predictable.

Let us take an example I believe is relatively uncontroversial. Let us consider a married woman who is raped at gunpoint by a stranger in an alley. No one would contend that this person acted with full consent, so much so that she is not culpable at all. But let us imagine that this woman was kidnapped (again, at gunpoint) and tied up in a room in her captor's house. The captor then says, "Tomorrow, I am going to rape you." Is this woman's full consent somehow not impaired because she knows this will happen tomorrow instead of today?

Since one example suffices to show that mitigating circumstances can be applied prospectively and not just retroactively, then I think my case has been proven. Of course, I am not saying that this doctrine cannot be applied to past sins, in the context of a conscience exam before communion. In fact, Pope Francis is in favor of such conscience exams: he lays out in detail how these conscience exams should be done in the pastoral accompaniment of the divorced and remarried.[77] However, we cannot restrict the Holy Father's discipline to such a limited view. If we wish to make sense of the part where Pope Francis teaches about the "not

---

77. See *AL* 300: "*Useful in this process is an examination of conscience* through moments of reflection and repentance. The divorced and remarried should ask themselves: how did they act towards their children when the conjugal union entered into crisis; whether or not they made attempts at reconciliation; what has become of the abandoned party; what consequences the new relationship has on the rest of the family and the community of the faithful; and what example is being set for young people who are preparing for marriage. A sincere reflection can strengthen trust in the mercy of God which is not denied anyone."

The Teaching on Mitigating Circumstances

yet fully the objective ideal," we must assume that the "past vs. future" objection does not hold.

Conclusion

At the end of this chapter, I think we can draw the following conclusions:

- A mortal sin requires three conditions: grave matter, full knowledge, and full consent.
- A sin with grave matter, but without full knowledge and full consent, is not mortal sin, but venial sin.
- Mortal sins preclude the sinner from the Eucharist, whereas venial sins do not.
- Subjective culpability can be diminished if full knowledge and full consent are impaired.
- Diminished subjective culpability in no way interferes with the objectively evil nature of the sin.
- An intrinsically evil sin can have diminished culpability and still remain intrinsically evil. (It is one thing to say that a sin is not justified in any circumstance and another thing to say that there are circumstances where the sinner is not fully culpable.)
- This doctrine is not new. The only "novelty" comes from extending it to the divorced and remarried.
- Ignorance is not overcome by simply restating doctrine to the sinner.
- Consent can be limited by many factors, not just coercion.
- *Amoris Laetitia* deals mostly with full consent, not full knowledge.

Chapter 8

The Problem of Scandal

ONE OF THE MOST sensible concerns raised by many of *Amoris Laetitia*'s critics has to do with the matter of scandal. Scandal, as defined by the *Catechism*, has a very different meaning than the one assumed in common parlance:

> Scandal is an attitude or behavior which leads another to do evil. The person who gives scandal becomes his neighbor's tempter. He damages virtue and integrity; he may even draw his brother into spiritual death. Scandal is a grave offense if by deed or omission another is deliberately led into a grave offense.[1]

The critics would argue that *Amoris Laetitia* would induce scandal in the faithful, since admitting divorced and remarried people to communion would seem to convey the idea that their lifestyle was somehow validated.[2] Onlookers would watch this and say to themselves: "If these people can divorce and remarry and still be admitted to the Eucharist, why can't I do the same? It's all good, after all!" This would be a "supreme counter-witness"[3] to the church's teaching on marriage.

---

1. CCC 2284.
2. As an example, see Meenan, "The Loss of This One Key Distinction Is Fueling Much of the Confusion around *Amoris Laetitia*": "Furthermore, those in such public and manifest sin who receive Communion also offer a scandal to the faithful, whose consciences may be deformed and led astray, left wondering, well, is adultery therefore really so bad? Is marriage truly indissoluble? Does cohabiting outside of matrimony exclude one from grace, Communion, and ultimately eternal life with the blessed?"
3. Expression aptly used by Buttiglione, *Risposte amichevoli*, 45.

Indeed, one of the two reasons why Pope St. John Paul II did not accept this opening of the sacraments to those who had been civilly divorced and remarried is precisely how this practice could lead to scandal.[4]

> However, the Church reaffirms her practice, which is based upon Sacred Scripture, of not admitting to Eucharistic Communion divorced persons who have remarried. . . . *Besides this, there is another special pastoral reason: if these people were admitted to the Eucharist, the faithful would be led into error and confusion regarding the Church's teaching about the indissolubility of marriage.*[5]

However, for the purpose of better delineating what scandal means on this topic, it is worth noting that John Paul II did not close the possibility of communion to all divorced and remarried couples. In the same document (in fact, in the same section), we see an exception, if certain conditions are met:

> Reconciliation in the sacrament of Penance which *would open the way to the Eucharist, can only be granted to those who,* repenting of having broken the sign of the Covenant and of fidelity to Christ, are sincerely ready to undertake a way of life that is no longer in contradiction to the indissolubility of marriage. This means, in practice, that when, for serious reasons, such as for example the children's upbringing, a man and a woman cannot satisfy the obligation to separate, they *"take on themselves the duty to live in complete continence, that is, by abstinence from the acts proper to married couples."*[6]

In other words, if the divorced and remarried couple accepts living in complete continence (i.e., cease to live *more uxorio*), then they can undergo the sacrament of Reconciliation and, afterwards, the Eucharist.

Nevertheless, this raises a question: If one of the reasons why divorced and remarried couples cannot be admitted to the Eucharist rests on how this would lead the other faithful into error regarding the church's teaching about the indissolubility of marriage, how can this danger be avoided if communion is given to divorced and remarried couples practicing complete continence? After all, whether a couple has intercourse or not is something very personal and intimate: it would probably be

---

4. Buttiglione, *Risposte amichevoli*, 39.
5. FC 84.
6. FC 84.

unknown to most people in the pews.⁷ So, how do we reconcile this apparent oversight in the document?

John Paul II does not say. *Familiaris Consortio* is not clear on this issue. Fortunately, in spite of this, the church did not fall into great confusion. This is what happens when people try, with good intentions and solicitous obedience and docility, to put in practice the manifest will of the pope.

As far as I know, the way this apparent contradiction has been resolved in practice has been to transfer the sacramental life of these couples to the internal forum—i.e., to a private setting, known only to them and their pastor. In the internal forum, the couple would work together with the priest to live their lives as best as they could, in accordance with the mandates of the gospel and with the help of the sacraments, far away from prying eyes and scandalous judgments from bystanders.

❖❖❖

This brings us full circle back to *Amoris Laetitia*. To oppose *Amoris Laetitia*'s sacramental discipline based on the objection of scandal, it is necessary to first ascertain whether the apostolic exhortation's provisions lend themselves to scandal or not. If we read carefully, we can see that scandal is, indeed, a concern for Pope Francis too:

> I am in agreement with the many Synod Fathers who observed that "the baptized who are divorced and civilly remarried need to be more fully integrated into Christian communities in the variety of ways possible, *while avoiding any occasion of scandal*."⁸

Also, as I said in previous chapters, we can use the criteria adopted by the bishops of Buenos Aires as a benchmark to evaluate whether our

---

7. Fernández, "El capítulo VIII de *Amoris Laetitia*," 453: "When we talk about the need to avoid scandal, it is important to highlight that this only happens when people 'flaunt' their situation as if it were right (cf. 297). Otherwise, the scandal could also occur when the first marriage has been declared null, since many who will witness that couple partaking of Communion will probably not know of the nullity of their previous marriage. *Also, they would not be able to know whether the couple is living as brother and sister, or not.* The objective fault is not 'manifest,' in the sense that it cannot be confirmed from the outside, and everyone deserves the benefit of the doubt. Let us leave that matter—in fact, unverifiable—in the intimacy of the discernment of the faithful with their pastor."

8. *AL* 299.

conclusions match the Holy Father's. These criteria seem to shed even more light on this topic:

> It may be convenient *that an eventual access to the sacraments be done in a reserved manner*, especially when conflicting situations are foreseen. But at the same time, we must not fail to accompany the community so that it grows in a spirit of understanding and acceptance, *without implying confusion in the teaching of the Church about the indissolubility of marriage*.⁹

By saying that this access to the sacraments should be done in a reserved manner, the Buenos Aires bishops (and, therefore, the pope) seem to be talking precisely about the "internal forum" solution¹⁰ as a way to avoid scandal.¹¹

❖❖❖

There is, however, another part of *Amoris Laetitia* that may help clarify even further: the much contentious footnote opening the possibility of communion to some divorced and remarried couples:

> In certain cases, this can include the help of the sacraments. . . . I would also point out that the Eucharist "*is not a prize for the perfect, but a powerful medicine and nourishment for the weak*."¹²

This draws attention to a very troublesome problem in the church today, especially among Catholics who are well-read and knowledgeable about the faith: If one knows that only people who are not in mortal sin can receive the Eucharist, one may start to associate communion with a state of righteousness. From there on, one may begin to deduce that a presence in the communion line means a validation of this person's life.¹³

9. Bishops of the Pastoral Region of Buenos Aires, "Carta del Santo Padre Francisco."

10. The internal forum, in fact, is explicitly mentioned by Pope Francis in *AL* 300: "What we are speaking of is a process of accompaniment and discernment which "guides the faithful to an awareness of their situation before God. Conversation with the priest, *in the internal forum*, contributes to the formation of a correct judgment on what hinders the possibility of a fuller participation in the life of the Church and on what steps can foster it and make it grow."

11. For more information on the internal forum, see Smith, "The Internal Forum." Travers also proposes the possibility of taking communion "in a parish where the person is not known" ("*Amoris Laetitia* and Canon 915," 383).

12. *AL* n351.

13. As an example, see Olson, "Three Reasons for Excluding Obstinate Sinners."

The medicinal aspect of the Eucharist has been lost in our collective minds. The Eucharist is no longer viewed as a vehicle of grace to help us live a better life, and to help us in our daily struggles with sin. Maybe in theory this is still acknowledged. Yet in practice it is no longer perceived as so. For how can someone assume that taking the Eucharist is a validation of one's life if someone views the Eucharist as a way to improve, as a help to grow into a holier state? Actively seeking a change for the better always implies that the current state is not being validated as acceptable.

In recent years, these knowledgeable Catholics' worldview has shifted to such a degree that orthodoxy seems to mandate a kind of Eucharistic policing of the communion lines.[14] These orthodox faithful then self-ascribe to themselves the role of protecting the Eucharist from being taken from those whom they think unworthy, even if they have no ecclesiastical authority to do so.

And herein lies a great problem, for the very seed of scandal is found in this mindset. It is only by judging the interior dispositions of another person's soul from his external acts that we are able to get scandalized. If we saw the Eucharist as a way to help remedy the interior sinfulness of the divorced and civilly remarried people, and not as a reward for their external actions, then we would have no trouble in accepting their access to communion, provided they are not in mortal sin (and we would have no way to know that, for we cannot judge the state of another person's soul).

❉❉❉

What about the scandal for the other faithful, i.e., those not as knowledgeable in the faith? We are living in an age of profound lack of religious education among the pews. Many of them do not view divorce and remarriage as intrinsically evil. Is there concern that they will be scandalized by the implementation of *Amoris Laetitia*?

According to my experience, the fear of scandal among these Catholics is overrated among orthodox ranks. First of all, since Western and urban settings have lost the sense of community and become massified and depersonalized, many churchgoers have no idea who the person standing beside them is, let alone their marital status.

---

14. Olson, "Three Reasons for Excluding Obstinate Sinners."

# The Problem of Scandal

But most importantly, most people who go to communion nowadays have no idea what the Eucharist really is,[15] or how solemn this sacrament is. In my experience, they will go into the communion lines, without any conscience exam or without undergoing the sacrament of penance.[16] They do this out of a sense of misguided liturgical duty.[17] They think this is what is expected of them to do at that time: they see everyone else doing it, and that this is the time to do it, so they do it.

This is a very sad state of affairs, but there is, at least, a very small consolation: these people are not in danger of getting scandalized when they see a civilly divorced and remarried person taking communion. Many will be astonished to know that the church does not allow communion to people in those circumstances.[18] This will come, in fact, as a surprise to many divorced and remarried Catholics, who have no idea about the ban themselves.[19]

In this respect, papal critics are really approaching the problem from the wrong angle. Yes, they should be catechizing the masses about the church's unchanging teaching on the indissolubility of marriage. This is especially important in light of the crisis of values and family we are experiencing today (I will explore these social transformations with more detail in chapter 10 of this book). However, they should *also* be

---

15. Smith, "Just One-Third of U.S. Catholics Agree with Their Church That Eucharist Is Body, Blood of Christ."

16. Travers, "*Amoris Laetitia* and Canon 915," 413: "Those of us who are pastors know, of course, that even before the publication of AL Chapter Eight large numbers of Catholics in irregular marriage situations have completely ignored the previous discipline, receiving the Sacraments. . . . For such persons, AL Chapter Eight is hardly a 'blip' on their 'radar screens', if they are aware of it at all, and will have no significant effect on their behavior."

17. See Benedict XVI, "The Church and the Scandal of sexual abuse": "The way people often simply receive the Holy Sacrament of communion as a matter of course shows that many see communion as a purely ceremonial gesture."

18. This happened in Portugal when the Cardinal-Patriarch of Lisbon issued his own guidelines on how to implement *Amoris Laetitia*. Those guidelines, while faithful to the mind and will of the pope, mentioned the "brother and sister" option for some divorced and remarried couples. This generated controversy, and the media handled it as if the cardinal had introduced new restrictions, not as if he was enforcing the previous *status quo*. Francis quelled this controversy by sending a letter to the cardinal, praising his guidelines, as we shall see in chapter 17 of this book. See Faria, "Católicos recasados devem ser aconselhados a abster-se de ter relações sexuais."

19. See Longley, "*Amoris Laetitia*: Pope Francis has created confusion where we needed clarity." Referring to the previous sacramental discipline, Longley affirms: "I have never heard of a parish applying it."

catechizing the masses about the true meaning of the Eucharist. And they should be doing this also by instructing people about how to view the Eucharist as a medicine and not as a reward, so as to minimize scandal when sinners receive communion.

If one of the main reasons to withhold communion is the possibility of scandal, then a way to deal with this is to minimize the possibility of scandal. This way, we can help people receive the benefits of sacramental grace, especially if they are in a situation that makes it hard for them to live according to the gospel mandates. Catholics should be overjoyed that any person who is not in mortal sin is able to receive the host, and should strive as much as possible to maximize attendance to this sacrament. For the Eucharist will indeed be a privileged source of grace for the sinner to stop sinning—which is the point. Knowledgeable Catholics should, therefore, endeavor to remove hurdles that may preclude sinners from the Eucharist, especially if (as in the case of scandal) those obstacles lie not on the sinners themselves, but on others. Apologists should take this opportunity: since most uncatechized Catholics are a kind of a clean slate, they should be instructed also against the error of seeing the Eucharist as a prize for the perfect and not as a medicine for the weak.[20]

❄ ❄ ❄

However, this is not what papal critics have been doing. Instead of rejoicing with the possibility of sacramental help for their brothers and sisters caught up in sin, they will cling to their views of the Eucharist as a reward for good behavior. In doing so, they will push back against the apostolic exhortation's opening of communion to people who they view as in an external state of grave sin. And herein lies another great danger of scandal, often overlooked by papal critics. As Rocco Buttiglione says, there is a distinction between the scandal to the simple, and the scandal to the wise.[21] Giving communion to people in an objective state of sin is not the only way to give scandal. We give scandal whenever we push people away from the church through our public example. As the *Catechism* states:

---

20. Almeida, "*Amoris Laetitia*—reflexões," 384–85: "Since matrimony is not simply a private matter between Jesus and me, so receiving the Eucharist is not simply a private matter. It involves the whole community. So, just like the pastor must help form the conscience of the couple in question, he should also help form the conscience of the community, so as to avoid the integration of the remarried couples in a way that results in scandal."

21. Buttiglione, *Risposte amichevoli*, 95.

> *Scandal is grave when given by those who by nature or office are obliged to teach and educate others.* Jesus reproaches the scribes and Pharisees on this account: he likens them to wolves in sheep's clothing.[22]

If a divorced and remarried person is set on a course of conversion that would eventually lead him to change his life, and then desists from that course because someone with no authority has kept him from the Eucharist, when the pope has allowed it, then what happened was scandal. Furthermore, if papal critics believe that *Amoris Laetitia* may create scandal by undermining the church's teaching on the indissolubility of marriage, why are they propagating this erroneous interpretation of the exhortation? They should be clearing that misconception, instead of undermining the whole document and/or papal primacy in the process of defending the church's doctrine on marriage.

There are, however, even other ways to create scandal. The disobedience against the pope has spun completely out of control in certain places, especially on social media. Commenters who were once Catholicism's staunch defenders now wield arguments to undermine papal authority,[23] insult the pope,[24] liken him to the Antichrist,[25] and spread a number of conspiracy theories against him.[26] Who would want, when on the fence, to convert to a church like this? I personally know of people who have not crossed the Tiber because of the division they witness inside the church on this issue. Not because of the doctrine, mind you, but because of the division.

I have also seen liberal Catholics denounce the double-standard of those who previously viewed the pope as the ultimate authority and who used to put down others as "cafeteria Catholics" for not changing deep-seated views incongruent with papal teachings.[27] Those liberal Catholics will point to conservatives and say to the uncatechized masses: "See? They also disobey the pope when they disagree with him! All their words

---

22. *CCC* 2285.

23. I again refer the reader to my article "Sola Traditio," published on *WPI*.

24. As an example, see Wynne, "Viganò Champions Virgin Mary After Pope Francis Smear."

25. Doody, "Bishop Who Called Pope Francis the Antichrist Defies Polish Church Order to Stay Silent."

26. These are documented at *WPI* in the "Conspiracy Theories Archives."

27. As an example, see Reese, "Comment: Francis Opens the Door to 'Cafeteria' Catholics." See also Ramos, "Conservatives In Their Pushback."

about assent to papal teaching were just politically motivated! Turn the tables on them and watch them act just the same!"

This, too, is scandal.

Papal detractors who loudly proclaim their criticisms on social media, or who broadcast them on Catholic television, or who sell it through books, are committing the sin of scandal, a grave matter per the *Catechism*.[28] It is, therefore, extremely ironic for them to argue that we should turn other people away from the Eucharist on account of grave matter. As Pope Francis warns us in *Amoris Laetitia*:

> The Eucharist demands that we be members of the one body of the Church. *Those who approach the Body and Blood of Christ may not wound that same Body by creating scandalous distinctions and divisions among its members.* This is what it means to "discern" the body of the Lord, to acknowledge it with faith and charity both in the sacramental signs and in the community; *those who fail to do so eat and drink judgment against themselves.*[29]

Public critics should heed this cautionary warning from their pope and change their attitudes and behaviors. Jesus warns us about judging others, for the same measure we mete out shall be used to measure us.[30] He also tells us that we should remove the beam from our eye before trying to remove the mote from our brother's eye.[31] Finally, he says:

> It is impossible that scandals should not come: but woe to him through whom they come. It were better for him, that a millstone were hanged about his neck, and he cast into the sea, than that he should scandalize one of these little ones.[32]

Those who invoke scandal as a reason to oppose *Amoris Laetitia* should be very wary of giving scandal themselves. I invite them to reconsider their position, or at least, not to make it public in order to avoid the real and grave possibility of scandal.

---

28. See *CCC* 2284–85.
29. *AL* 186.
30. Matt 7:1–2.
31. Matt 7:3–5.
32. Luke 17:1–2.

CHAPTER 9

The *Dubia*

WHEN WE ARE DEALING with the subject of clarifications of *Amoris Laetitia*, the *dubia* are inevitably bound to come up. On September 19, 2016, four cardinals (Carlo Caffarra, Joachim Meisner, Raymond Burke, and Walter Brandmüller) sent a letter to Pope Francis with five questions (*dubia* in Latin, singular *dubium*) in order to clarify the true meaning of the apostolic exhortation's eighth chapter. Having received no answer from the Holy Father, they made their initiative public on November 14, 2016.[1]

From that point onward, the cry for an answer to the *dubia* has become commonplace, especially in sectors of the church which do not seem to agree with the interpretation laid out in previous chapters.[2] At the date of the publication of this book, the pope remains silent on this matter, and has chosen to clarify his document through alternative venues: namely, by publishing the Buenos Aires criteria in the *AAS*, as previously mentioned.

A question, therefore, should be raised: are these *dubia* really such an effective way to clarify *Amoris Laetitia*, that they need necessarily be answered?

---

1. Pentin, "Full Text and Explanatory Notes of Cardinals' Questions on '*Amoris Laetitia*.'"

2. As an example, see O'Connell, "Dissenters' Conference on '*Amoris Laetitia*' Hears Call for an Answer to the *Dubia*."

What Are Dubia?

According to the cardinals themselves, *dubia* are "formal questions brought before the pope and to the Congregation for the Doctrine of the Faith asking for clarifications on particular issues concerning doctrine or practice."[3] In this "age-old practice," the inquiries are "worded in a way that requires a 'Yes' or 'No' answer, without theological argumentation."[4]

This format is meant to ensure clarity. If theological argumentation was used to answer these questions, a situation could arise where the doubt would not be resolved, namely if the answer was worded in an equivocal or confusing way. In this sense, an unequivocal "yes" or "no" answer must be given.[5]

A cursory search on the Vatican website features several CDF answers to many *dubia* throughout the years.[6] In all of them, we can see that questions were indeed answered unequivocally in the affirmative or in the negative, thereby confirming the format postulated by the cardinals.

Of course, it can be argued that simply replying in the affirmative or in the negative may not dispel confusion, but actually increase it, if the reasons for those answers are not explained. This is why many of these answers do not stand alone, but are accompanied with a commentary from the CDF, either as an explanation after the answers,[7] or as a separate document.[8] However, these explanations are not inserted into the actual answers, which must be answered simply "yes" or "no" (at most, with a very brief paragraph).[9]

---

3. Pentin, "Full Text and Explanatory Notes of Cardinals' Questions on '*Amoris Laetitia*.'"

4. Pentin, "Full Text and Explanatory Notes of Cardinals' Questions on '*Amoris Laetitia*.'"

5. I have seen three excellent attempts to answer the *dubia*, but they require some theological argumentation. I highly recommend López, "Para comprender *Amoris Laetitia*," 436–39; Buttiglione, *Risposte amichevoli*, 171–75; and Almeida, "*Amoris Laetitia*—reflexões," 377–82.

6. See the complete list of documents at http://www.vatican.va/roman_curia/congregations/cfaith/doc_doc_index.htm.

7. As an example, see CDF, "Concerning 'Uterine Isolation.'"

8. Also as an example, see CDF, "Concerning the Reply."

9. See CDF, "Responses to Certain Questions."

The Wording of the Dubia

One thing we can gather from reading previous *dubia* published by the CDF before Francis's election is how they were formulated in a way that sheds clarity at the issues at hand. The wording of these questions is meant to understand the mind and will of the pope on what is being questioned. This is, in fact, the self-evident purpose of this process: to ascertain, in certain doubtful aspects, what the true doctrine or practice of the church is, by taking recourse to the judgment of the Vicar of Christ. The *dubia* cardinals acknowledge this, for they themselves say: "The great Tradition of the Church teaches us that the way out of situations like this is recourse to the Holy Father, asking the Apostolic See to resolve those doubts, which are the cause of disorientation and confusion."[10]

Given what I explained above, let us then proceed to examine a *dubium* posed in relation to *Amoris Laetitia*:

> 1) It is asked whether, following the affirmations of *Amoris Laetitia* (300–305), it has now become possible to grant absolution in the sacrament of penance to, and thus to admit to holy Communion, a person who, while bound by a valid marital bond, lives together with a different person *more uxorio* without fulfilling the conditions provided for by *Familiaris Consortio*, 84, and subsequently reaffirmed by *Reconciliatio et Paenitentia*, 34, and *Sacramentum Caritatis*, 29. Can the expression "in certain cases" found in Note 351 (305) of the exhortation *Amoris Laetitia* be applied to divorced persons who are in a new union and who continue to live *more uxorio*?[11]

In this *dubium*, the cardinals ask whether *Amoris Laetitia*'s sacramental provisions apply to divorced persons who are in a new union and who continue to live *more uxorio*. We already have gathered, from chapter 4 of this book, that the answer to this question is clearly "yes," albeit in only some cases. However, please note how the *dubium* is worded in a way in which an affirmative answer seems to conflict with other authoritative church documents from previous pontificates, namely *Familiaris*

---

10. Pentin, "Full Text and Explanatory Notes of Cardinals' Questions on '*Amoris Laetitia*.'"

11. Pentin, "Full Text and Explanatory Notes of Cardinals' Questions on '*Amoris Laetitia*.'"

Consortio, Reconciliatio et Paenitentia and *Sacramentum Caritatis*[12] (I will devote the next section of this book to showing why this is not so).

A similar pattern emerges in every single one of the other questions. *Dubium* three contrasts *Amoris Laetitia* with canon law and with the Gospel itself, whereas *dubia* two, four, and five try to do the same with specific paragraphs from John Paul II's encyclical *Veritatis Splendor* (which are always qualified as "based on Scripture and Tradition").

This is compounded by the fact that, when the cardinals made the *dubia* public, they attached to them an explanatory note where the correct interpretation of *Amoris Laetitia* (as we have seen in chapters 4 and 5) seems to be refuted by those same authoritative references. For example, regarding *dubium* 1, it is said that (emphasis as in the original):

> It would seem that admitting to Communion those of the faithful who are separated or divorced from their rightful spouse and who have entered a new union in which they live with someone else as if they were husband and wife would mean for the Church to teach by her practice one of the following affirmations about marriage, human sexuality, and the nature of the sacraments:
>
> • A divorce does not dissolve the marriage bond, and the partners to the new union are not married. However, *people who are not married can under certain circumstances legitimately engage in acts of sexual intimacy*.
> • *A divorce dissolves the marriage bond*. People who are not married cannot legitimately engage in sexual acts. The divorced and remarried are legitimate spouses and their sexual acts are lawful marital acts.
> • A divorce does not dissolve the marriage bond, and the partners to the new union are not married. People who are not married cannot legitimately engage in sexual acts, so that the divorced and civilly remarried live in a situation of habitual, public, objective and grave sin. However, admitting persons to the Eucharist does not mean for the Church to approve their public state of life; the faithful can approach the Eucharistic table even with consciousness of grave sin, and receiving absolution in the sacrament of penance does not always require the purpose of amending one's life. *The sacraments, therefore, are*

---

12. Almeida, "*Amoris Laetitia*—reflexões," 378: "The question is specious. It is no accident that the cardinals asked Francis to limit himself to answering 'yes' or 'no,' a tactic very similar of the Pharisees towards Jesus, and precisely in the question that allowed Jesus to teach on the topic of matrimony (cf. Matt 19:3)."

detached from life: Christian rites and worship are on a completely different sphere than the Christian moral life.[13]

In writing this way, it seems like the Cardinals are not submitting *dubia*, but actually providing a point-by-point refutation. Please note that all the implications (in italics) conflict with church doctrine. We already know that implication number one is false, since there is no way an intrinsically evil act can be done "legitimately" (we are discussing subjective culpability, not the objectively evil nature of the sin). Implication number two is also false, since nowhere does *Amoris Laetitia* sanction divorce. As for implication number three, it has been worded in a way that is also misleading: no one is defending that the sacraments are detached from life, but rather that Christians who are not in mortal sin can receive communion, as is usual practice in many other sins.

One day after making the *dubia* public, Cardinal Burke gave an interview to the *National Catholic Register*. In this interview, the cardinal was asked what would happen if the Holy Father "fails to give the clarification of the Church's teaching that you hope to achieve." Burke replied:

> Then we would have to address that situation. There is, in the Tradition of the Church, the practice of correction of the Roman Pontiff. It is something that is clearly quite rare. *But if there is no response to these questions, then I would say that it would be a question of taking a formal act of correction of a serious error.*[14]

Obviously, in this context, an answer of "yes" or "no" would not help clarify, but would actually increase confusion. In this case, an answer in accordance with the pope's manifest mind and will would be contrasted with other parts of church doctrine in the terms defined according to the *dubia*, and eventually trigger a "formal correction."[15] This would cause confusion, not only regarding the true interpretation of *Amoris Laetitia*, but also about the role of the papacy itself.

---

13. Pentin, "Full Text and Explanatory Notes of Cardinals' Questions on '*Amoris Laetitia*.'"

14. Pentin, "Cardinal Burke on *Amoris Laetitia* Dubia." See López, "Para comprender *Amoris Laetitia*," 435: "Some declarations, complementary to the letter, seem to be clothed in a threatening tone. Cardinal Burke affirmed that if Francis did not answer his questions within a certain deadline, the four cardinals would issue a 'formal act of correction' to the successor of Peter."

15. For a very interesting article about how narrow the limits are for a correction of the pope, see Baker, "Is it Virtuous to Criticize the Pope?"

Making the Dubia *Public*

Another characteristic of *dubia* from previous pontificates is that they were made public by the CDF, not by the inquirers. I have no knowledge of such *dubia* being made public by the questioners before the answers were published by the CDF. If they were, they certainly did not create such an impact in the media as the *Amoris Laetitia dubia*.

The four cardinals' private letter to Pope Francis, containing the *dubia*, is dated September 19, 2016. The *dubia* were made public on November 14, 2016. This means that the cardinals gave the pope and the CDF less than two months to answer. We are dealing with a universal church, with a worldwide reach and a wide array of concerns. Was a two month deadline reasonable?

Let us examine some precedents. On July 11, 2005, the United States Conference of Catholic Bishops sent two *dubia* to the CDF concerning some bioethical aspects on artificial nutrition and hydration.[16] This came in the wake of a highly controversial case: Terri Schiavo, a woman in an irreversible persistent vegetative state, had been removed from her feeding tube, an act which precipitated her death in March 31, 2005.[17] This situation gathered considerable attention, both nationally and abroad, and was quickly picked up by right-to-death movements trying to capitalize on it to further their political agenda.[18] Certainly, the notoriety of such a case would demand a quick response to these crucial *dubia*. Yet, they were answered by the CDF only on August 1, 2007,[19] more than two years after they were issued.

Other examples exist: on July 2, 1982, Cardinal Silvio Oddi issued five *dubia* on the interpretation of the decree *Ecclesiae Pastorum*, which were answered only on July 7, 1983—one year later.[20] A much quicker example was an answer to a November 16, 1966, letter of a Cleveland chaplain, which came on March 1, 1967: an astonishing three and a half months.[21]

A more bizarre case is the one involving Archbishop Marcel Lefebvre. This bishop became the most visible face of the opposition to Vatican

---

16. CDF, "Commentary."
17. Koch, "The Challenge of Terri Schiavo."
18. Koch, "The Challenge of Terri Schiavo."
19. See CDF, "Responses to Certain Questions."
20. CDF, "Replies to Questions."
21. CDF, "Epistola ad Episcopum Clevelandensum."

II,[22] having earned the displeasure and correction of Pope St. Paul VI. In 1970, he founded the International Priestly Society of St. Pius X (SSPX),[23] a fraternal order of priests devoted to preserving Catholicism as it was practiced before the council. The SSPX was canonically suppressed in 1975, and the archbishop was suspended *a divinis*.[24] Yet Lefebvre kept the society functioning, in open rebellion against the pope's stipulations.

On November 6, 1985, Lefebvre issued thirty-nine *dubia* about the teachings on religious liberty, as defined in the Vatican II declaration *Dignitatis Humanae*.[25] A reply from an anonymous member of the CDF (or Cardinal Ratzinger, then prefect of the CDF, according to some sources) was sent to him on March 9, 1987.[26] For all the urgency to address one of the most visible wounds in the post-conciliar church at the time, the CDF took more than one year to reply. I will come back to these Lefebvrian *dubia* shortly.

Returning to the five *Amoris Laetitia dubia*, we should consider not only the timing, but also the way in which they were made public.[27] They were released to several Catholic news outlets in various languages around the world, all at the same time.

Can we assume the cardinals were trying to pressure the pope to answer in a certain way? We could only answer such a question if we had a window to their soul. I do not, and, therefore, must assume the most

---

22. Vere, "Canonical History of the Lefebvrite Schism": "Defiant in their belief that the Second Vatican Council had undermined the Church during the post-conciliar era, Archbishop Lefebvre and his followers had come to believe that a grave crisis infected the Church.... Lefebvre pursued an active role at the Second Vatican Council, often being identified by various participants and observers as a cornerstone of the ultra-conservative camp."

23. Vere, "Canonical History of the Lefebvrite Schism."

24. Vere, "Canonical History of the Lefebvrite Schism."

25. Lefebvre, *Religious Liberty Questioned*.

26. This CDF reply has not been made public in the official Vatican website. It was a private letter, and we know of its existence because it was leaked by sources close to the SSPX. A French account of this reply can be read at *La crise intégriste*, "Réponses de La Congrégation Pour La Doctrine de La Foi Aux *Dubia* Présentés Par Mgr Lefebvre." A Portuguese translation is also available: Ratzinger, "Respostas Às *Dubia*."

27. López, "Para comprender *Amoris Laetitia*," 435: "The letter of the Cardinals is certainly cordial. Notwithstanding, it is regrettable that they made it public, since it seemed that it had been originally written as a private letter. On many *occasions, when an originally private letter is made public without the recipient's approval, one commits a grave moral error. Worse yet, it is not strange that taking recourse to these media resources can be construed as a way to exert pressure.*"

charitable interpretation. The cardinals justify their decision to make the *dubia* public thus: "The Holy Father has decided not to respond. We have interpreted his sovereign decision as an invitation to continue the reflection and the discussion, calmly and with respect. And so we are informing the entire people of God about our initiative, offering all of the documentation. . . . We hope that no one will judge us unjustly, as adversaries of the Holy Father and people devoid of mercy. What we have done and are doing derives from the deep collegial affection that unites us to the pope, and from an impassioned concern for the good of the faithful."[28]

Be that as it may, and whether the cardinals intended for it or not, the fact remains that as soon as they were made public, the *dubia* took on a life of their own, metastasizing outside the boundaries set down by the cardinals in their letter and into the context of social media strife, as I will proceed to explain.

The Misuse of the Dubia

Since the *dubia* have been made public, they have been used by papal critics on social media as a way to challenge or avoid *Amoris Laetitia* and the clarification provided by the pope on this matter. Thus, instead of serving as a way of clarification—as they were purported to be—they have become an obstacle to said clarification.

This obviously does not mean that everyone who wants the *dubia* answered is acting in bad faith. There are people who are actually confused by *Amoris Laetitia*, whether this confusion arises from the exhortation itself or from negative misinformation being spread by critical sources. These Catholics would certainly want the *dubia* answered as a way to resolve their doubts. However, we must also be attentive to the problems caused by the *dubia*, especially when they are invoked by some people who use them in flawed ways. Stephen Walford warns us against these problems, in an open letter directed at the *dubia* cardinals:

> You may or may not be aware that there is a growing section of traditionalists and even some conservative Catholics who see you as the standard bearers for the rejection of this papacy. I know from experience that some of it is deeply troubling. The

---

28. Pentin, "Full Text and Explanatory Notes of Cardinals' Questions on '*Amoris Laetitia*.'"

abuse from many, including those who run websites and Traditionalist blogs aimed at the Holy Father and those who are loyal to him, is nothing short of satanic. You are their role models and that is an intolerable situation. In reality, there is no confusion but only outright rejection and defiance towards the legitimate Pope and his magisterial teachings. If all the Cardinals had accepted and defended Pope Francis's clear teaching, there would have been no fuel for the dissenting fire.[29]

This problem must be addressed, or otherwise we risk allowing the resistance to *Amoris Laetitia* to feed off itself. From my years long experience in online debates, there are five ways in which the *dubia* can be used to undermine *Amoris Laetitia*. We should be mindful of these five errors, lest they become a hurdle for clarification on this issue.

First, the *dubia* can be used to shut down debate. Sometimes, when discussing *Amoris Laetitia*, the critic will reply that he cannot give assent to it, because it is unclear what the pope taught. If you proceed to clarify the meaning of the document to this person, he will often retort that this is just the opinion of the apologist, but not an official reading.[30] Sometimes, the only thing the apologist does is quote the Buenos Aires criteria verbatim, since the pope defined them as the only possible interpretation. But that is not enough, according to the critic.[31] It does not matter whether

29. Walford, "Open Letter to the Four *Dubia* Cardinals." See also López, "Para comprender *Amoris Laetitia*," 435: "I ask myself, are the cardinals unaware that their questions, now made public, directly or indirectly strengthen those who for years have suspected of Paul VI, John Paul II, Benedict XVI and the Second Vatican Council? Are they unaware that some sectors more associated with fantastic conspiracy theories, to ideological conservatisms alien to the Gospel, to moralism—so criticized by Pope Ratzinger—are celebrating their stance? Maybe they are unaware. Maybe they undervalue it. Or maybe they simply heartily desire to extinguish 'doubts' and are trying to get closer to the Pope with an impetus to learn, not to question the Magisterium."

30. O'Reilly, "*Amoris Laetitia* and the Confusion of Those Contradicting the Magisterium of John Paul II": "No such history supports any discipline suggested by Mr. Walford or a Walfordian *Amoris Laetitia*; indeed it might arguably be asserted of Pope Francis that not only has he not 'repeated' his doctrine, but that he has not as of yet even affirmed it once himself. That is, due to his failure to affirm the nature of his teaching as requested in the *Dubia*." This author, in fact, has the habit of calling "Walfordian interpretation" to the interpretation favored by the pope, so as to make it seem like it is only Stephen Walford's personal opinion, robbing it of its legitimate authority.

31. See Montagna, "Cardinal Burke Makes 'Final Plea' for Clarity to Pope Francis on *Dubia* Anniversary": "Contrary to what some have claimed, we cannot consider the Pope's letter to the bishops of the region of Buenos Aires, written shortly before receiving the *dubia* and containing comments on the bishops' pastoral guidelines, an adequate response to the questions posed."

the pope has clarified the document or not: it will only be really clarified when the pope answers the *dubia*. The pope not only needs to clarify, he needs to clarify in a pre-specified way.[32] Since the pope has not done so, the critic will feel justified in ignoring the pope's actual clarification. In other words, instead of clarifying *Amoris Laetitia*, the *dubia* have become a way to hinder clarification.

This reasoning can also be employed on other fronts besides the *Amoris Laetitia* debate. When the pope makes a speech or any kind of intervention his critics disagree with, it is not unusual to read in the comment section someone asking, "Answer the *dubia!*"[33] In other words, the pope is supposedly not free to act or teach something until he complies with their requests on an unrelated issue. This, in fact, hinders the Holy Father's mission and freedom to teach.

Second, the *dubia* have been used to propagate many incorrect notions about the pope and his primacy. I have heard people argue that, as long as Francis does not answer the *dubia*, then *Amoris Laetitia* is not official or magisterial.[34] Or that, until he answers the *dubia*, *Amoris Laetitia* is just his personal opinion.[35] This is not correct. For example, *Ecclesiae Pastorum* was not placed on hold between 1982 and 1983 while Cardinal Oddi awaited for an answer to his *dubia* about this document. In fact, since most of the previous *dubia* were not made public until after

---

32. Montagna, "Cardinal Burke Makes 'Final Plea' for Clarity to Pope Francis on *Dubia* Anniversary."

33. One such example happened on Twitter on May 23, 2020. Father John LoCoco tweeted about the uncanny coincidence between Pope Francis's extraordinary *Urbi et Orbi* blessing on March 27, 2020, and the subsequent drop of incidence of COVID-19 cases in Italy. A user named Steve Dallas then made the following comment: "If the bishop of Rome has all this time to perform miracles, why can't he answer the *Dubia*?"

34. When *LifeSiteNews* tweeted an article titled "Pope Francis: *Amoris Laetitia* is 'the Magisterium of the Church' on divorced and remarried," on December 7, 2019, a Twitter user named Gerald Baggot, commented: "Can it be fairly said that it is Magisterium when it is subject to an unanswered dubia?" Another user, named Julie Krezmien replied: "No. It's proof it is not magisterial. 3 years + 3 mo, still waiting. Silence proves errors. #Dubia."

35. I have even seen people making an argument that the pope was canonically obliged to answer the *dubia*, something that is explicitly contradicted by actual canon law. See canon 331: "The office uniquely committed by the Lord to Peter, the first of the Apostles, and to be transmitted to his successors, abides in the Bishop of the Church of Rome. He is the head of the College of Bishops, the Vicar of Christ, and the Pastor of the universal Church here on earth. *Consequently, by virtue of his office, he has supreme, full, immediate, and universal ordinary power in the Church, and he can always freely exercise this power.*"

they were answered, a Catholic would never know if he should assent to a certain papal teaching or not, because he would not know whether a *dubium* would be awaiting a reply from the CDF or not.

The pope need only teach in his official capacity as the successor of Peter. Whether a *dubium* is awaiting an answer or not is beside the point. An answer to a *dubium* is meant to clarify an authoritative teaching, not to confer authority on the teaching itself. A person in good faith can ask *dubia* to better understand what the pope is saying, but the *dubia* cannot be used in a way that would disrupt the pope's teachings and official acts themselves. Doing so is a distortion of their purpose. It would mean that, contrary to what the *Catechism* says, the pope could not exercise his full, supreme, universal power over the church unhindered,[36] since the *dubia* would take precedence over him. Also, this could backfire. For example, a liberal bishop could theoretically prevent *Humanae Vitae* from being binding by continuously asking *dubia* about it over and over again.

Third, the *dubia* have bred the "clarity vs. confusion" dichotomy, so much abused when discussing Francis's pontificate. According to the *dubia* cardinals, they were asking for "clarification," since they had noted "a grave disorientation and great confusion" about certain church matters. From that point on, it has become commonplace to argue that the pope is "unclear" and promotes "confusion." These adjectives have spilled out of the *Amoris Laetitia* debate and into every single instance of Francis's pontificate.[37] Since (as we have seen) some critics will not accept any kind of clarification besides answering the *dubia*, then the pope is not addressing "confusion" until he does answer them.[38] This means that the pope's clarification, and the interpretation he seems to favor on the implementation of *Amoris Laetitia*, gets labeled as "confusion."[39] Ironi-

---

36. *CCC* 882; *Code of Canon Law*, c. 331.

37. As an example, see Kilpatrick, "Tumult in the Church: Is the Confusion Intentional?"

38. Seifert, "The Church After *Amoris Laetitia*": "In my view, all other Cardinals, bishops, and all Catholics should support the four (now three living) Cardinals and ask the Pope, together with the *dubia* Cardinals, to give a final clear and unambiguous answer to these *dubia*, an answer that might restore clarity and truth, and dispel the immense confusion that reigns now and which nobody who has eyes to see and a mind to think, can deny. Not the *dubia*, but not answering them in the truth and with unambiguous clarity, sows distrust in the Pope and confusion."

39. See Montagna, "Cardinal Burke Makes 'Final Plea' for Clarity to Pope Francis on *Dubia* Anniversary."

cally, it is not unusual to find the word "confusion" being used to spread confusion about Francis's teachings.

Besides the clarity vs. confusion dichotomy, the *dubia* have also bred a fourth mistake: the "just asking questions"[40] trope. The *dubia* are questions that have, in effect, created hurdles to the implementation of *Amoris Laetitia*. So some papal critics have started challenging it further by "simply asking questions." In fact, many times, asking questions is not needed at all. When confronted with a refutation, the critic can equivocate his position by claiming he was not affirming anything, only asking questions, even if a cursory search of his previous comments does not yield any question mark whatsoever.

Finally, it is not unusual to find people asking the *dubia* in one breath and answering them in the other. Often, they will say something like "Of course the pope could easily answer; here, let me show you what he should answer."[41] When he does so, the critic cannot claim to be confused, otherwise he would not know how to answer. He is, in fact, not confused about what the church teaches (or should teach, in his opinion), but rather thinks that *others* are the ones who are confused and the pope should clarify by setting the *others* right.

This is, again, a misuse of the *dubia*. These were meant for a person who actually feels confused about the pope's intentions on a certain doctrine or practice. This person asks questions in order to better submit to the pope's manifest mind and will. But the critics do not seem to use the *Amoris Laetitia dubia* that way. Since, for them, the "correct answer" to the first *dubium* invariably conflicts with the Buenos Aires criteria, the "clarification" they seek would, in effect, be less of a clarification and more of a retraction.

---

40. Lawler, "The Rhetorical Strategy to Debunk the *Dubia*": "If you want to push the argument further, accuse the four cardinals of spreading confusion. They say that *Amoris Laetitia* is the source of the confusion; let's take the offensive, and steal that argument away from them. Remember how, in high school, your teacher said, 'There's no such thing as a stupid question?' Forget that! . . . Especially if you are not a bishop—and therefore will probably not be seen as an authority figure in the Church—act astonished that anyone would dare to question what a Roman Pontiff has written. Never mind that the four cardinals are only asking questions."

41. The most notable example is Cardinal Walter Brandmüller, one of the *dubia* cardinals, providing the "correct" answer to the *dubia* he himself issued. See Hickson, "Cardinal Brandmüller on How the *Dubia* Should Be Answered."

Whether the Dubia *Should Be Answered*

Of course, given these five ways the *dubia* have derailed the debate around *Amoris Laetitia* (and around all of Francis's pontificate), one may be tempted to argue: Maybe the pope should answer the *dubia* fast and be done with it. If the pope answered the *dubia*, then he would theoretically void the critics of these arguments.

Nevertheless, answering the *dubia* in this environment is not as innocuous as it might seem. As I said, the *dubia* should not have been made public in the way they were, and we have been experiencing the bitter fruits of this oversight since then. Answering the *dubia* in this context could be seen as validating this way of acting. This could backfire severely in the future, even against those who are now the *dubia*'s fiercest defenders. Whether the cardinals intended for this to happen or not, the fact of the matter is that the *dubia* have been exploited to undermine a magisterial document. In this sense, it is not unthinkable that a future cardinal or bishop could, knowing full well how the *Amoris Laetitia dubia* played out, try to do the same to pressure a pope in illegitimate ways. We cannot validate that by granting these *dubia* an answer (which would imply they were legitimately posed).

Still, one can argue that, prudentially, the risk of not answering the *dubia* outweighs the dangers I have mentioned before. In this case, we should ask ourselves: What good would answering the *dubia* do? Should the pope overturn the fruits of a two-year synodal process of discernment by the world's bishops in communion with the see of Peter, on account of *dubia* posed by four cardinals, especially since the concerns raised by them had already been discussed?[42]

Also, is it really certain that answering would dispel the confusion? Would the critics stand down and say "Roma locuta est"? We have precedents showing that this might not be as straightforward as it might seem at first glance:

In February 4, 2019, during his official trip to the United Arab Emirates, Pope Francis signed a joint declaration with the Grand Imam of Al Azhar, Ahmed el-Tayeb, one of the leading authorities in Muslim Sunni world, laying the groundwork for a new stage of cooperation between

---

42. In this regard, I recommend reading chapter 9 of the book *The Wounded Shepherd*, by Austen Ivereigh. It is the most detailed account of the family synods I have encountered.

Islam and Catholicism for a more fraternal and peaceful future.[43] This declaration, however, was strongly condemned by the usual papal critics, because of this isolated snippet:

> *The pluralism and the diversity of religions,* colour, sex, race, and language *are willed by God in His wisdom,* through which He created human beings.[44]

Many claimed that this statement was heterodox,[45] since they believed it affirmed that God willed other religions ("false religions") besides the Catholic faith. Deeply ingrained conspiracy theories about the pope being a freemason bent on creating a syncretic, one-world religion started to emerge in social media.[46]

During the in-flight press conference after this historical visit,[47] and since the controversy had already exploded at the time, Pope Francis clarified that the document "does not pull away one millimeter from Vatican II." This is typical of Pope Francis: while he acknowledges that there was a development ("[it is a] step forward that comes after 50 years, from the Council, that must be developed") he assures us that each development (like *Amoris Laetitia* or the *Catechism* revision on the death penalty) has been made in continuity with previous teachings.

While some papal critics simply dismissed this continuity as self-evidently impossible, some apologists took up the task of trying to find an accurate interpretative lens through which they could read this declaration in continuity with Catholic doctrine.[48] One of the justifications which gained more traction came from theologian Chad Pecknold, who made a distinction between God's active will and permissive will.[49] God

---

43. Vatican News, "Document on Human Fraternity for World Peace and Living Together."

44. Vatican News, "Document on Human Fraternity for World Peace and Living Together."

45. Montagna, "Pope Francis under Fire for Claiming 'Diversity of Religions' Is 'Willed by God.'" See also Chapman, "Arbp. Vigano: Pope Francis Is Teaching 'Blatant Heresy . . . a Terrible Blasphemy.'"

46. For example, see the replies to the article on Gloria.tv, "Viganò: Not Even The Most Optimistic Freemason Would Have Dreamed Francis' Papacy."

47. Catholic News Agency, "Full Text of Pope Francis' in-Flight Press Conference from Abu Dhabi."

48. My own attempt was published on *WPI*: "Pluralism and the will of God . . . is there another way to look at it?"

49. Farrow, "Pope Francis Signs Peace Declaration on 'Human Fraternity' with

actively willed Catholicism but he only *tolerated* (on account of man's freedom) the existence of other religions. Since everything that happens comes about through God's will, we call this tolerance of evils "God's permissive will."

In this context, during an *ad limina* visit to the Vatican, Bishop Athanasius Schneider asked Francis to clarify the meaning of this polemical passage. Schneider then relayed this information to *LifeSiteNews*, a media outlet very critical of the pope. According to him, the pope explicitly stated he could share the contents of their exchange on this point: "You can say that the phrase in question on the diversity of religions means the permissive will of God."[50]

Later on, in one of his general audiences, Pope Francis clarified even further: "Why does God allow many religions? God wanted to allow this: scholastic theologians used to refer to God's *voluntas permissiva*" (i.e., permissive will).[51]

One would think Francis had clarified his meaning, in a way considered orthodox by his detractors. After all, Bishop Schneider's interview was hailed as a victory at the time, since the title of the news item was that he had "won" a clarification. But it was not so. Two months after this, the same bishop said to the same *LifeSiteNews*:

> "Up to now, neither the pope, nor an office of the Holy See speaking in his name, have made a public correction with direct reference to the dubious passage concerning the 'diversity of religions'" in the Abu Dhabi statement, Bishop Schneider explains in an interview. . . . He insists that the correction given to him by the pope during an audience on March 1 has only a "private character," and he explains that he gave the pope on the same day a letter asking him to "rescind" the formulation on the "diversity of religions." [52]

In other words, the clarification was not enough. A retraction was needed. I do think it would not be implausible for such a thing to happen if Francis answered the *dubia*, since many critics are convinced of the heterodoxy of the Buenos Aires interpretation. So Pope Francis has

---

Grand Imam."

50. Montagna, "Exclusive: Bishop Schneider Wins Clarification on 'Diversity of Religions' from Pope Francis."

51. Francis, "General Audience of April 3, 2019."

52. Hickson, "Bp. Schneider: Pope Must Formally Correct Statement That God Wills False Religions."

adopted a position of silence instead. I have explained elsewhere why this is consistent with Francis's life history, theology, and thought.[53]

Whether the Dubia *Have Been Answered*

We now know that there may be legitimate reasons to not answer the *dubia*. However, a more bizarre query can be raised: can we not say the *dubia* have indeed been answered? Papal critics will reply: most obviously not. Of course, if by "answering the *dubia*," we mean an official "yes" or "no" answer to each of the five questions, then the critic is right: the *dubia* have not been answered. However, must *dubia* always be answered this way?

Again there is a precedent we should take into account: I once again recall the thirty-nine *dubia* issued by Archbishop Lefebvre, in defiance of the Second Vatican Council's teaching on religious freedom. When the CDF replied, it subverted the expectations: contrary to what is customary, it did not reply to the *dubia* in a "yes" or "no" fashion. Instead, it provided an extensive theological study and argumentation to address Lefebvre's concerns:

> Given the multiple aspects involved in the *dubia*, each one of them would end up in an exposition of the almost totality of doctrine on religious liberty. . . . Besides, an attempt to focus on each *dubium* would be, in many cases, insufficient. Often, the *dubia* contain apparently accessory nuances, but which are determinant for an affirmative or negative answer. Consequently, it is not just for a matter of brevity (to avoid duplications), but above all of clarity and precision, that we prefer to give a detailed answer to the fundamental points raised by the aforementioned questions.[54]

In other words, in certain delicate situations, the CDF (and, obviously therefore, the pope) may opt to reply to the *dubia* in a way that does not conform with the traditional molds. In this case, the CDF once again explained the rationale behind the controversial teaching, thereby engaging in theological argumentation—something supposedly, the *dubia* are

---

53. I recommend my article "Silence, the shield against suspicious man," published in *WPI*.

54. This is my translation of the leaked CDF letter, published in Portuguese: Ratzinger, "Respostas Às Dubia."

meant to avoid.⁵⁵ Lefebvre was understandably not pleased with this reply. In the next year, he consecrated four SSPX priests as bishops without the pope's authorization, thereby incurring automatic excommunication.⁵⁶

It seems like Pope Francis has taken a similar approach in this case. Instead of replying each *dubia* in the affirmative or in the negative, and when confronted by the cardinals with the problem of "divergent, conflicting interpretations" for his apostolic exhortation, Francis decided to restate *Amoris Laetitia* once more. He did so by making his mind and will clearly manifest by unequivocally pointing out to the Buenos Aires criteria as the only possible interpretation.⁵⁷ Any additional clarification should take this fact as the starting point.

Conclusions

The *dubia* cardinals posed their questions in order to clarify *Amoris Laetitia*'s true interpretation. Unfortunately, the *dubia* have severely failed in this regard. The cardinals affirmed that their *dubia* were an "act of justice and charity."⁵⁸ Of justice, because they professed that the Petrine ministry is the ministry of unity, and that to Peter, to the pope, belongs the service of confirming in the faith; of charity, because they said they wanted to help the pope to prevent divisions and conflicts in the church.⁵⁹ However, the *dubia* have, on the contrary, fomented disunity with the Petrine ministry, and created divisions and conflicts within the

---

55. The *dubia* cardinals explain that "What is peculiar about these inquiries is that they are worded in a way that requires a 'Yes' or 'No' answer, without theological argumentation." See Pentin, "Full Text and Explanatory Notes of Cardinals' Questions on '*Amoris Laetitia*.'"

56. Vere, "Canonical History of the Lefebvrite Schism."

57. See Fernández, "El capítulo VIII de *Amoris Laetitia*," 451: "If we are interested in knowing how the Pope himself interprets what he has written, the answer is very explicit in his commentary on the guidelines by the Bishops of the Buenos Aires Region." See also Ryan, "Weakness, and Wounded and Troubled Love," 137n14: "Again, what I have outlined above is relevant to the *dubia* of the four cardinals. A key element in any reply is the distinction between 'intrinsic evil' considered as either 'formal sin' (grave matter, full knowledge, and adequate freedom of consent) or 'material sin' (grave matter with defective knowledge and/or freedom)."

58. Pentin, "Full Text and Explanatory Notes of Cardinals' Questions on '*Amoris Laetitia*.'"

59. Pentin, "Full Text and Explanatory Notes of Cardinals' Questions on '*Amoris Laetitia*.'"

church. In other words, they have done the opposite of what they were meant to do in the first place.

The cardinals decided to make the *dubia* public because they interpreted the pope's silence as an invitation to continue the reflection and discussion, calmly and with respect.[60] Unfortunately, the *dubia* have been used as a way to shut down reflection and discussion, as a way to feed suspicion about the pope's intentions (thereby eschewing calm), and as a way to disrespect the pope.

Most importantly, far from helping clarify the meaning of *Amoris Laetitia*, the *dubia* have sowed even more confusion, since they do not allow the pope's actual clarification to thrive. In this sense, we can only conclude that the *dubia* are manifestly ineffective in achieving their end, and are showing themselves to be, in fact, extremely counterproductive. A better way to clarify the document is studying the Holy Father's manifest mind and will, either in the words and character of the apostolic exhortation itself or in his manner of speaking in other interventions of his (as I tried to show in chapters 4 and 5 of this book). Therefore, it is my humble opinion that the intent of the *dubia* would be better served if the two surviving cardinals (at the time of the publication of this book) would retract them and replace them with an unequivocal, unconditional, and public endorsement of the Buenos Aires criteria.[61] This would help clarify the document much more than answering the *dubia*.

However, since the *dubia* are already out, thereby sowing suspicion that *Amoris Laetitia* contradicts previously established teaching (namely *Familiaris Consortio*, *Veritatis Splendor*, and canon 915), I will dedicate the following section of this book to proving that these contradictions do not exist. For now, I would like to conclude with an invitation to consider the following quote from Pope St. Pius X:

---

60. Pentin, "Full Text and Explanatory Notes of Cardinals' Questions on '*Amoris Laetitia*.'"

61. See Walford, "Open Letter to the Four *Dubia* Cardinals": "I will end by humbly asking you to reconsider your position on this issue. . . . If all the Cardinals had accepted and defended Pope Francis's clear teaching, there would have been no fuel for the dissenting fire. In the desire for the Unity of the Church around Peter, it is essential to affirm the Pope has the authority—ratified in heaven—to make disciplinary changes for the good of some divorced and remarried souls, and so I ask you to bring to an end this situation by accepting the constant Tradition of the Church that Popes are free from error in matters of faith and morals and that derives from the specific prayer of Jesus himself: 'I have prayed for you that your faith may not fail' (Luke 22:32)."

When we love the Pope, there are no discussions regarding what he orders or demands, or up to what point obedience must go, and in what things he is to be obeyed; when we love the Pope, we do not say that he has not spoken clearly enough, almost as if he were forced to repeat to the ear of each one the will clearly expressed so many times not only in person, but with letters and other public documents; we do not place his orders in doubt, adding the facile pretext of those unwilling to obey—that it is not the Pope who commands, but those who surround him; we do not limit the field in which he might and must exercise his authority; we do not set above the authority of the Pope that of other persons, however learned, who dissent from the Pope, who, even though learned, are not holy, because whoever is holy cannot dissent from the Pope.[62]

---

62. Pius X, "Discorso."

Section III

A HARMONIOUS DEVELOPMENT

CHAPTER 10

The Anatomy of a Development
A Proposal

IN THE NEXT THREE CHAPTERS, I will try to show how *Amoris Laetitia* can be reconciled with a series of authoritative documents usually cited by papal critics as proof that the exhortation contradicts previous doctrine. However, before proceeding with this, I wish to make some brief reflections on how the church develops its doctrine and practice, and to propose a model that may help illustrate my points in the remainder of the book, for those who may find them unclear.

Papal critics understand how crucial this question is.[1] They argue, and rightfully so, that if the church can contradict itself, then its reliability as a divinely instituted guide would be questionable. We would never be able to determine whether the church would be teaching error or not, and would need to rely on personal interpretation to make those determinations. This, in turn, would make the church redundant, since people do not need a church for them to make their own personal interpretations on matters of faith and morals.

---

1. See Ferrara, "*Amoris Laetitia*: Anatomy of a Pontifical Debacle": "Just as God cannot contradict Himself, the Magisterium cannot contradict itself. For the Magisterium is the teaching office of the Church; it presents what the Church teaches, which is not determined by the latest utterance of the current Pope. Therefore, whatever contradicts the constant prior teaching of the Church cannot possibly belong to the Magisterium."

However, after papal critics accurately grasp this problem, they go on to make the point that the current pope is unreliable,[2] which is precisely the position we were seeking to avoid in the first place. They usually try to bypass this conundrum by appealing to the reliability of the church's tradition, by which they mean the teachings prior to the current pope's election.[3] But this does not solve the problem, for if this pope in particular is unreliable, then there is no reason to assume the previous ones were reliable. If divine protection is not enough to prevent Francis from teaching error in matters of faith and morals today, what prevents us from entertaining the thought that this failure has not started before Francis? Maybe the sedevacantists are correct in assuming the church went astray at the time of the Second Vatican Council.[4] Maybe Protestants are correct in assuming that the clerical apostasy happened at the time of Emperor Constantine.[5] Either way, to ascertain this, we would have to rely on a personal interpretation of tradition.[6] In other words, we are exactly in the place we wanted to steer clear of.

Logically, then, we must assume that Pope Francis is reliable when he teaches in matters of faith and morals. But then, if Francis seems to contradict his predecessors, does this mean the church was not reliable before Francis? Again this would not solve the problem, it would only shift it to other pontiffs. We are left to conclude that both Francis *and* his predecessors are reliable. Therefore, the contradictions between them must be reconcilable through reason, even if this is not apparent at first glance.

There are two key concepts that can be helpful with this task: first, the notion that, even if doctrine cannot contradict itself, it can develop; second, the distinction between "doctrine" and "discipline."

---

2. Ferrara, "*Amoris Laetitia*: Anatomy of a Pontifical Debacle": "Every Catholic worthy of the name has a duty to resist this attempted overthrow of the perennial Magisterium by a wayward Pope who clearly has no respect for the teaching of his own predecessors."

3. Ferrara, "*Amoris Laetitia*: Anatomy of a Pontifical Debacle."

4. "CMRI's Theological Position: The Chair of Peter Today Is Vacant," Religious Congregation of Mary Immaculate Queen.

5. "The Great Apostasy," Rome Corrupted Christianity.

6. Ferrara, "*Amoris Laetitia*: Anatomy of a Pontifical Debacle": "Nor can it be argued that the faithful have no capacity to recognize these contradictions but rather must blindly presume that somehow they do not exist. This is the Catholic Church, whose deposit of Faith is objectively knowable, not a gnostic sect headed by the Oracle of Rome, who announces what 'Jesus wants' today."

Starting with the concept of doctrinal development, we must distinguish between two different perspectives: discontinuity and actual development.

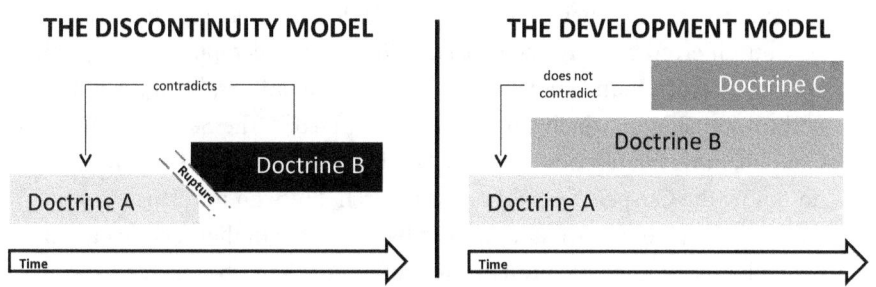

Figure 1. Doctrinal evolution models

In the discontinuity model, there can be breaks in tradition. This means that a doctrine that was believed until a certain point may be abandoned and replaced by another doctrine, completely contradictory with the first: in other words, a doctrinal rupture. Someone with a progressive mindset may have no problems with this model, since for them doctrinal progress is good in itself, regardless of consistency. For an orthodox Catholic, however, this is a problematic view, since it assumes that the church can teach something completely contradictory before and after the rupture. A religion can morph into its opposite while still retaining the same label. An abstract view of progress, instead of the magisterium, is viewed as the doctrinal compass to what we must turn to, in order to gauge the will of God.

The truly Catholic model is the development model. Here, we do not see breaks with tradition, nor ruptures. Rather, each doctrine builds upon the previous ones, while not contradicting them. Of course, doctrine does not remain static. It evolves, but always in continuity with its previous pronouncements. Since there is no doctrinal contradiction, the church's reliability is safeguarded. In other words, we can always turn to the church to guide us, both before and after the development has taken place.

However, there are some nuances we must take into account. While the developed doctrine remains the same, this does not mean that it may not bear the *appearance* of rupture. It might seem like a doctrine has been abandoned and replaced with a new one, just like in the discontinuity model. There are differences though. Doctrine can develop in ways that eventually make it unrecognizable, just like the top floor of a building can be completely different from the ground floor.[7] Yet the foundations remain, and the building is the same building.

A good example is the doctrine of *extra ecclesiam nulla salus* (i.e., "outside the church there is no salvation"). Some assert that the Catholic Church erred by introducing discontinuity in this topic. In 1215, the Fourth Lateran Council taught that "there is one universal Church of the faithful, outside of which no one at all is saved."[8] The Second Vatican Council, however, teaches, "Those who, through no fault of their own, do not know the Gospel of Christ or his Church, but who nevertheless seek God with a sincere heart, and, moved by grace, try in their actions to do his will as they know it through the dictates of their conscience—those too may achieve eternal salvation."[9] Is there a rupture here? Or is it an illusion?

One of the ways such an illusion may occur is when there is a shift in doctrinal emphasis.

Figure 2. Doctrinal development with shift of emphasis

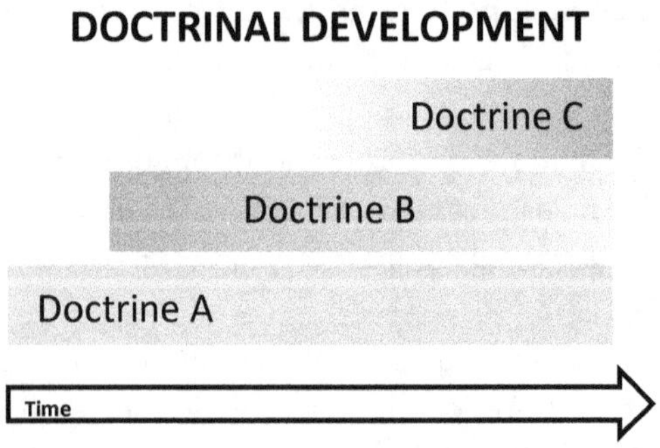

DOCTRINAL DEVELOPMENT

Doctrine C

Doctrine B

Doctrine A

Time →

Slightly adjusting the development model graph, we can perceive how a shift of emphasis might work to produce this illusion. In Figure 2, we can

---

7. In chapter 15, I will quote Cardinal Newman's metaphor of doctrinal development as a caterpillar becoming a butterfly, even though the former does not resemble the latter in the least.

8. Lateran IV, "Confession of Faith."

9. *LG* 16.

see that doctrine B shifts over time from a shade of dark gray to light gray. This denotes how the church, over time, begins to de-emphasize this part of doctrine. As far as doctrine C is concerned, it evolves in the opposite way, with ever greater emphasis. At a certain point, doctrine B might have a shade of gray so light, it might even resemble pure white. In other words, it might seem like it was abandoned in favor of doctrine C. Thus, there is an apparent rupture.

However, if we look at Figure 2 holistically, we can see it is not so. Doctrine C does not contradict doctrine B. Therefore, there is no doctrinal contradiction, no rupture, no discontinuity. In fact, one of the sure signs that doctrine B has not been abandoned can be found in the very existence of doctrine C. The latter builds upon the former. Therefore, if doctrine C exists, then doctrine B must exist too, otherwise doctrine C would have no sure ground to stand on.

Regarding our example of *extra ecclesiam nulla salus*, it is possible to argue that the teachings of the Second Vatican Council were already present since apostolic times. *Lumen Gentium* mentions "those who in shadows and images seek the unknown God,"[10] a clear reference to the discourse of St. Paul in the Areopagus.[11] There are also patristic writings sustaining this interpretation of Vatican II.[12] However, during medieval times, those patristic writings were relatively forgotten in favor of other teachings from other church fathers, more restrictive in nature.[13] A shift of emphasis took place then, similar to the shift in the opposite direction that would happen during the twentieth century.

Is it possible to reconcile both, though? At the pivot of this doctrinal development stands Pope Pius XII, who issued a condemnation against the rigorist interpretation of *extra ecclesiam nulla salus* proposed by Fr. Leonard Feeney.[14] In his encyclical *Mystici Corporis Christi*, he wrote about those who "by an unconscious desire and longing . . . have a certain relationship with the Mystical Body of the Redeemer" (i.e., the Catholic Church).[15] This draws from the age-old tradition of baptism of desire, according to which catechumens who were martyred before being

10. *LG* 16.

11. Acts 17:22–23.

12. A good summary of those patristic quotes, and of all the development involving *extra ecclesiam nulla salus*, can be found in Mazza, "Extra Ecclesiam Nulla Salus."

13. Mazza, "Extra Ecclesiam Nulla Salus."

14. "Church Texts Condemning Father Leonard Feeney," RomanCatholicism.org.

15. Pius XII, *Mystici Corporis Christi*, 103.

baptized were also saved. Pius XII taught that non-Catholics with this "unconscious desire and longing" "cannot be sure of their salvation."[16] This wording implies that we do not have an absolute certainty on whether they are saved or excluded from salvation, thereby validating *Lumen Gentium*'s opening: "they *may* achieve salvation."

In short, the possibility that salvation may be attainable to those who are not within the visible boundaries of the church hinges, according to Pius XII, on the idea that non-Catholics may have a "certain relationship"[17] with the church. Those who are not "formally part of the Church" are not saved by their own actions, or by the religions they formally belong to, but through this "mysterious relationship with the Church."[18] In short, this development presupposes what it apparently and allegedly contradicts: outside the church there is no salvation. It is only through this mysterious relationship with the church that those who are apparently (and only apparently) outside it are saved. This doctrinal development builds itself on the foundations of the previous formulation, even if at first glance they seem self-evidently contradictory.

I dare say this is exactly what happens with *Amoris Laetitia*. As I mentioned in chapter 7 of this book, *Amoris Laetitia* relies on the teaching on mitigating circumstances. In the same chapter, I have detailed how mitigating circumstances do not contradict other parts of doctrine, namely the objectively evil nature of all intrinsically evil acts. In fact, in that very same chapter, I make a distinction between the doctrine of mitigating circumstances and situation ethics. Adopting the latter would be to adopt the illegitimate model of doctrinal discontinuity, since it contradicts the objectively evil nature of some sins. But the former is a legitimate development.

Therefore, if *Amoris Laetitia* grounds itself on the teaching on mitigating circumstances, while the previous church pronouncements (which I will talk about in the next three chapters) based themselves on the doctrine of the objectively evil nature of sin, there can be no doctrinal contradiction. In fact, mitigating circumstances presuppose the doctrine of the objectively evil nature of sin. Mitigating circumstances diminish subjective culpability, and there can be no culpability in an act that is not evil. The teachings build upon each other.

---

16. Pius XII, *Mystici Corporis Christi*, 103.
17. Pius XII, *Mystici Corporis Christi*, 103.
18. John Paul II, *Redemptoris Missio*, 10.

What we have observed is a shift of emphasis. Francis chose to emphasize subjective culpability, while his predecessors chose to emphasize the objectively evil nature of sin. Papal critics observe this shift of emphasis and wrongly conclude that a de-emphasizing of the objectively evil nature of sin means that this part of doctrine was abandoned in favor of a new, contradictory teaching. This is, however, erroneous. A papal critic might rightfully disagree on whether this shift of emphasis is prudent, but he cannot mistake said shift of emphasis with doctrinal contradiction. There is an organic and faithful continuity between the last pontiffs.[19]

❊ ❊ ❊

Now, we must turn to the second point: the distinction between doctrine and discipline. Although I am not aware of any magisterial definition of those two concepts, they play a crucial role in church life and theology (as I mentioned in chapter 1). "Doctrine" usually refers to the teaching of the church,[20] while "discipline" refers to the practical applications of this teaching.[21] Doctrine can develop, but not contradict itself.[22] Disci-

---

19. López, "Entender a Wojtyla para comprender a Bergoglio," 38. A very interesting and overlooked continuity has been explored in the fifth chapter of Stephen Walford's book *Pope Francis, the Family, and Divorce*: the continuity between Francis's *Amoris Laetitia* and Benedict XVI's *Caritas in Veritate*.

20. Williams, "Doctrine," 802: "The word doctrine . . . is used both in the active sense of the imparting of knowledge and in the passive sense of what is taught."

21. Boudinhon, "Ecclesiastical Discipline": "More frequently, however, discipline is considered objectively, that is, as being the precepts and measures for the practical guidance of subjects. Thus understood ecclesiastical discipline is the aggregate of laws and directions given by the Church to the faithful for their conduct both private and public. . . . If we eliminate laws merely formulated by the Church as the exponent of natural or Divine law, there remain the laws and directions laid down and formulated by ecclesiastical authority for the guidance of the faithful; this is the restricted and more usual acceptation of the word discipline."

22. Vatican I, *Dei Filius*, chap. 4: "For, the doctrine of faith which God revealed has not been handed down as a philosophic invention to the human mind to be perfected, but has been entrusted as a divine deposit to the Spouse of Christ, to be faithfully guarded and infallibly interpreted. Hence, also, that understanding of its sacred dogmas must be perpetually retained, which Holy Mother Church has once declared; and there must never be recession from that meaning under the specious name of a deeper understanding. 'Therefore . . . let the understanding, the knowledge, and wisdom of individuals as of all, of one man as of the whole Church, grow and progress strongly with the passage of the ages and the centuries; but let it be solely in its own genus, namely in the same dogma, with the same sense and the same understanding.' [Vincent of Lerins, *Commonitorium*, 23, 3]."

plines, on the other hand, vary across time and space and can, therefore, change.[23]

This does not, of course, mean that we can exaggerate the scope of these changes: disciplines can never contradict established doctrine.[24] Yet disciplines can indeed be contradictory with other disciplines.[25] So, for instance, there is obligatory celibacy in place for most priests of the Latin church,[26] but the Eastern Catholic churches[27] and some personal ordinariates of former Anglicans[28] allow the ordination of previously married men.

Knowing this, I will complete my model with the interplay between doctrine and discipline, by contrasting two different hermeneutics: the hermeneutic of discontinuity and the hermeneutic of reform.[29]

The hermeneutic of discontinuity is based on doctrinal discontinuity (see Figure 3). As the secular world, always fickle, keeps shifting its culture, its ideas, and its circumstances, it imposes on the church ruptures

---

23. Boudinhon, "Ecclesiastical Discipline": "That ecclesiastical discipline should be subject to change is natural since it was made for men and by men. To claim that it is immutable would render the attainment of its end utterly impossible, since, in order to form and direct Christians, it must adapt itself to the variable circumstances of time and place, conditions of life, customs of peoples and races, being, in a certain sense, like St. Paul, all things to all men. . . . While the Faith of the Church remains the same in all ages, it is not so with her discipline. This changes with time, grows old with the years, is rejuvenated, is subject to growth and decay."

Sheehan, *Apologetics and Catholic Doctrine*, 209: "The rules or legislation of the Church (often called discipline): These do change, and have regularly changed over the centuries, some of them differing from one country to another even at the same time. Among countless examples are: the holy days of obligation outside of Sunday; the penance required on Fridays; the length of the fast prescribed before Holy Communion; the rules and ceremonies connected with a mixed marriage; the liturgical laws governing Mass and other rituals; Communion for the laity under one or both kinds; the celibacy of the clergy in the Latin Church; and so on. . . . Christ never promised that the pastors of the Church would always act with prudence and effectiveness. The wisdom of certain decisions (not doctrinal or moral) is open to discussion. Thus a new bishop or pope is free to change his predecessor's directives." See also López, "Para comprender *Amoris Laetitia*," 460–61.

24. Sheehan, *Apologetics and Catholic Doctrine*, 209.

25. Sheehan, *Apologetics and Catholic Doctrine*, 209.

26. *CCC* 1579.

27. *CCC* 1580.

28. CDF, "Declaration."

29. The characteristics of both of these hermeneutics are superbly explained by Benedict XVI in his "Address of His Holiness Benedict XVI to the Roman Curia."

both in doctrine and in discipline. Mind you, these ruptures do not arise organically out of an internal doctrinal development, but are imposed from the outside by changes in worldly perceptions. Doctrine follows changes of widespread ideas and values, while discipline follows changes in behaviors. Also, since both doctrinal and disciplinary changes arise from the secular world, there might not be a consistency between theory and practice. In fact, changes in practice might even precede changes in theory, so that new doctrines are created to justify the new disciplines.

The hermeneutic of reform works differently. First of all, at the doctrinal level, it is based on actual development: doctrines build upon the previous ones without contradicting each other, as we have seen. Nevertheless, since the world changes its culture and circumstances, the best practical way to apply doctrine (i.e., disciplines) may vary in the same way. This is the reason why we need a living magisterium. It is up to the church to discern at any given time what the best practice is, always in accordance with doctrine.

Figure 3. Hermeneutics models

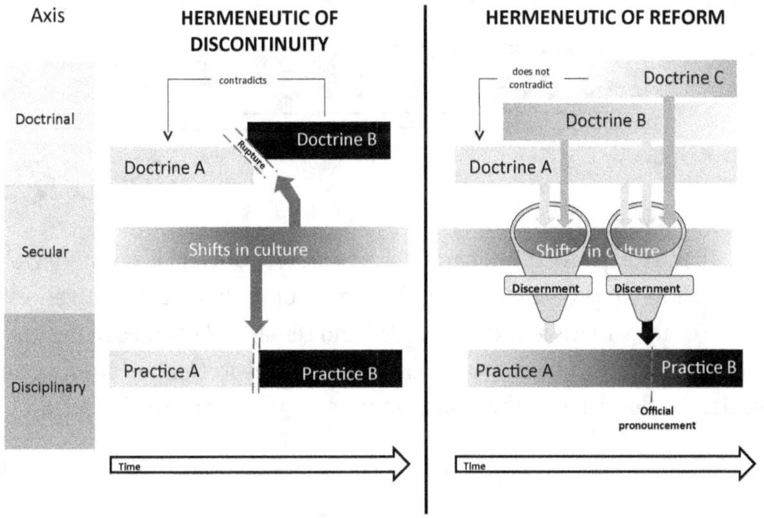

Practices may vary, and sometimes even contradict each other. However, they will never contradict doctrine, since they are born from an ecclesial discernment, taking into consideration the wealth of doctrine in the *depositum fidei*. Discipline follows doctrine, even if discernment takes into account worldly circumstances and events. Also, doctrinal development may provide new insights into how to tackle new secular problems,[30] and different doctrinal emphases may also help to meet the different expectations and needs of the secular world.[31]

Bearing all this in mind, this is my perception of what happened in the case of *Amoris Laetitia* and the issue of communion to the divorced and civilly remarried.

Figure 4. Hermeneutics of reform for the divorced and remarried

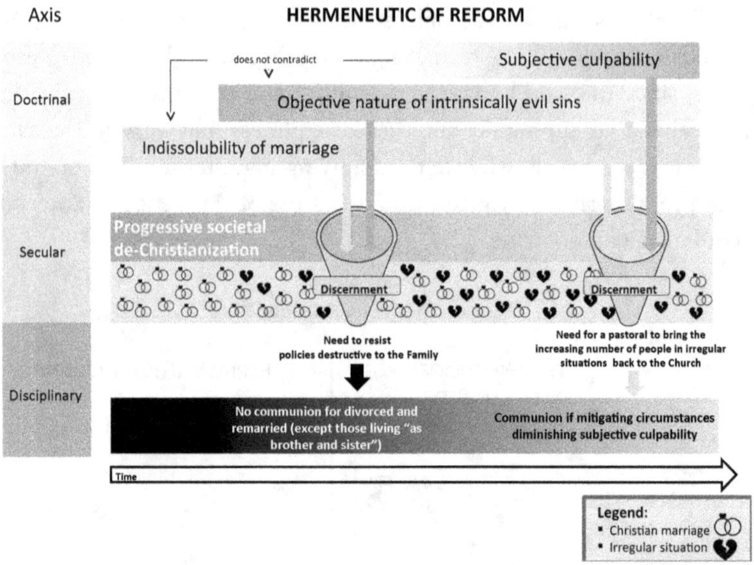

As I already explained in chapter 7, in a purely doctrinal point of view, the teaching on subjective culpability does not nullify the objectively evil nature of the situation of the divorced and remarried couples living *more uxorio*. In fact, it builds upon it and presupposes it. Neither does it contradict the doctrine on the indissolubility of marriage (see chapter 6).

---

30. See the church's teachings against *in vitro* fertilization, or weapons of mass destruction, which could not have been formulated in apostolic times, but still draw from timeless Christian ethics.

31. An example of this is Francis's contested change of the *Catechism*'s reference to the death penalty. While in previous centuries the church chose to emphasize justice, nowadays the church chooses to emphasize human dignity, thereby responding to the yearning of the modern world in this regard, and also responding to the evolution of modern prison and criminal systems.

Let us now take a look at what happened in the secular world. From the 1960s onward, there was a progressive loss of influence of the Catholic Church on secular affairs, particularly on sexual matters. This progressive de-Christianization of an increasingly hedonistic society led to a boost in divorce rates, namely in the USA. Baby boomers were the first cohort to divorce and remarry in large numbers during young adulthood.[32] In this sense, it is not strange that Pope St. John Paul II discerned, precisely in the 1980s and 1990s, that it was urgent to counter this trend by taking a strong stand against further erosion of the marriage institution. Therefore, a sacramental discipline was established whereby the divorced and civilly remarried were prevented from taking communion precisely because their situation objectively contradicted the union between Christ and church signified by the Eucharist (see next chapter).

Time has passed and the situation has shifted somewhat. Granted, the de-Christianization of society and the policies destructive to the family continue unabated. However, these have moved away from divorce and into other fields, like that of homosexual unions. The overall divorce rates may still be increasing, but the newest generations seem to be divorcing at a slower rate.[33] Yet there are now people who were born in this modern culture and whose values and actions were molded by this society. Rocco Buttiglione applies John Paul II's concept of "societal structures of sin"[34] to this situation: modern society would predispose people born in it to sin, hindering their ability to recognize the truth and to choose it accordingly.[35] A person living in a structure of sin will have a diminished responsibility for the sins practiced in that structure and because of such structure.[36]

The sacredness and indissolubility of marriage are concepts totally foreign to people born in this culture, even if theoretically understandable to them. They were educated in and by a "throwaway culture of the ephemeral."[37] Catholicism still pervades the culture, but as a muffled in-

---

32. Brown and Lin, "The Gray Divorce Revolution."

33. Kennedy and Ruggles, "Breaking Up Is Hard to Count."

34. As an example see John Paul II, *Sollicitudo Rei Socialis*, 36. In this context, theologian Juliano Almeida also brings up John Paul II and Pius XII's concept of "loss of the sense of sin," and also Benedict XVI's concept of the "dictatorship of relativism" (see Almeida, "*Amoris Laetitia*—reflexões," 377).

35. Buttiglione, *Risposte amichevoli*, 64.

36. Buttiglione, *Risposte amichevoli*, 68.

37. *AL* 39, 125, 191.

fluence drowned in the noise of innumerable other voices. In other words, it is like a hidden treasure, shining between the cracks in the dirt, but only perceptible to those who actually and actively seek it.

In this sense, it is not unusual for those born in this generation to come to contact with the fullness of the Catholic faith only later in life,[38] many times after they have made mistakes. Sometimes, these mistakes include entering into irreversible irregular situations, like a divorce and remarriage, with children in need of family stability and a heterodox spouse unwilling to follow the neophyte in his or her newly found faith.[39] These people call for the church for guidance, and it is manifestly insufficient to tell them that they should have known better in the past.[40]

We know that even before he ascended to the papacy, Jorge Mario Bergoglio[41] was concerned with the pastoral accompaniment of the growing multitudes of divorced and remarried people.[42] After his election, he convened two synods of bishops, who agreed that a new pastoral approach needed to be implemented while retaining the sound and perennial orthodox teachings of the church.[43] Aware of the changing times, Francis wanted to privilege other strategies of pastoral processes, focusing on caring for the sinner rather than on fighting culture wars.[44]

---

38. Buttiglione, *Risposte amichevoli*, 68: Rocco Buttiglione draws attention to how the modern practice of infant baptism, where the person is introduced in the church without a catechumenal path, may compound this problem. See also p. 140.

39. Buttiglione, *Risposte amichevoli*, 40: "Divorce is a mass phenomenon, and it risks becoming a mass apostasy if the divorced and remarried abandon the Church and stop giving a Christian education to their children.... The number of the divorced has become too great, and of course the number of those who may be subjectively in the grace of God may also have increased. It is necessary to develop a new pastoral strategy."

40. This seems to be the main answer from Fr. Joseph Levine to a case-study designed by Fr. Paul Keller, which we will explore with further detail in chapter 16. See Levine, "How Not to Minister."

41. Pope Francis's birth name.

42. See Ivereigh, *Wounded Shepherd*, 248–50.

43. Schönborn, "Conversation with Cardinal Schönborn": "We are led in a living manner to draw a distinction between the continuity of the doctrinal principles and the discontinuity of perspectives or of historically conditioned expressions. This is the function that belongs to the living magisterium: to interpret authentically the Word of God, whether written or handed down."

44. López, "Para comprender *Amoris Laetitia*," 422. See also p. 421 and its quote of *AL* 32.

The pontiff and bishops in communion with him sought to achieve this through recourse to the teaching on mitigating circumstances. This teaching already existed at the time of John Paul II, but the latter chose to emphasize the doctrine of the objectively evil nature of irregular situations instead. This was in his purview, just as it is up to Pope Francis to choose to emphasize the doctrine of mitigating circumstances according to his discernment of the present situation. This does not mean that John Paul II was wrong: his discernment of the situation at the time led him to make a well-adjusted decision in that specific context. This conclusion, however, was not definitive, for the changing state of affairs would come to warrant different decisions at other times. As Stephen Walford posits: "*Amoris Laetitia* is a document that had to come, to show that as historical circumstances change, the Church has the ability to maneuver into a new position: one that is not powerless to help."[45]

This new discipline issuing from Francis may (partially) change the previous discipline, but is nevertheless based in orthodox principles which do not contradict in the slightest the doctrines of the indissolubility of marriage and the intrinsically-evil nature of these irregular situations. In this sense, Cardinal Schönborn explains how this "positive pastoral style is also a way of expounding doctrine in a gentle manner, linking it to the profound motivations of men and women. The totality of doctrine is expressed, but in a fresh and new way that a large public can read. This is a beautiful illustration of what St. John XXIII said at the opening of the council: the truths are unchangeable, but the way of uttering them and proposing them must be renewed."[46]

From that perspective, Fr. Thomas Ryan maintains that *Amoris Laetitia* could arguably be viewed as an instance of development of doctrine—a matter of ongoing theological discussion and of reception within the church community.[47] Importantly, in such doctrinal developments, earlier teachings need to be read "in the light of the new development."[48]

45. Walford, *Pope Francis, the Family, and Divorce*, 63.
46. Schönborn, "Cardinal Schönborn on 'The Joy of Love.'"
47. Ryan, "Weakness, and Wounded and Troubled Love," 146.
48. Ryan, "Weakness, and Wounded and Troubled Love," 145. In the same vein, Cardinal Schönborn answers in his May 1, 2017, interview to *La Civiltà Cattolica*: "As we read the Council of Nicaea in the light of the Council of Constantinople, and Vatican I in the light of Vatican II, so now we must read the previous statements of the magisterium about the family in the light of the contribution made by 'The Joy of Love.'" This is an inversion of what papal critics have usually done, since they usually read new developments in light of the old ones.

In conclusion, *Amoris Laetitia* is a legitimate development. There is no doctrinal contradiction, no heresy, no apostasy.

❦ ❦ ❦

Of course, papal critics may object, what I said is only correct if we are dealing with discipline and not doctrine.[49] If, however, the access of the divorced and remarried to communion is a matter of doctrine, then Francis cannot change this without contradicting previous popes. This would be an illegitimate action on the pope's behalf, since doctrines (unlike disciplines) cannot contradict each other.

For me, it is obvious that the change is a matter of discipline and not of doctrine,[50] since whether a specific divorced and remarried person can receive the Eucharist is a practical application of doctrinal principles involving the concepts of mortal sin, adultery, and divorce. Secondly, as we will see in the next chapters, the church documents underlying the previous Eucharistic ban talk about reaffirming a "practice."

But let us assume that there are doubts about whether we are talking of doctrine or discipline. Here, I think we should apply a kind of tautological thinking. We know that doctrine cannot change, while disciplines can. Pope Francis has *changed* the requirements for a divorced and remarried person to be allowed to receive the Eucharist. Then logically, this can only have happened if we are talking about a discipline and not a doctrine, since by definition, the latter cannot change.

The only other option is the venue taken by papal critics: that doctrine cannot change and Pope Francis illegitimately tried to change doctrine.[51] This position, however, is either untenable for a Catholic, or at least should be taken only after exhausting all other possible explanations. We should favor a position that safeguards all that is at stake: from the doctrine of intrinsically evil acts to the doctrine of mitigating

---

49. See Brother André Marie [pseud.], "*Amoris Laetitia* and the 'Authentic Magisterium.'"

50. This view is taken by others too, notably including Cristoph Schönborn in his interview with *La Civiltà Cattolica*; Fernández, "El Capítulo VIII de *Amoris Laetitia*," 459–61; López, "Para comprender *Amoris Laetitia*," 437; Buttiglione, *Risposte amichevoli*, 144; Walford, "Pope Francis, the Family, and Divorce," 152–53; Almeida, "*Amoris Laetitia*—reflexões," 374, 387. NB: This does not in any way mean that there is not a doctrinal development underlying the change in discipline. Yet, the change itself is disciplinary, not doctrinal.

51. Ferrara, "*Amoris Laetitia*: Anatomy of a Pontifical Debacle."

circumstances; from the doctrine of the indissolubility of marriage to the doctrine of the papal primacy and indefectibility of the church.

To settle this matter, I will now proceed to analyze each of the church documents that papal critics usually pit against *Amoris Laetitia*, so as to show how they are eventually reconcilable. We will start with the most important one, since this is what the previous sacramental discipline was rooted in: *Familiaris Consortio*.

CHAPTER 11

Does *Amoris Laetitia* Contradict *Familiaris Consortio*?

WHEN TRYING TO PROVE that *Amoris Laetitia* contradicts established doctrine, papal critics will usually refer to *Familiaris Consortio* as proof of this alleged contradiction.[1] *Familiaris Consortio* was a post-synodal apostolic exhortation promulgated by Pope St. John Paul II in 1981. It is interesting that papal critics will sometimes ascribe a low magisterial weight to *Amoris Laetitia* (a post-synodal apostolic exhortation),[2] while assigning a definitive, infallible nature to the sacramental discipline laid out in *Familiaris Consortio*, another post-synodal apostolic exhortation.[3]

    1. As an example, see the interview given by philosopher Robert Spaemann to the *Catholic News Agency*: "Article 305 together with footnote 351—in which it is stated that believers can be allowed to the sacraments 'in an objective situation of sin' 'because of mitigating factors'—directly contradicts article 84 of Pope John Paul II's exhortation *Familiaris Consortio*. . . . *That it is an issue of a breach emerges doubtlessly for every thinking person who knows the respective texts*."

    2. Burke, "'*Amoris Laetitia*' and the Constant Teaching and Practice of the Church": "Pope Francis makes clear, from the beginning, that the post-synodal apostolic exhortation is not an act of the magisterium."

    3. Burke, "Interview With Cardinal Burke . . . (Part 2) Discriminating Mercy": "In more recent times, paragraph 84 of Pope St. John Paul II's apostolic exhortation *Familiaris Consortio* has pronounced the Church's constant teaching. So then, that type of reversal is simply not possible." See also Skojec, "Is *Amoris Laetitia* an Expression of the Ordinary and Universal Magisterium?": "An example of the infallible ordinary magisterium that would likely fall under this first category (and possibly the second; that is, of things related to divine truths) is *Familiaris Consortio* 84. . . . An example of a something that does not correspond in any way to divinely-revealed truth, to truths so related, or even to ordinary teaching on faith and morals would be *AL* 301. . . . This last

Still, the question remains: does *Amoris Laetitia* contradict *Familiaris Consortio* or not?

Of course, the answer to this question depends on whether we are talking about matters of doctrine or discipline. As I explained in my previous chapter, I posit that we are talking about a sacramental discipline. Since disciplines can and do change, how can we know if they are legitimate? First of all, a change in discipline must be done by someone with authority in the church, like the pope. This is particularly true for sacramental discipline. As the Council of Trent states:

> It [the Council] furthermore declares, that this power has ever been in the Church, that, in the dispensation of the sacraments, their substance being untouched, it may ordain,—or change, what things soever it may judge most expedient, for the profit of those who receive, or for the veneration of the said sacraments, according to the difference of circumstances, times, and places.[4]

Of course, while even non-infallible magisterial pronouncements require religious submission of mind and will, the same is not true regarding disciplines. However, as I have shown in chapter 2, disciplines promulgated by the church are not without divine assistance and also require adherence from the faithful. This means that, even if the faithful may respectfully disagree with the prudence of a particular discipline, and propose that it be changed, the same faithful cannot on the other hand postulate that a discipline approved by the church is erroneous, or that the church is not the final arbiter on the matter.

With this in mind, let us review *Familiaris Consortio* as far as communion for the divorced and civilly remarried is concerned.

❈ ❈ ❈

The Sacramental Discipline

Regarding access to the Eucharist for the divorced and remarried, *Familiaris Consortio* stipulates:

---

example is irreconcilable with the [former], which [is] infallible magisterial teachings related directly to divinely-revealed truth. And that's a problem."

4. Council of Trent, "21st Session, chap. II."

> The Church reaffirms her *practice*, which is based upon Sacred Scripture, of not admitting to Eucharistic Communion divorced persons who have remarried. They are unable to be admitted thereto from the fact that their state and condition of life objectively contradict that union of love between Christ and the Church which is signified and effected by the Eucharist. Besides this, there is another special pastoral reason: if these people were admitted to the Eucharist, the faithful would be led into error and confusion regarding the Church's teaching about the indissolubility of marriage.
>
> Reconciliation in the sacrament of Penance which would open the way to the Eucharist, can only be granted to those who, repenting of having broken the sign of the Covenant and of fidelity to Christ, are sincerely ready to undertake a way of life that is no longer in contradiction to the indissolubility of marriage. This means, in practice, that when, for serious reasons, such as for example the children's upbringing, a man and a woman cannot satisfy the obligation to separate, they "take on themselves the duty to live in complete continence, that is, by abstinence from the acts proper to married couples."[5]

In other words, the Eucharist is to be given only to those divorced and remarried couples who, having ceased to live *more uxorio*, celebrated the sacrament of Reconciliation beforehand.

Are we dealing with doctrine or discipline? *Familiaris Consortio* is very clear that the church is "reaffirming her *practice*." Therefore we are dealing with a "practice," a matter of sacramental discipline,[6] which can be overturned if done authoritatively and without contradicting established doctrine.[7] *Amoris Laetitia* has been promulgated by the pope,

---

5. *FC* 84.

6. See Almeida, "*Amoris Laetitia*—reflexões," 374. Referring to *FC* 84: "I highlight the word practice, to bring attention to the fact that John Paul II did not affirm that it was a doctrine founded in Holy Scripture, but rather a practice."

7. Almeida, "*Amoris Laetitia*—reflexões," 373–74: "So, any wise interpretation of *Amoris Laetitia* must acknowledge that it absolutely cannot be a change in the doctrine given by Christ to the Church, something that is not allowed even to the Roman pontiff. What we see here is a change in practice following an interpretation of doctrine." See also Buttiglione, *Risposte amichevoli*, 144: "Something has changed in the pastoral approach and something has changed from the point of view of ecclesiastical discipline.... Certainly, nothing has changed regarding the theology of matrimony." See also Fernández, "El Capítulo VIII de *Amoris Laetitia*," 459–60: "The norm does not admit exceptions, as an objective qualification based in an absolute moral precept, but it admits a discernment relatively to its disciplinary consequences.... Is this

who has the authority to do so. So, we need only to focus on whether there has been any contradiction in doctrine.

Familiaris Consortio bases its sacramental discipline on two reasons: one pastoral and one doctrinal. The pastoral one has to do with scandal[8] and I have already tackled this topic in chapter 8. The doctrinal one is that the divorced and remarried couple's "state and condition of life objectively contradict that union of love between Christ and the Church which is signified and effected by the Eucharist" (a reasoning that came to be known as *Ipse Namque*).[9] Besides this, I can recognize in *Familiaris Consortio* another doctrinal reason for this sacramental discipline: it was based on sacred scripture.[10]

So, does *Amoris* contradict these two doctrinal statements? The answer is "no." *Amoris Laetitia* does not say that the previous sacramental discipline was not based on sacred scripture. The fact that it instituted a new sacramental discipline does not mean that the previous one was not based on sacred scripture, just like it does not mean that the new

---

change possible and acceptable? Can Francis incorporate John Paul II's teachings and simultaneously open a previously closed door? Yes, because the Church can evolve in its comprehension of its own doctrine, and of its disciplinary consequences." Finally, see López, "Para comprender *Amoris Laetitia*," 437: "The prohibition to access the Eucharist in situations of grave matter as in Canon 915 . . . rests on a disciplinary, not doctrinal norm, that the Pope can modify. . . . On the contrary, the impossibility to access the Eucharist in mortal sin is of a doctrinal, not merely disciplinary order."

8. See Buttiglione, *Risposte amichevoli*, 39, 155.

9. It is interesting that, while papal critics defend the *Ipse Namque* as being the "constant teaching of the church," it is possible to argue that it was actually an innovation from St. John Paul II. This does not mean that it is illegitimate, but it certainly weighs in favor of it not being as perennial as previously thought. See Ivereigh, *Wounded Shepherd*, 249–50, 361–62: "John Paul II added a startling new doctrine. The divorced and remarried were outside the sacraments, he said, because 'their state and condition of life objectively contradict that union of love between Christ and the Church which is signified and effected by the Eucharist.' This became known, after its original Latin, as the *ipse namque* clause, and it *was troubling to theologians who were concerned for doctrinal continuity* because it had appeared nowhere in the synod and had no provenance in the Church's teaching documents on marriage. The metaphorical description of the Church as the 'bride of Christ' had never been wrapped into eucharistic theology, and certainly it had never been used to bar the remarried from receiving the sacraments. . . . Ipse Namque has no provenance in the councils (Trent, Vatican I, Vatican II) nor in the two papal encyclicals on marriage: neither *Casti Connubii* of 1930 nor *Humanae Vitae* of 1968."

10. See Almeida, "*Amoris Laetitia*—reflexões," 374: "Many things in the Bible evolved significantly over time, from the use of veils by women in the Church (cf. 1 Cor 11:6) to many norms relatively to excommunications."

discipline is not based on the deposit of the faith. In fact, if we admit that two disciplines can contradict each other, and both be legitimate, we must assume that both are, by definition, based on the same deposit of faith (of which scripture is a part).

Likewise, *Amoris Laetitia* never says that the divorced and remarried person's state in life does not objectively contradict the union between Christ and the church. There is no textual evidence for this claim. In fact, *Amoris Laetitia* does indeed proclaim the analogous nature between marriage and the union of Christ and the church:

> The sacrament of marriage is not a social convention, an empty ritual, or merely the outward sign of a commitment. The sacrament is a gift given for the sanctification and salvation of the spouses, since "their mutual belonging is a real representation, through the sacramental sign, of the same relationship between Christ and the Church." . . . *Christian marriage is a sign of how much Christ loved his Church* in the covenant sealed on the cross, yet it also makes that love present in the communion of the spouses. By becoming one flesh, *they embody the espousal of our human nature by the Son of God*. That is why "in the joys of their love and family life, he gives them here on earth a foretaste of the wedding feast of the Lamb". *Even though the analogy between the human couple of husband and wife, and that of Christ and his Church, is "imperfect," it inspires us to beg the Lord to bestow on every married couple an outpouring of his divine love.*[11]

After this, Francis clearly says that "any breach of the marriage bond is against the will of God,"[12] and he approvingly quotes the Bible to proclaim that the Lord "hates divorce."[13] Hence, we cannot affirm that *Amoris Laetitia* contradicts the doctrinal point that the divorced and remarried couple's "state and condition of life objectively contradict that union of love between Christ and the Church which is signified and effected by the Eucharist." We can say, however, that *Amoris Laetitia* develops and complements this statement, by showing that this analogy is "imperfect," since the couple is composed of sinful people who can never become as perfect as Christ.

In conclusion, *Amoris Laetitia* and *Familiaris Consortio* do not contradict themselves in matters of doctrine, only of sacramental discipline.

---

11. *AL* 72–73.
12. *AL* 291.
13. *AL* 123.

But if *Amoris Laetitia* acknowledges the doctrinal foundations of the previous sacramental discipline, how can it propose a different one?

❦ ❦ ❦

A Shift of Emphasis

When an apologist points out that *Amoris Laetitia* is perfectly compatible with the orthodox doctrine of mitigating circumstances, the papal critic will usually (and correctly) point out that the previous sacramental discipline was never about subjective guilt. Rather, the divorced and remarried were excluded because their state in life objectively contradicts Catholic marriage.[14] From this correct assessment, he will incorrectly extrapolate that it is not possible, therefore, to institute a new sacramental discipline not taking into account solely the objective state, but also subjective guilt.[15] Of course, we have already established that disciplines can vary over time and even contradict each other, as long as they do not contradict doctrine. But if disciplines cannot contradict doctrine, how can they be contradictory among themselves?

One of the ways (if not the only way) this can be achieved is if both disciplines draw their conclusions from different parts of doctrine. Mind you, the doctrine is the same, but it has different parts: in our example, one part is the objectively evil nature of sin and the other part is the subjective guilt of the sinner. One discipline can ground itself in the former and another discipline can ground itself in the latter. Since, as we have already seen in chapter 7, both parts of doctrine are not contradictory, then neither discipline contradicts doctrine. Ergo, both disciplines are valid.

In other words, when the papal critic says "sacramental discipline for the divorced and remarried has never been about subjective culpability, but about the objective nature of their state," he is actually engaging in a kind of tautology. A different sacramental discipline will inevitably base itself on a different part of doctrine. If two contradictory disciplines were based in the same part of doctrine, then it would be highly likely that at least one of them would contradict doctrine. Since *Amoris Laetitia* allows communion for some divorced and remarried people, then it cannot base itself on the objective state of life of those sinners, like *Familiaris*

---

14. As an example, see Hitchens, "Sacraments Don't Need Fixing."
15. Hitchens, "Sacraments Don't Need Fixing."

Consortio does. If it did, then its sacramental discipline would indeed be invalid. Since its sacramental discipline is based on a different reasoning, then it is legitimate (I provided a detailed explanation on "shifts of emphasis" in my previous chapter).

In summary, papal critics think that *Amoris Laetitia* has to do with doctrinal change, when in fact it has to do with a shift of emphasis vis-à-vis doctrine. John Paul II chose, in his sacramental discipline, to emphasize the objectively evil nature of divorce and remarriage,[16] while Francis chose to emphasize the subjective culpability of the sinner. Both are legitimate, both are orthodox.[17] This is not a doctrinal change. Rather, it is a disciplinary change based on a doctrinal swing, like the harmonious and continuous movement of a pendulum. Or perhaps a better expression would be that we are observing "a paradigm shift."[18]

---

16. Juliano Almeida argues that *Familiaris Consortio* implicitly acknowledges that divorced and remarried people may not be in mortal sin, since *FC* 84 affirms that Catholics who "have rejected the Lord's command and *are still living in this state* will be able to *obtain from God the grace of conversion and salvation*, provided that they have persevered in prayer, penance, and *charity*." Yet *CCC* 1861 affirms that mortal sin "results in the loss of charity and the privation of sanctifying grace." Therefore, a Catholic in the situation mentioned in *FC* 84 is not necessarily in a state of mortal sin (see Almeida, "*Amoris Laetitia*—reflexões," 375). See also Schönborn, "Conversation with Cardinal Schönborn": "Saint John Paul II did indeed distinguish a variety of situations. He saw a difference between those who had tried sincerely to salvage their first marriage and were abandoned unjustly, and those who had destroyed a canonically valid marriage through their grave fault. . . . John Paul II already presupposes implicitly that one cannot simply say that every situation of a divorced and remarried person is the equivalent of a life in mortal sin that is separated from the communion of love between Christ and the Church. Accordingly, he was opening the door to a broader understanding, by means of the discernment of the various situations that are not objectively identical."

17. See Walford, *Pope Francis, the Family, and Divorce*, 63: "With its focus on subjective guilt, [*Amoris Laetitia*] balances the objective sin approach taken by John Paul II in *Familiaris Consortio*." See also Ryan, "Weakness, and Wounded and Troubled Love," 143: "*Familiaris Consortio* 84 and John Paul II's focus on the objective situation of those who are divorced and remarried and its implications for the sexual aspect of the relationship. Francis (unobtrusively) balances this with consideration of the subjective situation and the dispositions of the parties involved."

18. One of the first people to use this expression was actually Archbishop Victor Manuel Fernández, one of the ghostwriters of *Amoris Laetitia*, in an interview to *La Stampa*, on March 12, 2018, "Without the gaze of faith, the Pope is reduced to a character." For more information on the different paradigms at play, see Worgul, "*Amoris Laetitia*."

Hermeneutic of Continuity

Some frequently invoke the expression "hermeneutic of continuity" to justify their personal interpretations of tradition and to put down any other interpretations (even authoritative ones).[19] This term was coined—so it is argued—by Pope Benedict XVI to denote the true way to develop doctrine, in contrast with the illicit "hermeneutic of rupture." There are two problems with this reasoning. First of all, critics sometimes use the expression "hermeneutic of continuity" to quell any and all development coming from magisterial sources, so that it ceases to be a way to properly evaluate doctrinal development and becomes only a justification to not develop at all.[20] Secondly (and most importantly), in his seminal speech instituting this term, Benedict did not use the expression "hermeneutic of continuity," but rather "hermeneutic of *reform* (in continuity)."[21]

Reform implies change. However, as Benedict says in his speech, doctrine cannot change, even if it develops. Doctrine is not reformable. So, how is reform to be undertaken? The only possible answer is: reform is to be done at others levels, like the disciplinary or pastoral levels. But

---

19. See the *National Catholic Register*'s interview with Stephan Kampowski, "A Handbook for faithfully interpreting *Amoris Laetitia*": "One must remember that any interpretation of *Amoris Laetitia* that suggests that the divorced in a new union could approach the sacraments without first taking on the commitment to change their objective way of life (by separating, or by living like brother and sister), introduces a chasm between life and liturgy, between ethos and sacrament, putting into question not only marriage as an objective reality of the Church, but the very sacramentality of the Church herself.... A hermeneutic of continuity is the only legitimate one for interpreting magisterial texts. A manner of reading the difficult passages of Chapter 8 that clearly contradicts the previous magisterium—in particular, with respect to the concrete practice, John Paul II's *Familiaris Consortio* ... —is not simply implausible but, theologically speaking, illegitimate."

20. As an example, see Boniface [pseud.], "What Is the Hermeneutic of Continuity?"

21. See Benedict XVI, "Address of His Holiness": "On the one hand, there is an interpretation that I would call 'a hermeneutic of discontinuity and rupture'; it has frequently availed itself of the sympathies of the mass media, and also one trend of modern theology. *On the other, there is the 'hermeneutic of reform', of renewal in the continuity* of the one subject-Church which the Lord has given to us. *She is a subject which increases in time and develops*, yet always remaining the same, the one subject of the journeying People of God.... *The hermeneutic of discontinuity is countered by the hermeneutic of reform.*"

if there is a new discipline, there are certain practical implications: some practices that used to be performed are abandoned; some practices that were not performed until then are adopted. Nevertheless, what matters is whether this reform is done in continuity—doctrinal continuity.

So in order to ascertain whether *Amoris Laetitia* and *Familiaris Consortio* are in continuity, we should not focus on whether their sacramental disciplines contradict each other or not. Rather, we should see if *Amoris Laetitia* flows from a doctrinal continuity with *Familiaris Consortio*. I do believe this to be the case, for the seeds of *Amoris Laetitia* are all present in *Familiaris Consortio*, even if they had not yet bloomed at the time.

Familiaris Consortio does indeed acknowledge that there is a tension between the church's roles as a teacher and as a mother. It does so in the context of the church's teachings on artificial contraception, but I think this can shed light into Pope Francis's theology:

> As Mother, the Church is close to the many married couples who find themselves in difficulty over this important point of the moral life: she knows well their situation, which is often very arduous and at times truly tormented by difficulties of every kind, not only individual difficulties but social ones as well; *she knows that many couples encounter difficulties not only in the concrete fulfillment of the moral norm but even in understanding its inherent values.*[22]

Of course, John Paul II does not believe that, as mother, the church can ever compromise truth and moral norms. Again, this is not what we are talking about, as I hope to have shown in the course of this book. However, even if the church's pedagogy must always remain linked with her doctrine and never be separated from it, this pedagogy must "display its realism and wisdom . . . by making a tenacious and courageous effort to create and uphold all the human conditions—psychological, moral, and spiritual—indispensable for understanding and living the moral value and norm."[23] The pope then proceeds to enunciate some of those conditions: among them is the *frequent recourse to the sacraments* of penance and the Eucharist.

---

22. *FC* 33.
23. *FC* 33.

Right in the next paragraph, John Paul II urges priests to exercise a "unity of moral and pastoral judgment."[24] This unity "must be carefully sought and ensured, in order that the faithful may not have to suffer anxiety of conscience." The Holy Father talks about this pastoral judgment in the context of the moral *progress* of married people (that is the actual title of this section of the exhortation). He mentions how "man . . . knows, loves, and accomplishes moral good by *stages of growth*."[25] Both progress and growth are, by definition, gradual. This is why the "law of gradualness" is mentioned here for the first time.[26] This is the law where *Amoris Laetitia* rests.[27]

Granted, there is a difference between the law of gradualness and gradualness of the law. As I said before, this is a distinction that *Amoris Laetitia* also explicitly makes.[28] But still, the law of gradualness is defined as a "step-by-step advance."[29] Before we reached this section dealing with the moral progress of married couples, *Familiaris Consortio* had already delved on what gradualness means in a section entitled "Gradualness and Conversion":

> What is needed is a continuous, permanent conversion which, while requiring an interior detachment from every evil and an adherence to good in its fullness, is *brought about concretely in steps which lead us ever forward*. Thus a dynamic process develops, one which *advances gradually with the progressive integration* of the gifts of God and the demands of His definitive and absolute love in the entire personal and social life of man. Therefore an educational growth process is necessary, in order that *individual believers, families, and peoples, even civilization itself*, by beginning from what they have already received of the mystery of Christ, *may patiently be led forward*, arriving at a

---

24. *FC* 34.

25. *FC* 34.

26. *FC* 34.

27. See Calmeyn, "Accompagnamento e legge di gradualità": "It is the classical notion of the 'path in the Good,' also called 'the law of gradualness' that allows us to understand *Amoris Laetitia*'s real contribution, and the way the document positions itself in Tradition. . . . *Amoris Laetitia* offers us a law of gradualness that is its true content." In fact, according to this essay, the law of gradualness was "considered as one of the main contributions resulting from the meeting proceedings" of the 1980 Synod on the Family, which eventually led to the post-synodal exhortation *Familiaris Consortio*.

28. *AL* 295.

29. *FC* 34.

richer understanding and a fuller integration of this mystery in their lives.[30]

In other words, what has been stated before about the law of gradualness does not apply solely to married couples, but to anyone, even entire civilizations. Therefore, we cannot exclude the divorced and remarried from this process. In fact, Pope St. John Paul II is very explicit in stating that pastoral care should be extended to families in "irregular situations" (the same terminology used in *Amoris Laetitia*):[31]

> The Church's pastoral concern will not be limited only to the Christian families closest at hand; it will extend its horizons in harmony with the Heart of Christ, and will show itself to be even more lively for families in general and for those families in particular which are *in difficult or irregular situations*. For all of them the Church will have a word of truth, goodness, understanding, hope, and deep sympathy with their sometimes tragic difficulties. To all of them she will offer her disinterested help so that they *can come closer to that model of a family which the Creator intended* from "the beginning" and which Christ has renewed with His redeeming grace. *The Church's pastoral action must be progressive*, also in the sense that it must follow the family, *accompanying it step by step in the different stages of its formation and development*.[32]

Also, even if *Familiaris Consortio* did not go as far as *Amoris Laetitia* regarding sacramental discipline, it certainly laid out the foundations for *Amoris Laetitia*, by saying:

> Pastors must know that, for the sake of truth, they are obliged to *exercise careful discernment of situations*. There is in fact a difference between those who have sincerely tried to save their first marriage and have been unjustly abandoned, and those who through their own grave fault have destroyed a canonically valid marriage. Finally, there are those who have entered into a

---

30. *FC* 9.

31. Interestingly, theologian Juliano Almeida claims that a major advance might actually have come about with *Familiaris Consortio*, since this exhortation only mentions the word "adultery" once (*FC* 12), and not as a reference to Catholics in an "irregular situation," but to Israel's infidelity to God's covenant. The adjective "adulterous" does not exist in *Familiaris Consortio*. In fact, John Paul II never uses the word "sin" when referring to the divorced and remarried (see Almeida, "*Amoris Laetitia*—reflexões," 375).

32. *FC* 65.

second union for the sake of the children's upbringing, and who are sometimes subjectively certain in conscience that their previous and irreparably destroyed marriage had never been valid.[33]

Of course, there are even more staggering parallels between *Amoris Laetitia* and *Familiaris Consortio*. In fact, the points of agreement between both documents as regards education of children and the missionary vocation of families are so abundant that they would require a chapter of their own. It cannot be denied that there is a great continuity from *Familiaris Consortio* to *Amoris Laetitia*. If *Amoris Laetitia* implements reforms (namely sacramental reforms), it does so in continuity with *Familiaris Consortio* and the doctrinal principles laid therein.

Anyway, we should bear in mind that *Familiaris Consortio* does not claim to have the last word on the matter. *Familiaris Consortio* urges a greater dialogue between pastors and laity, pastors and families, and theologians and experts in family matters. "In this way the teaching of the Magisterium becomes better understood and the way is opened to *its progressive development*."[34]

It seems to me to be undeniable that this dialogue is precisely what Pope Francis sought to undertake with the two synods of the bishops on the family.

❖ ❖ ❖

The Only Rupture

It is precisely in this part of *Familiaris Consortio*, where Pope St. John Paul II appeals for a greater dialogue, that we can find the only rupture between *Familiaris Consortio* and the church today. However, when I mention "the church" here, I am not referring to Pope Francis or to the bishops in communion with him. Those are, by definition, the magisterium.[35] The church in rupture with *Familiaris Consortio* is composed of Catholics who refuse to assent to the magisterium. For *Familiaris Consortio* is very clear in this regard:

> Priests and deacons, when they have received timely and serious preparation for this apostolate, must unceasingly act towards

---

33. FC 84.
34. FC 73.
35. CCC 100.

> families as fathers, brothers, pastors, and teachers, assisting them with the means of grace and enlightening them with the light of truth. *Their teaching and advice must therefore always be in full harmony with the authentic Magisterium of the Church*, in such a way as to help the People of God to gain a correct sense of the faith, to be subsequently applied to practical life. *Such fidelity to the Magisterium will also enable priests to make every effort to be united in their judgments, in order to avoid troubling the consciences of the faithful.* . . .
>
> But it is useful to recall that the proximate and obligatory norm in the teaching of the faith—also concerning family matters—*belongs to the hierarchical Magisterium*. Clearly defined relationships between theologians, experts in family matters, and the Magisterium are of no little assistance for the correct understanding of the faith and for promoting—within the boundaries of the faith—legitimate pluralism.[36]

In short, those who are now spreading all sorts of arguments to undermine the authority of the magisterium, both in theory (by defending that a Catholic need not assent to non-infallible magisterial pronouncements), and in practice (by disrupting the reforms defined in *Amoris Laetitia*), are actually the ones who are acting within a hermeneutic of rupture with *Familiaris Consortio*.

They sometimes decry "dialogue" as if this meant a subtle way to introduce heterodoxy into what has been clearly defined before in *Familiaris Consortio*. By doing so, they are not being consistent with the document they claim to defend, since it actively asks for such dialogue to take place. More grievously, with their actions, they have put themselves outside the boundaries of legitimate dialogue: for the obligatory norm on the teaching of the faith, including family matters and their practical application, belongs to the hierarchical magisterium.

---

36. *FC* 73.

CHAPTER 12

Does *Amoris Laetitia* Contradict *Veritatis Splendor*?

THE SECOND MAGISTERIAL DOCUMENT most frequently invoked by papal critics is *Veritatis Splendor* (*VS*). This encyclical, also written by Pope St. John Paul II, would allegedly stand in complete contradiction with *Amoris Laetitia*.[1] The main purpose of *Veritatis Splendor* would be to condemn subjectivism in moral theology, and *Amoris Laetitia*'s main purpose would be to introduce such subjectivism. Therefore, *Amoris Laetitia* would be at odds with *Veritatis Splendor*—it should be viewed as erroneous and dismissed.

Is there truth to this claim? As usual, this argument stems from misconceptions on the reading of both documents. To know whether *Veritatis Splendor* condemns *Amoris Laetitia*, we need to understand what exactly is being condemned in *Veritatis Splendor*.

❊❊❊

What Veritatis Splendor *Stands Against*

Veritatis Splendor was promulgated in response to some currents of thought in moral theology that had become fashionable in certain theological quarters in the wake of the Second Vatican Council. Let us explore each of these theological currents rejected by *Veritatis Splendor*:

---

1. As an example, see Brugger, "'*Amoris Laetitia*' vs. '*Veritatis Splendor*.'"

1. *Situation Ethics:*[2] Morality is not based on universal moral laws, but on the real and concrete conditions or circumstances in which men must act, and according to which the conscience of the individual must judge and choose.[3]

> Certain currents of modern thought have gone so far as to exalt freedom to such an extent that it becomes an absolute, which would then be the source of values. . . . The individual conscience is accorded the status of a supreme tribunal of moral judgment which hands down categorical and infallible decisions about good and evil. To the affirmation that one has a duty to follow one's conscience is unduly added the affirmation that one's moral judgment is true merely by the fact that it has its origin in the conscience. . . . Conscience is no longer considered in its primordial reality as an act of a person's intelligence, the function of which is to apply the universal knowledge of the good in a specific situation and thus to express a judgment about the right conduct to be chosen here and now. Instead, there is a tendency to grant to the individual conscience the prerogative of independently determining the criteria of good and evil and then acting accordingly.[4]

2. *Subjectivism/Individualism:*[5] The idea that morality is subjective.

> *But in this way the inescapable claims of truth disappear, yielding their place to a criterion of sincerity, authenticity, and 'being at peace with oneself,' so much so that some have come to adopt a radically subjectivistic conception of moral judgment.* . . . Certain tendencies in contemporary moral theology, under the influence of the currents of subjectivism and individualism just mentioned, involve novel interpretations of the relationship of freedom to the moral law, human nature, and conscience, and propose novel criteria for the moral evaluation of acts. *Despite their variety, these tendencies are at one in lessening or even denying the dependence of freedom on truth.*[6]

---

2. For an example of a papal critic accusing *Amoris Laetitia* of situation ethics, see the "Situation Ethics" section of McCusker, "Key Doctrinal Errors and Ambiguities of *Amoris Laetitia.*"

3. Pius XII, *Soyez les bienvenues*, 4.

4. VS 32.

5. See Gaudron, "*Amoris Laetitia*: A Triumph of Subjectivism."

6. VS 32, 34.

3. *Relativism:*[7] The idea that we can never grasp ultimate truth in itself, but only its appearance in our way of perceiving.[8]

> This relativism becomes, in the field of theology, a lack of trust in the wisdom of God, who guides man with the moral law. *Concrete situations are unfavourably contrasted with the precepts of the moral law, nor is it any longer maintained that, when all is said and done, the law of God is always the one true good of man.*[9]

4. *Teleological ethical systems*:

    4.1 *Consequentialism:*[10] Morality that "claims to draw the criteria of the rightness of a given way of acting solely from a calculation of foreseeable consequences deriving from a given choice."[11]

    4.2 *Proportionalism:*[12] Morality that, "by weighing the various values and goods being sought, focuses rather on the proportion acknowledged between the good and bad effects of that choice, with a view to the 'greater good' or 'lesser evil' actually possible in a particular situation."[13]

5. *"Fundamental Option" Theory:*[14]

    > [The idea that] an individual could, by virtue of a fundamental option, remain faithful to God independently of whether or not certain of his choices and his acts are in conformity with specific moral norms or rules. *By virtue of a primordial option for charity, that individual could continue to be morally good, persevere in God's grace, and attain salvation,*

---

7. San Souci, "*Amoris Laetitia*: A Nod to the Dictatorship of Relativism."
8. Ratzinger, "Relativism: The Central Problem."
9. *VS* 84.
10. See the section "Consequentialist reasoning" in Brugger, "'*Amoris Laetitia*' vs. '*Veritatis Splendor*': You Say You Want a Revolution?"
11. *VS* 75.
12. See Twomey, "*Amoris Laetitia* and the chasm in modern moral theology." It is however, important to note, that the author does not claim that *Amoris Laetitia* is proportionalist, only that it echoes proportionalism.
13. *VS* 75.
14. See the "Fundamental Option" section of McCusker, "Key Doctrinal Errors and Ambiguities of *Amoris Laetitia*."

> even if certain of his specific kinds of behaviour were deliberately and gravely contrary to God's commandments as set forth by the Church.... Consequently, they go on to say, it is difficult, at least psychologically, to accept the fact that a Christian, who wishes to remain united to Jesus Christ and to his Church, could so easily and repeatedly commit mortal sins, as the 'matter' itself of his actions would sometimes indicate.... *The gravity of sin, they maintain, ought to be measured by the degree of engagement of the freedom of the person performing an act, rather than by the matter of that act.*[15]

If we pay close attention, we will see a common thread going through all of these erroneous currents of thought. They are all moral theories that deny the existence of one universal and immutable moral law as an objective standard to determine what is good and evil. In this respect, situation ethics would claim that the morality of an act depends on the circumstances; subjectivism, that morality rests on a subjective assessment of conscience; and the "fundamental option" theory, that it is contingent on one's intentions. Relativism could never assume one universal moral law, since it does not accept the existence of one single objective truth. Finally, the teleological ethical systems believe that moral values are influenced by a pre-moral order, including advantages and disadvantages accruing both to the agent and to all other persons possibly involved, such as, for example, health or its endangerment, physical integrity, life, death, loss of material goods, etc.[16]

To all of these erroneous currents of thought, Pope St. John Paul II answers with Catholic teaching: there exists a universal natural law, written in the heart of each man. This natural law allows people, by a common law, to build up a true communion of persons and, by God's grace, to practice charity.[17] Most emphatically, *Veritatis Splendor* deals with negative precepts of the universal moral law, which declare that certain acts are always seriously wrong according to their species (i.e., their objects), irrespectively of intentions and circumstances.[18] These acts are termed "intrinsically evil acts," and one such act is adultery.[19]

15. VS 68–69.
16. VS 75.
17. VS 51.
18. VS 79–80.
19. VS 52.

Amoris Laetitia has been accused of promoting the idea that adultery (i.e., divorced and remarried couples living *more uxorio*) can be justified in certain circumstances, because of the sinner's conscience.[20] Were this so, *Amoris Laetitia* would condone intrinsically evil acts, and therefore stand in opposition to *Veritatis Splendor*. Papal critics have pinned every single one of the aforementioned erroneous currents of thought on *Amoris Laetitia*. But is there any truth to these assertions?

❄ ❄ ❄

Veritatis Splendor *and Subjective Culpability*

As I stated in chapter 7, *Amoris Laetitia* grounds itself on the teaching of mitigating circumstances.[21] This teaching is articulated in the *Catechism of the Catholic Church*, promulgated by none other than John Paul II, the same author who penned *Veritatis Splendor*. So, if the Polish pope did not see any contradiction between the *Catechism* and the doctrine he laid out in *Veritatis Splendor*, then neither should we.

Veritatis Splendor deals with the objectively evil nature of sin, and especially of intrinsically evil acts. *Amoris Laetitia* deals with the subjective culpability of the sinner. The latter does not change the former. The fact that a sinner is more or less culpable does not change the object of the sin: it remains wrong. Therefore, we are talking about different planes, which do not generally intersect in those two documents, so that they cannot contradict each other. As I said in previous chapters, it is a matter of emphasis.

However, even if it is true that *Veritatis Splendor* focuses on the objectively evil nature of sin, it does not mean we cannot find vestiges of the teaching on mitigating circumstances in that encyclical.[22] In fact, *Veritatis Splendor* very categorically affirms the existence of invincible ignorance, as well as its impact on the culpability of the sinner:

---

20. See the section "Encouragement to adultery?" in McCusker, "Key Doctrinal Errors and Ambiguities of *Amoris Laetitia*."

21. In fact, in the same chapter of this book, I have already made the distinction between situation ethics and the discipline laid out in *Amoris Laetitia*.

22. We can also find vestiges of the law of gradualness in this encyclical. See Calmeyn, "Accompagnamento e legge di gradualità," particularly the sections "Camminare nel e verso il bene alla luce del kerygma" and "La legge di gradualità: da *Humanae vitae* ad *Amoris laetitia*."

> [An] error of conscience can be the result of an invincible ignorance, an ignorance of which the subject is not aware and which he is unable to overcome by himself. The Council reminds us that in cases where such invincible ignorance is not culpable, conscience does not lose its dignity, because even when it directs us to act in a way not in conformity with the objective moral order, it continues to speak in the name of that truth about the good which the subject is called to seek sincerely. . . . It is possible that the evil done as the result of invincible ignorance or a non-culpable error of judgment may not be imputable to the agent; but even in this case it does not cease to be an evil, a disorder in relation to the truth about the good.[23]

On the "full consent" side of the equation, *Veritatis Splendor* also talks about human weakness. It says that we should make allowance for God's mercy towards the sinner and also for understanding human weakness.[24] Of course, this weakness cannot be made the criterion of what is good, because otherwise the sinner would feel self-justified, so that he "would not ever feel the need to have recourse to God's mercy."[25] This is not what *Amoris Laetitia* tries to do. *Amoris Laetitia* never says that weakness is to be made the criterion of truth. In fact it explicitly rejects this notion, as we shall see later. Most importantly, it would be a complete betrayal of Francis's thought to believe that there are instances where we should not feel the need to have recourse to God's mercy. A major overtone of his pontificate is precisely how we always need God's mercy, without exception. A need for mercy presupposes the existence of sin, or of error.

Finally, the encyclical very distinctly delves into the distinction between mortal sin and venial sin (and, by extension, on mitigating circumstances):

> The Post-Synodal Apostolic Exhortation *Reconciliatio et Paenitentia* reaffirmed the importance and permanent validity of the distinction between mortal and venial sins, in accordance with the Church's tradition. And the 1983 Synod of Bishops, from which that Exhortation emerged, "not only reaffirmed the teaching of the Council of Trent concerning the existence and nature of mortal and venial sins, but it also recalled that *mortal sin is sin whose object is grave matter and which is also committed with full knowledge and deliberate consent.*" The statement of the Council

---

23. VS 61–62.
24. VS 104.
25. VS 104.

of Trent does not only consider the "grave matter" of mortal sin; it also recalls that its necessary condition is "full awareness and deliberate consent." ... In any event, *both in moral theology and in pastoral practice one is familiar with cases in which an act which is grave by reason of its matter does not constitute a mortal sin because of a lack of full awareness or deliberate consent on the part of the person performing it.* ... Clearly, situations can occur which are very complex and obscure from a psychological viewpoint, and *which influence the sinner's subjective imputability.*[26]

An even more staggering example is seen when John Paul II teaches that, although a good intention or particular circumstances cannot completely remove the evil out of an intrinsically evil act, it can diminish said evil.[27] I reiterate, John Paul II said circumstances can actually diminish evil— though not remove it.

In summary, *Veritatis Splendor*'s emphasis on intrinsically evil acts does not abrogate the doctrine of mitigating circumstances. In fact, it reasserts and reinforces it. Therefore, a sacramental discipline grounded on the teaching of mitigating circumstances, as the one in *Amoris Laetitia*, could never stand in contradiction to *Veritatis Splendor*.

❋ ❋ ❋

Amoris Laetitia *and Objective Evil*

However, some may still object that *Amoris Laetitia* is confusing and may actually not rest on the teaching of mitigating circumstances, but rather ground itself on one of those erroneous currents of thought condemned by *Veritatis Splendor*. In fact, all of those currents of thought have been attributed to *Amoris Laetitia* by its critics at some point. But this accusation could only hold if *Amoris Laetitia* did not assert the existence of an objectively evil nature for the sins for which we are discerning the culpability. Indeed, the apostolic exhortation cautions us several times not to read it through the lens of the errors *Veritatis Splendor* warns us against:

1. *Situation Ethics:*[28] "At the same time, it must be said that, precisely for that reason, *what is part of a practical discernment in particular*

---

26. VS 70.
27. VS 81.
28. See López, "Para comprender *Amoris Laetitia*," 423–24: "In the context of the moral teaching of the Church, this does not translate to an easy and misguided

circumstances cannot be elevated to the level of a rule. That would not only lead to an intolerable casuistry, but would *endanger the very values which must be preserved with special care.*"[29]

2. *Subjectivism/Individualism:*[30] "It is easy nowadays to confuse genuine freedom with the idea that each individual can act arbitrarily, as if there were no truths, values, and principles to provide guidance, and everything were possible and permissible."[31]

3. *Relativism:*[32] "A lukewarm attitude, any kind of relativism, or an undue reticence in proposing that ideal, would be a lack of fidelity to the Gospel and also of love on the part of the Church for young people themselves. To show understanding in the face of exceptional situations never implies dimming the light of the fuller ideal, or proposing less than what Jesus offers to the human being."[33]

4. *Teleological ethical system:*[34] The "personal and pastoral discernment of particular cases" advocated by *Amoris Laetitia* must be read

---

repeal of natural law, or an acritical assimilation of situation ethics, but to a prudential application of the precept to each case. This application admits no exceptions; but as we shall see, it allows for recognizing mitigating and contingent conditions that may interfere with the degree of culpability of each case." See also Buttiglione, *Risposte amichevoli*, 131–36. Finally, see chapter 7 of this book, section "Objective Evil vs. Subjective Guilt—A Wojtylan Tradition."

29. *AL* 304.

30. See Fernández, "El Capítulo VIII de *Amoris Laetitia*," 458: "It is still an 'objective situation of sin,' because there is still a clear Gospel proposition about matrimony that this situation does not objectively reflect. Francis, just like the Synod, sustains the existence of objective truths and universal norms, and never defended either subjectivism or relativism."

31. *AL* 34.

32. Fernández, "El Capítulo VIII de *Amoris Laetitia*," 458. See also López, "Entender a Wojtyla para comprender a Bergoglio," 41–42: "Why do we introduce the question of conscience? Is it a kind of subterfuge to justify some kind of relativism? The answer is negative. . . . If conscience is to subject its actions to the truth, the truth must be received in conscience."

33. *AL* 307.

34. Twomey, "*Amoris Laetitia* and the chasm in modern moral theology": "To return to the broader question as to the implications of the apostolic exhortation for fundamental moral theology, it seems to me that *AL*, though echoing many of the assumptions, and even using some of the language, of proportionalism, *avoids its pitfalls, namely the denial of intrinsically wrong acts (objective morality) or the notion of a fundamental option* (only mentioned in footnote #344, with reference to St. John Paul II's critique of the same)."

Does *Amoris Laetitia* Contradict *Veritatis Splendor*?

in this context: "Given that gradualness is not in the law itself, this discernment can never prescind from the Gospel demands of truth and charity, as proposed by the Church."[35]

As I said in chapter 6, we should avoid interpretations leading to unnecessary contradictions when interpreting a text. If Pope Francis condemns each erroneous current of thought in his apostolic exhortation, then we should heed his caveats. Instead of believing that Francis is being self-contradictory or confusing, we should take what he is saying at face value and acknowledge that we cannot interpret *Amoris Laetitia* through those errors.

It can also happen that imputing those erroneous currents of thought to *Amoris Laetitia* comes from a misreading, not of *Amoris Laetitia* itself, but of *Veritatis Splendor*. This can be particularly seen in the accusations that *Amoris Laetitia* subscribes to a "fundamental option" theory. At first glance, *Veritatis Splendor* seems to be damning indeed:

> Here an important pastoral consideration must be added. According to the logic of the [erroneous] positions mentioned above, an individual could, by virtue of a fundamental option, remain faithful to God independently of whether or not certain of his choices and his acts are in conformity with specific moral norms or rules. By virtue of a primordial option for charity, that individual could continue to be morally good, persevere in God's grace and attain salvation, even if certain of his specific kinds of behaviour were *deliberately and gravely* contrary to God's commandments as set forth by the Church.
>
> In point of fact, man does not suffer perdition only by being unfaithful to that fundamental option whereby he has made "a free self-commitment to God." With every *freely committed* mortal sin, he offends God as the giver of the law and as a result becomes guilty with regard to the entire law (cf. Jas 2:8–11); even if he perseveres in faith, he loses "sanctifying grace," "charity" and "eternal happiness."[36]

But please note the emphasized parts. Some papal critics used this quote to censure *Amoris Laetitia*'s pastoral approach, whereby a sinner might want to follow Christ while engaging in objectively sinful behaviors because of mitigating circumstances. However, *Veritatis Splendor*'s rebuttal only applies to *deliberate* behaviors, and to *freely-committed* mortal sins

35. *AL* 300.
36. *VS* 68.

(a pleonasm, for sure, but needed in order to avoid a misreading of the text). As we have seen in chapter 7, *Amoris Laetitia* deals mostly with sins with grave matter, but done without full consent. In other words, they are not deliberate, nor freely committed. Therefore, *Amoris Laetitia* does not contradict *Veritatis Splendor* in this instance.[37]

Likewise, when *Veritatis Splendor* condemns the notion that "*The gravity of sin* . . . ought to be measured by the degree of engagement of the freedom of the person performing an act, rather than by the matter of that act,"[38] it does not contradict *Amoris Laetitia*, for *Amoris Laetitia* never claims that subjective culpability interferes with the *gravity of the sin*, only with the subjective culpability of the sinner.

❋❋❋

Veritatis Splendor and the Seeds of *Amoris Laetitia*: The Case of the Rich Young Man

As I said in the previous chapter, we can go beyond the question: "Does *Amoris Laetitia* engage in a hermeneutic of rupture with *Veritatis Splendor*?" We can actually transcend the mere search for contradictions and ask ourselves: "Are *Amoris Laetitia*'s reforms in continuity with *Veritatis Splendor*?" From a reading of the first part of the encyclical, my answer is a resounding and surprising "yes." The seeds for *Amoris Laetitia* were all present in *Veritatis Splendor*, if we are sensitive enough to sense them.

In the introduction to *Veritatis Splendor*, Pope St. John Paul II fleshes out the biblical episode depicted in Matt 19:16–26, where a rich young man comes to Jesus Christ to ask him, "Good teacher, what good must I do to have eternal life?" John Paul II notes how the rich young man does not have a name, but rather that scripture says: "Someone came to him." The Polish pope then goes on to add that all of us are this "someone." In him we can recognize every person who, consciously or not, approaches Christ, and questions him about morality.[39] This is an essential and unavoidable question for the life of every man, for it is about the moral good which must be done, and about eternal life.[40] The Holy Father goes on to

---

37. Twomey, "*Amoris Laetitia* and the chasm in modern moral theology." See also Buttiglione, *Risposte amichevoli*, 150–56.

38. VS 69.

39. VS 7.

40. VS 8.

explain how Jesus, after being questioned, acts as a patient and sensitive teacher, and answers the young man by taking him by the hand, and leading him *step by step* to the full truth.[41]

First, Jesus asks: "Why do you call me good? No one is good but God alone." In other words, Jesus explains that asking about the good ultimately means to turn towards God, the fullness of goodness.[42] What man is and what he must do becomes clear as soon as God reveals himself, and the moral life presents itself as the response due to the many gratuitous initiatives taken by God out of love for man.[43]

Only after centering the answer on the goodness of God (the summit and source of all goodness), does Jesus go on to tell the young man: "Keep the commandments."[44] However, this answer does not satisfy the young man, who asks Jesus another question: "I have kept all these; what do I still lack?"[45] For the young man, *the question is not so much about rules to be followed, but about the full meaning of life.*[46] Here, John Paul II concludes that this full meaning of life can only come out of an encounter with Jesus Christ, the only response fully capable of satisfying the desire of the human heart. Precisely in this perspective, the Second Vatican Council called for a renewal of moral theology, so that its teaching would display the lofty vocation which the faithful have received in Christ.[47]

Conscious of the young man's yearning for something greater, *which would transcend a legalistic interpretation of the commandments*,[48] the good teacher invites him to enter upon the path of perfection: "If you wish to be perfect, go, sell your possessions and give the money to the poor, and you will have treasure in heaven; then come, follow me."[49] This is not a matter only of disposing oneself to hear a teaching and obediently accepting a commandment. More radically, it involves holding fast to the

---

41. VS 8.
42. VS 9.
43. VS 9.
44. VS 12.
45. VS 16.
46. VS 7.
47. VS 7.
48. VS 16.
49. VS 16.

very person of Jesus, partaking of his life and his destiny, sharing in his free and loving obedience to the will of the Father.[50]

The conclusion of Jesus's conversation with the rich young man is very poignant: "When the young man heard this, he went away sorrowful, for he had many possessions." Not only the rich man but the disciples themselves were taken aback by Jesus's call to discipleship, the demands of which transcend human aspirations and abilities: "When the disciples heard this, they were greatly astounded and said, 'Then who can be saved?'" But the master refers them to God's power: "With men this is impossible, but with God all things are possible."[51]

To imitate and live out the love of Christ *is not possible for man by his own strength* alone. He becomes capable of this love only by virtue of a gift received.[52] "The law of the Spirit of life in Christ Jesus has set me free from the law of sin and death."[53] With these words, the apostle Paul invites us to consider in the perspective of the history of salvation, which reaches its fulfillment in Christ, the relationship between the (old) law and grace (the new law). He recognizes the *pedagogic function of the law*,[54] which, by enabling sinful man to take stock of his own powerlessness and by *stripping him of the presumption of his self-sufficiency*, leads him to ask for and to receive "life in the Spirit."[55]

Love and life according to the gospel *cannot be thought of first and foremost as a kind of precept, because what they demand is beyond man's abilities.*[56] They are possible only as the result of a gift of God who heals,

---

50. VS 19.

51. VS 22.

52. VS 22.

53. Rom 8:2.

54. See Fernández, "El Capítulo VIII de *Amoris Laetitia*," 454: "Francis does not affirm that general moral laws cannot encompass all situations, nor that they cannot rule over the decision of conscience. On the contrary, he says that they 'set forth a good which can never be disregarded or neglected, but in their formulation they cannot provide absolutely for all particular situations' (AL 304). *It is the formulation of the norm* that cannot provide for every situation, *not the norm in itself*. . . . In this vein, the International Theological Commission, during the pontificate of Benedict XVI wrote that: 'Natural law could not, therefore, be presented as an already established set of rules that impose themselves a priori on the moral subject; rather, it is a source of objective inspiration for the deeply personal process of making a decision.'"

55. VS 23.

56. VS 23.

restores, and transforms the human heart by his grace.[57] And so we find revealed the authentic and original aspect of the commandment of love and of the perfection to which it is ordered: we are speaking of a possibility opened up to man exclusively by grace, by the gift of God, by his love.[58]

What I have expounded since the beginning of this segment consists almost entirely of *verbatim* quotes taken from *Veritatis Splendor*. It is very difficult not to note the similarities (especially in the last parts) between *Veritatis Splendor* and Pope Francis's theology, particularly his calls for us to transcend a purely legalistic and neo-Pelagian approach to the faith, heavily relying instead on God's grace to heal our weakness. In this sense, we can see how *Amoris Laetitia* evolves from *Veritatis Splendor* with an astounding continuity. In fact, the part where *Veritatis Splendor* concludes the telling of the story of the young rich man could have been written by Francis himself in *Amoris Laetitia*:

> The external precepts also mentioned in the Gospel dispose one for this grace or produce its effects in one's life. Indeed, the New Law is not content to say what must be done, but also gives the power to "do what is true." Saint John Chrysostom likewise observed that the New Law was promulgated at the descent of the Holy Spirit from heaven on the day of Pentecost, and that the Apostles "did not come down from the mountain carrying, like Moses, tablets of stone in their hands; but they came down carrying the Holy Spirit in their hearts . . . having become by his grace a living law, a living book."[59]

❖ ❖ ❖

---

57. *VS* 23.

58. *VS* 27.

59. *VS* 24. See also *VS* 104: "The Pharisee represents a 'self-satisfied' conscience, under the illusion that it is able to observe the law without the help of grace and convinced that it does not need mercy. . . . Accepting, on the other hand, the 'disproportion' between the law and human ability (that is, the capacity of the moral forces of man left to himself) kindles the desire for grace and prepares one to receive it." Please compare that excerpt with Francis's *Gaudete et Exsultate*, 49: "Those who yield to this pelagian or semi-pelagian mindset, even though they speak warmly of God's grace, 'ultimately trust only in their own powers and feel superior to others because they observe certain rules or remain intransigently faithful to a particular Catholic style.' When some of them tell the weak that all things can be accomplished with God's grace, deep down they tend to give the idea that all things are possible by the human will, as if it were something pure, perfect, all-powerful, to which grace is then added."

Veritatis Splendor, *the Magisterium, and the Development of Doctrine*

I would like to finish this chapter just like I finished the last one: not just by showing how *Amoris Laetitia* stands in continuity with previous papal documents, but how its critics stand in rupture with those same papal documents they claim to defend.

Veritatis Splendor makes a call for "an intense pastoral effort,"[60] which resides "not so much in doctrinal statements"[61] "as in constantly looking to the Lord Jesus."[62] It explains that clear and forceful presentation of moral truth can never be separated from a profound and heartfelt respect, born of that patient and trusting love which man always needs along his moral journey, a journey frequently wearisome on account of difficulties, weakness, and painful situations.[63] The church must always be careful (so says *Veritatis Splendor*) not to break the bruised reed or to quench the dimly burning wick.[64]

Of course, John Paul II is very clear that such pastoral efforts cannot prescind from the truths of the gospel and moral norms. However, he is also very clear that the task of interpreting these prescriptions was entrusted by Jesus to the apostles and their successors, with the special assistance of the spirit of truth.[65] Within the unity of the church, promoting and preserving the faith and the moral life is the task entrusted by Jesus to the apostles,[66] a task which continues in the ministry of their successors.[67] The task of authentically interpreting the word of God, whether in its written form or in that of tradition, has been entrusted only to those charged with the church's living magisterium, whose authority is exercised in the name of Jesus Christ.

This is apparent from the living tradition, which comes from the apostles, and which *progresses in the church under the assistance of the Holy Spirit.*[68] Within tradition, the authentic interpretation of the Lord's

60. VS 84.
61. VS 85.
62. VS 85, 87–88.
63. VS 95.
64. VS 95.
65. VS 25.
66. See Matt 28:19–20.
67. VS 27.
68. VS 27.

law *develops*, with the help of the Holy Spirit. The same spirit who is at the origin of the revelation of Jesus's commandments and teachings guarantees that they will be reverently preserved, faithfully expounded, and correctly applied in different times and places. The church, in her life and teaching, is thus revealed as "the pillar and bulwark of the truth,"[69] including the truth regarding moral action. Indeed, the church has the right always and everywhere to proclaim moral principles, and to make judgments about any human matter insofar as this is required by fundamental human rights or the salvation of souls.[70]

In this regard, there is a need to seek out and to discover the most adequate formulation for universal and permanent moral norms in the light of different cultural contexts, a formulation most capable of ceaselessly expressing their historical relevance, of making them understood, and of authentically interpreting their truth. This truth of the moral law—like that of the "deposit of faith"—unfolds down the centuries: the norms expressing that truth remain valid in their substance, but must be specified and determined "*eodem sensu eademque sententia*" in the light of historical circumstances *by the church's magisterium*, whose decision is preceded and accompanied by the work of interpretation and formulation characteristic of the reason of individual believers and of theological reflection.[71]

What I said above is also composed of almost word-for-word quotes taken from *Veritatis Splendor*. In the end, those who reject the capacity of the magisterium to authentically interpret how to develop the application of universal and permanent moral norms in the light of different cultural contexts are the ones interpreting *Veritatis Splendor* with a hermeneutic of rupture toward the encyclical itself.

---

69. 1 Tim 3:15.
70. VS 27.
71. VS 53.

Chapter 13

Does *Amoris Laetitia* Contradict Any Other Authoritative Church Statement?

IN THIS CHAPTER, I wish to focus very briefly on other church documents and pronouncements which are often used by papal critics to illustrate the alleged contradictions between *Amoris Laetitia* and previously established doctrine.

❖❖❖

The Council of Trent

Papal critics will sometimes affirm that *Amoris Laetitia* contradicts the Council of Trent's *Decree on Justification*:[1] "If any one saith, that the commandments of God are, even for one that is justified and constituted in grace, impossible to keep; let him be anathema."[2] This would be especially problematic, as this canon is infallibly proclaimed and cannot, therefore, be revoked by any church authority, not even a pope.

We must, however, take two facts into consideration. First, the Council of Trent is speaking in the context of the Protestant Reformation. This canon is meant to condemn erroneous ideas on justification issuing from Protestant leaders, and should be read with this historical context in

---

1. As an example, see the section "Inconsistency with the teaching of Trent on grace" from Brugger, "Five Serious Problems with Chapter 8 of *Amoris Laetitia*."
2. Council of Trent, 6th Session, c. XVIII.

Does *Amoris Laetitia* Contradict Any Other Church Statement? 181

mind.³ Second, as *Veritatis Splendor* itself makes clear in #69, the teaching concerning the distinction between mortal and venial sins also comes from the Council of Trent. After all, this ecumenical council also makes the following condemnation in the same *Decree on Justification*: "If any one saith, that a man . . . is able, during his whole life, to avoid all sins, *even those that are venial,*—except by a special privilege from God, as the Church holds in regard of the Blessed Virgin; let him be anathema."⁴ If the critics' interpretation of Trent is true, then how come grace does not stop man from sinning ever again, even venially? The issue is probably a bit more nuanced than it seemed at first glance.

The question remains, though: does *Amoris Laetitia* contradict Trent in this regard? Let us examine with more detail what the council has to say:

> But no one, how much soever justified, ought to think himself exempt from the observance of the commandments; no one ought to make use of that rash saying, one prohibited by the Fathers under an anathema,—that the observance of the commandments of God is impossible for one that is justified. For God commands not impossibilities, but, by commanding, both admonishes thee to do what thou art able, and to pray for what thou art not able (to do), and aids thee that thou mayest be able.⁵

Let us now see what *Amoris Laetitia* has to say about the very same topic:

> For the law is itself a gift of God which points out the way, a gift for everyone without exception; it can be followed with the help of grace, *even though each human being "advances gradually with the progressive integration of the gifts of God and the demands of God's definitive and absolute love in his or her entire personal and social life."*⁶

---

3. Guarino, *Disputed Teachings of Vatican II*, 29–30: "When an ecumenical council teaches about an issue, it normally addresses only one aspect of the faith, often an aspect that has been misunderstood. Consequently conciliar statements should not be expected to be fully rounded expositions of Christian truth. In fact, the church's reaction to an error may be so defensive and polemical that the rebuttal itself becomes one-sided and unilateral."

4. Council of Trent, 6th Session, c. XXIII.

5. Council of Trent, 6th Session, c. XI.

6. *AL* 295.

Please note, the law of God can be followed by everyone, without exception, with the help of grace. The first half of this quote (non-italicized) is a faithful restatement of the doctrine infallibly proclaimed in the Council of Trent. But then, Pope Francis complements it with additional information (the italicized part): following the law is brought about gradually and progressively. By doing this, Francis shows that he is not contradicting Trent, but actually developing it with a more accurate formulation,[7] more in keeping with the reality experienced by many Christians who struggle with their sins, while failing many times.

Also, this additional information with which Francis complements Trent was not invented by him—it is actually a direct quote from *Familiaris Consortio* #9. Thus, we can see yet again how Francis remains faithful to his predecessor's apostolic exhortation, notwithstanding the accusations of his critics. More importantly, we can see how the Holy Father masterfully integrates two different magisterial pronouncements, weaving them together in a seamless fashion. This is not a contradiction, otherwise *Familiaris Consortio* would contradict Trent. Rather, it is a doctrinal development, whereby we can read Trent in light of *Familiaris Consortio*, and by extension, *Amoris Laetitia*.

Another less common objection is that Trent also infallibly defined that "no one can know with a certainty of faith, which cannot be subject to error, that he has obtained the grace of God".[8] In other words, the divorced and remarried could never discern whether they are in mortal sin or not, and therefore, whether they could partake of communion. They should—so it is argued—simply not take communion in order to avoid the risk of sacrilege. However, if we took a literalist view of this proposition, as papal critics do, then *no one* would be able to *ever* take communion, since no one can ever be sure of being in a state of grace. As Archbishop Victor Fernández argues, one is never "certain" of being in a state of grace, "even if one does not have conscience of having violated a commandment." Therefore, we are talking about a certain "moral security" that the person is not in mortal sin. This "moral security can

---

7. See Guarino, *Disputed Teachings of Vatican II*, 30: "While this theologian considers all the definitions sanctioned by the Church to be irreformable, he believes them nonetheless to be capable of a more profound clarity and a more lucid formulation. A new council is able to perfect the definition of a preceding council by, for example, showing how a solemn but partial teaching is integrated into the ensemble of complex doctrine."

8. Council of Trent, 6th Session, chap. IX.

be attained through a personal and pastoral discernment, which cannot base itself only in general norms".[9]

I would also like to recall an interesting historical side note: when the Council of Trent was preparing to anathematize (in an infallible way) anyone who would say that marriage can be dissolved by the adultery of one of the spouses, and that the innocent spouse could then enter another marriage, some ambassadors from the Republic of Venice intervened in favor of a large number of Greeks living in their territories. These Greek Catholics had been allowed to follow their own Eastern practices on marriage,—namely that a man whose wife had committed adultery could remarry and receive the sacraments—as long as they accepted the rule of Latin bishops and the authority of the pope. Since the Council was directed at the Protestant Reformation, there was no reason to address these Eastern practices. Therefore, the final version of the canon was softened, only condemning someone who would say that the Church is mistaken when it teaches that the bond of marriage cannot be dissolved by the adultery of the other spouse. This in practice allowed the Greek Catholics in Venetian territories to keep receiving the sacraments even in a remarriage setting.[10]

❊❊❊

Sacramentum Caritatis

In 2007, Pope Benedict XVI also issued a post-synodal apostolic exhortation, named *Sacramentum Caritatis*. In this document, Benedict basically reaffirms *Familiaris Consortio* vis-à-vis communion for the divorced and remarried:

> The Synod of Bishops confirmed the Church's *practice*, based on Sacred Scripture (cf. Mark 10:2–12), of not admitting the divorced and remarried to the sacraments, since their state and their condition of life objectively contradict the loving union of Christ and the Church signified and made present in the Eucharist. . . . Finally, where the nullity of the marriage bond is not declared and objective circumstances make it impossible to cease cohabitation, the Church encourages these members of the faithful to commit themselves to living their relationship in

---

9. Fernández, "Para comprender Amoris Laetitia," 459–60.
10. Travers, "*Amoris Laetitia* and Canon 915," 322–24.

fidelity to the demands of God's law, as friends, as brother and sister; in this way they will be able to return to the table of the Eucharist, taking care to observe the Church's established and approved *practice* in this regard.[11]

Please note how Benedict XVI once again talks about a *practice* (i.e., a sacramental discipline), based on sacred scripture and on the *Ipse Namque*. His wording almost exactly mirrors the one in *Familiaris Consortio*,[12] so everything that I wrote in chapter 11 regarding *Familiaris Consortio* can be equally applied to *Sacramentum Caritatis*.

There is one other reason why it is important to bring up the case of *Sacramentum Caritatis*. Decades before his election to the papacy, Joseph Ratzinger had published an article precisely about communion for the divorced and remarried. In this 1972 essay, Ratzinger draws from such sources as Origen, St. Basil of Caesarea, Pope Gregory II, and Gratian (a famous ancient canon lawyer) to talk about a "concrete pastoral application, a more elastic practice, which was not indeed seen as entirely in conformity with the true faith of the Church, but which also could not be absolutely excluded. . . . It [was] contrary to Scripture and contrary to what was ordained from the beginning, but it [was] not [viewed as] entirely senseless—a custom that some of the leaders in the Church ventured in order to avoid still worse things."[13]

It must be noted that this pastoral approach is *not* the one advocated in *Amoris Laetitia*. It was a much more lax practice, more akin to the Eastern Orthodox churches, or to Cardinal Kasper's proposed "penitential path"[14] (see chapter 3). *Amoris Laetitia*'s pastoral approach is based on the sound, well-established, and orthodox doctrine about the distinction between mortal and venial sins when making a conscience exam

---

11. Benedict XVI, *Sacramentum Caritatis*, 29.

12. This does not mean that *Sacramentum Caritatis* did not have some developments relatively to *Familiaris Consortio*. As Archbishop Victor Fernández explains, "While John Paul II asked the divorced and remarried couples who could not satisfy the obligation to separate, to 'take on themselves the duty to live in complete continence' (FC 84), Benedict proposed to them, more gently, that they 'strive' (in Spanish *esforzarse*, even if the English version has 'commit') 'to live their relationship in fidelity to the demands of God's law, as friends, as brother and sister' (#29b)" (Fernández, "Para comprender *Amoris Laetitia*," 453).

13. Ratzinger, "On the Question of the Indissolubility of Marriage."

14. See Walter Kasper's address to the Consistory of Cardinals on February 21, 2014 ("Cardinal Kasper's Proposal," *Inside The Vatican*). Note the similarities with Ratzinger's essay in the section "The Practice of the Early Church."

for receiving the Eucharist, taking into account mitigating circumstances that may diminish subjective culpability. In contrast, the practice depicted in Ratzinger's essay was as follows: "the second marriage does not become a properly ecclesial marriage. It remains a tolerated marriage, and the reception of the sacraments is permitted by way of tolerance (today termed economy)."[15] From this, young Joseph Ratzinger proposed: "If in the second marriage moral obligations to the children, to the family, and so also to the woman have arisen, and no similar commitments from the first marriage exist, and if thus for moral reasons the abandonment of the second marriage is inadmissible, and on the other hand practically speaking abstinence presents no real possibility (*magnorum est*, says Gregory II), the opening up of community in Communion after a period of probation appears to be no less than just and to be fully in line with the Church's tradition."[16]

Later on, Ratzinger retracted his conclusions. As prefect for the CDF under Pope St. John Paul II, he upheld the sacramental discipline as laid out in *Familiaris Consortio* (as we shall see later in this chapter). Already as Pope Benedict XVI, he promulgated *Sacramentum Caritatis*, which on this topic follows *Familiaris Consortio* to the letter, as we have seen. Later on, he republished all his previous theological writings in the collection *Opera Omnia*. Instead of republishing his 1972 essay as it was, he rewrote the conclusions in order to accommodate his predecessor's practice.[17]

If Benedict retracted his conclusions, then we should not use this essay to advance any idea contrary to the author's wishes. After all, even young Ratzinger admits that this approach goes against scripture and church teaching. However, the article remains noteworthy for two reasons. First, Benedict's retraction applies to his theological conclusions, not to the historical findings he previously based those conclusions on. Therefore, people of a more traditionalist bent should be more cautious before they defend a certain practice on the basis that it is what the church always and everywhere has done, since the time of the apostles—as is usually claimed.[18] Reality and history are often much more complex

15. Ratzinger, "On the Question of the Indissolubility of Marriage."
16. Ratzinger, "On the Question of the Indissolubility of Marriage."
17. This rewritten conclusion has been translated into English by Matthew Scherry and published in the blog *Chiesa Expressonline* (Magister, "In the Synod on the Family Even the Pope Emeritus Is Speaking Out").
18. As an example, see Pentin, "Thousands of Priests Worldwide Call for Clarification of *Amoris Laetitia*": "It is also essential that the Church's discipline must always

than what is presented by people with an idealized vision of the church and of the past. Sometimes, the church is more lax now than in previous times, and sometimes more rigorous. We should not view this as a threat to the church's infallibility or to its teaching charism, but humbly accept that there are legitimate developments, both in the past (the development that led the West to eschew the more lax practice and that brought about what people today refer to as the "traditional" understanding), and in the present (as in *Amoris Laetitia*'s discipline).

Secondly, and most importantly, the way Ratzinger reacted to John Paul II's magisterial pronouncement should serve as an example. Even if Ratzinger had previously written on this topic, he did not try to defend himself and his ideas after John Paul II published his apostolic exhortation. Ratzinger did not try to accommodate the pope's clear teachings to his findings. He simply assented to what his pontiff taught and actively defended it. In this regard, people who invoke Benedict/Ratzinger as a model should not do so simply because they perceive him as an ally, or as someone who agrees with them on this matter. They should see him also as a model of a private theologian willing to review his work in light of his fidelity to the pope. And they should follow his example, especially with respect to Francis.

❈ ❈ ❈

Canon 915

Another common objection[19] has to do with canon 915 of the 1983 Code of Canon Law, which states:

> Those upon whom the penalty of excommunication or interdict has been imposed or declared, and *others who obstinately persist in manifest grave sin*, are not to be admitted to holy communion.

---

follow her *dogmatic teaching*. In particular, since at the present time there is much confusion, it is necessary to make clear that Holy Communion cannot be given to someone choosing to live in a sexual relationship with a person other than their validly espoused husband or wife. . . . Requesting such a clarification, *which reiterates the perennial teaching of the Church*, is an act of filial love by faithful sons of the Church who turn to our Supreme Shepherd seeking his paternal guidance."

19. As an example, see Peters, "On the Appearance of the Pope's Letter to the Argentine Bishops in the *Acta Apostolicae Sedis*."

Accordingly, those who would obey Pope Francis's provisions would be in violation of canon law. If Francis would like to introduce his sacramental discipline, he would have to amend canon law accordingly.[20]

However, please note that canon 915 refers to "manifest" grave sin. In other words, any grave sin covered by this canon would have to be manifest. I already dealt with the question of scandal in chapter 8 of this book. I will also return to this point later. But for now, I would like to consider this canon's precursor: the previous 1917 Code of Canon Law.

This old code labeled divorced and remarried people (then called "bigamists") as simply "infamous," not necessarily "*manifest* infamous." Bigamists were excommunicated only if they had spurned the "admonitions of the Ordinary."[21] The canon that excluded the "*manifest* infamous" from the Eucharist, on the other hand, applied to those "*publicly* unworthy."[22] Scott Smith, the author of the *Reduced Culpability* website, has gathered a wealth of references from authoritative canon law commentators,[23] mostly pre-Vatican II,[24] on this topic. Even though he grants that this was not "unanimously agreed by all commentators," and that there was a "familiar discussion" and "controversy" as to the norms to be used, the "majority view"[25] was that only the *manifestly* infamous bigamists were excluded from the Eucharist. Scott Smith then concludes that the 1917 code "did not provide an absolute, automatic, and exceptionless ban on the reception of Holy Communion by the divorced and remarried. Rather these Commentators understood that under the 1917 Code, the divorced and remarried could not be refused Holy Communion in two circumstances": "Good Faith" and "Occult in Fact."[26]

This is consistent with another historical fact: in 1975 (when the old code was still in force), the bishops of the United States requested clarification on whether divorced and remarried couples could be admitted to the sacraments. Archbishop Jerome Hamer, then secretary of the CDF,

---

20. Peters, "On the Appearance of the Pope's Letter to the Argentine Bishops in the *Acta Apostolicae Sedis*."

21. Peters, *1917 Code of Canon Law*, c. 2356.

22. Peters, *1917 Code of Canon Law*, c. 885.

23. Smith, "*Amoris Laetitia* and the 1917 Code of Canon Law."

24. And many of whom were praised by none other than Dr. Edward Peters, one of the most prominent critics of the Buenos Aires interpretation on account of canon 915.

25. Smith, "*Amoris Laetitia* and the 1917 Code of Canon Law."

26. Smith, "*Amoris Laetitia* and the 1917 Code of Canon Law."

replied to them: "These couples *may be allowed to receive the sacraments on two conditions*, that they try to live according to the demands of Christian moral principles and that they receive the sacraments in churches in which they are not known so that they will not create any scandal."[27]

Also, Cardinal Schönborn said in an interview[28] that he asked then-Cardinal Ratzinger, in 1994, whether "it is possible that the *old praxis, that was taken for granted, and that I knew before the Council,* is still valid?" (This old praxis was the "possibility, in the internal forum with one's confessor, of receiving the sacraments, provided that no scandal was given.") The response from the prefect of the CDF at the time was, according to Schönborn, very clear: "There is no general norm that can cover all particular cases."[29]

Of course, the 1917 Code of Canon Law has been superseded by the current one. We must try to ascertain whether *Amoris Laetitia* is compatible with the 1983 code, not the 1917 one. However, our incursions on the previous Code of Canon Law illustrate how the praxis of denying communion to all divorced and remarried people on account of their objective state is not as perennial and immutable as papal critics make it out to be.

Pope St. John Paul II promulgated the 1983 Code of Canon Law in accordance with the provisions delineated in *Familiaris Consortio* (see chapter 11). Later on, in the year 2000 (i.e., still during John Paul II's pontificate), the Pontifical Council for Legislative Texts (PCLT) issued a declaration, where it was stated:

> Authors offer various interpretations of the above-cited canon [915] that exclude from its application the situation of those who are divorced and remarried. For example, since the text speaks of "grave sin," it would be necessary to establish the presence of all the conditions required for the existence of mortal sin, including those which are subjective, necessitating a judgment of a type that a minister of Communion could not make ab externo; moreover, given that the text speaks of those who "obstinately" persist in that sin, it would be necessary to verify an attitude of defiance on the part of an individual who had received a legitimate warning from the Pastor. . . .

---

27. CDF, "Letter of Clarification," 1284/66. See also the analysis given to this letter by Walford, *Pope Francis, the Family, and Divorce,* 165–66.

28. Schönborn, "Conversation with Cardinal Schönborn."

29. Schönborn, "Conversation with Cardinal Schönborn."

The phrase "and others who obstinately persist in manifest grave sin" is clear and must be understood in a manner that does not distort its sense so as to render the norm inapplicable. The three required conditions are:

a. grave sin, understood *objectively*, being that the minister of Communion *would not be able to judge from subjective imputability*;
b. obstinate persistence, which means the existence of an *objective situation of sin* that endures in time and which the will of the individual member of the faithful does not bring to an end, *no other requirements (attitude of defiance, prior warning, etc.) being necessary* to establish the fundamental gravity of the situation in the Church;
c. the manifest character of the situation of grave habitual sin.[30]

In other words, this PCLT declaration interprets canon 915 in a way that only takes into account the objective situation of sin. It explicitly rules out the discernment of subjective culpability (per *Amoris Laetitia*) and the necessity of an act of defiance of a warning from the pastor (as in the 1917 Code of Canon Law).

However, there is one additional condition that must necessarily be present: "*manifest character* of the grave sin." This condition exists to allow the exception laid out in *Familiaris Consortio*: those who, though divorced and civilly remarried (and publicly known to be so), seek to live in perfect continence, as brother and sister. As the PCLT says:

Given that the fact that these faithful are not living *more uxorio* is *per se* occult, while their condition as persons who are divorced and remarried is *per se manifest*, they will be able to receive Eucharistic Communion only *remoto scandalo*.[31]

So, the divorced and remarried couples who cease to live *more uxorio* are not excluded from the Eucharist, as long as they will take communion in a way that will not cause scandal.[32] In fact, scandal seems to be the substantive reason for the PCLT's decision:

30. PCLT, "Declaration," 1, 2.
31. PCLT, "Declaration," 2.
32. See López, "Para comprender *Amoris Laetitia*," 437: "The prohibition to access the Eucharist in a situation of grave sin, as expressed in Canon 915, is grounded on the possibility of affecting the order of the community, and generate scandals and similar situations. In other words, it is a disciplinary, not doctrinal norm, that the Pope

> In effect, the reception of the Body of Christ when one is *publicly unworthy* constitutes an objective harm to the ecclesial communion: it is a behavior that affects the rights of the Church and of all the faithful to live in accord with the exigencies of that communion. *In the concrete case of the admission to Holy Communion of faithful who are divorced and remarried, the scandal, understood as an action that prompts others towards wrongdoing, affects at the same time both the sacrament of the Eucharist and the indissolubility of marriage.* That scandal exists even if such behavior, unfortunately, no longer arouses surprise: in fact *it is precisely with respect to the deformation of the conscience that it becomes more necessary for Pastors to act, with as much patience as firmness, as a protection to the sanctity of the Sacraments* and a defense of Christian morality, and for the correct formation of the faithful.[33]

This immediately precedes the PCLT definition of those who are excluded from the Eucharist by canon 915. In other words, it is meant as context for the bans. I have already dealt with the problem of scandal in chapter 8, namely in how both *Amoris Laetitia* and the Buenos Aires criteria explicitly state how communion can only be given to the divorced and civilly remarried in a reserved manner, and avoiding any occasion of scandal.

Nevertheless, even with this caveat, can we interpret canon 915 in accordance with *Amoris Laetitia*'s sacramental discipline, as defined by the manifest mind and will of the pope? Let us consider canon 16:

> §1 Laws are *authentically interpreted by the legislator* and by that person to whom the legislator entrusts the power of authentic interpretation.
>
> §2 *An authentic interpretation* which is presented by way of a law has the same force as the law itself, and must be promulgated.

The legislator is the pope. Did *Amoris Laetitia* give an authentic interpretation of canon 915? We cannot deny that *Amoris Laetitia* deals with the same substance as canon 915 regarding divorced and remarried people and their access to the Eucharist. Nonetheless, *Amoris Laetitia* is an apostolic exhortation. In other words, it is exhortative in nature, not legislative. However, both *Familiaris Consortio* and *Sacramentum Caritatis*

---

can modify or, even without modifying it, make exceptions to it based on the canonical principle of 'salus animarum.'"

33. PCLT, "Declaration," 1.

are apostolic exhortations too. So, by the same token, they cannot be an authentic interpretation of canon 915 either, especially given that neither mention this canon by name.[34]

Still, canon 16 says that laws may be authentically interpreted, not only by the legislator (the pope), but also by "that person to whom the legislator entrusts the power of *authentic interpretation*." This refers to the PCLT, which has the authority to issue authentic interpretations. We should bear in mind, however, that in this specific case, the PCLT issued a "declaration," not an "authentic interpretation." This is not the same in canon law: the PCLT at times issues declarations clarifying a law's meaning and applicability, but these are not authentic interpretations.[35]

Since *Amoris Laetitia* and the PCLT seem to disagree, it seems that there may be reasonable doubt about how to implement canon 915, especially in light of the precedents of the 1917 Code of Canon Law, as mentioned above. In this case, we should consider canon 17:

> Ecclesiastical laws are to be understood according to the proper meaning of the words considered in their text and context. *If the meaning remains doubtful or obscure, there must be recourse to parallel places*, if there be any, to the purpose and circumstances of the law, and *to the mind of the legislator*.

In other words, even if *Amoris Laetitia* is not an authentic interpretation of canon 915, we can still take recourse to it to know the mind of the pope as to how this canon should be applied.[36] In fact, chapters 4 and 5 of this book were written precisely to ascertain the mind of the pope on this

---

34. In fact, *Familiaris Consortio* precedes canon 915. Of course, canon 915 cites *Familiaris Consortio*, but this is not what I am arguing. What I am arguing is that *Familiaris Consortio*, being an apostolic exhortation, is not an "authentic interpretation" of the canon. "Authentic interpretation" has a very well defined meaning.

35. For more information on this topic, I also recommend reading the section "Authentic Interpretation" in Smith, "Public Scandal." See also Travers, "*Amoris Laetitia* and Canon 915," 319–20: "In terms of its canonical status, the Council's declaration was not an *authentic interpretation* of canon 915 that would have required the approval of the Supreme Pontiff in order to have definitive effect in the nature of a law. Neither was it approved by the Holy Father 'in specific form' [*in forma specifica*] so as to adopt the declaration as his own, thereby overriding any otherwise applicable canon law to the contrary." Also on the Vatican website it is possible to see that the PCLT document in question has been filed under "Declarations" and not as an "*Interpretatio authentica*." For a list of "authentic interpretations" issued by the PCLT (which does not include canon 915), see the table in Wikipedia, s.v. "Interpretation (Canon Law)."

36. See once more Smith, "Public Scandal."

matter. By knowing the mind of the legislator, we know how we should understand canon 915.

Of course, the PCLT explicitly mentions that the phrase "and others who obstinately persist in manifest grave sin" is clear. But it is undeniable that the meaning of that sentence ceased to be clear as soon as Pope Francis published *Amoris Laetitia*. In fact, the "lack of clarity" and "confusion" allegedly created by *Amoris Laetitia* is one of the main arguments coming from papal critics,[37] so it would be very strange if they would deny that this confusion exists as to how to understand canon 915. If there is no clarity in how we should interpret canon 915, then we must take recourse to the mind of the legislator. And the mind of the legislator (as I proved in chapters 4 and 5) is, in turn, perfectly clear regarding the access of the divorced and remarried to the Eucharist.[38] Therefore, canon 915 should be applied accordingly.[39]

But can we really interpret canon 915 in a way that supports Francis's magisterial developments on this matter, using well-established principles of canonical construction? Patrick Travers, Vicar General and Judicial Vicar of the Diocese of Juneau, Alaska, has written masterfully on this topic. First, he cites canon 18:

> Laws which establish a penalty or *restrict the free exercise of rights* or which contain an exception to the law are subject to a *strict interpretation*.

Strict interpretation is the restriction of the proper meaning of the words of a law in a way that reduces its effect to that minimum beyond which the law would be rendered meaningless or absurd[40]. Since canon 915 is a law that restricts the exercise of the right to receive the Holy Eucharist[41], its construction must also take account of the principle of strict interpretation.[42]

---

37. See Longley, "*Amoris Laetitia*: Pope Francis Has Created Confusion Where We Needed Clarity."

38. To be clear, what I am arguing here is that the *application of canon 915* is not clear in this setting, not that the true interpretation of *Amoris Laetitia* is unclear.

39. Another source of interest to interpret canon law in accordance with the pope's manifest mind and will can be seen in Miller, "Understanding and Implementing *Amoris Laetitia* Chapter VIII."

40. Travers, "*Amoris Laetitia* and Canon 915," 399–400.

41. *Code of Canon Law*, c. 912: "Any baptized person not prohibited by law can and must be admitted to holy communion."

42. Travers, "*Amoris Laetitia* and Canon 915," 399.

Does *Amoris Laetitia* Contradict Any Other Church Statement?

Reverend Travers then proceeds to interpret each of the terms used in canon 915 according to this principle. Since canon 915 excludes from communion those who obstinately persist in manifest *grave sin*, and since John Paul II himself admitted that the church sometimes has been imprecise on how she defines "grave sin,"[43] it is important to define what is meant by this term. Does "grave sin" mean "sin with grave matter" or "mortal sin"? Reverend Travers brings attention to canon 988 on the sacrament of penance:

> §1 Each of the Christian faithful is bound by the obligation of confessing in species and number all *grave sins* [*omnia peccata gravia*] committed after baptism and not yet directly remitted by the keys of the Church nor acknowledged in individual confession, of which he has knowledge after diligent self-examination.
>
> §2 It is to be recommended to the Christian faithful that they confess even *venial sins* [*peccata venialia*].

Here, "grave sin" is contrasted with "venial sin", thereby equating the term with "mortal sin".[44] If we apply this definition of "grave sin" to canon 915, then this canon is consistent with *Amoris Laetitia*.

I would like to address a final objection: the PCLT declaration claims its interpretation of canon 915 is a matter of "divine law," and that "no ecclesiastical authority may dispense the minister of Holy Communion from this obligation in any case, nor may he emanate directives that contradict it."[45] But the PCLT does not have the authority to define a certain interpretation (especially one that is not an "authentic interpretation") as a divine law in contradiction with the magisterium of a pope. This would violate canon law itself, for canon 331 states:

> The office uniquely committed by the Lord to Peter, the first of the Apostles, and to be transmitted to his successors, abides in the Bishop of the Church of Rome. He is the head of the College of Bishops, the Vicar of Christ, and the Pastor of the universal Church here on earth. Consequently, *by virtue of his office, he has supreme, full, immediate, and universal ordinary power in the Church, and he can always freely exercise this power.*

---

43. John Paul II, *Reconciliatio et Paenitentia*, 17.

44. Travers, "*Amoris Laetitia* and Canon 915," 403. Additional evidence for this interpretation can be seen also in pages 404–05.

45. PCLT, "Declaration," 1, 4.

Neither can it be used to judge the pope as in violation of canon law, for canon 1404 also states: "The First See is judged by no one." In the end, trying to use canon law to refute the magisterium is manifestly condemned by none other than Pope St. John Paul II:

> A more dangerous reductionism is that which claims to interpret and apply the laws of the Church in a manner that is detached from the teaching of the Magisterium. According to this view, only formal legislative acts and not doctrinal pronouncements would have disciplinary value. It is obvious that those operating from this reductionist perspective could sometimes come up with two different solutions to the same ecclesial problem: one drawn from the texts of the Magisterium, and the other drawn from canonical texts. At the root of such a conception is an impoverished idea of canon law that identifies it only with the positive dictate of the norm. This is not right.[46]

✵✵✵

The Letters of the Congregation for the Doctrine of the Faith

In 1994, then Cardinal Joseph Ratzinger, prefect of the CDF at the time, issued a letter to the bishops of the Catholic Church concerning the reception of Holy Communion by the divorced and remarried members of the faithful. In this letter, the CDF reaffirmed the practice of "not admitting the divorced and remarried to Holy Communion. The structure of the Exhortation [*Familiaris Consortio*] and the tenor of its words give clearly to understand that this practice, which is presented as binding, cannot be modified because of different situations."[47] In other words, only the objective situation of the divorced and remarried couple should be considered. Later on, in 1998, given some theological objections raised by this letter, the CDF issued another letter to counter them.[48]

Some papal critics have tried to pit these CDF letters against the Buenos Aires interpretation of *Amoris Laetitia*.[49] There are, however,

---

46. John Paul II, "Address of John Paul II."
47. CDF, "Letter to the Bishops."
48. CDF, "Concerning Some Objections."
49. As an example, see Hickson, "Head of CDF Declines to Comment on *Dubia* of Four Cardinals": "During the interview Cardinal Müller signals as strongly as he

some problems with this approach. First and foremost, the CDF's authority does not supersede that of the pope. Claiming otherwise would contradict canon 331, as I said above, for in that case the pope would not have supreme, full, immediate, and universal ordinary power over the church, but would have to answer to the CDF. This is an inversion of the hierarchy of authority within the church. So, if the CDF says that the previous sacramental discipline is "binding,"[50] that it "cannot be modified,"[51] or that reception of communion by the divorced and remarried is "intrinsically impossible,"[52] and if the pope says otherwise, then it is the CDF that must yield, not the pope.

One of the ways to bypass this problem is to grant papal authority to the CDF letters. I have seen papal critics do this in two ways. Some have claimed that the letters were written by Pope Benedict XVI, so they have his authority.[53] This is erroneous, since Joseph Ratzinger would only be elected pope some years later. Even if his writings as cardinal and prefect of the CDF merit our respect, he did not receive retroactive papal authority on everything he wrote previously to his election.

The other way is to point out that the 1994 letter has the authority of Pope St. John Paul II, who "gave his approval to this letter, drawn up in the ordinary session of this Congregation, and ordered its publication."[54] *Donum Veritatis* explicitly says that documents issued by the CDF and expressly approved by the pope participate in the ordinary magisterium

---

can in the circumstances that he is on the side of the four cardinals who submitted the *dubia* to Pope Francis. He does this by going out of his way to emphasise that *Amoris Laetitia* must be interpreted according to the Congregation for the Doctrine of the Faith's *Letter to the Bishops of the Catholic Church concerning the reception of Holy Communion by the divorced and remarried members of the faithful* (1994). This definitive reiteration of the Church's magisterial doctrine on communion for the divorced and remarried was an explicit correction of the main architect of *Amoris Laetitia*'s 'innovative' approach to the issue, Cardinal Kasper." See also Brugger, "'*Amoris Laetitia*' vs. '*Veritatis Splendor*': You Say You Want a Revolution?."

50. CDF, "Letter to the Bishops."
51. CDF, "Letter to the Bishops."
52. CDF, "Concerning Some Objections."
53. To be fair, most people who wield this argument are commenters on social media who are lacking proper formation.
54. CDF, "Letter to the Bishops."

of the successor of Peter.⁵⁵ In other words, the papal critic points out that these letters are part of John Paul II's ordinary magisterium.⁵⁶

However, Reverend Travers has argued that this papal approval of the CDF letters lacked proper form (*forma specifica*), which should contain the explicit words "*in forma specifica approbavit*" in the approval formula. Thus, it "remained only the action of a dicastery of the Holy See, subject to the normally applicable canon law, rather than the action of the Holy Father himself, which could derogate from that law".⁵⁷

However, let us take for granted the critic's assessment that these CDF letters are magisterial. Can these letters be definitive and, therefore, binding even on future popes?⁵⁸ This would be true if they were really definitive, but we must remember that there are several levels in the magisterium. According to *Donum Veritatis*, these letters would be a part of John Paul II's *ordinary* magisterium. As I have explained in chapter 1, the ordinary magisterium, though authoritative, is not infallible (i.e., definitive). Definitive pronouncements of the magisterium come only in the form of extraordinary magisterium or ordinary and universal magisterium (see chapter 1). The former is done by the pope speaking *ex cathedra*, or by an ecumenical council. The CDF has, therefore, no authority to do either. As for the universal and ordinary magisterium, it falls to the pope to authoritatively interpret if a church teaching belongs to it or not. In other words, that competence does not belong to the CDF, nor has the CDF done so in this specific situation.⁵⁹

Definitive pronouncements cannot be done by proxy. Also, we must be mindful of canon law: "No doctrine is understood to be infallibly defined unless this is manifestly demonstrated."⁶⁰

---

55. *DV* 18.

56. See O'Reilly, "*Amoris Laetitia* and the Confusion of Those Contradicting the Magisterium of John Paul II": "This CDF letter, 'expressly approved' by the Pope John Paul II, participates 'in the ordinary magisterium of the successor of Peter' (cf *DV* 18)."

57. Travers, "*Amoris Laetitia* and Canon 915," 315.

58. O'Reilly, "*Amoris Laetitia* and the Confusion of Those Contradicting the Magisterium of John Paul II": "This wording is quite clear, it is irreformable. Not even the Pope can change this 'doctrine and discipline' because of different situations."

59. It is true that in the 1994 letter, the CDF mentions the "universal Magisterium," but only to say that the task to authentically interpret scripture and tradition belongs to the universal magisterium. Even if the CDF mentioned this in the context of discussing the previous sacramental discipline, the CDF never says that this discipline belongs to the ordinary and universal magisterium.

60. *Code of Canon Law*, c. 749, §3.

As part of the ordinary magisterium of Pope John Paul II, the CDF recalls the "doctrine and discipline of the Church in this matter," as defined by *Familiaris Consortio*. That *Amoris Laetitia* does not contradict *Familiaris Consortio* at a *doctrinal* level is something I have already explained in chapter 11. We are then left with the matter of discipline.

When the CDF defines that the previous "practice" (i.e., "discipline") is presented as "binding," and that it "cannot be modified because of different situations," we should interpret it as being applicable to the previous sacramental discipline, as laid out in *Familiaris Consortio*.[61] It was indeed binding and could not be modified because of different situations while it was in effect. However, we cannot say the same now that *Amoris Laetitia* has been published, and a new sacramental discipline was approved. This does not mean that these letters were not authoritative, or that they were wrong. It simply means that disciplines can and do change.

There are two more notes of interest regarding these CDF letters. First, the 1994 letter says that *Familiaris Consortio*'s sacramental discipline is a "constant and universal practice." Papal critics take this wording to justify their contention that this discipline has been the way the church has dealt with this problem during its 2,000 years of history. Therefore, a newcomer pope cannot simply change it. However, the letter does not lend itself to such reading. Doing so would be to deny historical facts, as I have been showing through the course of this chapter. In the same letter, Cardinal Ratzinger mentions "pastoral solutions [which] have been proposed by a few Fathers of the Church and in some measure were practiced,"[62] in which some divorced and remarried couples could receive communion. Ratzinger then goes on to say:

> These [pastoral solutions] never attained the consensus of the Fathers and in no way came to constitute the common doctrine of the Church nor to determine her discipline. It falls to the universal Magisterium, in fidelity to Sacred Scripture and Tradition, to teach and to interpret authentically the depositum fidei.[63]

Of course, this raises the question: what if the magisterium of a pope decided that such pastoral solutions could determine discipline? We can answer this question in two ways: 1) it is in the pope's purview to do so

---

61. In fact, the 1994 letter specifically mentioned *Familiaris Consortio* in points 5 and 9, and quotes it *verbatim* to make its point.

62. CDF, "Letter to the Bishops," 4.

63. CDF, "Letter to the Bishops," 4.

and then the CDF's objections are muted; or 2) the pope is impeded from doing so because the CDF said so. Papal critics take the latter position. In so doing, they do not notice that they are, in fact, contradicting the last sentence of that quote: that it falls on the magisterium to teach and interpret authentically the *depositum fidei*. They prefer to think that, when the magisterium does so, it is not doing it in fidelity to sacred scripture and tradition. But who has the authority to determine this besides the magisterium? They are, in fact, usurping the magisterium of its task of being the authoritative interpreter of tradition. They are contradicting the CDF letter with the pretense of defending it.

The second and final note is that, even if the CDF letters only take into account the objective situation of the divorced and remarried couples, they do not *explicitly* condemn the provisions laid out in *Amoris Laetitia*. Contrary to the PCLT document mentioned in the previous segment, the CDF letters never deal with mitigating circumstances diminishing subjective culpability.

The interpretations rejected by the CDF letters are: 1) the Eastern practice of tolerating second marriages on account of the principle of "*oikonomia*" (from which the so-called "Kasper proposal" could flow);[64] 2) the giving of communion to people who are convinced of the nullity of their previous marriage, although unable to demonstrate it in the external forum (namely applying the principles of *epikeia* and *aequitas canonica*);[65] and 3) the idea that personal conscience is considered to be able, on the basis of one's own convictions, to come to a decision about the value of the new union and approach communion when one considers himself authorized according to a judgment of conscience to do so (i.e., the situation ethics and subjectivism condemned in *Veritatis Splendor*, and which I dealt with in the previous chapter).[66] In chapter 3 of this book, I have already explained the differences between these proposals and the Buenos Aires criteria (the only interpretation to which the pope gave official recognition).

---

64. See CDF, "Concerning Some Objections," 2; see also CDF, "Letter to the Bishops," 3 ("when they have gone through a long period of reflection and penance, or also when for morally valid reasons they cannot satisfy the obligation to separate").

65. See CDF, "Letter to the Bishops," 3, 7, 8, 9; also CDF, "Concerning Some Objections," 3.

66. See CDF, "Letter to the Bishops," 3, 7, 8; also CDF, "Concerning Some Objections," 3.

Absent from any consideration in the CDF letters, however, is a pastoral approach that takes into account subjective culpability and mitigating circumstances, like *Amoris Laetitia* proposes.[67] Since it is not considered in the CDF letters, it is not explicitly rejected by them.

Of course, one may object that, even if *Amoris Laetitia*'s discipline is not explicitly condemned by the CDF letters, it is nonetheless implicitly condemned, for the CDF letters only take into account the objective situation of the divorced and remarried. But still, even if this is true, it is also true that the CDF has an implicit exception to this general rule: *Familiaris Consortio*'s concession of admitting to the Eucharist couples who are living "as brother and sister." The 1994 letter is silent on this regard. If the CDF allows this implicit exception in attention to *Familiaris Consortio*'s magisterial instructions, it certainly can do the same for *Amoris Laetitia*'s magisterial provisions, which, again, are not explicitly condemned in it.

❊❊❊

---

67. Granted, *Amoris Laetitia* 298 mentions a case condemned by the CDF letters: "Those who have entered into a second union for the sake of the children's upbringing, and are sometimes subjectively certain in conscience that their previous and irreparably broken marriage had never been valid." However, it does *not* do it in the context of its sacramental discipline, but to contrast those cases with a "new union arising from a recent divorce, with all the suffering and confusion which this entails for children and entire families, or the case of someone who has consistently failed in his obligations to the family." The main focus of *Amoris Laetitia*'s sacramental discipline is the divorced and remarried with mitigating circumstances diminishing subjective culpability. Either way, it is noteworthy that the 1998 CDF document does not close the possibility of communion to all those who are subjectively certain of the nullity of their previous marriages, as stated in 3.c: "Admittedly, it cannot be excluded that mistakes occur in marriage cases. In some parts of the Church, well-functioning marriage tribunals still do not exist. Occasionally, such cases last an excessive amount of time. Once in a while they conclude with questionable decisions. Here it seems that the application of *epikeia* in the internal forum is not automatically excluded from the outset. This is implied in the 1994 letter of the Congregation for the Doctrine of the Faith, in which it was stated that new canonical ways of demonstrating nullity should exclude 'as far as possible' every divergence from the truth verifiable in the judicial process. . . . This question, however, demands further study and clarification. Admittedly, the conditions for asserting an exception would need to be clarified very precisely, in order to avoid arbitrariness and to safeguard the public character of marriage, removing it from subjective decisions."

The Catechism of the Catholic Church

Finally, the papal critic may appeal to the *Catechism*[68] in order to show an alleged contradiction between *Amoris Laetitia* and an authoritative document:

> If the divorced are remarried civilly, they find themselves in a situation that objectively contravenes God's law. Consequently, they cannot receive Eucharistic communion as long as this situation persists. For the same reason, they cannot exercise certain ecclesial responsibilities. Reconciliation through the sacrament of Penance can be granted only to those who have repented for having violated the sign of the covenant and of fidelity to Christ, and who are committed to living in complete continence.[69]

It is obvious from a plain reading of this passage that the *Catechism* is referring here to *Familiaris Consortio*'s sacramental discipline (which is not surprising, since it was published in 1992, when *Familiaris Consortio* was in effect).[70] In other words, it cannot take into account a sacramental discipline instituted later.

Of course, some object that, if the pope wanted to institute a new sacramental discipline, he would change the *Catechism* accordingly. Granted, the *Catechism* will probably have to be revised to accommodate the new practice. However, one cannot simply say that if the pope really wanted to implement *Amoris Laetitia*, he would have already changed the *Catechism*. The mind and will of the pope on this issue are clear, as I have already proven in chapters 4 and 5. Denying these truths with the justification that the pope has not changed the *Catechism* yet is to obfuscate reality.

---

68. As an example, see Peters, "The Law before '*Amoris*' Is the Law After": "The *Catechism of the Catholic Church* 2384 describes civil remarriage after divorce as 'public and permanent adultery' (something obviously gravely sinful), so, if Francis had wanted to authorize the administration of holy Communion to divorced-and-remarried Catholics (*and he did not want to repudiate* CCC 2384, 1650, etc.) he would have had to have wrought a change in the law contained in Canon 915." See also Brugger, "'*Amoris Laetitia*' vs. '*Veritatis Splendor*': You Say You Want a Revolution?"

69. CCC 1650. See also CCC 1665, 2384, and 2390.

70. See Ratzinger and Schönborn, *Introduction to the Catechism*, 27: "The individual doctrines which the Catechism presents receive no other weight than that which they already possess. The weight of the Catechism itself lies in the whole." In this sense, since CCC 1650 is based in *Familiaris Consortio*, one can argue that whatever has been said in this book regarding *Familiaris Consortio* is equally applicable to the *Catechism*.

So the mind and will of the pope are clear, but they stand in disagreement with the *Catechism*. Can the *Catechism* then be used as an instrument to forestall the pope's intentions? I think this would be a betrayal of the *Catechism* itself, since it states very clearly that the task of authentically interpreting tradition belongs to the magisterium of the pope and the bishops in communion with him.[71]

In fact, Pope Francis has already revised the *Catechism* once,[72] which means his authority extends over the *Catechism*. Interestingly, when Francis revised the *Catechism*, some papal critics pointed out that this is not a magisterial document, since they disagreed with this revision. Rather, the *Catechism*—so it is argued—only possesses the magisterial authority of the documents from which its teachings come.[73] Since the *Catechism* was referring to the discipline of *Familiaris Consortio*, and since this discipline has been superseded by the one in *Amoris Laetitia*, then the latter takes precedence over the *Catechism*. One cannot say the *Catechism* is not magisterial in one topic, and then use the *Catechism* as an authoritative document to contradict the pope's magisterium in another topic.

---

71. *CCC* 85, 100.

72. See the 1997 and 2018 versions of *CCC* 2267. Granted, many papal critics do not accept Francis's authority to revise the *Catechism* vis-à-vis the death penalty, but they never reject Francis's authority to revise the *Catechism* in itself, only in revising the *Catechism* in the way that he did.

73. Shadle, "The Death Penalty and the Development of Doctrine, Part II"

Chapter 14

A Very Interesting Precedent

In this chapter, I would like to focus not so much on church documents that allegedly contradict *Amoris Laetitia*, but on a document that actually validates it. This document provides precedent for some pastoral practices delineated in *Amoris Laetitia* and contested by papal critics. The reason why I say this precedent is interesting is because it has to do with *Humanae Vitae*.

Papal critics usually hold *Humanae Vitae* in the highest of regards, as a foundational encyclical to Catholicism's sexual ethics. They argue (probably correctly) that if Catholics would have upheld *Humanae Vitae*'s teachings on artificial contraception, the current widespread heterodoxy in other areas of sexuality would not have happened, since all of them (e.g., abortion, homosexuality, fornication, masturbation, pornography) presuppose the separation of the sexual act from its procreative intent.[1] In fact, the papal critics' admiration for this encyclical is so pronounced, that they often use it as a litmus test to gauge the orthodoxy of fellow Catholics.[2]

---

1. See Pentin, "Can *Humanae Vitae*'s Teachings Change?": "Many Catholics, especially in the pro-life movement, have long upheld *Humanae Vitae* as prophetic. They have based such a view on the fact that the widespread acceptance of birth control has separated the unitive and procreative meaning of sexual relations, leading to a trivialization of sexual relations that, in turn, has resulted in promiscuity, extensive abortion, and the arrival of same-sex 'marriage' that occurred in the context of the rapid normalization of homosexual behavior in Western nations."

2. As an example, see Patrick Coffin, as quoted in Gyapong, "Fifty Years Later, Birth-Control Predictions Even 'Crazier than He Thought'": "'The teaching of *Humanae Vitae* is almost a perfect litmus test for Catholic orthodoxy in other areas,' Coffin

It is, therefore, not unusual to find people applying a hermeneutic of suspicion to everything that Pope Francis says and does as if it was part of a plot to do away with this encyclical. For them, *Amoris Laetitia* is a slippery slope, the principles of which threaten to tear down the whole moral edifice of Catholic moral teaching, including *Humanae Vitae*.[3] These fears were particularly visible when they learned that Francis was taking the opportunity of the encyclical's 50th anniversary to set up a commission to study it.[4] They assumed that this commission would be a scheme to "reinterpret" *Humanae Vitae* in light of *Amoris Laetitia*.

Unsurprisingly, all of these fears turned out to be unfounded.[5] The commission that was supposedly going to overturn the encyclical finished its work by concluding that "*Humanae Vitae* needs no update."[6] Before that, *Amoris Laetitia* itself had already favorably quoted *Humanae Vitae* no less than six times.[7]

Of course, if the pastoral principles present in *Amoris Laetitia* were already applied to *Humanae Vitae* before Francis's pontificate, all of this line of reasoning would simply fumble. And in fact, this is actually the case. Some pastoral overtones from *Amoris Laetitia* have already been applied pastorally to *Humanae Vitae* since the pontificate of Pope St. John Paul II (the pope detractors most use to contrast with Francis). If no one

---

said. 'I never met a gay activist who believes in *Humanae Vitae*.'"

3. See Seifert, "Does Pure Logic Threaten to Destroy the Entire Moral Doctrine of the Catholic Church?" It is interesting that, in *Evangelii Gaudium* #39, Pope Francis uses similar terminology, but about preaching "certain doctrinal or moral points based on specific ideological options" instead of the Gospel. In that situation, "the edifice of the Church's moral teaching risks becoming a house of cards, and this is our greatest risk."

4. Seifert, "Does Pure Logic Threaten to Destroy the Entire Moral Doctrine of the Catholic Church?" See also Mattei, "De Mattei: The Plan Of 'Reinterpretation' For *Humanæ Vitæ*."

5. San Martín, "No, Virginia, There's No 'Secret Commission' on *Humanae Vitae*."

6. Gagliarducci, "*Humanae Vitae* Needs No Update, Commission Chair Says."

7. See most especially *AL* 82: "The Synod Fathers stated that 'the growth of a mentality that would reduce the generation of human life to one variable of an individual's or a couple's plans is clearly evident.' The Church's teaching is meant to 'help couples to experience in a complete, harmonious, and conscious way their communion as husband and wife, together with their responsibility for procreating life. *We need to return to the message of the Encyclical Humanae Vitae of Blessed Pope Paul VI, which highlights the need to respect the dignity of the person in morally assessing methods of regulating birth.*'" See also *AL* 68, 81 (with n86), 154 (with n156), and 222 (twice).

has ever argued that John Paul II has revoked *Humanae Vitae*, when he applied this pastoral approach specifically to this document, it is much more difficult to claim that *Amoris Laetitia* will do that, by indirectly applying these same pastoral principles. Let us then proceed to examine this matter.

❦ ❦ ❦

In 1989, during John Paul II's pontificate, the CDF headed by Joseph Ratzinger published a document named "Moral Norm of *Humanae Vitae* and Pastoral Duty." While this document upholds to the letter the doctrine of the intrinsically evil nature of artificial contraception, it also had this to say:

> *The same Christian moral tradition just referred to has also always maintained the distinction—not the separation and still less an opposition—between objective disorder and subjective guilt.* Accordingly, when it is a matter of judging subjective moral behaviour without ever setting aside the norm which prohibits the intrinsic disorder of contraception, it is entirely licit to take into due consideration the various factors and aspects of the person's concrete action, not only the person's intentions and motivations, but also the diverse circumstances of life, in the first place all those causes which *may affect the person's knowledge and free will*. This subjective situation, while it can never change into something ordered that which is intrinsically disordered, may to a greater or lesser extent modify the responsibility of the person who is acting. As is well known, *this is a general principle, applicable to every moral disorder, even if intrinsic*, it is accordingly applicable also to contraception.

Please note how this principle is applicable to every moral disorder, even if intrinsic. In other words, this logic is applicable to adultery too.

Later on, in 1997, the Pontifical Council for the Family, instituted by none other than John Paul II,[8] issued a *Vademecum* for confessors concerning some aspects of the morality of conjugal life. This *Vademecum* had a specific focus on "the problem of responsible procreation [which]

---

8. See Buttiglione, *Risposte amichevoli*, 145: "The Pontifical Council for the Family was then presided over by Cardinal Alfonso Lopez Trujillo, who was certainly not a reckless progressive."

represents a particularly delicate point in Catholic moral teaching relating to conjugal life."⁹

> If, on a doctrinal level, the Church has a solid awareness of the requirements of the Sacrament of Penance, it cannot be denied that a certain void has been forming with regard to implementing these teachings in pastoral practice. The doctrinal data, therefore, is the foundation supporting this "Vademecum," and it is not our task to repeat it here, although it is called to mind in various passages. We know well all the richness that has been offered to the Christian community by the Encyclical *Humanae Vitae*, illuminated then by the Encyclical *Veritatis Splendor*, and by the Apostolic Exhortations, *Familiaris Consortio* and *Reconciliatio et Paenitentia*. We also know how the Catechism of the Catholic Church has provided an effective and synthetic summary of the Church's doctrine on these subjects.[10]

In other words, by the Vatican's own admission, these pastoral provisions do not contradict *Humanae Vitae*, *Veritatis Splendor*, or *Familiaris Consortio*. This is noteworthy, since many of the directives in section 3 of the *Vademecum* ("Pastoral Guidelines for Confessors") very closely mirror some of the most controversial passages from *Amoris Laetitia*. Of course, the parallels are not perfect in every respect, but only in the ways I highlight in each segment. Let me then point out the most important examples:

※※※

The Principle of Good Faith—Subjective Ignorance

> The principle according to which it is preferable to let penitents remain in good faith in cases of error due to subjectively invincible ignorance, is certainly to be considered always valid, even in matters of conjugal chastity. And this applies whenever it is foreseen that the penitent, although oriented towards living within the bounds of a life of faith, would not be prepared to change his own conduct, but *rather would begin formally to sin*.[11]

---

9. Pontifical Council for the Family, "Vademecum," 1.
10. Pontifical Council for the Family, "Vademecum," Presentation.
11. Pontifical Council for the Family, "Vademecum," sec. 3, para. 8.

This provision is based on St. Alphonse Liguori's pastoral principle of the good faith, mentioned already in chapter 7 when discussing the issue of full knowledge. Please note that this seems to allow for some penitents who are not yet mature to change their own conduct, but who are certainly oriented on a path to do so later on, to remain in ignorance while the pastor keeps trying to nudge the person into the right direction. Otherwise, by losing their subjectively invincible ignorance, the sinner would begin to sin, not only in a material way, but also in a *formal* way. This mirrors another polemical passage in *Amoris Laetitia*, which states: "A subject may know full well the rule, yet have great difficulty in understanding 'its inherent values.'"[12]

❊❊❊

The Law of Gradualness

> *The pastoral "law of gradualness," not to be confused with the "gradualness of the law" which would tend to diminish the demands it places on us, consists of requiring a decisive break with sin* together with a progressive path towards total union *with the will of God and with his loving demands.*[13]

This bit about "law of gradualness" not being confused by "gradualness of the law" is expressed very clearly in *Amoris Laetitia* #295. Also, please note how there is no contradiction between requiring a "decisive break with sin" and a "progressive path towards total union with the will of God." Those go hand in hand together. But the path, while decisive, is still progressive. If it is progressive towards total union with the will of God,

---

12. *AL* 301. See also Buttiglione, *Risposte amichevoli*, 146–47: "The Pastoral Directives then recall the general principle of not disturbing those who live in good faith in an invincible error condition. . . . This text itself implicitly answers those who ask whether in some cases absolution can be given to those who live materially in one condition of habitual adultery. The answer is yes and this is not an innovation by *Amoris Laetitia*. It is rather the consequence of a rule that we find here formulated in relation to the morality of married life in a 1997 document. . . . This does not imply that the confessor should renounce the affirmation of the integral truth of Christian ethics. He simply has to find the right time and way to explain this truth, and make it understandable."

13. Pontifical Council for the Family, "Vademecum," sec. 3, para. 9.

then that means the total union is not instantaneously achieved (see my notes on "impenitent sinners" in chapter 6).¹⁴

❋❋❋

Rigorist Demands for Amendment

> Sacramental absolution is not to be denied to those who, repentant after having gravely sinned against conjugal chastity, demonstrate the desire to strive to abstain from sinning again, notwithstanding relapses. In accordance with the approved doctrine and practice followed by the holy Doctors and confessors with regard to *habitual penitents*, the confessor is to avoid demonstrating lack of trust either in the grace of God or in the dispositions of the penitent, *by exacting humanly impossible absolute guarantees of an irreproachable future conduct.*¹⁵

If we took the rigid interpretation of Trent used to contrast this council with *Amoris Laetitia*, then the emphasized part is heretical, since it talks about demanding "humanly impossible guarantees of an irreproachable future conduct." If this rigid version of Trent is right, it would always be possible for a sinner to change his conduct. Therefore, it would always be possible to demand such change of conduct as a condition for frequenting the sacraments.

Also, please note how this mirrors *Amoris Laetitia*'s footnote 364: "Perhaps out of a certain scrupulosity, concealed beneath a zeal for fidelity to the truth, some priests demand of penitents a purpose of amendment so lacking in nuance that it causes mercy to be obscured by the pursuit of a supposedly pure justice. For this reason, it is helpful to recall

---

14. See also the section "La legge di gradualità: da *Humanae vitae* ad *Amoris laetitia*" from Calmeyn, "Accompagnamento e legge di gradualità."

15. Pontifical Council for the Family, "Vademecum," sec. 3, para. 11. Also, Rocco Buttiglione draws attention to the term "habitual penitent" (*Risposte amichevoli*, 146): "The document opportunely distinguishes between occasional penitents and those with which there is a more or less formal relationship of spiritual accompaniment (the document uses the expression 'spiritual direction'). With the occasional penitent in general it is good to stick to a 'static' evaluation of the situation that is presented to him. With the habitual penitent it is possible and necessary to have a dynamic vision, projected towards the future. The document probably has in mind the application of this rule to contraception, but this indication also holds for the divorced and remarried."

the teaching of Saint John Paul II, who stated that the possibility of a new fall 'should not prejudice the authenticity of the resolution.'"

✻✻✻

Licit Cooperation with an Intrinsically Evil Act

Special difficulties are presented by cases of cooperation in the sin of a spouse who voluntarily renders the unitive act infecund. In the first place, it is necessary to distinguish cooperation in the proper sense, from violence or unjust imposition on the part of one of the spouses, which the other spouse in fact cannot resist. This cooperation can be licit when the three following conditions are jointly met:

1. when the action of the cooperating spouse is not already illicit in itself;
2. when proportionally grave reasons exist for cooperating in the sin of the other spouse;
3. when one is seeking to help the other spouse to desist from such conduct (patiently, with prayer, charity, and dialogue; although not necessarily in that moment, nor on every single occasion).[16]

Here, the *Vademecum* states that cooperation with an objectively evil act may be licit on account of an uncooperative spouse. Is it not possible that Pope Francis also had these cases in mind, whereby only one of the spouses is interested in following the church teaching? Some apologists very convincingly think so (see chapter 16).[17]

Of course, it can be argued that the two situations are not analogous: while in the case of contraception, only one of the partners is engaging in an intrinsically evil act, in the case of living *more uxorio* after a civil remarriage, both partners are engaging in such an act. As Rocco Buttiglione admits, in the case of the divorced and remarried, "the sexual act in itself is illicit and not the contraceptive act that is added to the sexual

---

16. Pontifical Council for the Family, "Vademecum," sec. 3, para. 13.

17. See also Buttiglione, *Risposte amichevoli*, 147: "The *Vademecum* also considers the fact that, in general, love is made by two. What to do if the other partner does not accept the moral rule that we must follow in our relationships? Obviously if one is forced to do something he would not want to do, he or she bears no moral responsibility for the act."

act, perhaps on the initiative of only one of the two spouses. Here the analogy with the cases considered by *Amoris Laetitia* disappears."[18] Yet, Buttiglione also adds: "It is true, however, that in the presence of these three criteria, the partner is completely free from fault. *Amoris Laetitia* in general does not deal with the lawfulness of the act but with the subjective culpability and the lessening of responsibility. In this sense a partial analogy remains. The first condition foreseen by the *Vademecum* is missing, and therefore the act is intrinsically evil; but the presence of the other two conditions may decrease subjective liability."[19]

There are other parallels. The *Vademecum* makes a clear distinction between those cases of licit cooperation and violence / unjust impositions on the part of one spouse, thereby showing how the Catholic Church does not narrow down the issue of consent to the libertarian concept of coercion.[20]

Finally, the cooperative spouse, while trying to help his or her partner from desisting from his or her conduct, does not necessarily need to do it "at that moment or on every single occasion." This contrasts starkly with the approach taken by papal critics, whereby we need to constantly remind the sinner of his sins and, after a formal notification, demand a complete and immediate end to the sinful behavior. Here, a more patient and realistic approach is allowed, more in keeping with *Amoris Laetitia*'s paradigm.

❧ ❧ ❧

In conclusion, many of *Amoris Laetitia*'s pastoral provisions were already in place for *Humanae Vitae* at the time of Pope St. John Paul II. The pontiff, who oversaw the Pontifical Council for the Family at the time, did not think that this pastoral approach somehow contradicted *Humanae Vitae*, nor the rest of his magisterium on intrinsically evil acts. This sets up a very curious precedent: the encyclical most revered by papal critics is actually a source of precedent, ultimately showing pastoral continuity between Francis and his predecessor, albeit with developments.

---

18. Buttiglione, *Risposte amichevoli*, 149.

19. Buttiglione, *Risposte amichevoli*, 149.

20. Buttiglione, *Risposte amichevoli*, 148. Here, Buttiglione also draws from precedents from Pope Pius XI's *Casti Connubii* to make this point.

Applying these pastoral principles never made anyone question whether *Humanae Vitae* or *Veritatis Splendor* were in danger. Therefore, neither should *Amoris Laetitia* arouse such concerns.

Chapter 15

The Newman Trial

SOMETIMES, WHEN PAPAL CRITICS try to assert that *Amoris Laetitia* is not a legitimate development, they take recourse to St. Vincent de Lérins.[1] They will rightly point out that any legitimate development should obey the two rules laid out by this saintly fifth-century monk (who is so prominent as to feature in the decrees of the First Vatican Council[2] and in *Veritatis Splendor*).[3] These rules, meant to distinguish between a true, legitimate development (*profectus fidei*), and a false development amounting to a corruption of the faith (*permutatio fidei*),[4] are as follows:

> *"id teneamus Quod ubique, quod semper, quod ab omnibus creditum est"*: i.e., that we *hold that faith which has been believed everywhere, always, by all.*[5]

---

1. As an example, see Pentin, "'Doctrinal Anarchy' as Bishops' Conflicting Positions on *Amoris Laetitia* Show": "'The first effect on the Church of doctrinal anarchy is division,' said Monsignor Nicola Bux, a former consulter of the Congregation for the Doctrine of the Faith during the pontificate of Benedict XVI. This is 'because of apostasy,' he added, 'which is the abandonment of Catholic thought, as defined by Saint Vincent of Lerins: *quod semper, quod ubique, quod ab omnibus creditur* [what has been believed everywhere, always, and by all].' St. Vincent was a 5th century Church father who distinguished the legitimate growth in understanding of divine revelation from the false alteration of religion and Catholic orthodox dogma. Msgr. Bux warned that the Church 'cannot change the faith and at the same time ask believers to remain faithful to it.'"

2. See Vatican I Council, *Dei Filius*, chap. 4.
3. See John Paul II, *Veritatis Splendor*, 53.
4. See Guarino, *The Disputed Teachings*, 12–15.
5. Vincent de Lérins, *Commonitorium*, chap. 2.

> "*in eodem sensu eadamque sententia*": i.e., the doctrine of the church should develop only in its own kind, that is to say, *in the same doctrine, in the same sense, and in the same meaning.*[6]

These rules seem, on the surface, to contradict the possibility of any and all doctrinal development. Far from so. In fact, the chapter where St. Vincent de Lérins expounds on "*in eodem . . .*" is precisely titled "On Development in Religious Knowledge."[7] The saint notes:

> But some one will say, perhaps, Shall there, then, be no progress in Christ's Church? Certainly; all possible progress. For what being is there, so envious of men, so full of hatred to God, who would seek to forbid it? Yet on condition that it be real progress, not alteration of the faith. For progress requires that the subject be enlarged in itself, alteration, that it be transformed into something else. The intelligence, then, the knowledge, the wisdom, as well of individuals as of all, as well of one man as of the whole Church, ought, in the course of ages and centuries, to increase and make much and vigorous progress; but yet only in its own kind; that is to say, in the same doctrine, in the same sense, and in the same meaning.[8]

After correctly bringing up St. Vincent de Lérin's rules to ascertain whether a development is legitimate or not, the papal critic will often incorrectly jump to the conclusion that *Amoris Laetitia* does not constitute a legitimate development, since it allegedly does not hold to the faith which has been believed everywhere, always, by all, and not in the same sense and meaning.[9] Having therefore asserted that *Amoris Laetitia* does not fulfill these criteria, the critic will look up to St. Vincent so as to know how to respond: "What, if some novel contagion seek to infect not merely an insignificant portion of the Church, but the whole? Then it will be his care to cleave to antiquity, which at this day cannot possibly be

---

6. Vincent de Lérins, *Commonitorium*, chap. 23.
7. Vincent de Lérins, *Commonitorium*, chap. 23.
8. Vincent de Lérins, *Commonitorium*, chap. 23.
9. As an example, see "Theological Terrorism," Catholic Truth: "From now on, says [Cardinal] Schönborn, all the previous magisterial texts concerning marriage and the family 'have to be read in the light of *Amoris Laetitia*. [*AL*]' But, hang on ... The Church has always tested the authenticity, the veracity of teachings by examining them in the light of Catholic Tradition: that which has been believed always, everywhere, by all. . . . No longer do we apply the litmus test of judging beliefs against what has always been believed in the Church, always, everywhere, and by all, but we must put those traditional teachings under scrutiny to see if they comply with the New Morality."

seduced by any fraud of novelty."[10] They will use this argument to cleave to a personal interpretation of antiquity/tradition, completely separated from the magisterium of the church. On my end, this seems like a complete distortion of this theologian's thought, for even a cursory reading of his writings shows a great affinity with the Catholic Church.[11]

When asked to justify why he feels that *Amoris Laetitia* violates the Vincentian Canon, the papal critic will most likely say that it is obvious how *Amoris* constitutes a novelty and a departure from previous doctrine.[12] By doing this, he will ignore St. Vincent's own warning that: "*There may supervene shape, form, variation in outward appearance*, but the nature of each kind must remain the same."[13]

❖❖❖

Pope Francis does not ignore the theology of St. Vincent de Lérins. In his preface to Stephen Walford's book about *Amoris Laetitia*, Francis mentions a "magisterial hermeneutic of the Church, always in continuity (without ruptures), yet always maturing." The Holy Father then goes on to quote St. Vincent's rule: "*ut annis scilicet consolidetur, dilatetur tempore, sublimetur aetate*"[14] (i.e., that doctrine is to be consolidated by years, enlarged by time, refined by age).

10. Vincent de Lérins, *Commonitorium*, chap. 3.

11. In fact, the Vincentian Canon was formulated as a reply to those who accused ecumenical councils of introducing unscriptural novelties. See Guarino, *The Disputed Teachings*, 2, 13: "[Vincent] acknowledged that terms such as 'consubstantial' (*homoousios*) and 'God-bearer' (*Theotokos*)—terms that had been consecrated by early ecumenical councils—were not found in the New Testament. And yet he thought these words were legitimate representations of biblical teaching, fully congruous with scriptural witness. . . . Indeed, a significant part of Vincent's work seeks to respond to those who believed that the Creed of Nicaea could be rewritten with rather less emphasis on the one divine nature (consubstantiality) shared by the Father and Jesus Christ. . . . Proper development is exemplified by the Councils of Nicaea and Ephesus (with their insistence on the divinity of Jesus and on his divine-human unity.) Where does one find deformations and corruptions, Vincent's dreaded *permutationes fidei*? One such place is in the various fourth-century imperial attempts to reverse the Council of Nicaea by reformulating the creed without the word *homoousios*. Such attempts also represent 'changes'—but changes that are now alterations of the Christian faith."

12. See again "Theological Terrorism," Catholic Truth: "We speak often enough about the diabolical disorientation—the turning away from the right path—predicted by Our Lady at Fatima, but it is now crystal clear that the enemies within the Church are determined to literally turn the Church and Christ's teaching upside down."

13. Vincent de Lérins, *Commonitorium*, chap. 23.

14. Vincent de Lérins, *Commonitorium*, chap. 23.

This is not the first time Pope Francis has invoked St. Vincent de Lérins. He cited this very same passage when justifying his also very controversial *Catechism* revision on the death penalty.[15] The Holy Father also cited this Vincentian quote in an interview to *La Civiltà Cattolica*[16] and also in a homily.[17]

Pope Francis's concept of doctrinal development is not as reductive as the one papal critics often employ. Francis's idea of development of doctrine is highly influenced by principles he laid out in *Evangelii Gaudium* #222–30: "time is greater than space," and "unity prevails over conflict." From the first principle, we know that "A constant tension exists between fullness and limitation. . . . This principle enables us to work slowly but surely, without being obsessed with immediate results. It helps us patiently to endure difficult and adverse situations, or inevitable changes in our plans. It invites us to accept the tension between fullness and limitation, and to give a priority to time."[18] As for the second principle, it states that, "The message of peace is not about a negotiated settlement but rather the conviction that the unity brought by the Spirit can harmonize every diversity. It overcomes every conflict by creating a new and promising synthesis. Diversity is a beautiful thing when it can constantly enter into a process of reconciliation and seal a sort of cultural covenant resulting in a 'reconciled diversity.'"[19]

It seems like we are being presented with two conflicting ideas of doctrinal development. The papal critics assume Francis is contradicting St. Vincent, while the Vicar of Christ claims to be consistent with the saint's theology. Of course, a Catholic should automatically know which of these two narratives is the correct one, based on its authority alone. However, since this principle seems to be more and more questioned

---

15. Francis, "To Participants in the Meeting."

16. Francis, "Big Heart Open to God."

17. Francis, "Dio Delle Sorprese." After quoting St. Vincent, the pope invites us to pray to the Lord so as to receive the grace of discernment to not to fall in immobility and rigidity and to not close our hearts—a wise counsel.

18. Francis, *Evangelii Gaudium*, 222–23. Stephen Walford's book contains an excellent chapter explaining precisely how we can apply the principle "time is greater than space" to *Amoris Laetitia* (Walford, *Pope Francis, the Family, and Divorce*, 113–36). See also Ryan, "Weakness, and Wounded and Troubled Love," 141: "God is patient enough to allow time to do its work rather than to be feverishly concerned with people's lives as tidy spaces and well-groomed gardens—captured in the parable of the wheat and the weeds, a key metaphor for Pope Francis."

19. Francis, *Evangelii Gaudium*, 230. See also Francis, *Querida Amazônia*, 104.

nowadays, let us then proceed to test whether *Amoris Laetitia* corresponds to a legitimate development or not.

We already established that mere appearance of contradiction is not enough to ascertain whether a development violates the Vincentian Canon. Then, how to know for sure? Fortunately, we can take recourse to another saintly theologian, who has expounded with greater detail about the conditions of a legitimate development: Saint Cardinal Henry Newman. In his excellent *Essay on the Development of Christian Doctrine*, Newman has mentioned seven notes of genuine developments that allow us to distinguish them from doctrinal corruptions.

Of course, these seven notes apply only to doctrinal developments. Disciplinary developments are, as I said in chapters 10 and 11, much more flexible (in fact, there can actually be disciplinary changes). However, I also explained how *Amoris Laetitia*'s disciplinary change came in the wake of some doctrinal development, or doctrinal shifts of emphasis (see figure 4 in chapter 10). Let us then explore the doctrines of *Amoris Laetitia* at the root of this sacramental discipline (namely the teaching of mitigating circumstances), and check them against the backdrop of Newman's seven notes of doctrinal development.

❀❀❀

First Note: Preservation of Type

St. Vincent de Lérins compares doctrinal development "to the growth of the body, which, though in the process of years is developed and attains its full size, yet remains still the same. There is a wide difference between the flower of youth and the maturity of age; yet they who were once young are still the same now that they have become old, insomuch that though the stature and outward form of the individual are changed, yet his nature is one and the same, his person is one and the same. An infant's limbs are small, a young man's large, yet the infant and the young man are the same."[20]

Cardinal Newman picks up this analogy, but complements it in a way that allows much more outward variation. While St. Vincent only considers the analogical value of a human being's physical growth, Cardinal Newman mentions the physical growth of a butterfly:

---

20. Vincent de Lérins, *Commonitorium*, chap. 23.

> *This is readily suggested by the analogy of physical growth.... The adult animal has the same make as it had on its birth; young birds do not grow into fishes, nor does the child degenerate into the brute, wild or domestic.... However, as the last instances suggest to us, this unity of type, characteristic as it is of faithful developments, must not be pressed to the extent of denying all variation, nay, considerable alteration of proportion and relation, as time goes by, in the parts or aspects of an idea. Great changes in outward appearance and internal harmony occur in the instance of the animal creation itself. The fledged bird differs much from its rudimental form in the egg. The butterfly is the development, but not in any sense the image, of the grub.*[21]

In another place, Newman explains that a "popular leader may go through a variety of professions, he may court parties and break with them, he may contradict himself in words, and undo his own measures, yet there may be a steady fulfillment of certain objects, or adherence to certain plain doctrines, which gives a unity to his career, and impresses on beholders an image of directness and large consistency which shows a fidelity to his type from first to last."[22]

In my opinion, even if the church seems to have contradicted itself in words, even if it wobbles between more conservative and more liberal factions, and even if it undid its own measures (i.e., disciplines) from the time of *Familiaris Consortio*, there is consistency in the big picture. The objective "in need of being steadily fulfilled," as Newman calls it, is winning the salvation of souls, particularly those entrapped in the sins of the age. There is consistency in adherence to the plain doctrines of the indissolubility of marriage and the objectively evil nature of adultery, as *Amoris Laetitia* itself repeatedly admits (and as I explained in previous chapters, namely 6), and also to the plain doctrine of the distinction between mortal and venial sins.

It is also interesting how Newman takes much of his time explaining the principle of "preservation of type" by taking on the example of St. Peter and the eating of unclean animals (explicitly forbidden by the old law):

> It must have been an extreme shock to St. Peter to be told he must slay and eat beasts, unclean as well as clean, though such command was implied already in that faith which he held and

---

21. Newman, *Development of Christian Doctrine*, 171–172, 175.
22. Newman, *Development of Christian Doctrine*, 173.

> taught; a shock, which a single effort, or a short period, or the force of reason would not suffice to overcome. *Nay, it may happen that a representation which varies from its original may be felt as more true and faithful than one which has more pretensions to be exact.* . . . The Samaritans who refused to add the Prophets to the Law, and the Sadducees who denied a truth which was covertly taught in the Book of Exodus, were in appearance only faithful adherents to the primitive doctrine. *Our Lord found His people precisians in the obedience to the letter; He condemned them for not being led on to its spirit, that is, to its developments.* The Gospel is the development of the Law; yet, what difference seems wider than that which separates the unbending rule of Moses from the "grace and truth" which "came by Jesus Christ"?[23]

In other words, simply following the older paradigm to the letter does not mean we are adhering to the faith as we should. Preservation of type rules out the argument I mentioned in the beginning of this chapter, whereby some papal critics will claim that we should adhere to previous paradigms by default if we believe the magisterium has fallen into error (what I call the "pseudo-antiquity criterion"). For Newman also explains:

> *Nay, one cause of corruption in religion is the refusal to follow the course of doctrine as it moves on, and an obstinacy in the notions of the past.* . . . An idea does not always bear about it the same external image; this circumstance, however, has no force to weaken the argument for its substantial identity, as drawn from its external sameness, when such sameness remains. On the contrary, for that very reason, unity of type becomes so much the surer guarantee of the healthiness and soundness of developments, when it is persistently preserved in spite of their number or importance.[24]

But then, if so much variation is possible, how can we really be sure we are dealing with preservation of type? Later on in his essay, Newman takes a significant amount of time trying to explain this by taking recourse to the history of the Catholic Church in the first centuries. The chapter is so lengthy that I can do nothing but summarize it. Simply put, even in the midst of a cacophony of heresies and novelties, the preservation of type would lay in the church labeling itself Catholic. For Christianity is

---

23. Newman, *Development of Christian Doctrine*, 176–77.
24. Newman, *Development of Christian Doctrine*, 177–78.

meant to be universal, while heresies are the product of factionalism and partisanship. Christianity traces its roots to Christ himself, while heresies trace them to men who give their names to them (Arius to the Arians, Nestorius to the Nestorians, etc.).[25]

Of course, papal critics nowadays are following non-authoritative authors instead of the Vicar of Christ, and they are following ideological-political movements (traditionalism, conservatism, libertarianism) instead of the church. However, since the papal critics of today do what no heresiarch, *per* Newman, ever did (which is to appropriate the label of Catholicism for themselves), then we must proceed with our reading of the essay. Later in the text, Newman identifies the Catholic Church (and therefore, the one containing the preservation of type) with the one maintaining its communion with the see of Peter:

> One man was raised up for her [the church's] deliverance. . . . Who was the destined champion of her who cannot fail? Whence did he come, and what was his name? He came with an augury of victory upon him, which even Athanasius could not show, it was Leo, the Bishop of Rome. Leo's augury of success, which even Athanasius had not, was this, that he seated in the Chair of Peter and the heir of his prerogatives. . . . St. Peter Chrysologus had urged this grave consideration: . . . to submit yourself to everything to what has been written by the blessed Pope of Rome; for St. Peter, who lives and presides in his own See, gives the true faith to those who seek it.[26]

This is how we know where the preservation of type lies. In fact, Newman finishes his chapter on the preservation of type with a list of visible signs of Christianity. This list has such an uncanny resemblance with the church under Pope Francis, it becomes impossible not to recognize it, or even be stricken in awe at the similarities:

> If there is now a form of Christianity such, that it extends throughout the world, though with varying measures of prominence or prosperity in separate places—that it lies under the power of sovereigns and magistrates, in various ways alien to its faith—that *flourishing nations and great empires, professing or tolerating the Christian name, lie over against it as antagonists—* that schools of philosophy and learning are supporting theories, and following out conclusions, hostile to it, and establishing an

---

25. Newman, *Development of Christian Doctrine*, 257–59.
26. Newman, *Development of Christian Doctrine*, 306–307.

exegetical system subversive of its Scriptures—that it has lost whole Churches by schism, and *is now opposed by powerful communions once part of itself*—that it has been altogether or almost driven from some countries—that in others its line of teachers is overlaid, its flocks oppressed, its Churches occupied, its property held by what may be called a duplicate succession—*that in others its members are degenerate and corrupt, are surpassed in conscientiousness and in virtue, as in gifts of the intellect, by the very heretics it condemns*—that heresies are rife and bishops negligent within its own pale—and that amid its disorders and its fears there is but one Voice for whose decisions the peoples wait with trust, one Name and One See to which they look with hope, and that name Peter, and that see Rome—such a religion is not unlike the Christianity of the fifth and sixth centuries.[27]

❈❈❈

Second Note: Continuity of Principles

Saint Newman continues his essay by expounding on the "continuity of principles." These principles must be distinguished from doctrine:

> Principles are abstract and general, doctrines relate to facts; doctrines develope, and principles at first sight do not; doctrines grow and are enlarged, principles are permanent; doctrines are intellectual, and principles are more immediately ethical and practical. . . . Doctrines are developed by the operation of principles, and develope variously according to those principles.[28]

In this sense, principles are a better test of heresy than doctrine;[29] for, according to Newman, it is better to have principles without doctrine, than doctrine without principles (although, neither situation is commendable, of course).

> A development, to be faithful, must retain both the doctrine and the principle with which it started. Doctrine without its correspondent principle remains barren, if not lifeless. . . . On the other hand, principle without its corresponding doctrine may be considered as the state of religious minds in the heathen

---

27. Newman, *Development of Christian Doctrine*, 321–22.
28. Newman, *Development of Christian Doctrine*, 178, 180.
29. Newman, *Development of Christian Doctrine*, 181.

world, viewed relatively to Revelation; that is of the "children of God who are scattered abroad."[30]

That *Amoris Laetitia* is faithful to doctrine was the point of all my previous chapters. But what about principles? Newman enumerates some specimens of Christian principles, meant to be taken as exemplificative and not exhaustive. Among these, I will highlight at least two: 1) supremacy of faith, and 2) scripture.

On the supremacy of faith, I would like to point out how papal critics often complain about how reconciling Pope Francis with orthodoxy is a violence against the intellect.[31] "It would be like proclaiming that 2+2=5," is a slogan frequently deployed.[32] But, even if our faith does not contradict reason, Newman is very clear that one of the principles of Christianity is that belief precedes reason:

> I do not mean of course that the Fathers were opposed to inquiries into the intellectual basis of Christianity, but that they held that men were not obliged to wait for logical proof before believing: on the contrary, that the majority were to believe first on presumption and let the intellectual proof come as their reward.[33]

I started this book precisely by explaining how it would be futile to read my apologetics if the reader was not open to the possibility of *Amoris Laetitia* being orthodox in the first place. If someone reads this book with the fixed and unalterable presupposition that it is irrational to believe in the orthodoxy of *Amoris Laetitia*, then no arguments will avail, no matter how well constructed. This is why, in chapter 9, I mentioned that answering the *dubia* would very likely not serve any purpose at all; for they, instead of being means of clarification (as they were purported to be), on the contrary induced a state of close-mindedness among many who wield the *dubia* as arguments.

---

30. Newman, *Development of Christian Doctrine*, 181.
31. As an example, see "Church Crisis," Catholic Truth: "I'm afraid that I sometimes feel impatience with certain enquirers, especially if they are members of the older generation, when we were all taught very clearly that our Catholic Faith could never contradict Reason. Therefore, it seems to me, any (older) person of average intelligence should know, through their Catholic sense, that everything, from the introduction of a new Mass right up to and including *Amoris Laetita*, cannot be from God."
32. I tackle this argument in my article "2+2=5?," published at *WPI*.
33. Newman, *Development of Christian Doctrine*, 330.

Any person who is confused by *Amoris Laetitia* will need to be willing to undertake the jump of faith beforehand and give Pope Francis the benefit of the doubt. Only afterwards will the arguments of this book and of other authors find a more fertile soil, for it will open the reader's intellect to new perspectives. It is not an invitation to embrace irrationality, but of foregoing rigid mental schemes that one may confuse with the only rational approach possible.

"Believe first, and reason will be satiated afterwards" is one of the principles of Christian faith according to Newman. Every Catholic knows this, for they would not have embraced their faith if they were not open to accept premises that at a first glance, look irrational: e.g., that God was made man, that Jesus resurrected from the dead, or that Christ is physically present in the Eucharist.

The second principle is scripture. Here, many papal critics[34] will immediately bring out the biblical passages where Jesus instituted the indissolubility of marriage,[35] and point out that there is no biblical precedent for giving communion to the divorced and remarried.[36] Of course, we already established that *Amoris Laetitia* does not contradict indissolubility of marriage. But most importantly, Newman very explicitly explains how this is not the scriptural hermeneutics he has in mind:

> Now it was Scripture that was made the rule on which this development proceeded in each case, and *Scripture moreover interpreted in a mystical sense*; and whereas at first certain texts were inconsistently confined to the letter ... the very course of events, as time went on, interpreted the prophecies about the Church more truly.... This is but one specimen of a certain law of Church teaching, which is this—*a reference to Scripture throughout, and especially in its mystical sense*.... On the other hand, the School of Antioch, which adopted the *literal interpretation was, as I noticed above, the very metropolis of heresy*.... Diodurus and

---

34. Baklinski, "Bishop Schneider: 'Discernment' Now Means to 'Allow to Sin'": "Following the teachings of Jesus Christ, the Catholic Church has always taught that the marriage bond validly contracted between a husband and wife cannot be broken 'till death do us part.' This teaching is largely based on the words of Jesus, who taught that 'what God has joined together, let no one separate' (Mark 10:9). The Church teaches that those who engage in sexual relations outside of a valid marriage commit adultery, which is prohibited by the Sixth Commandment."

35. Mark 10:9.

36. This is not completely accurate. Stephen Walford gathered the scriptural evidence for the teaching of mitigating circumstances in his book, *Pope Francis, the Family, and Divorce*, 83.

> Theodore of Mopsuestia, who were the most eminent masters of literalism in the succeeding generations, were, as we have seen, the forerunners of Nestorianism. The case had been the same in a still earlier age—*the Jews clung to the literal sense of the Scriptures and hence rejected the Gospel; the Christian Apologists proved its divinity by means of the allegorical.*[37]

In other words, scripture should not be interpreted in the literalist sense, but in the mystical sense. How can we interpret scripture in the mystical sense in this situation? In *Amoris Laetitia*, Pope Francis mentions two such biblical instances:

> Many people feel that the Church's message on marriage and the family does not clearly reflect the preaching and attitudes of Jesus, who set forth a demanding ideal yet never failed to show compassion and closeness to the frailty of individuals like the *Samaritan woman* or the *woman caught in adultery*."[38]

How can we not notice the patience with which Jesus Christ guided the Samaritan woman at the well?[39] At first he came to her and introduced himself as the water of life; only as she opened up her heart did he mention how she lived in adultery, since she had remarried four times. This is—so Francis says—how Jesus treated the Samaritan woman: by addressing her desire for true love, in order to free her from the darkness in her life and to bring her to the full joy of the gospel. In like manner, people in irregular situations require a constructive response seeking to transform them into opportunities that can lead to the full reality of marriage and family in conformity with the gospel. These couples need to be welcomed and guided patiently and discreetly.[40]

As for the woman caught in adultery,[41] Jesus saved her from a literalist and legalistic application of the law, even before she stopped sinning (or even, as far as we know, before she repented of her sin). The Pharisees were condemning her, demanding that she be stoned. In like manner, Pope Francis warns us of the error of those who, rather than offering the healing power of grace and the light of the gospel message, would "indoctrinate" that message, turning it into "dead stones to be hurled at

---

37. Newman, *Development of Christian Doctrine*, 338–39, 343.
38. *AL* 38.
39. John 4:4–26.
40. *AL* 294.
41. John 7:53—8:11.

others."⁴² A pastor cannot feel that it is enough simply to apply moral laws to those living in "irregular" situations, as if they were stones to throw at people's lives.⁴³

In both biblical instances, Jesus is the one who takes the initiative. He is the one who comes to the sinners first, even before they stopped sinning. He comes not with condemnations for their dissolute lives, but with a profound love for them, coupled with patience and understanding. Yes, he eventually says: "Go and sin no more." That is, of course, important and indispensable. But that was not the first step:

> The example of Jesus is a paradigm for the Church. . . . In this way he demonstrated the true meaning of mercy, which entails the restoration of the covenant (cf. John Paul II, *Dives in Misericordia*, 4). This is clear from his conversations with the *Samaritan woman* (cf. Jn 1:4–30) and with *the woman found in adultery* (cf. Jn 8:1–11), *where the consciousness of sin is awakened by an encounter with Jesus's gratuitous love.*⁴⁴

By interpreting scripture *in the mystical sense*, as Newman urges us to do, we can see that *Amoris Laetitia* fulfills, in fact, one of the many principles laid out as part of a legitimate development. I would also like to mention a cautionary example from Newman himself, about those who separate doctrine from principles, and which seems very apropos:

> Protestantism, viewed in its more Catholic aspect, is doctrine without active principle; viewed in its heretical, it is active principle without doctrine. Many of its speakers, for instance, use eloquent and glowing language about the Church and its characteristics: some of them do not realize what they say, but *use high words and general statements about "the faith," and "primitive truth," and "schism," and "heresy," to which they attach no definite meaning; while others speak of "unity," "universality," and "Catholicity," and use the words in their own sense and for their own ideas.*⁴⁵

❖❖❖

---

42. *AL* 49.
43. *AL* 305.
44. *AL* 64.
45. Newman, *Development of Christian Doctrine*, 182.

Third Note: Power of Assimilation

Newman defines power of assimilation as "nothing more than a mere accretion of doctrines or rites from without."[46] Just like in the first note, Newman used the analogy of the physical growth of a living being to illustrate how doctrine develops:

> In the physical world, whatever has life is characterized by growth, so that in no respect to grow is to cease to live. It grows by taking into its own substance eternal materials; and this absorption or assimilation is completed when the materials appropriated come to belong to it or enter into its unity. . . . Doctrines and views which relate to man are not placed in a void, but in the crowded world, and make way for themselves by interpenetration, and develope by absorption. . . . They are modified, laid down afresh, thrust aside, as the case may be. A new element of order and composition has come among them; and its life is proved by this capacity of expansion, without disarrangement or dissolution. . . . Thus a power of development is a proof of life, not only in its essay, but especially in its success; for a mere formula either does not expand or is shattered in expanding. A living idea becomes many, yet remains one.[47]

Practically speaking, this means that Catholicism is not only polemical, but unitive. In other words, it must be capable, while retaining its own identity, of absorbing its antagonists, as Aaron's rod devoured the rods of the sorcerers of Egypt.[48] As Newman notes, the first centuries' heresies had no stay or consistency, yet they contained elements of truth amid the errors. Catholicism, in the collision with those heresies, broke into pieces its antagonists, and divided the spoils.[49] The church, therefore, operates by rejecting the evil of those heresies without sacrificing the good; and the conduct of popes, councils, fathers, betokens the slow, painful, anxious taking up of new truths into an existing body of belief.[50]

For Newman, the doctrines even of heretical bodies are indices and anticipations of the mind of the church.[51] The gospel, on the other hand,

---

46. Newman, *Development of Christian Doctrine*, 380.
47. Newman, *Development of Christian Doctrine*, 185–86.
48. Newman, *Development of Christian Doctrine*, 355.
49. Newman, *Development of Christian Doctrine*, 359.
50. Newman, *Development of Christian Doctrine*, 366.
51. Newman, *Development of Christian Doctrine*, 362.

has a certain virtue and grace which changes the quality of opinions and actions that are incorporated in it, and makes them right and acceptable to its divine author, whereas before they were infected with evil, or at best shadows of the truth.[52]

> The phenomenon, admitted on all hands, is this—That great portion of what is generally received as Christian truth is, in its rudiments or in its separate parts, to be found in heathen philosophies and religions.... Mr. Milman argues from it—"These things are in heathenism, therefore they are not Christian," we on the contrary, prefer to say, these things are in Christianity, therefore they are not heathen.... The distinction between these two theories is broad and obvious. The advocates of the one imply that Revelation was a single, entire, solitary act, or nearly so, introducing a certain message; whereas we, who maintain the other, consider that Divine teaching as been in fact, what the analogy of nature would lead us to expect at sundry times and in divers manners, various, complex, progressive, and supplemental of itself.[53]

When papal critics accuse *Amoris Laetitia* of being a capitulation to liberal talking points about conscience, mercy, and non-judgmentalism, they are missing the point. *Amoris Laetitia*, as a legitimate development, is bound to assimilate the adversaries of Catholicism, filtering out the evil and retaining the good. That it retained the good, I already proved in the rest of this book. However, the papal critic observes this assimilation and wrongly concludes that there was no development, but corruption. Nevertheless, as Newman says, "That an idea more readily coalesces with these ideas than with those does not show that it has been unduly influenced, that is, corrupted by them, but that it has an antecedent affinity with them."[54] This affinity is what Pope Francis seeks to explore for the benefit of souls.

❦❦❦

---

52. Newman, *Development of Christian Doctrine*, 368.
53. Newman, *Development of Christian Doctrine*, 380, 382.
54. Newman, *Development of Christian Doctrine*, 187.

Fourth Note: Logical Sequence

Logical sequence, according to Newman, includes a *progress* of the mind from one judgment to another:[55]

> Minds develope *step by step, without looking behind them or anticipating their goal*, and without either intention or promise of forming a system. Afterwards, however, this logical development which the whole wears becomes a test, that the process has been a true development, not a perversion or corruption from its evident naturalness.[56]

This step by step terminology seems to mirror Francis's pastoral approach; but for now we do not want to use this fourth note as a way to prove the law of gradualness, but rather to know if this note applies to the developments undertaken in *Amoris Laetitia*. I think that, in both chapters 7 and 14 of this book, I have shown how the doctrinal basis underlying *Amoris Laetitia*'s sacramental discipline seem to follow from general practices and teachings already laid out beforehand in the *Catechism* and the *Vademecum* for other sins of the flesh, thereby showing the logical sequence between *Amoris Laetitia* and these other authoritative church documents (see also chapter 10). Is this consistent with what Newman understands as "logical sequence"? I think it is hard to deny this, since Newman used, as an example to illustrate this fourth note of legitimate developments, precisely a relaxation of sacramental discipline regarding adulterous sinners. When explaining the fourth note, Newman mentions how, during primitive Christianity, plenary forgiveness of sin was conferred through baptism, a once-in-a-lifetime event. This, however, raised a problem:

> What could be done for those who had received the one remission of sins, and had sinned since? Some who thought upon the subject appear to have conceived that the Church was empowered to grant one, and one only, reconciliation after grievous offences. Three sins seemed to many, at least in the West, to be irremissible: idolatry, murder, and *adultery*. But such a system of *Church discipline, however suited to a small community, and even expedient in times of persecution, could not exist in Christianity, as it spread into the* orbis terrarum, *and gathered a net of every kind. A more indulgent rule gradually gained ground*; yet the Spanish Church adhered to the ancient rule even in the fourth

---

55. Newman, *Development of Christian Doctrine*, 383.
56. Newman, *Development of Christian Doctrine*, 190–91.

century, and a portion of Africa in the third, and in the remaining portion *there was a relaxation only as regards the crime of incontinence* (i.e. adultery).[57]

Newman goes on to mention how it was heretics (Montanists and Novatians) who wanted to adhere to the "primitive rule," and decried the "laxity" of their fellow Catholics. In the meantime, this relaxation of discipline was the starting point for many subsequent true developments. Those developments are now so ingrained in our Catholic DNA, that we take them for granted: the sacrament of penance[58] and the doctrine of purgatory.[59] These were needed to extend forgiveness to those who had sinned again (namely through adultery) after baptism had washed their sins away for the first time.

❊❊❊

Fifth Note: Anticipation of Its Future

That *Amoris Laetitia*'s sacramental discipline could be anticipated (even if people with no ability to foresee the future might have missed it at the time) is shown precisely in chapters 7 and 14, since the new discipline is grounded on the teaching of mitigating circumstances laid out beforehand. Anyone who knew this teaching might have anticipated that it might be applied to the situation of divorced and remarried people, even if the previous sacramental discipline seemed to exclude this possibility. The fact that this pastoral paradigm, though formerly present for other sins, was not fully realized until later, does not detract from the legitimacy of this development. Newman explains that ideas may lay dormant during extended periods of time, though they may be theoretically anticipated:

> Since, when an idea is living, that is, influential and effective, it is sure to develope according to its own nature, and the tendencies, which are carried out in the long run, may under favorable circumstances show themselves early as well as late, and logic is the same in all ages, *instances of a development which is to come, though vague and isolated, may occur from the very first, though*

---

57. Newman, *Development of Christian Doctrine*, 384.
58. Newman, *Development of Christian Doctrine*, 385–86.
59. Newman, *Development of Christian Doctrine*, 388–93.

a lapse of time be necessary to bring them to perfection. And since developments are in great measure only aspects of the idea from which they proceed, and all of them are natural consequences of it, it is often a matter of accident in what order they are carried out in individual minds; and it is in no wise strange that here and there definite specimens of advanced teaching should very early occur, which in the historical course are not found till a late day. The fact, then, of such early or recurring intimations of tendencies which afterwards are fully realized, is a sort of evidence that those later and more systematic fulfillments are only in accordance with the original idea.[60]

❊ ❊ ❊

Sixth Note: Conservative Action upon Its Past

Most papal critics who try to use Newman as an argument against *Amoris Laetitia* usually do so by invoking the sixth note: conservative action upon its past.[61] In fact, Newman says (much in the vein of St. Vincent de Lérins):

> As developments which are preceded by definite indications have a fair presumption in their favour, so *those which do but contradict and reverse the course of doctrine which has been developed before them, and out of which they spring, are certainly corrupt*; for a corruption is a development in that very stage in

---

60. Newman, *Development of Christian Doctrine*, 195–96.

61. As an example, see Smith, "Pope Francis on the Development of Doctrine": "For that we need to turn to Bl. John Henry Newman. The pope's remarks come just a couple of days after Newman's feast. It is a little surprising that Francis did not mention Newman, since Newman's *Essay on the Development of Christian Doctrine* has long been the *locus classicus* for an orthodox discussion of the development of doctrine. Or maybe not so surprising. In the *Essay*, Newman identifies several 'notes' (he does not go so far as to call them 'tests') of an authentic development of doctrine. *Among these notes is 'conservative action' upon a doctrine's past. Newman writes that a true development 'is an addition which illustrates, not obscures, corroborates, not corrects, the body of thought from which it proceeds; and this is its characteristic as contrasted with a corruption.'* In other words, Newman tells us that an authentic development will never result in black becoming white or up down. *When Francis talks about doctrine becoming 'clearly contrary' to a 'new understanding of Christian truth,' it seems that he rejects Newman's notion that a development of doctrine is conservative of the doctrine's past.* He seems to believe that authentic developments can correct, not corroborate, the body of thought from which they proceed."

which it ceases to illustrate, and begins to disturb, the acquisitions gained in its previous history. . . . A true development, then, may be described as one which is conservative of the course of antecedent developments being really those antecedents and something besides them: it is *an addition which illustrates, not obscures, corroborates, not corrects, the body of thought from which it proceeds*; and this is its characteristic as contrasted with a corruption.[62]

Most likely, the papal critic will assert that *Amoris Laetitia* is self-evidently a corruption, not a development, based on these grounds. However, if we keep reading Newman on his sixth note, we will see there is more to that. The saintly cardinal, in fact, when explaining this note, takes a long time dispelling Protestant accusations that Catholic traditions are a self-evident corruption, without a conservative action with the past.

> When *Roman Catholics are accused of substituting another Gospel for the primitive Creed*, they answer that they hold, and can show that they hold, the doctrines of the Incarnation and Atonement, as firmly as any Protestant can state them. To this it is replied that they do certainly profess them, but that *they obscure and virtually annul them by their additions; that the* cultus *of St. Mary and the Saints is no development of the truth, but a corruption and a religious mischief to those doctrines of which it is the corruption, because it draws away the mind and heart from Christ*. But they answer that, so far from this, it subserves, illustrates, protects the doctrine of our Lord's loving kindness and mediation. Thus the parties in controversy join issue on the common ground, that a developed doctrine which reverses the course of development which has preceded it, is no true development but a corruption; also, that what is corrupt acts as an element of unhealthiness towards what is sound.[63]

Just like Catholics do with the Protestants in the example above, I too join the papal critic on the common ground that a doctrine reversing the course of development which has preceded it, is no true development, but a corruption. Where we disagree, as in the quote above, is on whether *Amoris Laetitia* really does possess a conservative action on its past or not. In effect, I have dedicated section III of this book to showing how

---

62. Newman, *Development of Christian Doctrine*, 199.
63. Newman, *Development of Christian Doctrine*, 202.

Amoris Laetitia constitutes a harmonious development with previous magisterial pronouncements.

Just because a development seems to contradict past teaching, it does not mean that it does not possess a conservative action upon its past. In fact, Newman talks about a "great law which is seen in developments generally, that changes which appear at first sight to contradict that out of which they grew, are really its protection or illustration."[64] He goes on to exemplify this law by bringing up the Protestant allegation that Marian doctrines draw away from Christ. Newman argues that the *Theotokos*, far from hindering the dogma of the Incarnation, actually protects it.[65]

In the same line of argument, papal critics postulate that *Amoris Laetitia* hinders the perennial and irrevocable doctrine of the indissolubility of marriage. However, as I have said previously, not only does *Amoris Laetitia* not contradict the indissolubility of marriage (as per chapter 6 of this book), it actually is its protection: it acknowledges the present situation, and seeks the best way to lead this secularized culture back to full communion with perennial doctrine, without allowing it to be dismissed, derided, or trampled on (see chapter 10).

On the other hand, Newman is also perfectly clear that "conservative action on the past" does not mean a rigorous and intransigent adherence to the past:

> Though none could surpass the later Jews in its literal observance, nevertheless this did not save them from the punishments attached to the violation of it. *If this be so, the literal observance is not its true and evangelical import.* . . . Now the Jews of our Lord's day did not keep this covenant, for they incurred the penalty; *yet they kept the letter of the Commandment rigidly*, and were known among the heathen far and wide for their devotion to the "Lord God of their fathers who brought them out of the land of Egypt," and for their abhorrence of the "gods whom He had not given them." *If then adherence to the letter was no protection to the Jews, departure from the letter may be no guilt in Christians.*[66]

A development may have conservatism with the past, without this being apparent, because what is being conserved may be latent until its full manifestation.

64. Newman, *Development of Christian Doctrine*, 422.
65. Newman, *Development of Christian Doctrine*, 425–36.
66. Newman, *Development of Christian Doctrine*, 424.

> If we take the simplest and most general view of its history, as existing in an individual mind, or in the Church at large, we shall see in it an instance of this peculiarity. *It is the birth of something virtually new, because latent in what was before.* Thus we know that no temper of mind is acceptable in the Divine Presence without love; it is love which makes Christian fear differ from servile dread, and true faith differ from the faith of devils; yet in the beginning of the religious life, fear is the prominent evangelical grace, and love is but latent in fear, and *has in course of time to be developed out of what seems its contradictory. Then, when it is developed, it takes that prominent place which fear held before, yet protecting not superseding it. Love is added, not fear removed*, and the mind is but perfected in grace by what seems a revolution.[67]

In other words, there was an addition, not a loss. But what was added was latent before, so it seems contradictory at first. I already explained, in my comments on the fifth note, how I think *Amoris Laetitia*'s discipline lay dormant in the *Catechism* and the *Vademecum*. This discipline is an offshoot of the teaching on mitigating circumstances, already existent in the past. This pastoral practice was then added to the church, but not as a loss, since the doctrine of the indissolubility of marriage remains intact.

What is a doctrinal loss is the venue taken by most papal critics in the last years, whereby they seek to dispute *Amoris Laetitia*, by subtracting from Catholicism something that has always been constitutive of it: the deference and obedience owed to papal teachings, even non-infallible ones. This fundamental part of Catholicism has been ceaselessly undermined in the past few years, in a way that is certainly not conservative with many past magisterial pronouncements. It is much more in accordance with the sixth note to acknowledge *Amoris Laetitia*'s orthodoxy, than accepting the presuppositions underlying many of the arguments advanced against it.

✧ ✧ ✧

Seventh Note: Chronic Vigour

Regarding the seventh note, Cardinal Newman explains:

---

67. Newman, *Development of Christian Doctrine*, 420.

> Since the corruption of an idea, as far as the appearance goes, is a sort of accident or affection of its development, being the end of a course, and a transition-state leading to a crisis, it is, as has been observed above, a brief and rapid process. While ideas live in men's minds, they are ever enlarging into fuller development: they will not be stationary in their corruption any more than before it; and dissolution is that further state to which corruption tends. Corruption cannot, therefore, be of long standing; and thus duration is another test of a faithful development. *Si gravis, brevis; si longus, levis.* . . . The course of heresies is always short. . . . Thus, while a corruption is distinguished from decay by its energetic action, it is distinguished from a development by its transitory character.[68]

Of course, given that *Amoris Laetitia* has been published only a few years ago, it is impossible to ascertain whether it fulfills the seventh note or not. Only time will tell. Still, the way that *Amoris Laetitia* has withstood the wave of criticisms against it from influential sectors of the church, so much so that the wave has already lost most of its impetus, so that critics had to keep the momentum going by moving on to criticizing Francis on other topics, is an encouraging sign that *Amoris Laetitia* will endure the test of time. In the meantime, an increasing number of bishops is promulgating guidelines in communion with the pope's manifest mind and will. When something faces considerable opposition and overwhelming odds, and still stands, this is a sign that it comes from the Holy Spirit.

✿✿✿

In conclusion, I think *Amoris Laetitia* fulfills all seven notes of a true development, thereby passing the "Newman trial." So, I would like to finish this chapter with a final quote from the saint himself. This quote does not come from his essay on doctrinal development, but from another of his writings, about assent. I think it should be deeply meditated upon, since it seems to address a certain mindset at the root of much of the opposition to *Amoris Laetitia* (and, for what is worth, it does not apply solely to converts):

> A man is converted to the Catholic Church from his admiration of its religious system, and his disgust with Protestantism. That admiration remains; but, after a time, he leaves his new faith, perhaps returns to his old. The reason, if we may conjecture,

---

68. Newman, *Development of Christian Doctrine*, 203, 205.

may sometimes be this: he has never believed in the Church's infallibility; in her doctrinal truth he has believed, but in her infallibility, no. *He was asked, before he was received, whether he held all that the Church taught, he replied he did; but he understood the question to mean, whether he held those particular doctrines "which at that time the Church in matter of fact formally taught," whereas it really meant "whatever the Church then or at any future time should teach."* Thus, he never had the indispensable and elementary faith of a Catholic, and was simply no subject for reception into the fold of the Church. This being the case, when the Immaculate Conception is defined, *he feels that it is something more than he bargained for* when he became a Catholic, and accordingly he gives up his religious profession. *The world will say that he has lost his certitude of the divinity of the Catholic Faith, but he never had it.*[69]

---

69. Newman, *An Essay in Aid of a Grammar of Assent*, 240.

Section IV

SOME PRACTICAL EXAMPLES

CHAPTER 16

A Case Study

SOME PEOPLE, CONFUSED ABOUT how *Amoris Laetitia* might be applied in real life, will ask for concrete examples. This is fair—often we clarify by exemplifying. However, we must take note that examples may be counterproductive in this case, if we cling too rigidly to them. I remind the reader of this passage of *Amoris Laetitia*, already quoted in chapter 1:

> *If we consider the immense variety of concrete situations such as those I have mentioned*, it is understandable that neither the Synod nor this Exhortation could be expected to provide a new set of general rules, canonical in nature and applicable to all cases. *What is possible is simply a renewed encouragement to undertake a responsible personal and pastoral discernment of particular cases.* . . . It is true that general rules set forth a good which can never be disregarded or neglected, but in their formulation *they cannot provide absolutely for all particular situations.*[1]

In other words, the case study I am about to explore is meant to be exemplificative, not exhaustive. Other practical applications may arise that do not resemble this case study in most of its particulars, as long as mitigating circumstances are present. The purpose of this case study is simply to help establish *Amoris Laetitia*'s legitimacy. As long as there is a single possible and orthodox application for *Amoris Laetitia* (according to the Buenos Aires criteria), then the allegations against its theoretical illegitimacy are refuted.

1. *AL* 300, 304.

Also, since I am not a pastor, I think I should defer to someone with greater expertise and experience on the pastoral guidance of souls. Therefore, the case study I am about to analyze was designed, not by me, but by a priest, Fr. Paul Keller, who then published it at Crux.[2] As Fr. Keller says in the preamble, the following case study, while pastorally realistic, represents no specific person or case he had encountered. So, without further ado, let us consider it.

❀❀❀

Fr. Keller brings us the case of "Irma," a woman from El Salvador. Irma was, once, a merely "cultural" Catholic. In other words, she was brought up in a profoundly Catholic culture, but never properly catechized on the seriousness and theological particulars of her religion. She married her boyfriend in the Catholic Church. He was a very respectful and good man at the time.

However, after they got married, her new husband joined a gang and became an alcoholic and a drug addict. He started having affairs and, worse, became physically and verbally abusive towards her.

One day, he left the house and never came back. Irma was left to fend for herself for months. So she decided to divorce him and immigrate to the USA, where she had family who took her in. There she found another man: Tony, a gentle and considerate person, whom she eventually civilly married. He was not Catholic, though, even if he was supportive of her religion.

Eventually, Irma had a daughter, whom she named Araceli. As a cultural Catholic, Irma decided she wanted to baptize her daughter in the Catholic Church. So Irma started to attend Mass. This is when she started her conversion process, becoming more and more attracted to a deeper understanding of her faith. She developed a particular interest in the Eucharist, and a great yearning to receive communion. Fr. Keller accompanied her case for almost two years, and that's when the question was raised:

"But, Father, can't I receive Communion?"

❀❀❀

Let us stop for a moment to consider what has happened so far. First of all, Irma is divorced. Though the church does not condone divorce,

---

2. Keller, "Case Study in Communion."

there are instances where it tolerates it: "If civil divorce remains the only possible way of ensuring certain legal rights, the care of the children, or the protection of inheritance, it can be tolerated and does not constitute a moral offense."[3] I think this particular case, with violence and abandonment from her first spouse, is one instance where the church can tolerate divorce.

Either way, the intrinsically evil act was actually her remarriage. It can be argued that she should not have remarried. However, what happened, happened; and she is now stuck in this irregular situation. Simply rehashing about what she *should* have done will not solve her problems now.[4]

What is happening now is this: Irma has a new mate, who sustains her (both materially and emotionally), and a daughter in need of a stable family. Therefore, separating from Tony would cause a significant amount of harm to her and to her child. She is also growing in her faith and closeness with God. So what options are available to her?

One can say that she should proceed with an annulment. Fr. Keller, however, affirms this will not be possible for three reasons: 1) Irma immigrated to the US illegally, so she brought no church or legal documents with her when she came to the States; 2) she does not know where her first spouse is; 3) she has no grounds to request the annulment, since her first spouse's problems were caused by addictions that only developed *after* they were married.

Then, all that is left for Irma, per *Familiaris Consortio*, is for her to live in perfect continence with Tony, as if they were brother and sister. Irma would have no problem abiding by this, but there is a problem: Tony is not a Catholic, and is not open to that possibility. Irma fears (and

---

3. CCC 2383.

4. Fr. Joseph Levine wrote an article trying to disprove Fr. Keller's case study (Levine, "How Not to Minister"). This refutation basically does not give any concrete solutions to the problem, apart from simply restating doctrine, and making a passing reference to a "Marian solution" (i.e., pray the rosary, have a relationship with Mary), which will not quell Irma's Eucharistic thirst. Basically, Fr. Levine's answer is that "you can't solve every problem," and that Irma should not have gotten into that situation in the first place. Of course, the problem can indeed easily be solved if the priest applies the provisions laid out by the Vicar of Christ in *Amoris Laetitia*. It also shows the impoverishment of the pastoral solutions presented to the divorced and remarried before *Amoris Laetitia*, and why a new pastoral paradigm was sorely needed.

understandably so), that Tony might think this is too much for him to bear and leave her.[5]

So, all pre-*Amoris Laetitia* options failed Irma. What is left? Let us resume the story.

❖ ❖ ❖

"But, Father, can't I receive Communion?"

Fr. Keller explains that Irma is heartbroken about the prospect of not being able to receive the sacrament, ever. The good priest has a counseling degree and he notes how her despair is starting to erode her spiritual and psychological health whenever she attends Mass without being able to receive communion. After she gets home, she starts crying. Tony, who at first had voiced interest in learning more about the faith, is now refusing to attend Mass because he cannot bear the anguish that all of this is causing her. Even little Araceli is starting to question why mommy goes to Mass if it makes her so sad.

Is this a case where we can apply *Amoris Laetitia*'s concession for the divorced and remarried? *Amoris Laetitia* is clear that any process of discernment must involve someone with "humility, discretion and love for the Church and her teaching, in a sincere search for God's will and a desire to make a more perfect response to it."[6] Fr. Keller has discerned that this applies to Irma, since she does not pretend that the church's teaching is wrong, nor is she unwilling to comply, though her spiritual and psychological health are involuntarily being hampered because of her separation from the Eucharist.

Per *Amoris Laetitia*, we can start our process of discernment in this particular case. The next step is to ascertain the following: Irma cannot receive the Eucharist if she is in mortal sin, for she would then be eating and drinking her own condemnation. Also, we must be careful lest giving her communion in public may induce someone into scandal.

Mortal sin has three conditions: grave matter, full knowledge, and full consent. If Irma has sexual relations with Tony, she will be engaging in intercourse with someone with which she is not married to. In other words, it will be adultery, an intrinsically evil sin, and grave matter. As far as full knowledge is concerned, we understand from this story that

---

5. In this sense, this practical case seems to be consistent with the example granted also by Victor Fernández in "El Capítulo VIII de *Amoris Laetitia*," 457.

6. *AL* 300.

Fr. Keller has duly informed Irma of the seriousness of her situation. She understood and accepted it. Therefore, we must now turn to full consent.

Irma would like to live "as brother and sister" with Tony, but he will not agree with this arrangement. In fact, there is a real danger that, if Irma pushes too hard, Tony will leave her and deprive Araceli of her father figure. This is certainly a case where, if certain expressions of intimacy are lacking, the good of the children suffers.[7] Can we say that Irma is engaging in intercourse with "full consent"?

If Irma had her way, she would live in accordance with the prescriptions of the church. However, there are external pressures inducing her into actions she does not fully want to perform in the first place. The *Catechism* states, in its section on mortal vs. venial sin, that external pressures may diminish the voluntary and free character of the offense.[8] Also, in its section on freedom, the *Catechism* also states that imputability and responsibility for an action can be diminished or even nullified by fear and other psychological or social factors.[9]

Since the *Catechism* is very clear that venial sin occurs when someone disobeys the moral law in a grave matter but without complete consent,[10] Irma may, after an examination of conscience, discern with a certain moral security that she very likely is not in a state of mortal sin.

Granted, she will have to be on her toes, lest she starts using this venue as a "permission" to access the Eucharist and as an excuse to indulge in intercourse with Tony. Francis says we should avoid the grave danger of misunderstandings, such as the notion that any priest can grant exceptions.[11] Also, the Buenos Aires criteria are clear that it is not convenient to speak of "permits" to access the sacraments, but of a process of discernment accompanied by a pastor.[12] Therefore, Fr. Keller will need to keep accompanying Irma. She will have, in every Mass, to perform a conscience exam to ascertain whether she has sinned with full consent or not.

What about the question of scandal? Fr. Keller is very clear that, apart from him, no one in his parish knows of Irma's circumstances. All

---

7. *AL* n329.
8. *CCC* 1860.
9. *CCC* 1733.
10. *CCC* 1862.
11. *AL* 300.
12. Bishops of the Pastoral Region of Buenos Aires, "Criterios básicos."

the information he gathered from Irma's past is bound by the seal of confession. There is no danger of scandal.[13] Besides, he could easily give her communion away from prying eyes, in the internal forum.

※ ※ ※

"But, Father, can't I receive Communion?"

The Vicar of Christ, after two synods with the successors of the apostles, has published an apostolic exhortation, where it is written: "Because of forms of conditioning and mitigating factors, it is possible that in an objective situation of sin—which may not be subjectively culpable, or fully such—a person can be living in God's grace, can love, and can also grow in the life of grace and charity, while receiving the Church's help to this end."[14] In certain cases this can include the help of the sacraments,[15] while avoiding any occasion of scandal.[16]

To clarify even further, an authoritative interpretation of this exhortation, the Buenos Aires criteria, states as follows: "If it is recognized that, in a specific case, there are limitations that mitigate liability and guilt, particularly when a person considers that he would fall on a further fault damaging the children of the new union, *Amoris Laetitia* opens the possibility of access to the sacraments of Reconciliation and the Eucharist."[17]

So, when Irma asks whether she can receive communion, the answer is "yes."[18] The only reason not to allow her to receive the Eucharist would be a stubborn clinging to the previous sacramental discipline, in defiance of the pope's manifest mind and will. This would mean laying a heavy cross on this poor woman, a load that is not needed because the Vicar of Christ, entrusted with the task of binding and loosing, has said so. Papal critics should be wary of not tying Irma's shoulders to a heavy and insupportable burden, while they themselves are not willing to lift a

13. Keller, "Case Study in Communion."
14. *AL* 305.
15. *AL* n351.
16. *AL* 299.
17. Bishops of the Pastoral Region of Buenos Aires, "Criterios básicos."
18. Besides Fr. Levine's article, there has been another author who has tried to refute Fr. Keller's case study: Dr. Edward Peters, in his essay "Conscience can't be the final arbiter on who gets Communion." Dr. Peters takes recourse mostly to canon law, namely canon 915, to make his case. I have addressed this objection, and most others that he presents in his essay, in the previous chapters of this book.

finger to help her,[19] which would mean for them simply to acknowledge that their theoretical constructs of what is licit or not may be wrong, and that they should follow the magisterium instead of their own personal opinions (no matter how theologically informed). Surely for them, the stakes are much lower. Yet, according to them, the full weight of this situation must be endured by Irma, and the pope should uncharitably stop correcting them by bringing up terms like "rigidity."

※ ※ ※

Fr. Keller is faced with a choice: either he is faithful to the pope's directives and gives communion to Irma; or he, on account of some preconceived idea, decides that she is not eligible and withholds communion from her. Let us explore the most likely outcome of the latter strategy.

We know that Irma's spiritual and psychological health is suffering from this impasse. She is on the verge of a breakdown. If this keeps up, surely Irma will face a very serious temptation: in order to safeguard her own well-being she may be convinced that she will have to drop out of her newly found Catholic faith. Tony is certainly already moving her in that direction, as he has stopped attending Mass. I am certain that many of her friends and relatives will say the same thing. Even Araceli, inadvertently, is pushing her in that direction—as a child, she does not want mommy to keep going to Mass if that makes her so sad. Also, we must not neglect the dangerous possibility that this breakdown may drive Irma into suicide.

Things will not go so well for Tony and Araceli either. Fr. Keller is rightfully concerned that the end of this relationship will harm all three people involved. Tony does not want to take part in Mass anymore, and Araceli will grow up in a family environment vitiated by this situation. I am fairly certain that, if this keeps up (or if, God forbid, Irma takes her own life), Tony and Araceli will eventually turn virulently anti-Catholic.

But that is not the venue Fr. Keller took. In his story, he tells Irma: "If you sincerely believe in your conscience that this is how Christ can aid your growth in holiness, then yes: you may go to Communion."

He goes on to describe that, after Mass the following Sunday, Irma goes and greets the good priest with tears of joy in her eyes. She proclaims: "For all these years at every Mass, when it was time for Communion, I have felt as if Jesus turned his back to me. Today, for the first time, I felt

19. Matt 23:4.

as if Jesus embraced me and told me that he loved me." Her spiritual and psychological welfare is no longer in jeopardy.

Having partaken of the Eucharist, Irma has now received sacramental grace that will help her heal her internal wounds and keep growing and maturing in her faith. She is now strengthened to persevere and try, progressively, to bring herself more and more in alignment with the church's demands, by trying to bring Tony with her into the fold.

In fact, Tony, who until then had refused to attend Mass, accompanies her when she greets Fr. Keller. He has moist eyes. We must bear in mind that, before all of this kerfuffle, Tony had voiced an interest in learning more about the Mass and the Catholic Church. The mental and spiritual blockade that all these circumstances had placed on Tony's heart have been lifted and he can return to his journey back to the church. Fr. Keller has reasonable hope that Tony might eventually become Catholic and, perhaps after another two or three children, be able to embrace a life "as brother and sister." By patiently and continuously nudging him in that direction every single day, both Irma and Keller might be able to help his soul be saved too. Surely, Irma will need grace to be able to endure this task.

Furthermore, Araceli will be able to grow up in a steady and loving environment. Most importantly, she will have her mother's example to look up to, and her father will also not cause undue obstacles to her religious formation. If, as Fr. Keller hopes, Tony eventually converts and starts living "as brother and sister" with Irma, what testimony of Christian temperance and faith will these parents give to young Araceli! Certainly, she will be better equipped to respond to the current society's increasing hedonism and secularism. Who knows—she might embrace the consecrated life, or a saintly marriage of her own (which will certainly follow the example of her chaste parents).

We should not forget another person in this picture: the one who might be reading these words and who may find out that he has been deceived by misinformation into considering disobedience from the Vicar of Christ in order to deprive people like Irma from receiving the sacramental grace that would help them bear their circumstances. This is a heavy price to pay for such a small benefit. I beseech those who might be reading this to stop and reconsider: their situation is not as difficult and convoluted as Irma's. What needs to be done is quite simple, even if some might find it difficult: to take the leap of faith of Jesus's promise that he guides an indefectible church and preserves it through a visible head—the pope, the Vicar of Christ. If you find this difficult, do not despair of Christ's mercy, but consider how much more difficult it might be for Irma to ask her to face the decision between tearing her family apart or face the psychological and spiritual damage her separation from the Eucharist causes her. Then, maybe, we *all* may be able to start our progressive path towards God's salvation, each one of us with his own cross, without burdening others, and rather trying to help each other as much as possible.

CHAPTER 17

The Portuguese Reception

TAKING INTO ACCOUNT WHAT we have learned in previous chapters, I think Portugal has been exemplary in the way it has applied *Amoris Laetitia* at the diocesan level. The Portuguese Episcopal Conference has not promulgated a single document covering all national territory, but three dioceses have issued guidelines meriting a closer look: Lisbon, Leiria-Fatima, and Braga.

Historically and traditionally, Portugal is a very Catholic country. In a 2011 census, eighty-one percent of the total population identified as Catholic.[1] However, it is also a highly secularized country. A study done by the Catholic Church in 2001 showed that only nineteen percent of the total population attends Mass every Sunday.[2]

This secularization extends to matrimonial behavior as well. In 2007, only 47.3 percent of total marriages were Catholic.[3] In 2018, 58.7 percent of marriages ended in divorce,[4] making Portugal the European country with the highest rate of divorce.[5]

In this sense, I believe the Portuguese church sees *Amoris Laetitia* as a major opportunity to rebuild family and marriage in this country (see chapter 10). Also, all Portuguese guidelines we are going to explore have

---

1. Instituto Nacional de Estatística, *Censos 2011 Resultados Definitivos—Portugal*, 530. It is likely that this percentage has decreased since.
2. "Recenseamento Da Prática Dominical," Ecclesia.pt.
3. Instituto Nacional de Estatística, *Estatísticas Demográficas 2007*, 13.
4. "Número de Divórcios Por 100 Casamentos," Pordata.pt.
5. Cabral, "Portugueses são os europeus que mais se divorciam."

specific particularities making them unique and worthy of attention at the international level as well.

The Lisbon Notes

In February 2018, the Cardinal-Patriarch of Lisbon, D. Manuel Clemente, issued a document regarding the reception of chapter VIII of *Amoris Laetitia*.[6] Through this intervention, Cardinal Clemente allowed the sacraments to certain divorced and remarried couples with mitigating circumstances diminishing subjective culpability. By doing so, Clemente joined the ever growing number of bishops who are faithful to *Amoris Laetitia* as interpreted by the pope's manifest mind and will.

Cardinal Clemente is one of the most accomplished intellectuals in contemporary Portuguese society. His intellectual prowess, scholarship, and culture is acknowledged, even among the most secular elites in Portugal. It is no wonder his analytical mind was able to not only interpret the document accurately, but also present it in a clear and systematic way.

He is also perfectly orthodox, having been one of the most instrumental personalities in thwarting a recent attempt to legalize euthanasia in Portugal.[7] In fact, he is not biased in favor of the solution postulated by *Amoris Laetitia*: from the Family Synod[8] up to the very day after the apostolic exhortation was published,[9] Clemente was apparently against allowing divorced and remarried people to receive communion unless they lived in total continence. However, when confronted with the Buenos Aires criteria, and the overwhelming evidence for the pope's favored interpretation, the good cardinal reevaluated his stance. In this way, he perfectly showed how to unite mental aptitude with humility, so that the intellect is not a stumbling block to obedience, but rather a tool that allows oneself to perfect said obedience.

---

6. The original (Clemente, "Nota"), in Portuguese, can be consulted in the official site of the Lisbon Patriarchate. The English translation (Clemente, "Lisbon's Document"), which I will use from now on, has been undertaken by my friend Filipe d'Avillez, a journalist of *Rádio Renascença*, a Catholic radio station. Both sources can be found in the bibliography.

7. Less than two months after the publication of the Lisbon Notes, Clemente urged every deputy in parliament to vote against a bill that would legalize euthanasia in Portugal. See "Eutanásia," *Agência Ecclesia*.

8. "Bispos divididos," *Jornal Sol*.

9. Tavares, "Patriarca diz que Papa não validou comunhão de divorciados."

In his notes, Cardinal Clemente did not limit himself to following the pope's directives. He also illustrated the continuity between Pope Francis and the previous pontiffs, by quoting St. John Paul II's *Familiaris Consortio* and Benedict XVI's *Sacramentum Caritatis*.

What is more, Clemente has shown how it is possible to be faithful to *Amoris Laetitia*'s sacramental discipline while at the same time being clear on church doctrine. The patriarch stresses the church's teaching on the indissolubility of marriage; how seeking an annulment and (if not possible) sexual continence are the preferred options; and, in particular, how the discernment process should not stagnate in the irregular situation with mitigating factors, but should rather strive to evolve to a fuller realization of the Christian ideal.

One of the things I appreciated more in these notes (and the reason why I decided to include them in this book) was that they did not try to artificially fit *Amoris Laetitia* into a preconceived idea. The Lisbon guidelines try to interpret the pope's manifest will on its own terms. This is something that should be present in any attempt at adequately interpreting *Amoris Laetitia* (see chapters 4 and 5). Cardinal Clemente analyzes the text, not so much through the lens of his personal interpretation, but rather by letting the authoritative texts speak for themselves through extensive quoting of the source material—be it *Amoris Laetitia* itself, the Buenos Aires criteria, or the interpretation advanced by the papal cardinal vicar for the diocese of Rome, Agostino Vallini. By doing so, he arrives at the conclusion that we should "bear in mind exceptional circumstances and the possibility of the sacraments."

Clemente concludes his notes with a hierarchy of procedures which undeniably provides clarity on how these situations should be managed. This hierarchy of procedures also showcases the necessary steps to be followed before considering *Amoris Laetitia*'s sacramental provisions. He does not shun (in fact, he highlights) the necessity of the divorced and remarried person to try to regularize his or her situation (namely through an annulment) and to ascertain if the "brother-sister" approach is possible. Also, he brings attention to the necessary steps *after* the opening up of the sacraments, so that the person may strive for the eventual fulfillment of the Christian ideal of marriage in its entirety:

> Bearing all this in mind, I present herein some operative guidelines:

a. To accompany and integrate people into the life of the community, in line with the post-synodal Apostolic Exhortations *Familiaris Consortio*, 84, *Sacramentum Caritatis*, 29, and *Amoris Laetitia*, 299 (see appendix).
b. Carefully examine the specificity of each case.
c. Not to exclude recourse to the diocesan tribunal, whenever there is doubt concerning the validity of the marriage.
d. In cases in which validity is ascertained, not to neglect the proposal of a life in continence in the new situation.
e. To bear in mind exceptional circumstances *and the possibility of the sacraments*, in line with the aforementioned apostolic exhortation and documents.[10]
f. To continue the process of discernment, bringing the practice ever closer to the ideal of Christian marriage and sacramental consistency.[11]

Of course, some papal critics could reply that the Lisbon Notes are just one interpretation among many (see chapter 3). However, this is not the case. A few months later, Pope Francis himself wrote a letter to Clemente, which the cardinal made public:

> I am writing to thank you for having sent me, during the past Lent, the Note you addressed to the priests of the Patriarchate concerning the application of the VIII Chapter of the Apostolic Exhortation *Amoris Laetitia*.
>
> This deep reflection of yours filled me with joy, as I recognised in it the effort of a pastor and father who, aware of the duty to accompany his faithful, wished to start with his priests so that they can better fulfill their ministry.
>
> Today, the reality of married life is one of the fields where this accompaniment is most delicate and necessary. That is why

---

10. Previously, the cardinal had quoted AL 305 ("Because of forms of conditioning and *mitigating factors*, it is possible that in *an objective situation of sin—which may not be subjectively culpable*, or fully such—a person can be living in God's grace, can love and can also grow in the life of grace and charity, while receiving the Church's help to this end"), and then complemented it: "In other, more complex cases, and when a declaration of nullity has not been obtained, the above mentioned option may not, in fact, be feasible. Nonetheless, a path of discernment is still possible. *If it comes to be recognized that, in a specific case, there are limitations that mitigate responsibility and culpability* (cf. 301–302), especially when a person believes they would incur a subsequent wrong by harming the children of the new union, Amoris Laetitia *offers the possibility of access to the sacraments of Reconciliation and Eucharist* (cf. footnotes 336 and 351)."

11. Clemente, "Lisbon's Document."

> I wished to call the Bishops to a long synodal path which might prove propitious—despite the inevitable difficulties—to the maturing of shared guidelines which would benefit the entire People of God.
>
> Therefore, in expressing my gratitude, I would like to take advantage of the opportunity to encourage my Brother Cardinal and his collaborators in the pastoral ministry—*in primis* the priest—to carry on, with wisdom and patience, in their commitment to accompany, discern, and integrate the fragility which shows itself in many forms in couples and their ties.[12]

This is an important development. Apart from the Buenos Aires criteria, I have no knowledge of any other set of guidelines from any other diocese or Bishop Conference receiving so much praise and support from Pope Francis. Regardless, it seems obvious that Cardinal Clemente "got it right" on what the pope intended *Amoris Laetitia* to be. Therefore, both this papal letter and the Lisbon Notes can be read as a clear and unequivocal manifestation of the pontiff's mind and will on this matter, thereby strengthening the evidence even more in favor of the interpretation advanced in this book.

This means that people who are genuinely confused about *Amoris Laetitia* have one more resource where they can lean on to know what the apostolic exhortation actually means. Catholics may look up to the Lisbon Notes for clarity, guidance, and fidelity to the pope.

※ ※ ※

The Leiria-Fatima Approach

In June 2018, António Marto, the Portuguese bishop of Leiria-Fatima, was made cardinal. This may be seen as a validation of his ministry, since Marto has been said to be supportive of the pope's approach,[13] namely by adopting a merciful demeanor toward sinners and an attitude of closeness to ordinary people. It is also interesting to note that the sanctuary of Fatima falls under this diocese's jurisdiction. It was here that Our Lady of Fatima appeared to three little shepherds, which led to it becoming a hub

---

12. Francis, "Letter to the Cardinal Patriarch of Lisbon." Once again, the English translation was done by Filipe d'Avillez (d'Avillez, "Pope Francis' Letter of Thanks to Patriarch of Lisbon on *Amoris Laetitia* Note").

13. Luxmoore, "New Portuguese Cardinal Expected to Bring Church 'Closer to People.'"

of sanctity, a treasure for the Catholic Church, and, unfortunately, also a pretext for many who wish to resist Francis's reforms.[14]

It is, therefore, extremely significant that in the days immediately preceding his elevation to the cardinalate, Bishop Marto published his own pastoral note on how to interpret *Amoris Laetitia*, to which he attached a practical guide on how to implement the document in his diocese. It is plausible that, prior to its official publishing, the good bishop has sent his guidelines to Pope Francis, who knew at least the gist of them prior to nominating him as cardinal. Even before that, Marto was on record as having been able to see beyond the polemics and confusion around *Amoris Laetitia* and to truly grasp what the apostolic exhortation was all about:

> Pope Francis, in an ingenious way, introduced a change in discipline without putting in question the doctrine on marriage and family.[15]

The reason why I bring up these guidelines is because they exhibit some peculiarities that may reflect and illustrate the pope's thought and approach in ways other guidelines do not. First of all, the Leiria-Fatima practical guide (just like *Amoris Laetitia* itself and the Buenos Aires criteria) tries to re-center the discussion on what is truly important, unlike the controversy that pretends to make it all about the issue of communion for the divorced and civilly remarried. The document states in its introduction:

> The various agents involved (the person or "remarried" couple and their spiritual director) must accept that this is not about a process to gain access to the sacraments, but rather a path to search for the will of God—which may or may not be to access the sacraments. . . . The first requisite for any discernment is interior freedom. Without it, any procedure becomes vitiated and, deep down, tries to force God to accept the will of those who "discern" and not the other way around.[16]

In other words, the most important thing is not whether these people gain access to the Eucharist (which may not happen), but whether they are helped to live holy lives through a close accompaniment. Only by

---

14. I write about this topic in my article "Reclaiming Fátima," published on *WPI*.

15. "Igreja/Família," *Agência Ecclesia* (my translation from the original Portuguese).

16. Marto, "Guia Prático."

being accompanied by someone with authority and orthodoxy will it be possible for them to understand God's will for their lives, instead of conflating their own wills with God's. The practical guide continues:

> Only freedom allows a distancing which may dispassionately evaluate the situation, in order to accept truly what is perceived to be the will of God. . . . *For this reason, it is necessary that discernment be accompanied by an element external to the couple, usually a pastor (priest), with experience in accompaniment and spiritual direction. The engagement with a third person is essential* (cf. *AL* 300). The function of this minister of the Church is to accompany this path from the beginning and serve as a *moral reference* to unblock personal and internal processes in one of the members of the couple, or in both together, helping them to free themselves from inordinate affections and desires relating to this topic of wounds that do not take reality into account, etc.[17]

In other words, this is not about a couple just deciding that they want to receive the Eucharist, without any change or work on their part. There must be a minister of the church present in the whole process. His task is not to validate, but to *engage*, therefore filtering out preconceptions and disordered expectations that may hinder this discernment, diverting it from the path to holiness.

On the other hand, Cardinal Marto is faithful to Francis's favored interpretation. He meets His Holiness's call to discern every situation on a case by case basis, without a one-size-fits-all approach. Also from the introduction:

> Naturally, these orientations we have provided here will have to be adapted to each situation and each person, for this is the essence of discernment. Other aspects to take into account when putting in practice this process of discernment are the ages of the people being accompanied, the duration of their current relationship, if they have been both sacramentally married or just one of them, if their relationship includes children or not, their faith experiences, their participation in the life of the Church, etc.[18]

Most importantly, Cardinal Marto manifests his faithfulness to *Amoris Laetitia* by allowing the opening of communion to some people who have

17. Marto, "Guia Prático."
18. Marto, "Guia Prático."

divorced and remarried. The final section of the guide is named, appropriately, "The Question of Access to the Sacraments":

> Concerning the access to the Sacraments, we propose the following two steps:
>
> 1. Make an exercise of conclusion of the discernment as follows: during one week, to pray and to live as if the decision was not to access the sacraments, to take conscience of what one is feeling, of the spiritual feelings, where peace or disturbance lie; on the following week, do the opposite. . . . Pray and live as the decision was to access the sacraments, taking note of the spiritual feelings that are experienced. In that way, it is possible to understand what God's calling is, what brings the most peace, what brings us most together with Him and with Christian life and with others.
> 2. To confirm, through a rational process, and in light of everything that has been read, prayed upon, shared, and heard, a list is to be done, with two columns, with the pros and cons of accessing the sacraments. At another time, do another list with the same process with the pros and cons of not accessing the sacraments. After selecting the pros and cons for each possibility, see what is more evident. As affirmed in the beginning, this may be 1) access the sacraments; 2) not access the sacraments; 3) not yet, there are necessary steps to be followed through in life and discernment must go on.
>
> After these . . . stages, with honesty before God, with all freedom and based on what has been learned through the entire process, the person or couple takes the decision that seems most in line with God's will.[19]

This is a very interesting approach, since it seems to integrate an Ignatian component to the matter of discernment (something certainly pleasing to Pope Francis's Jesuit streak).[20] Namely, it seems based on the spiritual motions described by Saint Ignatius of Loyola. The third and fourth rules of the saint's fourteen rules for "Discernment of the Spirits" are, respectively, "Spiritual Consolation" and "Spiritual Desolation." Whether

---

19. Marto, "Guia Prático."

20. See Ryan, "Weakness, and Wounded and Troubled Love," 140: "[*Amoris Laetitia*] reflects the blending of the virtue ethics of Aquinas with the Ignatian tradition of the discernment of conscience."

a particular choice brings consolation or desolation is used to discern whether a particular decision is informed by the Holy Spirit or by the spirit of darkness. By living one week as if he or she would receive the sacraments and the next as if he or she would not, by praying upon both decisions and by doing a list of pros and cons, the person who is discerning may try to understand which of the two possibilities gives spiritual consolation or desolation, in order to follow through with the former and avoid the latter.

At a first glance, this approach may appear somewhat strange. The divorced and remarried person makes a decision, acts upon it, and even documents it, sending a written record to the bishop and the parish priest (in case the latter is not the spiritual director).

It may seem like the decision is permanent, once made, but such is not necessarily so. Discerning whether someone is likely in a state of mortal sin is a continuous process when we are dealing with recurring, addicting sins like the sins of the flesh, or with mitigating circumstances that may fluctuate over time. Someone may have sinned in a venial way on account of limited liberty (e.g., because of addictive behavior) on one day, and then sinned in a mortal way the next day with the same sin, if he or she gave full consent then. This is especially true if the person becomes complacent.

However, this problem only arises if we get too much focused on the "access to the sacraments" part and ignore all the context around it. The "Question of Access to the Sacraments" is just the last part of the discernment process, stage four. Before a divorced and remarried person gets there he or she will have to undergo stages one, two, and three.

The first stage is seeking an attitude of righteous intention before God, humbly asking him for the grace of interior freedom. The second stage is seeking interior (and, if possible, exterior) reconciliation with one's past history, with every person involved, and with badly resolved situations. This includes Pope Francis's proposed "exam of conscience" as stated in *Amoris Laetitia* #300. The third stage is seeking what God's will is and evaluating the current relationship (stability, rearing of children, religious practice). Only then comes the fourth stage, discerning one's access to the sacraments by living and praying upon both possibilities and drawing up the pros and cons list. Each of these stages is filled with intense prayer, spiritual retreats, regular meetings with the spiritual director, and meditations on various passages from the gospel and *Amoris*

Laetitia that the Leiria-Fatima guidelines specifically propose for each step.

In other words, what we have here is a true formation of conscience. For many years, apologists have responded to the charges about primacy of conscience by replying that such a primacy only applied to well-formed consciences. Here we have a practical guide to forming good consciences, even in those who are currently living in an irregular marital situation.

By doing so, these guidelines mitigate the fear that a divorced and remarried person who may have decided to receive communion gets complacent, for before that there was a lengthy process whereby his or her conscience has been well-formed according to the gospel teachings and the doctrine of the church. As Francis declares, "The following conditions must necessarily be present: humility, discretion, and love for the Church and her teaching, in a sincere search for God's will and a desire to make a more perfect response to it. These attitudes are essential for avoiding the grave danger of misunderstandings, such as the notion that any priest can quickly grant 'exceptions,' or that some people can obtain sacramental privileges in exchange for favours."[21] If these attitudes are present, there is no fear that *Amoris Laetitia* may be abused to obtain sacrilegious communions. Cardinal Marto anticipates these dangers and faces them head-on, by instilling these attitudes on the person undergoing accompaniment from the beginning of the path.

This forming of consciences, not access to the sacraments, is the true focus of the Leiria-Fatima guidelines. António Marto has gone the extra mile as regards a fundamental part from *Amoris Laetitia* that seems to have been a bit overlooked by other guidelines: Francis's plea to "better incorporate individual consciences into the Church's practice."[22] Of course, for this to happen, an adequate formation of consciences duly accompanied by an orthodox pastor is paramount, so that these sinners may start a path of conversion, without falling into the extremes of excessive laxity or scrupulosity. Both of these extremes are hallmarks of an unaccompanied spiritual journey, which may drive the soul off from the way to holiness. By duly forming consciences, it is easier to make a proper exam of conscience and understand, at any given point, whether one is in a state of grace or of mortal sin. Only then may the sacraments truly exert their proper, medicinal function.

21. *AL* 300.
22. *AL* 303.

Section IV | Some Practical Examples

❊❊❊

The Braga Guidelines

The guidelines issued in 2017 by D. José Ortiga, the Archbishop of Braga, were the first to be made public and implemented in Portugal. They are the most extensive of the three guidelines we are covering in this chapter. However, they also combine the best of the two approaches mentioned before, blending them together in a seamless unit.

First of all, the Braga guidelines do not focus solely on how to apply chapter 8 of *Amoris Laetitia*. A significant amount of time is spent exploring the topics of education of families (whether regular or irregular),[23] an adequate preparation for matrimony,[24] and the pastoral accompaniment for young couples.[25] In this way, the Braga guidelines also implement the mostly ignored chapters 6 and 7 of *Amoris Laetitia*. Hopefully this will help to preemptively and proactively reduce the amount of divorces that would make chapter 8's pastoral provisions necessary. By not focusing only on the controversial eighth chapter, the Braga document actually follows the pope's manifest mind and will in a previously unexplored way, since Francis also decried an excessive focus on chapter 8 (see chapter 5 of this book).

Regarding the application of chapter 8, the Braga episcopal letter follows a similar set of priorities to the Lisbon notes. The first help given to divorced and remarried couples is legal aid in order to ascertain whether there are grounds for an annulment.[26] Just like in the Lisbon document, it is proposed that the couple live in total continence, as brother and sister, especially if they are both Christians with a solid faith journey.[27] Notwithstanding the difficulties of this approach, the Braga guidelines propose an examination of conscience based on the suggestions laid out in *Amoris Laetitia* #300.[28] Recent divorcees are not included: only stable relationships with more than five years are considered for this discernment path (though some pastoral flexibility is granted depending on the

---

23. Ortiga, *Construir a Casa*, 7–13.
24. Ortiga, *Construir a Casa*, 13–20.
25. Ortiga, *Construir a Casa*, 20–25.
26. Ortiga, *Construir a Casa*, 26.
27. Ortiga, *Construir a Casa*, 33.
28. Ortiga, *Construir a Casa*, 29–31.

case).²⁹ Even if this discernment does not always end with the reception of the sacraments, mitigating circumstances diminishing subjective culpability should be taken into account. If the person is still living in God's grace,³⁰ he or she can have access to the sacraments of Reconciliation and the Eucharist,³¹ in a reserved manner so as to avoid scandal (even if the community should also be educated to understand and welcome these couples, simultaneously avoiding any confusion towards perennial doctrine on the indissolubility of marriage).³² Finally, this discernment process should always remain open to new stages of growth that may help the couple enter into a fuller communion with the teachings of the church.³³

After this theoretical exposition, the Braga guidelines specify the details of the discernment path in an annex to the main document. This discernment path is very similar to the Leiria-Fatima guidelines, and probably inspired the latter. Once again, this path is filled with Ignatian spirituality.³⁴ In fact, it makes an explicit mention to the motions of the spirit: consolation and desolation.³⁵

Finally, there is another aspect of the Braga guidelines that is worth mentioning. The document calls for the creation of a multidisciplinary office focused on aiding people in these irregular situations. This includes not only priests, but also psychologists, doctors, social assistants, and, in the case of the pursuit of an annulment in an ecclesiastical court, legal counsel.³⁶ This proposal did not die on paper, but was actually implemented one year later.³⁷

In this sense, these guidelines seek not to condemn (nor to validate) sinners, but truly to rehabilitate them: to approach sin not with a "take it or leave it, this way or the highway" approach, but as a work in progress; to catechize people by teaching them to deal with the concrete situations they are facing, and not by forcing conformity with a perfect framework

29. Ortiga, *Construir a Casa*, 33–34.
30. *AL* 305.
31. Ortiga, *Construir a Casa*, 32.
32. Ortiga, *Construir a Casa*, 34–35. See also chapter 8 of this book.
33. Ortiga, *Construir a Casa*, 35, 36–37.
34. Ortiga, *Construir a Casa*, 39–58.
35. Ortiga, *Construir a Casa*, 42.
36. Ortiga, *Construir a Casa*, 26.
37. "Família: Braga cria '«Centro de Escuta'» onde pode acompanhar divorciados que vivem em nova união," *Agência Ecclesia*.

that may seem out of reach for someone just starting their journey; to be truly Christ-like and not to feed into the stereotype of the judgmental church. This is Francis's project for the Catholic Church: the true answer, helping one soul at a time, with patience and love. We can see the good fruits of this project already blossoming in Portugal.

Conclusion

AT THE END OF THIS BOOK, I think I have proven beyond a reasonable doubt the following propositions:

- *Amoris Laetitia* is a magisterial document (chapter 1).
- As a magisterial document, its teachings on faith and morals demand religious submission of mind and will, even if they have not been infallibly defined (chapter 2).
- As a magisterial document, *Amoris Laetitia* must be interpreted according to the manifest mind and will of the pope (chapter 2).
- The manifest mind and will of the pope is very clear, both in *Amoris Laetitia* itself (chapter 4) and in other interventions from the Holy Father (chapters 5 and 17): certain divorced and remarried people can have access to communion, if they have mitigating circumstances diminishing subjective culpability, so that they are not in mortal sin.
- This is a change in sacramental discipline, not a doctrinal change, even though it can be argued that it is predicated on a doctrinal development (chapter 10).
- The faithful must accept the Holy Father's headship of the church, even when delineating disciplines (chapter 2).
- *Amoris Laetitia*'s sacramental discipline is grounded in orthodox doctrine (chapter 7) and solid precedents (chapters 7 and 14).
- The doctrine underlying this sacramental discipline does not conflict with any previous authoritative document (chapters 11, 12, and 13).
- This is a legitimate development (chapters 10 and 15).

- Any heterodox proposition attributed to *Amoris Laetitia* is based on misinterpretations of the document that do not hold up to closer scrutiny (chapter 6).

- Those who have been, in the last few years, trying to promote dissent against this document, by taking recourse to arguments that undermine papal primacy, are the ones who are at spiritual risk of falling out of communion with the Catholic Church (Introduction; chapters 1, 2, 11, and 12).

In conclusion: *Amoris Laetitia* is orthodox.

※ ※ ※

Since his election, Pope Francis has caused serious discomfort in a certain sector of the church. This faction had until then considered itself a hallmark of orthodoxy, even if it often denied or explained away vast parts of doctrine not amenable to its ideological or theological inclinations. *Amoris Laetitia* provided the outlet for that group to escape this conundrum. The members of this faction seized this opportunity to cast suspicion over the pope's orthodoxy, and have not stopped doing it ever since. In fact, while *Amoris Laetitia* was certainly the first incursion of theirs in this unexplored territory of decapitated Catholic (pseudo) orthodoxy, they have, over the years, aggregated more and more indictments to their litany of accusations: the death penalty revision of the *Catechism*, the *Interreligious Declaration on Human and Religious Freedom*, the Pachamama controversy, the papal plane interviews, Francis's homilies, etc. Each new accretion was accompanied by a barrage of news items from formerly faithful Catholic websites, scrutinizing every single act of the Holy Father and portraying it in the worst possible light, in order to validate a narrative that slowly took form and shape. They did this sometimes with open hostility and sometimes in more subtle ways, injecting negative propaganda under the guise of love for the pope (an unfortunately prevalent form of criticism today: Francis has accurately described it as "throwing stones and then hiding their hands").[1]

In this sense, I cannot but agree with Stephen Walford (one of the few to take up the task of defending the pontiff). In his open letter to the four *dubia* Cardinals, he calls the abuse aimed at the Holy Father by Catholic websites and blogs nothing short of satanic. It is undeniable

---

1. Francis, "Viagem Apostólica a Moçambique."

that the present antagonism against the Vicar of Christ, either covert or open, dripping constantly from those sources, cannot come from God. The enemy surely delights in it, as Catholics themselves do his bidding and undercut the visible head—the authoritative interpreter of scripture and tradition, the guarantor of unity of the whole church—in favor of a counterfeit Catholicism created by a "parallel magisterium" of pundits and biased media. Even while accusing their more liberal and secularized brethren of a pick-and-choose Catholicism, they have created their own brand of "cafeteria Catholicism." They have then branded this cafeteria as the "One True Church," to which every single person on earth must submit, even the Vicar of Christ and the successors of the apostles.

I cannot do more than pray and write arguments to counter this disinformation campaign. In this book, I have tried to prove *Amoris Laetitia*'s orthodoxy, since its denial has been, as I said, at the root of this widespread wave of dissent. I tried to cover the whole gamut of objections to *Amoris Laetitia*'s orthodoxy that I have encountered throughout the years of debates in social media. I am sure that, as the debate gets more and more specialized and academic, new objections are bound to surface. However, if this book will serve to disentangle the discussion from its present unfortunate state, and if it helps to dispel confusion and ameliorate the climate of suspicion against the successor of Peter, then my mission has been accomplished.

If discussion moves to higher theological grounds and someone finds any imprecision or error in anything I wrote, please attribute it not to ill will on my part. I have done my best. However, if theologians find such imprecisions and errors, I beseech them not to limit themselves to correct them, but to take the opportunity to mount their own defense of the Holy Father, armed with their knowledge and expertise. I remind them of their theological vocation, as defined in *Donum Veritatis*, to exercise their function in communion with the magisterium, and to be loyal to it.

For apologists also, I hope this book will provide them with arguments to fight back against so many false notions about the papacy that have infiltrated the Catholicosphere in the last few years. It is my firm belief that the online apologetics movement is in need of a serious overhauling. We cannot afford to have our apologetics sources populated by people who use their ministry, not as a way to defend the totality of doctrine, not as a way to defend the Holy Father from those who attack him, but rather as a way to reconcile Catholicism with extraneous ideas and ideologies, even in defiance of the pope and bishops. Formerly faithful apologists have caused severe damage to the church, by exploiting their credibility in order to weaken the papacy. We need a new generation of apologists, that really know what their proper function is: apologists moved not by politics or other kinds of sectarianism, but by a love for the church, the *real* church, the church in union with the magisterium. I hope this book will help to awaken this new generation. I invite them to not be intimidated by the media giants they have to confront, but to join the fray with more and better arguments than the ones expounded here. The salvation of so many people, who know no other Catholicism than the one presented by these formerly faithful apologists, cries for our action.

Finally, I hope that this book might have helped genuinely confused Catholics to have a little more clarity on this issue. I hope, at least, that their suspicions against the Holy Father might have been attenuated somewhat, so that they may give him another chance and start reading him with a new perspective.

As for those who are not open to the arguments of this book, but who are reading it with the sole intent of refuting them, I conclude with the finale of Newman's *Essay on the Development of Doctrine*:

> And now, dear Reader, time is short, eternity is long. Put not from you what you have here found; regard it not as mere matter of present controversy; set out not to refute it, and looking about for the best way of doing so; seduce not yourself with the imagination that it comes of disappointment, or disgust, or restlessness, or wounded feeling, or undue sensibility, or other weakness. Wrap not yourself round in the association of years past; nor determine that to be truth which you wish to be so, nor make an idol of cherished anticipations. Time is short, eternity is long.

❖❖❖

Ad maiorem Dei gloriam inque hominum salutem.
Fiat voluntas Tua.
Regina Sacratissimi Rosarii Fatimae, Ora pro nobis.
Sancte Petre, ora pro nobis.
Amen.

Recommended Reading

Bishops of the Pastoral Region of Buenos Aires. "Criterios básicos para la aplicación del capítulo VIII de '*Amoris laetitia*'. Texto de los Obispos de la Región de Buenos Aires (Argentina)." *Vida Nueva*, September 21, 2016. https://www.vidanuevadigital.com/documento/criterios-basicos-para-la-aplicacion-del-capitulo-viii-de-amoris-laetitia-texto-de-los-obispos-de-la-region-de-buenos-aires-argentina/.

Buttiglione, Rocco. *Risposte Amichevoli Ai Critici Di Amoris Laetitia*. Ragione & Fede. Milano: Edizioni Ares, 2017.

Clemente, Manuel. "Nota para a receção do capítulo VIII da exortação apostólica '*Amoris Laetitia*.'" February 6, 2018. https://www.patriarcado-lisboa.pt/site/index.php?id=8626.

Fernández, Victor. "El capítulo VIII de Amoris Laetitia: lo que queda después de la tormenta." *Medellín* XLIII, no. 168 (May–August 2017) 449–68.

Francis. *Amoris Laetitia*. Libreria Editrice Vaticana, 2016. Vatican.va.

Ivereigh, Austen. *The Wounded Shepherd*. Henry Holt and Co., 2019. Kindle. See especially chapter 9, pp. 247–77.

López, Rodrigo Guerra. "Entender a Wojtyla para comprender a Bergoglio. El carácter personalista de Amoris laetitia." *Metafísica y Persona* 11, no. 21 (January–June 2019) 37–50.

———. "Para Comprender Amoris Laetitia. Premisas y argumentos, respuesta a dudas y objeciones, camino y esperanza." *Medellín* XLIII, no. 168 (May–August 2017) 409–47.

Ortiga, José. *Construir a Casa sobre a Rocha*. Edição Arquidiocese de Braga, 2017.

Pié-Ninot, Salvador. "L'Ultima Parola." *L'Osservatore Romano*, March 17, 2017.

Ryan, Thomas. "'Weakness, and Wounded and Troubled Love' in *Amoris Laetitia*: Pope Francis as Pastor." *Australasian Catholic Record* 94, no. 2 (2017) 131–47.

Schönborn, Christoph. "A Conversation with Cardinal Schönborn on '*Amoris Laetitia*.'" Interview by Antonio Spadaro. *La Civiltà Cattolica* English Edition, March 1, 2017. https://www.laciviltacattolica.com/conversation-cardinal-schonborn-amoris-laetitia/.

Travers, Patrick J. "*Amoris Laetitia* and Canon 915: A Merciful Return to the «Letter of the Law»." Pts. 1 and 2. *Periodica de Re Canonica* 107, no. 1 (2018) 297–326; no. 3 (2018) 367–418.

Walford, Stephen. *Pope Francis, the Family, and Divorce: In Defense of Truth and Mercy*. New York: Paulist, 2018.

Bibliography

Acta Apostolicae Sedis. Libreria Editrice Vaticana. Vatican.va.

Agência Ecclesia. "Eutanásia: Voto Do Parlamento Tem de Ter Em Conta as Manifestações Da Sociedade 'insistentemente No Sentido Do Não'—Cardeal-Patriarca." March 27, 2018.

———. "Família: Braga cria 'Centro de Escuta' onde pode acompanhar divorciados que vivem em nova união." January 17, 2018.

———. "Igreja/Família: Bispo de Leiria-Fátima Sublinha Mudança Promovida Pelo Papa." April 12, 2016.

Almeida, Juliano. "Amoris Laetitia—reflexões sobre o capítulo VIII." *Encontros Teológicos* 33, no. 2 (August 2018) 371–88.

Altieri, Christopher R. "From What, Precisely, Are *Amoris Laetitia* 'Dissenters' Dissenting?" *Catholic World Report*, January 5, 2018. https://www.catholicworldreport.com/2018/01/05/from-what-precisely-are-amoris-laetitia-dissenters-dissenting/.

Arntz, Veronica A. "Guest Op-Ed: *Amoris Laetitia* and the New Church of Francis." *Rorate Cæli* (blog), August 4, 2016. https://rorate-caeli.blogspot.com/2016/08/amoris-laetitia-and-new-church-of.html.

Baker, Joanne. "Is it Virtuous to Criticize the Pope?" *Homiletic & Pastoral Review*, April 20, 2019.

Baklinski, Pete. "Bishop Schneider: 'Discernment' Now Means to 'Allow to Sin.'" LifeSite, January 31, 2018. https://www.lifesitenews.com/news/faithful-bishop-discernment-and-pastoral-accompaniment-really-mean-to-allow/.

Barr, Jeff. "Render Unto Caesar: A Most Misunderstood New Testament Passage." Ludwig von Mises Institute, July 3, 2018. https://mises.org/wire/render-unto-caesar-most-misunderstood-new-testament-passage.

Bellarmine, Robert. "On the Roman Pontiff: An Extract from St Robert Bellarmine, *De Romano Pontifice*, Lib. II, Cap. 30." Translated by James Larrabee. Accessed September 10, 2021. http://strobertbellarmine.net/bellarm.htm.

Belloc, Hilaire. *The Great Heresies*. Immortal, 2018.

Belmonte, Charles. "God's Church." In *Faith Seeking Understanding*, edited by Charles Belmont, Vol. 1. Studium Theologiae Foundation, 2006. http://fsubelmonte.weebly.com/introduction-to-theology.html.

Benedict XVI. "Address of His Holiness Benedict XVI to the Roman Curia Offering Them His Christmas Greetings," December 22, 2005. Vatican.va.

———. "The Church and the Scandal of Sexual Abuse." Translated by Anian Christoph Wimmer. Catholic News Agency, April 10, 2019.
———. *Deus Caritas Est*. Libreria Editrice Vaticana, 2005. Vatican.va.
———. *Introduction to Christianity*. 2nd ed. San Francisco, CA: Communio, 2004.
———. *Jesus of Nazareth: From the Baptism in the Jordan to the Transfiguration*. New York: Doubleday, 2007.
———. *Sacramentum Caritatis*. Libreria Editrice Vaticana, 2007. Vatican.va.
Bishops of the Pastoral Region of Buenos Aires. "Criterios básicos para la aplicación del capítulo VIII de '*Amoris laetitia*'. Texto de los Obispos de la Región de Buenos Aires (Argentina)." *Vida Nueva*, September 21, 2016. https://www.vidanuevadigital.com/documento/criterios-basicos-para-la-aplicacion-del-capitulo-viii-de-amoris-laetitia-texto-de-los-obispos-de-la-region-de-buenos-aires-argentina/.
"Bispos divididos." *Jornal Sol*, July 31, 2015. https://sol.sapo.pt/artigo/404932/bispos-divididos.
Boniface [pseud.]. "What Is the Hermeneutic of Continuity?" *Unam Sanctam Catholicam* (blog), September 1, 2013. http://unamsanctamcatholicam.blogspot.com/2013/09/what-is-hermeneutic-of-continuity.html.
Bordeyne, Philippe. "Divorcés remariés : quels changements ?" *La Croix*, June 28, 2017. https://croire.la-croix.com/Definitions/Lexique/Divorces-remaries/Divorces-remaries-quels-changements.
Boudinhon, Auguste. "Ecclesiastical Discipline." In *The Catholic Encyclopedia*, Vol. 5. New York: Robert Appleton Company, 1909. http://www.newadvent.org/cathen/05030a.htm.
Brockhaus, Hannah. "A Catholic 'Paradigm Shift' Would Be Corruption, Not Development—Cardinal Muller." Catholic News Agency, February 22, 2018. https://www.catholicnewsagency.com/news/37820/a-catholic-paradigm-shift-would-be-corruption-not-development---cardinal-muller.
Brother André Marie [pseud.]. "*Amoris Laetitia* and the 'Authentic Magisterium.'" *Catholicism.Org* (blog), December 5, 2017. https://catholicism.org/amoris-laetitia-authentic-magisterium.html.
Brown, Susan L., and I-Fen Lin. "The Gray Divorce Revolution: Rising Divorce Among Middle-Aged and Older Adults, 1990–2010." *The Journals of Gerontology Series B: Psychological Sciences and Social Sciences* 67, no. 6 (November 1, 2012) 731–41. https://doi.org/10.1093/geronb/gbs089.
Brugger, E. Christian. "'*Amoris Laetitia*' vs. '*Veritatis Splendor*': You Say You Want a Revolution?" *National Catholic Register*, April 7, 2018. https://www.ncregister.com/commentaries/amoris-laetitia-vs-veritatis-splendor-you-say-you-want-a-revolution.
———. "The Catholic Conscience, the Argentine Bishops, and 'Amoris Laetitia.'" Catholic World Report, September 20, 2016. https://www.catholicworldreport.com/2016/09/20/the-catholic-conscience-the-argentine-bishops-and-amoris-laetitia/.
———. "Five Serious Problems with Chapter 8 of Amoris Laetitia." Catholic World Report, April 22, 2016. https://www.catholicworldreport.com/2016/04/22/five-serious-problems-with-chapter-8-of-amoris-laetitia/.
———. "A Tale of Two Interpretations of 'Amoris Laetitia.'" *National Catholic Register*, April 25, 2017. https://www.ncregister.com/commentaries/a-tale-of-two-interpretations-of-amoris-laetitia.

Bibliography

Burke, Raymond. "'*Amoris Laetitia*' and the Constant Teaching and Practice of the Church." *National Catholic Register*, April 12, 2016. https://www.ncregister.com/news/amoris-laetitia-and-the-constant-teaching-and-practice-of-the-church.

———. "Interview With Cardinal Burke . . . (Part 2) Discriminating Mercy: Defending Christ And His Church With True Love." Interview by Don Fier. *The Wanderer*, August 14, 2017. https://thewandererpress.com/catholic/news/frontpage/interview-with-cardinal-burke-discriminating-mercy-defending-christ-and-his-church-with-true-love-2/.

Buscemi, Georges, et al. "Open Letter to the Bishops of the Catholic Church," April 30, 2019. https://www.documentcloud.org/documents/5983408-Open-Letter-to-the-Bishops-of-the-Catholic.html.

Buttiglione, Rocco. "L'Approccio Antropologico di San Giovanni Paolo II e quello Pastorale di Papa Francesco." *La Stampa*, February 2017.

———. *Risposte Amichevoli Ai Critici Di Amoris Laetitia*. Ragione & Fede. Milano: Edizioni Ares, 2017.

Cabral, Luís Pedro. "Portugueses são os europeus que mais se divorciam." *Jornal Expresso*, August 3, 2019. https://expresso.pt/sociedade/2019-08-03-Portugueses-sao-os-europeus-que-mais-se-divorciam.

Calmeyn, Laetitia. "Accompagnamento e legge di gradualità." *L'Osservatore Romano*, May 18, 2019.

Catholic Church, ed. *Catechism of the Catholic Church*. Libreria Editrice Vaticana, 1993. Vatican.va.

Catholic Dictionary. CatholicCulture.org. Accessed September 27, 2021. https://www.catholicculture.org/culture/library/dictionary/##.

Catholic News Agency. "Full Text of Pope Francis' in-Flight Press Conference from Abu Dhabi," February 5, 2019. https://www.catholicnewsagency.com/news/40492/full-text-of-pope-francis-in-flight-press-conference-from-abu-dhabi.

———. "Retired Archbishop Disciplined after Calling Pope Francis a 'Heretic.'" February 27, 2020. https://www.catholicnewsagency.com/news/43704/retired-archbishop-disciplined-after-calling-pope-francis-a-heretic.

Catholic Truth. "Church Crisis: Educating The Masses," November 21, 2016. https://catholictruthscotland.com/2016/11/21/church-crisis-educating-the-masses/.

———. "Theological Terrorism: Hierarchy Turning Christ's Church Upside Down," July 8, 2016. https://catholictruthscotland.com/2016/07/08/theological-terrorism-hierarchy-turning-christs-church-upside-down/.

Chapman, Michael W. "Arbp. Vigano: Pope Francis Is Teaching 'Blatant Heresy . . . a Terrible Blasphemy.'" *CNSNews*, April 23, 2020. https://www.cnsnews.com/commentary/michael-w-chapman/arbp-vigano-pope-francis-teaching-blatant-heresy-terrible-blasphemy.

Chaput, Charles. "Pastoral Guidelines for Implementing Amoris Laetitia." *Nova et Vetera* 15, no. 1 (2017) 1–7. https://doi.org/10.1353/nov.2017.0000.

Chesterton, G. K. *The Catholic Church and Conversion*. New York: MacMillan, 1926. https://www.ewtn.com/catholicism/library/the-catholic-church-and-conversion-13705.

"Clarence Darrow Quotes." Quotepark.com. Accessed September 22, 2021. http://quotepark.com/authors/clarence-darrow/.

Clemente, Manuel. "Lisbon's Document on the Reception of Chapter VIII of the Apostolic Exhortation '*Amoris Laetitia*.'" Translated by Filipe D'Avillez, February

7, 2018. https://actualidadereligiosa.blogspot.com/2018/02/lisbons-document-on-reception-of.html.

———. "Nota para a receção do capítulo VIII da exortação apostólica '*Amoris Laetitia*,'" February 6, 2018. https://www.patriarcado-lisboa.pt/site/index.php?id=8626.

Code of Canon Law. Accessed September 9, 2021. Vatican.va.

Congregation for the Doctrine of the Faith. "Commentary," August 1, 2007. Vatican.va.

———. "Concerning Some Objections to the Church's Teaching on the Reception of Holy Communion by Divorced and Remarried Members of the Faithful." Accessed September 14, 2021. Vatican.va.

———. "Concerning the Reply of the Congregation for the Doctrine of the Faith on the Teaching Contained in the Apostolic Letter *Ordinatio Sacerdotalis*," October 28, 1995. Vatican.va.

———. "Concerning 'Uterine Isolation' and Related Matters," July 31, 1993. Vatican.va.

———. "Declaration on Behalf of Some Clergy and Laity Formerly or Actually Belonging to the Episcopal (Anglican) Church for Full Communion with the Catholic Church, 1st April 1981," March 31, 1981. Vatican.va.

———. "Doctrinal Commentary on the Concluding Formula of the *Professio Fidei*." Accessed September 9, 2021. Vatican.va.

———. "Epistula Ad Episcopum Clevelandensum circa Dubia Proposita de Foetus Vel Membrorum Corporis Humani Crematione." Accessed September 14, 2021. Vatican.va.

———. "Instruction *Donum Veritatis* on the Ecclesial Vocation of the Theologian," December 29, 1975. Vatican.va.

———. "Letter of Clarification to Archbishop Joseph Bernardin," March 21, 1975. Vatican.va.

———. "Letter to the Bishops of the Catholic Church Concerning the Reception of Holy Communion by the Divorced and Remarried Members of the Faithful ," September 14, 1994. Vatican.va.

———. "Replies to Questions on the Interpretation of the Decree *Ecclesiae Pastorum*," July 7, 1983. Vatican.va.

———. "Responses to Certain Questions Concerning Artificial Nutrition and Hydration," August 1, 2007. Vatican.va.

"*Correctio Filialis de Haeresibus Propagatis*." July 16, 2017. https://www.correctiofilialis.org/.

Council of Trent. "6th Session," January 13, 1547. http://www.thecounciloftrent.com/.

———. "13th Session, Chapter VII," October 11, 1551. http://www.thecounciloftrent.com/.

———. "21st Session, Chapter II," July 16, 1562. http://www.thecounciloftrent.com/.

———. *Catechism*, 1566. Translated by John A. McHugh and Charles J. Callan. http://www.saintsbooks.net/books/The%20Roman%20Catechism.pdf.

d'Avillez, Filipe. "Pope Francis' Letter of Thanks to Patriarch of Lisbon on Amoris Laetitia Note." *Actualidade Religiosa* (blog), July 12, 2018. http://actualidadereligiosa.blogspot.com/2018/07/pope-francis-letter-of-thanks-to.html.

Domingues, Claire. "Pope Francis's Decentralization: Structural, Not Doctrinal." *Where Peter Is* (blog), August 17, 2020. https://wherepeteris.com/pope-franciss-decentralization-structural-not-doctrinal/.

Bibliography

Doody, Cameron. "Bishop Who Called Pope Francis the Antichrist Defies Polish Church Order to Stay Silent." *Novena News*, February 27, 2020. https://novenanews.com/bishop-francis-antichrist-defies-polish-church/.

Ecclesia.pt. "Recenseamento Da Prática Dominical," July 11, 2002. http://www.ecclesia.pt/rpd/totais.htm.

Esteves, Junno Arocho. "Church Wounded by Internal Tensions, Pope Tells Jesuits in Romania." *Crux*, June 13, 2019. https://cruxnow.com/vatican/2019/06/church-wounded-by-internal-tensions-pope-tells-jesuits-in-romania.

Faria, Natália. "Católicos recasados devem ser aconselhados a abster-se de ter relações sexuais." *Público*, February 8, 2018. https://www.publico.pt/2018/02/08/sociedade/noticia/recasados-catolicos-devem-ser-aconselhados-a-viver-como-irmaos-1802394.

Farrow, Mary. "Pope Francis Signs Peace Declaration on 'Human Fraternity' with Grand Imam." Catholic News Agency, February 4, 2019. https://www.catholicnewsagency.com/news/40483/pope-francis-signs-peace-declaration-on-human-fraternity-with-grand-imam.

Fastiggi, Robert. "Responding to the Five *Dubia* from *Amoris Laetitia* Itself." *La Stampa*, March 12, 2018. https://www.lastampa.it/vatican-insider/en/2018/03/12/news/responding-to-the-five-dubia-from-amoris-laetitia-itself-1.33989886.

Faust, Ed. "Because I Said So." The Fatima Center, January 22, 2019. https://fatima.org/news-views/because-i-said-so/.

Fernández, Victor. "El capítulo VIII de Amoris Laetitia: lo que queda después de la tormenta." *Medellín* XLIII, no. 168 (May–August 2017) 449–68.

———. "Without the gaze of faith, the Pope is reduced to a character." Interview by Andrea Tornielli. *La Stampa*, March 12, 2018. https://www.lastampa.it/vatican-insider/en/2018/03/12/news/fernandez-without-the-gaze-of-faith-the-pope-is-reduced-to-a-character-1.33991135.

Ferrara, Christopher A. "*Amoris Laetitia*: Anatomy of a Pontifical Debacle." *The Remnant Newspaper*, April 18, 2016. https://remnantnewspaper.com/web/index.php/articles/item/2464-amoris-laetitia-anatomy-of-a-pontifical-debacle.

Focus News. "Is *Amoris Laetitia* Good News?" September 1, 2016. https://www.futurechurchnews.org/article/is-amoris-laetitia-good-news.

Fox, James. "Natural Law." In *The Catholic Encyclopedia*, Vol. 9. New York: Robert Appleton, 1910. http://www.newadvent.org/cathen/09076a.htm.

Francis. *Amoris Laetitia*. Libreria Editrice Vaticana, 2016. Vatican.va.

———. "Apostolic Constitution *Episcopalis Communio* of the Holy Father Francis on the Synod of Bishops." September 15, 2018. Vatican.va.

———. "A Big Heart Open to God: An Interview with Pope Francis." Interview by Antonio Spadaro. *America Magazine*, September 2013. https://www.americamagazine.org/faith/2013/09/30/big-heart-open-god-interview-pope-francis.

———. "Ceremony Commemorating the 50th Anniversary of the Institution of the Synod of Bishops," October 17, 2015. Vatican.va.

———. "Dio Delle Sorprese," May 8, 2017. Vatican.va.

———. *Evangelii Gaudium*. Libreria Editrice Vaticana, 2013. Vatican.va.

———. *Gaudete et Exsultate*. Libreria Editrice Vaticana, 2013. Vatican.va.

———. "General Audience," April 3, 2019. Vatican.va.

———. "In-Flight Press Conference from Lesbos to Rome," April 16, 2016. Vatican.va.

———. "Letter to the Cardinal Patriarch of Lisbon," June 26, 2018. https://agencia. ecclesia.pt/portal/wp-content/uploads/2018/07/Carda-do-Papa-Francisco-ao-cardeal-patriarca-de-Lisboa.pdf.

———. "Message of His Holiness Pope Francis for Lent 2016," October 4, 2015. Vatican.va.

———. "Prayer Vigil for the 19th 'Memorial and Commitment Day,'" March 21, 2014. Vatican.va.

———. *Querida Amazonia: Post-Synodal Exhortation to the People of God and to All Persons of Good Will*, February 2, 2020. Vatican.va.

———. "To Participants in the Meeting Promoted by the Pontifical Council for Promoting the New Evangelization ," October 11, 2017. Vatican.va.

———. "Viagem Apostólica a Moçambique, Madagascar e Maurício: Coletiva de Imprensa Durante o Voo de Retorno Da África," September 10, 2019. Vatican.va.

FutureChurch. "FutureChurch Calls on Bishops to Implement *Amoris Laetitia* and Enter into a New Era of Dialogue, Engagement and Accompaniment." April 9, 2016. https://www.futurechurch.org/press-releases/futurechurch-calls-on-bishops-to-implement-amoris-laetitia-and-enter-into-new-era-of.

Gabriel, Pedro. "2+2=5?" *Where Peter Is* (blog), April 19, 2018. https://wherepeteris.com/225-2/.

———. "Following Christ, but Not His Vicar." *Where Peter Is* (blog), July 9, 2019. https://wherepeteris.com/following-christ-but-not-his-vicar/.

———. "Pluralism and the Will of God . . . Is There Another Way to Look at It?" *Where Peter Is* (blog), March 12, 2019. https://wherepeteris.com/pluralism-and-the-will-of-god-is-there-another-way-to-look-at-it/.

———. "Reclaiming Fatima." *Where Peter Is* (blog), May 13, 2018. https://wherepeteris.com/reclaiming-fatima/.

———. "Silence: The Shield against Suspicious Man." *Where Peter Is* (blog), December 10, 2018. https://wherepeteris.com/silence-the-shield-against-suspicious-man/.

———. "Sola Traditio." Where Peter Is (blog), February 8, 2018. https://wherepeteris.com/sola-traditio/.

———. "The Crucified Church: Tensions with the Flavor of the Gospel." *Where Peter Is* (blog), February 10, 2020. https://wherepeteris.com/the-crucified-church-tensions-with-the-flavor-of-the-gospel/.

———. "Was Pope Benedict Forced to Resign?" *Where Peter Is* (blog), February 28, 2018. https://wherepeteris.com/was-pope-benedict-forced-to-resign/.

———. "When Heresy Pretends to Be Tradition." *Where Peter Is* (blog), April 3, 2019. https://wherepeteris.com/when-heresy-pretends-to-be-tradition/.

Gagliarducci, Andrea. "*Humanae Vitae* Needs No Update, Commission Chair Says." Catholic News Agency, May 23, 2018. https://www.catholicnewsagency.com/news/38475/humanae-vitae-needs-no-update-commission-chair-says.

———. "Interpreting *Amoris Laetitia* 'through the Lens of Catholic Tradition.'" Catholic News Agency, April 8, 2016. https://www.catholicnewsagency.com/news/33692/interpreting-amoris-laetitia-through-the-lens-of-catholic-tradition.

Gaillardetz, Richard R. "Infallibility and the Ordination of Women." *Louvain Studies*, no. 1 (1996) 3–24. https://doi.org/10.2143/LS.21.1.542232.

Gaudron, Matthias. "*Amoris Laetitia*: A Triumph of Subjectivism." SSPX District of Canada, April 18, 2016. https://sspx.ca/en/amoris-laetitia-sspx-gaudron.

Bibliography

Gisotti, Alessandro. "Kasper: The Faithful Understand *Amoris Laetitia*, Stop Accusations of Heresy." *Vatican News*, March 5, 2018. https://www.vaticannews.va/en/vatican-city/news/2018-03/cardinal-walter-kasper-amoris-laetitia-no-heresy.html.

Gloria.tv. "Viganò: Not Even The Most Optimistic Freemason Would Have Dreamed Francis' Papacy," November 22, 2019. https://gloria.tv/post/ZAR2rh2u3K3b36obpsjknTw1i.

Granados, José, Stephan Kampowski, and Juan Pérez-Soba. *Accompanying, Discerning, Integrating: A Handbook for the Pastoral Care of the Family According to Amoris Laetitia*. Emmaus Road, 2017.

Gregory the Great. *Pastoral Rule*. Edited by Philip Schaff, Henry Wace, and Kevin Knight. Translated by James Barmby. Vol. 12. Nicene and Post-Nicene Fathers, Second Series. Buffalo, NY: Christian Literature, 1895. https://www.newadvent.org/fathers/36012.htm.

Guarino, Thomas G. *The Disputed Teachings of Vatican II: Continuity and Reversal in Catholic Doctrine*. Grand Rapids, Michigan: William B. Eerdmans, 2018.

Gyapong, Deborah. "Fifty Years Later, Birth-Control Predictions Even 'Crazier than He Thought.'" Grandin Media, June 5, 2018. https://grandinmedia.ca/fifty-years-later-birth-control-predictions-even-crazier-thought/.

Harris, R. Laird. *Fundamental Protestant Doctrines*. 5 vols. Wilmington, DE: Bible Presbyterian Press, 1949.

Hickson, Maike. "Bp. Schneider: Pope Must Formally Correct Statement That God Wills False Religions." LifeSite, May 8, 2019. https://www.lifesitenews.com/news/bp-schneider-pope-must-formally-correct-statement-that-god-wills-false-religions/.

———. "Cardinal Brandmüller on How the *Dubia* Should Be Answered." *OnePeterFive* (blog), January 3, 2018. https://onepeterfive.com/cardinal-brandmuller-dubia-answered/.

———. "Head of CDF Declines to Comment on *Dubia* of Four Cardinals." *OnePeterFive* (blog), December 1, 2016. https://onepeterfive.com/head-cdf-declines-comment-dubia-four-cardinals/.

Hitchens, Dan. "The Sacraments Don't Need Fixing." *First Things*, August 2, 2016. https://www.firstthings.com/web-exclusives/2016/08/the-sacraments-dont-need-fixing.

Hoffman, Matthew. "Cardinal Burke's Critics Fall into Serious Errors about the True Nature and Authority of the Papal Magisterium." LifeSite, December 1, 2016. https://www.lifesitenews.com/opinion/cardinal-burkes-critics-fall-into-serious-errors-about-the-true-nature-and-/.

———. "Pope Praises Lisbon Guidelines That Allow Communion to Divorced and Remarried." LifeSite, July 17, 2018. https://www.lifesitenews.com/news/pope-francis-thanks-lisbon-patriarch-for-amoris-instruction-endorsing-commu/.

Holy See Press Office. "Presentation of the Post-Synodal Apostolic Exhortation *Amoris Laetitia*: The Logic of Pastoral Mercy." April 8, 2016. https://press.vatican.va/content/salastampa/en/bollettino/pubblico/2016/04/08/160408a.html.

Horst, Guido. "Leitartikel: Faktisches Schisma." *Die Tagespost*, January 16, 2017.

Houselander, Caryll. *The Reed of God*. New ed. Notre Dame, IN: Christian Classics, 2006.

Inside The Vatican. "Cardinal Kasper's Proposal." April 1, 2014. https://insidethevatican.com/magazine/editorial/dossier/cardinal-kaspers-proposal/.

Instituto Nacional de Estatística. *Censos 2011 Resultados Definitivos—Portugal*. Lisbon, Portugal, 2012.

———. *Estatísticas Demográficas 2007*. Lisbon, Portugal, 2008.

Irrazabal, Gustavo. "Amoris Laetitia y los divorciados en nueva unión." *Revista Teología* LIII, no. 120 (August 2016) 151–73.

Ivereigh, Austen. *The Wounded Shepherd*. Henry Holt, 2019. Kindle.

Jackson, Chris. "Why I'm Disregarding Laudato Si and You Should Too." *The Remnant Newspaper*, June 19, 2015. https://remnantnewspaper.com/web/index.php/fetzen-fliegen/item/1819-why-i-m-disregarding-laudato-si-and-you-should-too.

John of the Cross. *Ascent of Mt. Carmel*. Eternal Word Television Network. https://www.ewtn.com/catholicism/library/ascent-of-mt-carmel-12494.

John Paul II. "Address of John Paul II to the Participants in the Day of Study on the Theme 'Twenty Years of Canonical Experience,'" January 24, 2003. Vatican.va.

———. "Audience," March 24, 1993. Vatican.va.

———. *Evangelium Vitae*. Libreria Editrice Vaticana, 1995. Vatican.va.

———. *Ordinatio Sacerdotalis*. Libreria Editrice Vaticana, 1994. Vatican.va.

———. *Reconciliatio et Paenitentia*. December 2, 1984. Vatican.va.

———. *Sollicitudo Rei Socialis*. Libreria Editrice Vaticana, 1987. Vatican.va.

———. *Veritatis Splendor*. Libreria Editrice Vaticana, 1993. Vatican.va.

Joseph, Peter. "Catholic Magisterium." *The Catholic Answer*, September/October 1998.

Kampowski, Stephan. "A Handbook for faithfully interpreting *Amoris Laetitia*." Interview by Edward Pentin. *National Catholic Register*, Apr 18th, 2017. https://www.ncregister.com/news/a-handbook-for-faithfully-interpreting-amoris-laetitia.

Kasper, Walter. "An Interview with Cardinal Walter Kasper." By Matthew Boudway and Grant Gallicho. *Commonweal Magazine*, May 7, 2014. https://www.commonwealmagazine.org/interview-cardinal-walter-kasper.

Keller, Paul. "A Case Study in Communion for the Divorced/Remarried." *Crux*, January 7, 2017. https://cruxnow.com/commentary/2017/01/case-study-communion-divorcedremarried/.

Kennedy, Sheela, and Steven Ruggles. "Breaking Up Is Hard to Count: The Rise of Divorce in the United States, 1980–2010." *Demography* 51, no. 2 (April 1, 2014) 587–98. https://doi.org/10.1007/s13524-013-0270-9.

Kilpatrick, William. "Tumult in the Church: Is the Confusion Intentional?" *Catholic World Report*, December 6, 2019. https://www.catholicworldreport.com/2019/12/06/tumult-in-the-church-is-the-confusion-intentional/.

Koch, Thomas. "The Challenge of Terri Schiavo: Lessons for Bioethics." *Journal of Medical Ethics* 31, no. 7 (July 1, 2005) 376–78. https://doi.org/10.1136/jme.2005.012419.

La Civiltà Cattolica. "'Our Little Path': Pope Francis with the Jesuits in Thailand and Japan." December 5, 2019. https://www.laciviltacattolica.com/our-little-path-pope-francis-with-the-jesuits-in-thailand-and-japan/.

La crise intégriste (blog). "Réponses de La Congrégation Pour La Doctrine de La Foi Aux Dubia Présentés Par Mgr Lefebvre," March 9, 1987. https://lacriseintegriste.typepad.fr/weblog/1987/03/r%C3%A9ponses-de-la-congr%C3%A9gation-pour-la-doctrine-de-la-foi-aux-dubia-pr%C3%A9sent%C3%A9s-par-mgr-lefebvre.html.

Bibliography

Lateran IV. "Confession of Faith," November 11, 1215. https://www.papalencyclicals.net/councils/ecum12-2.htm.

Lawler, Phil. "Pope Francis Has Become a Source of Division." *Catholic Culture*, January 27, 2017. https://www.catholicculture.org/commentary/pope-francis-has-become-source-division/.

———. "The Rhetorical Strategy to Debunk the *Dubia*." *Catholic Culture*, December 16, 2016. https://www.catholicculture.org/commentary/rhetorical-strategy-to-debunk-dubia/.

———. "This Disastrous Papacy." *Catholic Culture*, March 1, 2017. https://www.catholicculture.org/commentary/this-disastrous-papacy/.

———. "Three Things the Pope Can't Say." *Catholic Culture*, December 2016. https://www.catholicculture.org/commentary/three-things-pope-cant-say/https://www.catholicculture.org/commentary/three-things-pope-cant-say/.

Lefebvre, Marcel. *Religious Liberty Questioned*. Kansas City, MO: Angelus, 2001.

Levering, Matthew. Christ and the Catholic Priesthood: Ecclesial Hierarchy and the Pattern of the Trinity. Chicago: Hillenbrand, 2010.

Levine, Joseph. "How Not to Minister to the Divorced and Remarried." Crisis Magazine, January 18, 2017. http://www.crisismagazine.com/2017/not-minister-divorced-remarried.

Leo XIII. Sapientiae Christianae. Libreria Editrice Vaticana, 1890. Vatican.va.

Liguori, Alphonsus. "Guide for Confessors." Edited by R. Schiblin, 1978. https://vdocuments.mx/st-alphonsus-liguori-guide-for-confessors.html.

Longley, Clifford. "*Amoris Laetitia*: Pope Francis Has Created Confusion Where We Needed Clarity." *The Tablet*, April 18, 2016. https://www.thetablet.co.uk/blogs/1/919/amoris-laetitia-pope-francis-has-created-confusion-where-we-needed-clarity.

López, Rodrigo Guerra. "Entender a Wojtyla para comprender a Bergoglio. El carácter personalista de Amoris laetitia." *Metafísica y Persona* 11, no. 21 (January–June 2019) 37–50.

———. "Para Comprender Amoris Laetitia. Premisas y argumentos, respuesta a dudas y objeciones, camino y esperanza." *Medellín* XLIII, no. 168 (May–August 2017) 409–47.

Luxmoore, Jonathan. "New Portuguese Cardinal Expected to Bring Church 'Closer to People.'" *Crux*, June 2, 2018. https://cruxnow.com/cardinals/2018/06/new-portuguese-cardinal-expected-to-bring-church-closer-to-people.

Magister, Sandro. "In the Synod on the Family Even the Pope Emeritus Is Speaking Out." *Chiesa Espressonline* (blog), December 3, 2014. http://chiesa.espresso.repubblica.it/articolo/1350933bdc4.html?eng=y&refresh_ce.

Mallett, Mark. "On Vatican Funkiness." *The Now Word* (blog), October 22, 2019. https://www.markmallett.com/blog/2019/10/22/on-vatican-funkiness/.

Mares, Courtney. "Pope Francis: Synodality Is What the Lord Expects of the Church." Catholic News Agency, November 29, 2019. https://www.catholicnewsagency.com/news/42963/pope-francis-synodality-is-what-the-lord-expects-of-the-church.

Marshall, Taylor. *The Crucified Rabbi: Judaism and the Origins of Catholic Christianity*. Origins of Catholic Christianity Trilogy, Vol. 1. Dallas, TX: Saint John, 2009.

———. Red Pilled on Pope Francis, 2018. https://www.youtube.com/watch?v=eJZ-NTid9bA.

Martin, David. "Did Francis Formally Profess Heresy?" *Canada Free Press*, March 6, 2017. https://canadafreepress.com/article/did-francis-formally-profess-heresy.

Marto, Antonio. "Guia Prático para o Percurso de Discernimento Acompanhado." In *O Senhor está perto de quem tem o coração ferido (Sl 34,19) – Nota Pastoral sobre os fiéis divorciados a viver em nova união*. 2018.

Mattei, Roberto de. "De Mattei: The Plan Of 'Reinterpretation' For *Humanæ Vitæ*." *Rorate Cæli* (blog), June 14, 2017. https://rorate-caeli.blogspot.com/2017/06/de-mattei-plan-of-reinterpretation-for.html.

———. "A Response to Edward Peters on the Buenos Aires Letter & Authentic Magisterium." *OnePeterFive* (blog), December 19, 2017. https://onepeterfive.com/de-mattei-a-response-to-edward-peters-on-the-buenos-aires-letter-authentic-magisterium/.

Mazurczak, Filip. "Polish Bishops' *Amoris Laetitia* Guidelines Stress Discernment and Compassion, in Continuity with Church Doctrine." *Catholic World Report*, June 12, 2018. https://www.catholicworldreport.com/2018/06/12/polish-bishops-amoris-laetitia-guidelines-stress-discernment-and-compassion-in-continuity-with-church-doctrine/.

Mazza, Michael. "*Extra Ecclesiam Nulla Salus*: Father Feeney Makes a Comeback." *Fidelity*, December 1994.

McCusker, Matthew. "Key Doctrinal Errors and Ambiguities of *Amoris Laetitia*." LifeSite, May 9, 2016. https://www.lifesitenews.com/opinion/key-doctrinal-errors-and-ambiguities-of-amoris-laetitia/.

McElwee, Joshua J. "Signers of Document Critiquing '*Amoris Laetitia*' Revealed." *National Catholic Reporter*, July 22, 2016. https://www.ncronline.org/news/vatican/signers-document-critiquing-amoris-laetitia-revealed.

Meenan, John. "The Loss of This One Key Distinction Is Fueling Much of the Confusion around *Amoris Laetitia*." LifeSite, February 23, 2017. https://www.lifesitenews.com/opinion/amoris-laetitia-mortal-and-grave-sin/.

Melina, Livio. "Le Sfide di Amoris laetitia per un teologo della morale." *Anthropotes* 33, no. 1 (2017) 233–50.

Messori, Vittorio, and Joseph Ratzinger. *The Ratzinger Report: An Exclusive Interview on the State of the Church*. San Francisco: Ignatius, 1985.

Milco, Elliot. "Francis's Argentine Letter and the Proper Response." *First Things*, September 14, 2016. https://www.firstthings.com/blogs/firstthoughts/2016/09/franciss-argentine-letter-and-the-proper-response.

Miller, Bruce. "Understanding and Implementing *Amoris Laetitia* Chapter VIII." *Anuario Argentino de Derecho Canónico*, 23, no. 1 (2017). https://repositorio.uca.edu.ar/handle/123456789/5517.

Montagna, Diane. "Cardinal Burke Makes 'Final Plea' for Clarity to Pope Francis on *Dubia* Anniversary." LifeSite, November 14, 2017. https://www.lifesitenews.com/news/cardinal-burke-makes-final-plea-for-clarity-to-pope-francis-on-dubia-annive/.

———. "Exclusive: Bishop Schneider Wins Clarification on 'Diversity of Religions' from Pope Francis, Brands Abuse Summit a 'Failure.'" LifeSite, March 7, 2019. https://www.lifesitenews.com/news/bishop-schneider-extracts-clarification-on-diversity-of-religions-from-pope-francis-brands-abuse-summit-a-failure/.

———. "JPII Institute Profs Dismissed for Interpreting Francis in Line with Tradition? Former President Speaks Out." LifeSite, August 5, 2019. https://www.lifesitenews.

com/news/jpii-institute-profs-dismissed-for-interpreting-francis-in-line-with-tradition-former-president-speaks-out/.

———. "Pope Francis under Fire for Claiming 'Diversity of Religions' Is 'Willed by God.'" LifeSite, February 5, 2019. https://www.lifesitenews.com/news/pope-francis-under-fire-for-claiming-diversity-of-religions-is-willed-by-go/.

Morrisey, F. G. "Apostolic Exhortation." In *New Catholic Encyclopedia*, Second Ed., 1:585–86. Washington, DC: Catholic University of America, 2003.

Moyski, Martina. "Clergy and Laity Offer Strong Response to Pope's 'Rigid' Comments." ChurchMilitant.com, September 13, 2019. https://www.churchmilitant.com/news/article/clergy-and-laity-respond-to-popes-rigid-comments.

Müller, Gerhard Ludwig. "Development, or Corruption?" *First Things*, February 20, 2018. https://www.firstthings.com/web-exclusives/2018/02/development-or-corruption.

Nelson, Jim. "Positivism." In *Encyclopedia of Critical Psychology*, edited by Thomas Teo, 1437–44. New York, NY: Springer, 2014. https://doi.org/10.1007/978-1-4614-5583-7_468.

Newman, John Henry. *An Essay in Aid of a Grammar of Assent*. London: Burns, Oates, & Co., 1874.

———. *An Essay on the Development of Christian Doctrine*. 6th ed. Notre Dame Series in the Great Books. Notre Dame, IN: University of Notre Dame Press, 1989.

Ochabski, David. "'Dr. William Lane Craig vs. Dr. Peter Atkins Highlight' (Video + Transcript)." *Random Thoughts. Christian Walk.* (blog), July 7, 2016. https://randomthoughtsinachristianwalk.wordpress.com/2016/07/07/dr-william-lane-craig-vs-dr-peter-atkins-highlight-video-transcript/.

O'Connell, Gerard. "Dissenters' Conference on '*Amoris Laetitia*' Hears Call for an Answer to the *Dubia*." *America Magazine*, April 22, 2017. https://www.americamagazine.org/faith/2017/04/22/dissenters-conference-amoris-laetitia-hears-call-answer-dubia.

Odero, José Miguel. "Introduction to Theology." In *Faith Seeking Understanding*, edited by Charles Belmont, Vol. 1. Studium Theologiae Foundation, 2006. http://fsubelmonte.weebly.com/introduction-to-theology.html.

Olson, Carl E. "Three Reasons for Excluding Obstinate Sinners." *Catholic World Report*, October 31, 2012. https://www.catholicworldreport.com/2012/10/31/three-reasons-for-excluding-obstinate-sinners/.

O'Neil, Arthur Charles. "Sin." In *The Catholic Encyclopedia*, Vol. 14. New York: Robert Appleton, 1912. http://www.newadvent.org/cathen/14004b.htm.

O'Reilly, Steven. "*Amoris Laetitia* and the Confusion of Those Contradicting the Magisterium of John Paul II." *Roma Locuta Est* (blog), November 9, 2017. https://romalocutaest.com/2017/11/09/amoris-laetitia-and-the-confusion-of-those-contradicting-the-magisterium-of-john-paul-ii/.

———. "Pope Francis, the Open Letter, and the Pesky Preface." *OnePeterFive* (blog), May 6, 2019. https://onepeterfive.com/pope-francis-the-open-letter-and-the-pesky-preface/.

Ortiga, José. *Construir a Casa sobre a Rocha*. Edição Arquidiocese de Braga, 2017.

Passos, João. "The Reception of the Post-Synodal Apostolic Exhortation *Amoris Laetitia*: Challenges and Ecclesial Tasks." *Espaços* 25, no. 1–2 (2017) 19.

Paul VI. *Humanae Vitae*. Libreria Editrice Vaticana, 1968. Vatican.va.

Pentin, Edward. "Archbishop Fernández Defends '*Amoris Laetitia*' From Its Critics." *National Catholic Register*, August 21, 2017. https://www.ncregister.com/blog/archbishop-fernandez-defends-amoris-laetitia-from-its-critics.

———. "Can *Humanae Vitae*'s Teachings Change?" *National Catholic Register*, July 13, 2018. https://www.ncregister.com/news/can-humanae-vitae-s-teachings-change.

———. "Cardinal Burke on *Amoris Laetitia Dubia*: 'Tremendous Division' Warrants Action." *National Catholic Register*, November 15, 2016. https://www.ncregister.com/news/cardinal-burke-on-amoris-laetitia-dubia-tremendous-division-warrants-action.

———. "'Doctrinal Anarchy' as Bishops' Conflicting Positions on *Amoris Laetitia* Show." *National Catholic Register*, June 17, 2017. https://www.ncregister.com/blog/doctrinal-anarchy-as-bishops-conflicting-positions-on-amoris-laetitia-show.

———. "Full Text and Explanatory Notes of Cardinals' Questions on '*Amoris Laetitia*.'" *National Catholic Register*, November 14, 2016. https://www.ncregister.com/blog/full-text-and-explanatory-notes-of-cardinals-questions-on-amoris-laetitia.

———. "Full Text of *Dubia* Cardinals' Letter Asking Pope for an Audience." *National Catholic Register*, June 19, 2017. https://www.ncregister.com/blog/full-text-of-dubia-cardinals-letter-asking-pope-for-an-audience.

———. "Thousands of Priests Worldwide Call for Clarification of *Amoris Laetitia*." *National Catholic Register*, February 1, 2017. https://www.ncregister.com/blog/thousands-of-priests-worldwide-call-for-clarification-of-amoris-laetitia.

Pepinster, Catherine. "The Pope's Liberal Supporters Feel That He's Let Them down." *The Guardian*, February 14, 2020. http://www.theguardian.com/commentisfree/2020/feb/14/pope-francis-liberal-supporters-let-down.

Peters, Edward. *The 1917 Or Pio-Benedictine Code of Canon Law: In English Translation with Extensive Scholarly Apparatus*. San Francisco, CA: Ignatius, 2001.

———. "Conscience Can't Be the Final Arbiter on Who Gets Communion." *Crux*, January 9, 2017. https://cruxnow.com/commentary/2017/01/conscience-cant-final-arbiter-gets-communion/.

———. "The Law before '*Amoris*' Is the Law After." *Catholic World Report*, April 10, 2016. https://www.catholicworldreport.com/2016/04/10/the-law-before-amoris-is-the-law-after/.

———. "A Non-Magisterial Magisterial Statement?" *In the Light of the Law* (blog), December 15, 2015. https://canonlawblog.wordpress.com/2015/12/15/a-non-magisterial-magisterial-statement/.

———. "On the Appearance of the Pope's Letter to the Argentine Bishops in the *Acta Apostolicae Sedis*." *In the Light of the Law* (blog), December 4, 2017. https://canonlawblog.wordpress.com/2017/12/04/on-the-appearance-of-the-popes-letter-to-the-argentine-bishops-in-the-acta-apostolicae-sedis/.

Pié-Ninot, Salvador. "L'Ultima Parola." *L'Osservatore Romano*, March 17, 2017.

Pius VI, *Auctorem Fidei*. 1794. http://ldysinger.stjohnsem.edu/.

Pius IX. *Syllabus of Errors*. Libreria Editrice Vaticana, 1864. https://www.papalencyclicals.net/pius09/p9syll.htm.

Pius X. "Discorso del Santo Padre Pio X ai Sacerdoti dell'Unione Apostolica in Occasione del Cinquantesimo Anniversario della Fondazione," November 18, 1912. Vatican.va.

———. *Pascendi Dominici Gregis*. Libreria Editrice Vaticana, 1907. Vatican.va.

Bibliography

———. *Promulgandi pontificias Constitutiones*. Libreria Editrice Vaticana, 1908. Vatican.va.
Pius XI. *Casti Conubii*. Libreria Editrice Vaticana, 1930. Vatican.va.
Pius XII. *Humani Generis*. Libreria Editrice Vaticana, 1950. Vatican.va.
———. *Mystici Corporis Christi*. Libreria Editrice Vaticana, 1943. Vatican.va.
———. *Soyez les bienvenues*. Libreria Editrice Vaticana, 1952. Vatican.va.
Pontifical Council for Legislative Texts. "Declaration Concerning the Admission to Holy Communion of Faithful who are Divorced and Remarried," June 24, 2000. Vatican.va.
Pontifical Council for the Family. "*Vademecum* for Confessors Concerning Some Aspects of the Morality of the Conjugal Life," February 12, 1997. Vatican.va.
Pope, Charles. "The Ambiguities of *Amoris Laetitia* Cannot Overrule the Unambiguous Teaching of the Church." *National Catholic Register*, December 14, 2016. https://www.lifesitenews.com/opinion/catholic-teaching-on-marriage-and-communion-is-unambiguous/.
Pordata.pt. "Número de Divórcios Por 100 Casamentos." Accessed June 1, 2020. https://www.pordata.pt/Portugal/N%C3%BAmero+de+div%C3%B3rcios+por+100+casamentos-531.
Poupard, Paul. "Christ and Science." In *Science and the Future of Mankind: Science for Man and Man for Science: The Proceedings of the Preparatory Session, 12–14 November 1999 and the Jubilee Plenary Session, 10–13 November 2000*, edited by Pontificia Accademia delle scienze, 484–94. Pontificiae Academiae Scientiarum Scripta Varia 99. Pontifical Academy of Sciences, 2001.
Ramos, Joshua. "Are Conservatives In Their Pushback Against Pope Francis The New 'Cafeteria Catholics'?" *Political Theology Network*, November 10, 2015. https://politicaltheology.com/are-conservatives-in-their-pushback-against-pope-francis-the-new-cafeteria-catholics/.
Ratzinger, Joseph. "Mass '*Pro Eligendo Romano Pontifice*': Homily of Card. Joseph Ratzinger." April 18, 2005. Vatican.va.
———. "On the Question of the Indissolubility of Marriage." Translated by Joseph Bolin, March 25, 2011. https://www.pathsoflove.com/texts/ratzinger-indissolubility-marriage/.
———. "Relativism: The Central Problem for Faith Today." EWTN Global Catholic Television Network, May 1996. https://www.ewtn.com/catholicism/library/relativism-the-central-problem-for-faith-today-2470.
———. "Respostas Às Dubia Apresentadas Por S. Ex.a. Revma. Dom Lefebvre—09 de Março de 1987." June 3, 2014. http://www.apologistascatolicos.com.br/index.php/concilio-vaticano-ii/liberdade-religiosa/655-respostas-as-dubia-apresentadas-por-s-ex-revma-dom-lefebvre.
Ratzinger, Joseph, and Christoph von Schönborn. *Introduction to the Catechism of the Catholic Church*. San Francisco: Ignatius, 1994.
Reese, Thomas. "Comment: Francis Opens the Door to 'Cafeteria' Catholics." The Catholic Register, October 13, 2017. https://www.catholicregister.org/opinion/guest-columnists/item/26183-comment-francis-opens-the-door-to-cafeteria-catholics.
Religious Congregation of Mary Immaculate Queen. "CMRI's Theological Position: The Chair of Peter Today Is Vacant." Accessed September 30, 2021. https://cmri.org/about-cmri/theological-position-sede-vacante-2/.

Reno, R. R. "A Failing Papacy." First Things, February 2019. https://www.firstthings.com/article/2019/02/a-failing-papacy.

RomanCatholicism.org. "Church Texts Condemning Father Leonard Feeney," May 14, 2008. https://web.archive.org/web/20080514013144/http://www.romancatholicism.org/feeney-condemnations.htm.

Rome Corrupted Christianity. "The Great Apostasy," July 3, 2013. https://romecorruptedchristianity.wordpress.com/2013/07/03/the-great-apostasy/.

Rothbard, Murray Newton. "War, Peace, and the State." In *Egalitarianism as a Revolt Against Nature and Other Essays*, 115–32. Auburn, Alabama: Ludwig von Mises Institute, 2000.

Ryan, Thomas. "'Weakness, and Wounded and Troubled Love' in *Amoris Laetitia*: Pope Francis as Pastor." *Australasian Catholic Record* 94, no. 2 (2017) 131–47.

San Martín, Inés. "No, Virginia, There's No 'Secret Commission' on *Humanae Vitae*." *Crux*, July 27, 2017. https://cruxnow.com/commentary/2017/07/no-virginia-theres-no-secret-commission-humanae-vitae/.

San Souci, Nicholas. "*Amoris Laetitia*: A Nod to the Dictatorship of Relativism." *Musings of a Mere Paper Boy* (blog), May 5, 2016. http://musingsofapaperboy.weebly.com/2/post/2016/05/amoris-laetitia-a-nod-to-the-dictatorship-of-relativism.html.

Scanlon, Regis. "The Flawed Strategy Behind Amoris Laetitia." *Homiletic & Pastoral Review*, August 18, 2017. https://www.hprweb.com/2017/08/the-flawed-strategy-behind-amoris-laetitia/.

Schneider, Athanasius. "Important: Bishop Athanasius Schneider Interview with *Rorate Caeli* on 'Profession of the Immutable Truths', Communion for 'Divorced and Remarried.'" *Rorate Cæli* (blog), January 6, 2018. https://rorate-caeli.blogspot.com/2018/01/important-bishop-athanasius-schneider.html.

Schneider, Matthew. "Does the Text of Amoris Laetitia Allow Communion for the Divorced and Remarried?" *Homiletic & Pastoral Review*, February 12, 2019. https://www.hprweb.com/2019/02/does-the-text-of-amoris-laetitia-allow-communion-for-the-divorced-and-remarried/.

Schönborn, Christoph. "Cardinal Schönborn on 'The Joy of Love': The Full Conversation." Interview by Antonio Spadaro. *America Magazine*, August 9, 2016.

———. "A Conversation with Cardinal Schönborn on '*Amoris Laetitia*.'" Interview by Antonio Spadaro. *La Civiltà Cattolica* English Edition, March 1, 2017. https://www.laciviltacattolica.com/conversation-cardinal-schonborn-amoris-laetitia/.

Seifert, Josef. "The Church after *Amoris Laetitia*: An Interview with Josef Seifert." Interview by Maike Hickson. *OnePeterFive* (blog), September 5, 2017. https://onepeterfive.com/the-church-after-amoris-laetitia-an-interview-with-josef-seifert/.

———. "Does Pure Logic Threaten to Destroy the Entire Moral Doctrine of the Catholic Church?" OnePeterFive, August 24, 2017. https://onepeterfive.com/josef-seifert-pure-logic-threaten-destroy-entire-moral-doctrine-catholic-church/.

———. "Famed Catholic Philosopher: How Can Christ and Our Lady Read *Amoris Laetitia* without Weeping?" LifeSite, June 9, 2016. https://www.lifesitenews.com/news/famed-catholic-philosopher-how-can-christ-and-our-lady-read-amoris-laetitia/.

Shadle, Matthew. "The Death Penalty and the Development of Doctrine, Part II." *Catholic Moral Theology* (blog), November 28, 2017. https://catholicmoraltheology.com/the-death-penalty-and-the-development-of-doctrine-part-ii/.

Sheehan, Michael. *Apologetics and Catholic Doctrine*. Edited by Peter Joseph. London: Baronius, 2009.

Siscoe, Robert. "Dogmatic Fact: The One Doctrine That Proves Francis Is Pope." *OnePeterFive* (blog), March 18, 2019. https://onepeterfive.com/dogmatic-fact-francis-pope/.

Skojec, Steve. "Is *Amoris Laetitia* an Expression of the Ordinary and Universal Magisterium?" *OnePeterFive* (blog), June 22, 2017. https://onepeterfive.com/is-amoris-laetitia-an-expression-of-the-ordinary-and-infallible-magisterium/.

———. "The Dictator of the Vatican." *Foreign Policy* (blog). Accessed September 21, 2021. https://foreignpolicy.com/2016/04/08/the-dictator-of-the-vatican-pope-francis-amoris-laetitia-divorce-communion/.

———. "We Worship Christ, Not the Pope. @Pontifex Is Fomenting Doctrinal Error and Souls Are at Stake." Twitter, December 17, 2016. https://twitter.com/SteveSkojec/status/810164784867852288?s=19&fbclid=IwAR1MDlUjZ-DLzykJtTUT3NjXDcIVlo-oHCLutaRaRRU3LEsTElp59YGf6eY.

Smith, Gregory A. "Just One-Third of U.S. Catholics Agree with Their Church That Eucharist Is Body, Blood of Christ." Pew Research Center, August 5, 2019. https://www.pewresearch.org/fact-tank/2019/08/05/transubstantiation-eucharist-u-s-catholics/.

Smith, P. J. "Pope Francis on the Development of Doctrine." *First Things*, October 16, 2017. https://www.firstthings.com/web-exclusives/2017/10/pope-francis-on-the-development-of-doctrine.

Smith, Scott. "*Amoris Laetitia* and the 1917 Code of Canon Law." *Reduced Culpability* (blog), February 13, 2018. https://reducedculpability.blog/2018/02/13/amoris-laetitia-and-the-1917-code-of-canon-law/.

———. "The Internal Forum." *Reduced Culpability* (blog), January 19, 2018. https://reducedculpability.blog/2018/01/19/the-internal-forum/.

———. "Public Scandal." Reduced Culpability (blog), January 18, 2017. https://reducedculpability.blog/2017/01/19/3-0-public-scandal/.

Spaemann, Robert. "Full text: Interview with Robert Spaemann on *Amoris Laetitia*." Interview by Anian Christoph Wimmer. Catholic News Agency, April 29, 2016. https://www.catholicnewsagency.com/news/33812/full-text-interview-with-robert-spaemann-on-amoris-laetitia.

Spencer, Robert. "The Truth about Pope Honorius." *Catholic Answers*, September 1, 1994. https://www.catholic.com/magazine/print-edition/the-truth-about-pope-honorius.

Tavares, Pedro Sousa. "Patriarca diz que Papa não validou comunhão de divorciados." *Diário de Notícias*, April 8, 2016. https://www.dn.pt/sociedade/patriarca-diz-que-papa-nao-validou-comunhao-de-divorciados-5117149.html.

Third Plenary Council of Baltimore. *Baltimore Catechism #3*. StGemma.com Web Productions, 2005. http://www.baltimore-catechism.com/.

Thomas à Kempis. *The Imitation of Christ*. Milwaukee: Bruce, 1940. https://ccel.org/ccel/kempis/imitation/imitation.

Thomson, J. Anderson, and Clare Aukofer. "Science and Religion: God Didn't Make Man; Man Made Gods." *Los Angeles Times*, July 18, 2011. https://www.latimes.

com/opinion/la-xpm-2011-jul-18-la-oe-thompson-atheism-20110718-story.html.

Travers, Patrick J. "*Amoris Laetitia* and Canon 915: A Merciful Return to the «Letter of the Law»." Pts. 1 and 2. *Periodica de Re Canonica* 107, no. 1 (2018) 297–326; no. 3 (2018) 367–418.

Twomey, D. Vincent. "'*Amoris Laetitia*' and the Chasm in Modern Moral Theology." *Catholic World Report*, September 1, 2017. https://www.catholicworldreport.com/2017/09/01/amoris-laetitia-and-the-chasm-in-modern-moral-theology/.

Vatican I. "Dogmatic Constitution on the Catholic Faith: *Dei Filius*," April 24, 1870. https://www.papalencyclicals.net/councils/ecum20.htm.

———. "First Dogmatic Constitution on the Church of Christ: *Pastor Aeternus*," July 18, 1870. https://www.papalencyclicals.net/councils/ecum20.htm.

Vatican II. "*Gaudium et Spes*," December 7, 1965. Vatican.va.

Vatican News. "Document on Human Fraternity for World Peace and Living Together: Full Text," February 4, 2019. https://www.vaticannews.va/en/pope/news/2019-02/pope-francis-uae-declaration-with-al-azhar-grand-imam.html.

Vennari, John. "Situation Ethics Enshrined—Q & A on Francis' *Amoris Laetitia*." *Catholic Family News* (blog), April 20, 2016. https://catholicfamilynews.com/blog/2016/04/20/2016-4-20-situation-ethics-enshrined-q-a-on-francis-amoris-laetitia/.

Vere, Peter John. "A Canonical History of the Lefebvrite Schism." MA thesis, Saint Paul University, 1999. https://www.catholicculture.org/culture/library/view.cfm?recnum=1392.

Vermeersch, Arthur. "Modernism." In *The Catholic Encyclopedia*, Vol. 10. New York: Robert Appleton, 1911.

Vincent of Lerins. *Commonitorium*. Edited by Philip Schaff and Henry Wace. Translated by C.A. Heurtley. From Nicene and Post-Nicene Fathers, Second Series. Buffalo, NY: Christian Literature, 1894. http://www.newadvent.org/fathers/3506.htm.

Voris, Michael. *Church of Nice!* Church Militant, 2012. https://www.youtube.com/watch?v=NxrIjE-WNVA.

Walford, Stephen. "Open Letter to the Four *Dubia* Cardinals." *La Stampa*, June 27, 2017. https://www.lastampa.it/vatican-insider/en/2017/06/27/news/open-letter-to-the-four-dubia-cardinals-1.34590559.

———. *Pope Francis, the Family, and Divorce: In Defense of Truth and Mercy*. New York: Paulist, 2018.

Ward, Maisie. *Gilbert Keith Chesterton*. New York: Sheed & Ward, 1943. https://www.gutenberg.org/ebooks/18707.

We Are Church Ireland. "Irish reform group welcomes exhortation, but regrets families 'had no deliberative voice' in synod." April 8, 2016. https://www.ncronline.org/blogs/ncr-today/reactions-pope-s-reflection-family-life

Weigel, George. "Caritas in Veritate in Gold and Red." *National Review*, July 7, 2009. https://www.nationalreview.com/2009/07/caritas-veritate-gold-and-red-george-weigel/.

Wikipedia. "Interpretation (Canon Law)." Last modified September 11, 2021, 15:46. https://en.wikipedia.org/wiki/Interpretation_(canon_law).

———. "Xenophanes." Last modified September 8, 2021, 22:16. https://en.wikipedia.org/wiki/Xenophanes.

Wilhelm, Joseph. "Heresy." In *The Catholic Encyclopedia*, Vol. 7. New York: Robert Appleton, 1910. http://www.newadvent.org/cathen/07256b.htm.

Williams, M. E. "Doctrine." In *New Catholic Encyclopedia*, Second Ed., 4:802–3. Washington, DC: Catholic University of America, 2003.

Williams, Thomas D. "When Ratzinger Said No: A History of the Kasper Proposal." *Crisis Magazine*, October 23, 2015. http://www.crisismagazine.com/2015/walter-kasper-the-same-yesterday-today-and-forever.

Wooden, Cindy. "Pope's Letter to Argentine Bishops on 'Amoris Laetitia' Part of Official Record." Catholic News Service, August 22, 2018. https://web.archive.org/web/20180822051150/http://www.catholicnews.com/services/englishnews/2017/popes-letter-to-argentine-bishops-on-amoris-laetitia-part-of-official-record.cfm.

Worgul, George. "*Amoris Laetitia*—Joy of Love or Scandal of Heresy?" *Spiritan Horizons* 13, no. 13 (October 1, 2018) 53–66. https://dsc.duq.edu/spiritan-horizons/vol13/iss13/10.

Wynne, Stephen. "Viganò Champions Virgin Mary After Pope Francis Smear." Church Militant, December 19, 2019. https://www.churchmilitant.com/news/article/abp-vigano-champions-virgin-mary.

www.ingramcontent.com/pod-product-compliance
Lightning Source LLC
Chambersburg PA
CBHW071232230426
43668CB00011B/1404